CUSTOMER SURVEY
Driving Corporate Culture for Business Success

RECEIVE £50 OFF YOUR NEXT REPORT P~~...~~ ~~...~~ U FILL IN AND RETURN THIS ~~...~~

D0587594

Please help Business Intelligence to ensure that its repor~~...~~ ~~...~~ relevant to the needs of its customers, by filling in and returning this snort survey.
To thank you for your time and trouble, when you return the survey, you will receive £50 off your next purchase of a Business Intelligence report!

1   Did you have any problems ordering, paying for or receiving the report? YES / NO
    If so, please give details..

2   Where did you obtain information about the report?
    Brochure from Business Intelligence   ☐   Review in magazine or newspaper   ☐
    Colleague   ☐   Conference   ☐
    Other...

3   Which of the following represents your overall rating of the report?
    Consistently interesting, relevant and informative   ☐   Mostly useful, will refer to again   ☐
    Average review of topic, nothing exceptional   ☐   Not very useful, dissatisfied   ☐
    Very poor, extremely dissatisfied   ☐   Other.......................................

4   Did you find the case studies to be...?
    Of great interest   ☐   Of some interest   ☐
    Of limited interest   ☐   Of no interest   ☐
    Other...

5   Did you find the analysis of the issues to be...?
    Practical and actionable?   ☐   Adequate, of some use?   ☐
    Of little use?   ☐   Other............................

6   Could you indicate the aspects of the report you most liked?...
    ....

7   Please give details of any aspects of the report you disliked?...
    ....

8   Please give details of any specific topics you felt we should have included or excluded?...............
    ....

9   Would this report encourage you to purchase other titles from BI? YES / NO

10 Which other report topics would interest you?...

Please send me a copy of your Reports catalogue, *The Edge* YES / NO

Name:... Job Title:...
Organisation:...
Address:...
.... Postcode:..
Telephone:.. Fax:...

NOW PLEASE DETACH AND FAX BACK TO BUSINESS INTELLIGENCE: 0181 879 1122

DRIVING CORPORATE CULTURE
FOR BUSINESS SUCCESS

How to Develop and Sustain

Winning Organizational Behaviours

that Support Strategic Change

JAMES CREELMAN

Business Intelligence Ltd
Third Floor
22-24 Worple Road
Wimbledon
London
SW19 4DD

Tel: +44 (0)181 879 3300
Fax: +44 (0)181 879 1122

Website: www.business-intelligence.co.uk

ISBN 1 898085 46 3

Typeset by David Brown, Heathfield, Sussex
Print Management by Graphic Direct, Basingstoke, Hampshire
Cover Illustration by Adrian Barclay

AUTHOR PROFILE

James Creelman is a business writer and consultant specializing in the fields of the balanced scorecard, organizational change, process management and improvement, and total quality management.

He was previously managing editor, Reports, for Business Intelligence. Prior to this he was editor of *The TQM Magazine*, *Managing Service Quality* and *Best Practice Magazine* for IFS International.

He is the author of two other Business Intelligence Reports, *Creating the Value-adding Finance Function* and *Building and Implementing a Balanced Scorecard*.

ACKNOWLEDGEMENTS

This Report would not have been possible without the help and advice of the following people, all of whom I gratefully acknowledge.

The following representatives from case study companies: Lucy Woods, CEO, BT Northern Ireland; Mike Campbell, senior vice president, human resources and labour relations, Michelle Meissner, director of human resource development, Continental Airlines; Johan Van der Hel, human resources manager, Coating Resins' business unit, DSM Resins; Edmund White, national head of internal communications, Ernst & Young; Sue Stoneman, customer service director, Lex Services plc; Andrew Geddes OBE, director, Inland Revenue Accounts Office, Cumbernauld, Scotland; Dick Kline, president, Peter Tait, vice president, total quality, Al Watt, ex-president, CBR's Vancouver-based business unit (now retired), Lehigh Portland Cement Company; Ian Hampton, human resources director, Bunbury, Western Australia plant, Millennium Inorganic Chemicals; Dr Christian Forstner, director, business excellence, Mark Derbacher, press officer, Siemens KWU; Peter Raine, head of total quality, Superdrug.

The following case report representatives: Dr Sudhanshu Palsule, head of learning and knowledge management, Anglian Water Services; Rupert Gavin, CEO, BBC Worldwide; Phil Nolan, managing director, Transco; Julian Stainton, CEO, Adrian Schuler, director of best practices, Western Provident Association.

The following consultants: Mark Krueger, managing director, Answerthink; Philip Sadler, chairman, Sarah Beety, public relations officer, Centre for Tomorrow's Company; Alison Rankin-Frost, head, Context Consulting; Dr Judd Robert Allen, Human Resources Institute; Garrey Melville, independent consultant; Dr David Clutterbuck, chairman, The ITEM Group; Dr David Chaudron, managing partner, Organized Change Consultancy; Dr George Labovitz, chairman, Lawrence Brink, vice president, marketing and product development, Alan Burleson, senior consultant, Organizational Dynamics Inc (ODI); Luca Mortara, managing director, ASI (UK); David Miller, managing director, Elaine Fear, principal consultant, ODR Europe; Nancy Blodgett, president, Performance Excellence Inc; Robin Cammish, managing director, QPA; Suzanne C Francis, senior vice president, Robert H Schaffer & Associates; John Childress, CEO, Mike Birtwistle, senior consultant, John Clayton, senior consultant, Senn-Delaney Leadership Consulting Group.

Finally, I would like to thank Julia Eccles for her work on analysing the 'Culture and Change Management' survey data, and Greg McCarthy, editor, Business Intelligence, for all his help and advice during the writing of this Report.

PREFACE

Driving Corporate Culture for Business Success was commissioned by Business Intelligence as part of its ongoing research programme into best practice thinking and developments in change management frameworks and systems.

Through ten focused chapters and 11 dedicated case studies, this Report explains how exemplary organizations throughout the world, and from differing industry and service sectors, are successfully transforming corporate culture in support of strategic or major change objectives. Indeed, the Report shows that understanding and leveraging the power of corporate culture is pivotal to long-term change success.

Throughout the Report, the advice and guidance of culture change consultants and academics is interwoven with the experiences of practitioners in the field. The intention being to provide readers with a rounded view of how to address and overcome the myriad, and often hidden, challenges in a culture change effort. A snapshot of each chapter follows.

Chapter 1: Introduction

This Chapter explains why understanding corporate culture is critical to succeeding with major change initiatives, stressing that most change failure is usually due to cultural problems. It looks at several definitions of corporate culture and provides a working definition for this Report. It also provides an overview of the key learning points from the Report.

A case study on Continental Airlines demonstrates best practice.

Chapter 2: Corporate Culture – The Key to Successful Business Transformation

Chapter 2 explains why a culture change effort has to be in support of strategic or major change initiatives. It examines research that suggests that culture has a powerful impact on bottom-line performance and shows that possessing a strong culture is not in itself a guarantee of success. Rather cultures must be adaptive to changing market-place and customer demands. It also shows that exemplary organizations actively orchestrate 'winning' cultures.

A case study on the Inland Revenue Accounts Office, Cumbernauld, Scotland, demonstrates best practice.

Chapter 3: 'Culture and Change Management' – Exclusive Research

This Chapter details the findings from the 'Culture and Change Management' survey, which was exclusively commissioned for this Report, of how organizations from Europe and from North America and the Rest of the World are actively managing and shaping corporate cultures. Based on the real life experiences of 236 responding organizations, the survey shows how well corporate cultures are defined and understood within organizations, how actively the culture is managed and how successful companies have been in changing their cultures. This Chapter provides a comparison against success objectives between companies with 'extremely well defined' cultures and those with 'very poorly defined' cultures.

A case study on Millennium Inorganic Chemicals, a survey respondent, demonstrates best practice.

Chapter 4: Leading Culture Change – The Role of the CEO and Senior Management Team

This Chapter explains why the leadership of the CEO and the senior management team is the single most critical success factor in a culture change effort. It explains why corporate leaders have to invest significant amounts of time and energy into a culture change effort and how they must personally live, and role model, the new cultural ethos. Also explored is the importance of vision, mission and value statements in providing direction and behavioural guidelines for the new culture.

A case study on KFC demonstrates best practice.

Chapter 5: Assessing the Cultural Challenges

Chapter 5 explains why it is judicious to assess the existing culture prior to a cultural change effort. Doing so will help senior management pinpoint the key cultural challenges ahead and therefore enable them to draw a roadmap from the existing to desired cultural states. The Chapter looks at several cultural assessment tools available and shows that central to culture change success is understanding the power of organizational subcultures and a company's 'unwritten' rules of behaviour.

Case studies on Superdrug and DSM Resins demonstrate best practice.

Chapter 6: Frameworks for Implementing and Driving Culture Change

This Chapter shows why it is vital to involve the whole of the employee-base when rolling out a cultural change initiative; key phases being 'unfreezing' the existing culture and 'refreezing' the new. It shows why piloting a culture change programme is often beneficial prior to organization-wide roll-out and the key role played by change facilitators and champions deep inside the company. It also explains why it is crucial to ensure that corporate measurement systems reinforce the new cultural ethos.

Case studies on BT Northern Ireland and Siemens KWU demonstrate best practice.

Chapter 7: Aligning Human Resources Management with Corporate Culture

This Chapter explains why human resource systems must be aligned with, and reinforce, the new culture. It shows why organizations must alter recruitment, performance appraisal, career development, recognition and incentives, and compensation mechanisms, and examines the challenges of each. The Chapter also shows why it is often injudicious to devolve responsibility for a corporate culture to the HR function, while showing how exemplary HR functions play a crucial enabling role in driving culture change deep into the organization.

A case study on Hyundai Car (UK) Ltd demonstrates best practice.

Chapter 8: The Communications Imperative – Messages, Media and Practices

Chapter 8 shows why internal communication mechanisms are vitally important in delivering the culture change message throughout the organization. It looks at the myriad of communication tools available, both traditional, eg cascade briefings and newsletters, and new, eg corporate intranets. This Chapter explains why communication mechanisms must be mutually reinforcing and that messages must be honest, timely and clearly support the new cultural ethos.

A case study on Ernst & Young demonstrates best practice.

Chapter 9: Mergers and Acquisitions – The Cultural Challenges

This Chapter explores the many cultural challenges within merger and acquisition (M&A) activities. Indeed it shows that M&A failure – and failure figures are frighteningly high – is normally due to cultural, and not strategic, reasons. It shows the importance of cultural due diligence prior to the merger or acquisition and explains why managing the cultural factors should be a key focus for a long time after organizations formally join together.

A case study on Lehigh Portland Cement Company demonstrates best practice.

Chapter 10: Conclusions and Key Learning Points

The final Chapter summarizes the key learning points from the Report and predicts what a 'high performing culture' will look like in the early years of the new millennium.

CONTENTS

Chapter 9: Mergers and Acquisitions – The Cultural Challenge

1

INTRODUCTION

Section A: Context

Understanding, and indeed leveraging corporate culture for competitive advantage is certainly on senior management's agenda. According to practitioners and commentators interviewed for this Report, it is fast climbing their list of priorities.

According to research for this Report there are several key reasons for this. First, the 1980s and 1990s have seen companies inundated with organizational change programmes, be they incremental, as in continuous improvement initiatives, or breakthrough, as in business process re-engineering projects. The evidence is that the volume of change programmes will grow further in the future.

This fact has been repeatedly demonstrated by original research by Business Intelligence throughout the 1990s. For example, 1995 research of 100 *Times* top 1000 companies for the report *Re-engineering: The Critical Success Factors* found that 60 per cent of organizations had attempted to re-engineer their business.[1]

Similarly research for the 1996 Business Intelligence report *Transforming HR to Support Corporate Change* found that 86 per cent of the 231 responding companies had implemented major change programmes.[2] Moreover research for the 1996 report *The Strategic Management of Internal Communication* found that, on an importance index of 0–10, respondents rated, at 8.6, 'supporting major change programmes' as *the* most important role of the internal communication function in the organization, thus suggesting a high level of change activity within their companies.[3]

The organizational change consultancy, Organizational Development Research (ODR) interviews senior executives on a yearly basis to study the volume, intensity and complexity of change programmes. For 1997 their research found that:[4]

- 48 per cent of organizations reported a greater volume of change than one year previous
- 65 per cent said the momentum of change was increasing
- 68 per cent stated that the complexity of the changes they are facing is on the rise.

According to ODR's data there is no evidence that this upwards trend is going to plateau. This belief is supported by the findings of 'Culture and Change Management',[5] a survey exclusively commissioned for this Report of the culture change activity within 236 mainly European and North American companies. A total of 79.32 per cent of respondents believed culture change to be currently a more important issue within their organization than five years ago. And 74.44 per cent believed it would become more important over the next five years. (This survey is touched on in section F of this Chapter and its findings are analysed in detail in Chapter 3).

Section B: Change Failure Rates

However, with change intensifying and with strategic implementation models such as the Balanced Scorecard and the European Foundation for Quality Management's (EFQM) Business Excellence Framework (see Chapter 6), and concepts such as knowledge management demanding senior management attention, organizations are having to accept one truth of corporate change endeavours – most fail to deliver lasting business success. Indeed, research for the report *Re-engineering: The Critical Success Factors* found that 90 per cent of re-engineering efforts failed to deliver breakthrough results.[6]

And experts interviewed for this Report would agree with the summation by John Childress, chief executive officer of the US-headquartered culture change specialists Senn-Delaney Leadership Consulting Group:

> "If you look at the failure rates for initiatives such as re-engineering, total quality management and information technology projects, they are normally around the 80 per cent mark. This is because companies fail to resolve the cultural issues that underpin any change initiative."

Indeed the cultural issues are often ignored completely. Culture is seen as something that can be either dealt with after the change effort, or alternatively something that will evolve naturally during the change programme, without any need for active management. Both approaches are fundamentally flawed. As Childress says:

> "Understanding the strengths and weaknesses of your current culture and comprehending how that culture is going to impact your change programme is critical, otherwise you can't go forward. Many excellent change programmes have been killed by the culture."

He explains why culture is often ignored:

> "The problem with addressing cultural factors in change programmes is that they're intangible. As you can't see them it's easier to concentrate on the

tangible, technical change factors. However, although invisible, culture is everywhere and to a large extent controls everything that goes on within the organization. So companies ignore them at their peril."

Indeed within the 1997 Business Intelligence report *Managing and Sustaining Radical Change*, the authors related evidence from ODR which showed that wherever a discrepancy exists between the objectives of change and the current culture, the culture always wins. They write:[7]

"Companies that sense the urgent need to make a shift in their performance and style of operation may first have to start with overhauling their cultures. This is the highest level of change that a business can undergo and is also the deepest because it must register at every level of the organization, from the CEO to the production line and sales operation. Otherwise the intended shift will not happen.

"FOR ODR, three essential management rules emerge from its study of corporate change:

1. Understand the powerful effect culture has on change.

2. Know that major change must be supported by culture.

3. Recognize that when counter-cultural changes are introduced, the existing culture must be altered."

As this Report will show, and Childress and other experts stress, understanding the potential cultural challenges *before* launching a change programme is a fundamental building block of success. This is dealt with in detail in Chapter 5.

Understanding cultural factors, research for this Report finds, is also an absolute prerequisite before and during a merger or acquisition (M&A). Given the current vertiginous growth in M&A activity and the fact that many experts now believe that M&A's high failure rates are due to cultural incompatibility, companies considering this approach to corporate growth would be injudicious not to consider these intangible issues. This is dealt with in detail in Chapter 9.

Section C: The People Factor

Corporate culture is also an agenda item because many senior management teams are finally waking up to the fact that it is people who make companies succeed, and that people's behaviour, commitment and ways of working are largely determined by the cultural context.

This is becoming much more important as we move from industrial-based to knowledge-based working paradigms. Recruiting, retaining and motivating knowledge workers will be much harder for organizations with a 'sick' culture than one which is healthy, challenging and inspiring. And people factors impact all stakeholder groups. As president and chief operating officer Greg Brenneman succinctly says in the Continental Airlines case study that accompanies this Chapter:[8]

"When the employees are happy, everyone is happy, from the customers to the shareholders."

Section D: Definitions of Culture

This brings us to possibly the most difficult part of any work on corporate culture, providing a working and meaningful definition of the word 'culture'. Indeed, understanding the word itself and how it applies in an organizational context has led to the publication of a plethora of books and articles proffering their own spin on the definition. For example, according to John Kotter and James Heskett in their best selling 1992 book *Corporate Culture and Performance*:[9]

> "Culture represents an interdependent set of values and ways of behaving that are common in a community, and tend to perpetuate themselves, sometimes over long periods of time."

In his seminal work, *Organizational Culture and Leadership*, the culture change specialist Edgar Schein wrote:[10]

> "... 'culture' [is] a pattern of basic assumptions – invented, discovered, or developed by a given group as it learns to cope with its problems of external adaptation and integral integration – that has worked well enough to be considered valid and, therefore, to be taught to new members as the correct way to perceive, think, and feel in relation to those problems."

Schein defines culture as existing on three levels. On the surface, or superficial level, there are artefacts, underneath there are values and behavioural norms, and at the deepest level is a core of beliefs and assumptions:[11]

1. **Artefacts**: These are defined as the visible, tangible, and audible characteristics of an organization which, according to Schein, can be divided into three categories, physical, behavioural and verbal manifestations:

   - Physical manifestations could include the buildings and offices, the internal layout, the design and logos, and the material objects of an organization.

   - Behavioural manifestations can be identified within traditions and customs, ceremonies and rituals, and the communication pattern of an organization.

   - Verbal manifestations can be found in the stories, myths, jokes, anecdotes, heroes, metaphors and jargon banded throughout the organization.

2. **Values and behavioural norms**: Values are defined as the social principles, goals and standards within a culture, which define what an organization cares about. They constitute the basis for making judgements, and can be referred to as an ethical or moral code. Behavioural norms are associated with values, and are defined as unwritten rules that are recognized by members of a particular group in both social and corporate cultures. Norms set boundaries and establish what sort of behaviour can be expected, or what is considered normal and acceptable to the members of that culture.

3. **Beliefs and assumptions**: These Schein defines as the core of the organization's culture. Assumptions represent what members believe to

be reality, and therefore influence what is perceived. They are invisible and taken for granted, existing outside everyday awareness. Members believe that their assumptions are the truth, and not open for question, and that they affect experiences within their cultural life. However, this also means that different members of an organization may have different assumptions about how their organization works, which may result in a variety of beliefs within one company.

In their book, *In the Eye of the Storm: Reengineering Corporate Culture*, Senn-Delaney chief executive John Childress and chairman Larry Senn define culture this way:[12]

"Corporate culture is a composite of the following:

1. shared values – what we think is important
2. beliefs – how we think things should be done
3. behaviours – the way we do things around here
4. heroes – the people who personify our corporate culture
5. systems – our written and unwritten policies and procedures.

"Corporate culture is created through the interaction of the critical determinants of culture:

1. corporate culture
2. leadership style
3. industry and environment
4. regional differences
5. employee base
6. key organizational tasks."

Commentators interviewed for this Report provided their own definitions. As examples, Robin Cammish, managing director of the change consultancy QPA, laconically states:

"A generic definition of corporate culture is very easy – it's the way we work around here."

Mark Krueger, managing director of the US-based Answerthink Consulting Group, says:

"The concept of corporate culture could be defined as a set of commonly held beliefs and attitudes that informally govern the conduct of an organization's corporate culture."

Finally Dr George Labovitz, chairman of the global consultancy Organization Dynamics Incorporated (ODI), provides this definition:

"Culture is the sum total of the behaviours of an organization. When I think of culture I'm struck with the parallel between corporate culture and individual personality. Personality is defined in psychology as the sum total of all of our behaviours. Culture is defined in a similar way – all the behaviours of an organization. So maybe what we ought to do is look at culture as the personality of an organization."

Labovitz also points out that culture exists at the macro level (eg I am Spanish) and at the micro level (the environment of the organization). He states that although the macro level culture must be understood and accounted for, it cannot be changed or controlled by the organization's management. However, he says:

> "Managers control the environment in which people work. So if they change the environment they will change the culture. And if they change the culture they will change the behaviour."

So as a short working definition based on the above examples:

> "corporate culture is the behaviour, personality and mind of the organization".

However, what this and all the above have in common is that they do not necessarily define a *winning* corporate culture. Indeed there may be diametrically opposite behavioural traits and multiple personalities within the organization. As with people this does not create a healthy state of mind or form the foundations for a productive existence.

For the purpose of this Report therefore a 'winning corporate culture' is described as:

> 'Where there exists a visible set of performing enhancing behaviours which together form a recognizable corporate personality and healthy organizational mind.'

> 'This organizational mind exists to deliver superior performance and as such is constantly learning about, and aligning with, changing customer and market demands.'

Section E: Success Examples

As the 11 dedicated case studies within this Report show, senior management teams have indeed created identifiable and performing enhancing behaviours, personalities and minds for their organizations. Moreover, in doing so they have typically improved the company's financial performance significantly. Here is a few examples of the successful culture change programmes studied in-depth within this Report.

Continental Airlines transformed itself from one of the worst performing US airlines to one of the best, in a four year period. At the start of the change programme the organization was facing bankruptcy for an unprecedented third time and the employees hated working for the company. Now the company is profitable (reporting a 1998 pre-tax profit of $770 million) and as for employee morale, Mike Campbell, the organization's senior vice president, human resources and labour relations, says:

> "In 1998 [we were] voted by *Fortune* magazine as one of the 100 best US companies to work for. Right now... employee morale could not be higher. We have a culture in which we are winning together. To use a sporting analogy we see ourselves as being a team that could win the superbowl."

Employees also hated working for the UK-based Inland Revenue Accounts Office, Cumbernauld, Scotland (the case study which accompanies Chapter 2). Indeed according to the Office's director, Andrew Geddes OBE, the culture could be defined in one word – "awful". However he says that following a wide reaching culture change initiative:

> "Today we have very high levels of customer and employee satisfaction and our financial performance has improved beyond recognition. We now deliver well within our budget on an annual basis and our unit costs show a year-on-year improvement in real terms.

> "We've moved from being a relatively obscure part of the Inland Revenue, and a poor performer at that, to a highly respected executive unit within the public sector and are recognized as a quality performer by much of the private sector."

At KFC (the case study which accompanies Chapter 4) the culture at the start of the change programme was so bad that annual staff turnover rates were between 150–180 per cent. Today, according to Mike Birtwistle, Senn-Delaney Leadership Consulting Group senior consultant, who worked with KFC during the culture change programme, "it's a people-focused, customer-focused culture. The hallmark of the culture is recognition and appreciation". Importantly, since launching the change effort KFC has experienced four years of growth, following several years without growth.

At Hyundai Car (UK) Ltd (a case study which accompanies Chapter 7), the culture at the start of the change programme was characterized as parochial, functional and suppressed, and it was also losing money. Today, the culture is positive, empowered, creative and customer-focused, and a £7 million deficit in 1995 was transformed into a £9 million profit in 1998.

An Adaptive Culture

But culture change is not just the preserve of poorly performing organizations. Indeed, research for this Report shows that one of the keys of successful and lasting cultural change is creating an 'adaptive' culture; one that is capable of continually refining or, if need be, dramatically refocusing, the corporate culture as the market demands (this is dealt with in detail in Chapter 2).

Ernst & Young (the case study which accompanies Chapter 8), for example, launched its culture change programme at a time of financial success. The now chairman Nick Lang recognized that customer demands on the professional services industry were going to change dramatically in the 1990s, and that he had to create a more client-focused and nimble firm in readiness for an increasingly competitive market-place. Today, as independent research shows, the firm is indeed client-focused and, as an exemplar knowledge management company, it is certainly nimble.

At BT Northern Ireland (a case study to accompany Chapter 6), the organization was certainly successful before the culture change and was already recognized as a benchmark organization for customer service. So culture change here was to transform a command and control, hierarchical, traditional and energy-sapping culture into an empowered one where employees could take charge of their own work, take considered risks and unleash their energy to drive customer-facing performance up another bar.

Section F: Culture and Corporate Strategy

As the case studies within this Report will show, the reasons for culture change vary from company to company. But what they all have in common is that a very clear rationale for culture change was identified and communicated at the start of the change effort. For, as explained in Chapter 2, there has to be a clear reason for culture change and it has to be in support of corporate strategy and/or powerful change objectives. As Childress and Senn state:[13]

> "This is not about change for change sake. This about competitive advantage, customer focus, increasing shareholder value, developing organizational capabilities."

Therefore, when culture change is referred to within this Report it is about changing culture to support clear business imperatives. For some of the case study companies, such as Ernst & Young and Continental Airlines, the culture was changed to support a significant strategic shift. For others, such as BT Northern Ireland and DSM Resins (a case study to accompany Chapter 5), it was to change the culture in order to better leverage employees' performance against essentially stable strategic goals (although these goals will normally be stretching).

When a 'change effort' or 'change programme' is referred to in the course of this Report, it relates to a performance enhancing initiative that is aligned to identifiable business objectives that will themselves be aligned to key strategic goals (be they signalling a dramatic shift from a previous strategy or a leveraging of an existing one).

Quite simply, if a change programme does not have a clear line-of-sight through to the strategic objectives, then it almost certainly is not worth doing in the first place, and equally certainly will quickly disappear in the face of more pressing business concerns. In short, culture change is essential to support organizational change efforts intent on leveraging strategic objectives.

Being clear as to the strategic objectives of culture change is an absolute prerequisite because changing corporate culture can be a long and difficult process. As David Miller, managing director of ODR Europe warns:

> "Organizations have to guard against getting sucked into culture change too quickly and senior management teams really have to think this through carefully and decide whether it is really worth doing.

> "We always press clients on the question 'do you really want to do this?'. For example, if you want to be customer-centric ask yourselves what will be

different in two years time, where are you now and how are you going to get there? [See Chapter 5 which will help organizations answer such questions.]

"Too often companies don't realize how much work goes into changing a culture and what it really takes to pull it off. And for most organizations it's a very, very long journey. Five years at least. And the amount of leadership time and commitment it takes is huge."

Jack Welch, chairman of US-headquartered General Electric and a pioneer of successful corporate transformation, explains:[14]

"When I try to summarize what I've learned since 1981 [the year he took the helm at GE], one of the big lessons is that change has no constituency. People like the status quo. They like it the way it was. When you start changing things, the good old days look better and better.... You've got to be prepared for massive resistance."

Identifying and dealing with this resistance is explored in detail in Chapters 5 and 6.

Dramatic Change

As the best practice companies profiled in this Report clearly show, culture can be changed and can be changed dramatically. The 'Culture and Change Management' survey found that organizations are in the main claiming to be successful with culture change efforts. Of the 236 responding organizations (mainly from Europe and North America) almost 60 per cent were able to assess the impact of the culture change process. Fifteen per cent stated it had exceeded its goals, 51.25 per cent claimed it had achieved its goals, while 33.75 per cent said it had failed to meet its goals. Thus a two in three success rate was reported.

However, such success claims should be treated with some caution. Rupert Gavin, CEO of BBC Worldwide (a case report in Chapter 8), says that testing whether a new culture has indeed been embedded would mean returning to an organization five years after the culture change programme and finding the same cultural values espoused, and that the programme was not reliant on the presence of the CEO who led the cultural transformation.

Companies may be too quick in claiming success. Any behavioural change may well be short-term, and employees may spring back to the old ways of doing things if the new culture is not nourished and reinforced over the long-term.

Section G: Key Success Factors

From the practitioners and advisers interviewed for the Report, there are a number of critical success factors for successful culture change. All of these points will be explored in great detail in subsequent chapters, but as a brief outline:

1. Culture change must be aligned to strategic objectives.

2. Recognize the importance of leadership. Senior management leadership of, and commitment to, the culture change effort must be evident. Lucy Woods, chief executive officer of BT Northern Ireland and key driver of its culture change programme puts it bluntly, "leadership is of fundamental importance. Without it positive culture change will not happen". Exemplary leadership approaches include how Woods drove change within her organization, how Gordon Bethune and Greg Brenneman led the culture change at Continental Airlines, how Nick Land drove change at Ernst & Young and how David Novak's leadership style transformed KFC.

3. There has to be a real commitment to change. Says Woods, "there must be a genuine desire to commit to change. It has to be real and it has to be consistent". Labovitz adds, "the kiss of death for a culture change programme is inconsistency".

4. Allocate resources – including your most important people. As Philip Sadler, chairman of the UK's Centre for Tomorrow's Company says, "people must have enough time for this, including those at the top".

5. Involve everybody. Says Sadler, "companies have to involve people at every level. If you don't do this, then nothing lasting will happen". All the organizations profiled paid particular attention to this, often through a 'branded' implementation approach. As examples, see the Better Ways initiative launched globally by Millennium Inorganic Chemicals (the case study that accompanies Chapter 3), Superdrug's Living the Mission programme (a case study in Chapter 5), BT Northern Ireland's Better Life initiative, and the VITA project at DSM Resins.

6. Identify new behaviours. Be clear as to the behaviours that are required within the new culture. Corporate values statements, if implemented deep within the organization and demonstrated by management (especially senior management) can be useful here. Case study companies Hyundai Car (UK) Ltd, Continental Airlines and KFC, for example, made values central to creating the new performance-enhancing company.

7. Align Human Resources. Human Resource strategies and policies must be aligned to the new corporate culture. Not least because how people are compensated and promoted speaks volumes for what the organization sees as important. Therefore companies must look to align their compensation, career development, appraisal, training and indeed recruitment policies. Equally important, formal and informal recognition programmes must be aligned with the new cultural ethos.

8. Communicate, communicate, communicate. Communication was recognized by all best practice companies as a prerequisite for successful culture change. But as Peter Raine, head of total quality at Superdrug, says, "[understand] that you have to deliver messages via a range of communication mechanisms again and again and again. Not everybody receives information in the same way or at the same time".

9. Systematically measure progress. As Labovitz says, "measures drive behaviour". So organizations must ensure that they underpin any culture

change initiative with a robust measurement framework. Companies such as Siemens KWU (a case study to accompany Chapter 6) and the Inland Revenue Accounts Office, Cumbernauld, put a lot of emphasis on the EFQM Business Excellence Model. Measures also ensure accountability for change is created at each level of the organization.

10. Maintain momentum. This is important because culture change should be a never-ending process and modification to culture should be made on an on-going basis. As Garrey Melville states, "there's a real danger that senior management sees this as a one-off exercise. However, if an organization wants to embed a new culture then it has to be revisited regularly and it has to be revised when needed".

The following Continental Airlines case study provides powerful lessons in how a 'sick' corporate culture was transformed into a 'winning' culture and how this had an almost unimaginable affect on the organization's financial performance.

CASE STUDY: CONTINENTAL AIRLINES

Summary

Continental Airlines has been transformed from a company facing bankruptcy to one that is consistently profitable. This has been achieved through a new corporate strategy, the Go Forward Plan, which has helped build a new, and winning, corporate culture.

Introduction

Headquartered in Houston, Texas, USA, global carrier Continental Airlines has about 48,000 employees and in 1998 reported a pre-tax profit of $770 million. This financial success is, in itself, a measure of the extraordinary turnaround in fortunes of this once perennially failing airline. As Mike Campbell, the organization's senior vice president, human resources and labour relations, says:

> "Within four years we have changed from one of the worst to one of the best performing airlines. We have turned the organization around from one that was failing to one that is very successful and indeed was, in 1998, voted by *Fortune* magazine as one of the best 100 US companies to work for.

> "Right now within Continental Airlines employee morale could not be higher. We have a culture in which we are winning together. To use a sporting analogy we see ourselves as being a team that could win the superbowl."

Corporate Culture – Pre-change

Such a confident assertion, to put it bluntly, would have been laughed out of sight by anybody involved in the organization in the early 1990s – by managers, staff, investors and customers alike. The company was, quite simply, awful. For example, in 1994, when its change programme was launched, Continental Airlines was facing bankruptcy for an unprecedented third time. President and chief operating officer (COO) Greg Brenneman, who first experienced the company while with the management consultancy Bain and Company, neatly expressed Continental Airlines problems pre-change in a 1998 article in the *Harvard Business Review*.[15]

> "In my six-odd years of working on turnarounds at Bain, I had never seen a company as dysfunctional as Continental. There was next to no strategy in place. Managers were paralysed with anxiety. The company had gone through ten presidents in ten years, so the standard operating procedure was to do nothing while awaiting new management. The product, in a word, was terrible. And the company results showed it. Continental ranked tenth out of the ten largest US airlines in all key customer-service areas as measured by

the Department of Transportation – on-time arrivals, baggage handling, customer complaints and involuntary denied boardings. And the company hadn't posted a profit outside of bankruptcy since 1978."

About employee morale he provided this example:[16]

> "When I arrived at Continental, it was a mean and lousy place to work.... A couple of weeks after I arrived, I was walking the ramp at Houston saying hello to our mechanics and baggage handlers, and helping to throw a bag or two, when I noticed that almost all the employees had torn the Continental logos from their shirts. When I asked one mechanic why he had done this, he explained, 'when I go to Wal-Mart tonight, I don't want anyone to know that I work for Continental'. His response still sends chills down my spine."

So how did the company address such massive and deeply ingrained financial and cultural problems? Campbell suggests that the fact that the company was so awful proved a somewhat perverse benefit. He says:

> "One of the advantages of being so bad is that you can only get better. It's much easier to change the culture when things are terrible than to change a negative culture when you are financially successful."

A New Leader

Cultural transformation started at Continental Airlines with the appointment of Gordon Bethune as chairman and chief executive officer in 1994. This in itself was greeted with disinterest from the employee-base; after all, Bethune was Continental's tenth CEO in ten years.

But Bethune would prove that it was possible to succeed at what many would perceive as the poisoned chalice of leading Continental Airlines. So what made the difference? Campbell recalls, "he came up with a strategic plan that could be devolved and he was a charismatic leader".

An early decision by Bethune was to dispense with Continental's historic competitive positioning as a low-cost carrier. In 1995 Bethune told the employees, "you can make a pizza so cheap, nobody will be willing to buy it".

This was clearly the case at Continental Airlines. The strategy was not a winning strategy. Therefore the strategic decision was made to refocus its competitive position around reliability and service rather than cost alone. This strategy was delivered through its Go Forward Plan.

The Go Forward Plan

First rolled-out company wide in 1995, the Go Forward Plan has four major components:

- Fly to Win.
- Fund the Future.

- Making Reliability a Reality.
- Working Together.

These four strategic components are still the same today and therefore form the basis for all annual business plans, although the underlying metrics will change.

Fly to Win

Fly to Win is essentially the company's marketing strategy. With an original goal of increasing revenues and delivering a profit (now it is achieving top quartile industry margins) the strategy focused on:

- improving its customer mix (from backpacks and flip-flops to suits and briefcase)
- expanding its alliances and international flying destinations
- revising marketing policies to enhance relationships with travel agents, corporations and frequent fliers
- to stop scheduling flights that lose money.

Fund the Future

Essentially the organization's financial plan, the Fund the Future element had the original strategic goal of securing liquidity. This was achieved by:

- tracking cash
- restructuring the balance sheet
- restructuring the fleet (reducing the number of fleet types from 13 to 4, matching aeroplane size with market size and eliminating above-market leases on aeroplanes)
- maximizing benefits from the underdeveloped US hubs in Houston, Texas, Newark and Cleveland
- selling non-strategic assets.

Make Reliability a Reality

This is the organization's product plan, with the strategic goal of improving the product to become an airline of preference, the original performance stretch-targets were to perform in the top 50 per cent of the industry against the key Department of Transport metrics of:

- on-time performance
- baggage mishandles
- customer complaints
- non-voluntarily denied boardings.

As shall be explained later in this case study, these stretch-targets were achieved somewhat quicker than many would have predicted. The plan also included intentions to:

- improve fleet image
- improve airline cleanliness
- improve food service.

Working Together

This is the organization's people plan, with the strategic goal of building a new corporate culture. Key elements of this plan were to:

- restore employee confidence in management (to be achieved by 'on-time' incentives, establishing a consistent and reliable flight schedule, improving communication, delivering a profit and introducing a profit sharing scheme)
- maintain peace among the work groups
- establish a results-oriented culture.

Rob Benson, pilot captain and former senior director, field services human resources, says:

> "In my opinion every company should have a strategy that covers the four elements of market, financial, product and people, whether it's in crisis or not."

Indeed this four-cornered approach does bear a striking similarity to the Balanced Scorecard, a strategy implementation framework used by an increasing number of companies (see Chapter 6 for further information).

Although a critical step in itself, creating the Go Forward Plan was not enough to transform the organization. Not least because, as Campbell points out, the employees had seen so many new strategies devised that they had essentially stopped taking notice. And, he adds, the management had promised so much in the past that they had failed to deliver, that any new initiative was greeted with a great deal of cynicism and mistrust.

Recognizing these significant barriers, Bethune and Brenneman sold the plan to Continental's management and employees with energetic zeal. Said Brenneman:[17]

> "We knew that the two of us could not save Continental on our own. But if we could get every employee headed in the same direction, we had a chance.

> "We knew that a major ending was on the horizon – either the old Continental was going to be entirely re-invented or it was going to go bankrupt... and would probably be liquidated."

On-time Bonus Plan

An early and powerful mechanism for overcoming the cultural scepticism, getting a demoralized workforce to buy-in to the new strategy and starting on the road to success against the Department of Transport metrics was an on-time bonus plan. Explains Campbell:

> "Basically the plan stated that if we ended in the top five out of the ten airlines tracked by the Department of Transportation for on-time scheduling then we would give everybody in the organization a $65 bonus for each month we achieved this position."

There was an immediate, and dramatic, improvement in performance as Campbell recalls:

> "In month one we moved from bottom to seventh. Consequently people started to believe that we could actually do it. Soon afterwards we climbed to fifth and then third, and we are now regularly coming first. For a company that had become used to being bottom this was an incredible achievement and was a powerful employee motivator."

According to Campbell the bonus plan, which rewarded all management and staff equally, removed a great deal of the divisiveness in the organization, which he stresses can be an unintended outcome if you reward sections of the employee-base and not others. He says:

> "We wanted to send a clear message that we would all win together or lose together."

Moreover, says Campbell, the bonus plan is a good example of Bethune's ability to focus employees onto simple yet successful performance improvement initiatives.

The on-time bonus has certainly been successful. When the leadership team of Continental Airlines made this offer it was paying about $6 million per month to reaccommodate its customers onto competitors' flights, and was receiving from competitors about $750,000 per month. As an on-time airline, the company pays out about $750,000 in reaccommodation expenses, while taking in about $4 million. Therefore, payments have changed from –$5.25 million per month to +$3.25 million, an improvement of $9 million per month. The on-time bonus costs about $2 million per month.

In 1998 $23 million was paid out as a bonus (now for being in the top three of the Department of Transportation's league table), meaning that $93 million has been distributed to employees over a four year period.

A Focus on People

The on-time bonus played an important first step in transforming Continental's culture and, in consequence, its financial performance. But the company realized that to build sustainable success required a significant investment in the 'people' part of the Go Forward Plan. As Michelle Meissner, director of human resource development, says:

> "We have found, as other research has, that external customer satisfaction correlates almost exactly with internal employee satisfaction. Therefore, to deliver a winning strategy in the eyes of our customers means we have to develop our people. We found that we had to focus on building four key employee deliverables:

1. The competence of the people working with us.
2. The collaboration, or the relationships, that we build with each other.
3. Their commitment to the organization.
4. The culture and character that we exhibit."

Consequently the organization focused development plans around these four areas. For the capability of 'culture and character', improvement initiatives were grouped under an 'Employee Participation' label.

Building Competence

Within Continental Airlines, 'building competence' is focused around:

- hiring the right people
- defining customer service
- setting challenging operational targets
- holding people accountable
- training on skills the customer values
- providing resources.

And crucially:

- providing leadership people can trust.

About the last point Meissner says:

> "It was imperative that we created, at all levels of the organization, leaders who could implement the strategy and who could support and enthuse employees."

Important here is that much of human resource (HR) activity is now owned and delivered by line managers. Says Benson:

> "We believe strongly in the leader-teach role. We've done this, not through a complex manual but through a small booklet. Sections within include, filling vacancies, paying employees, creating a winning environment, maximizing performance, handling employee leave and managing progressive discipline.
>
> "Supervisors no longer need to come to HR and ask how to do things."

Indeed this shows how HR itself has been transformed as part of the turnaround. Says Meissner:

> "1994 HR was transactional in nature. Our main job was answering telephone calls, resolving employee complaints about travel abuse and acting as the police for the corporation. HR was not adding value to the corporation.
>
> "However, the primary purpose of HR now is to develop intellectual capital. Our role is to align people and systems to get competitive advantage globally."

With regards to the most important alignment tool, the annual Go Forward Plan, this is first communicated to the top 500 managers who are then responsible for developing local plans and communicating the strategy to every employee. Consequently, the whole culture is focused on the Go Forward Plan.

A key tool for ensuring that cascade does indeed happen is the organization's leadership communication programme. At the end of each year employees rate their leaders' performance against ten dimensions. Articulated as questions the survey asks employees how well their leaders performed against, for example, 'communicating the Go Forward Plan', 'setting attainable local goals' and 'treating employees with dignity and respect'. As leader compensation is partly based on performance against these dimensions, it is clearly in the leader's best interest to ensure success. Interestingly, for the Fortune Top 100 Company rankings, employees are asked similar questions, providing further, and independent, data on managerial performance.

According to Meissner, critical to 'building competence' is staffing strategically. She recalls a time when securing employment within Continental was essentially through a pre-employment test called 'fogging the mirror'. She says:

> "If you could breathe and fog the mirror you were eligible for a job at Continental."

Although clearly apocryphal, this does serve as a powerful comparison to recruitment practices today. Meissner continues:

> "Now our recruitment process is completely different. We look for a motivational fit, meaning people who enjoy team-working, are willing to treat everyone with dignity and respect, can grow in their position, can add new ability to the organization and are imbued with a service ethic."

Importantly, as part of the induction process all new recruits become fully conversant with the Go Forward Plan and their role in meeting its goals. Says Meissner:

> "This is a strategic business orientation to the airline. We believe strongly that employing the right people with the right attitude who enjoy working for the organization will lead to customer satisfaction, which directly leads to revenue growth and profitability."

On the subject of leadership it is also important to point out that within a couple of months of launching the turnaround, the organization replaced 50 of its top 61 officers with about 20 new individuals. How this was done speaks volumes for the new cultural values of dignity and respect that would be pivotal to the change effort. Said Brenneman:[18]

> "Every turnaround involves creating a new culture. If you fire people inhumanely, you'll be left with a bunch of employees who don't trust the company or their co-workers. We needed to create a culture in Continental where people liked coming to work. We couldn't afford to have people hoarding ideas or sapping enthusiasm as we built our new organization. So when we let people go we went out of our way to be fair by honouring their contracts and letting them resign with dignity."

Building Collaboration

Says Benson:

> "Collaboration is a key tenet for us because every day all around the world Continental closes about 2000 airline doors. The moment of truth is when we close that door. All the people need to be aligned to make that happen – pilots, flight attendants, people who bring you to the airline, flight mechanics, the flight controllers, etc."

Pre-change, however, collaboration was poor within the airline, evidenced by its bottom position in the Department of Transport's 'on-time scheduling' league table. Unsurprisingly, therefore, the company has placed considerable emphasis on building collaboration. The on-time bonus mentioned earlier was important here, but the company has also put together cross-divisional work-groups to analyse how to improve performance against other Department of Transport performance metrics such as baggage handling and customer complaints.

What has also helped build collaboration is that the company sets the same standards of service for every scheduled flight and each employee is focused on the same four elements of the Go Forward Plan. Therefore, says Campbell, there is no dispute as to the key performance deliverables, so all employees can focus on the same service output.

An original difficulty with the concept of collaborative working was that, as of the mid 1990s, Continental Airlines was essentially the result of various mergers over preceding years, with companies such as People Express Airlines, New York Airlines, Eastern Airlines and Frontier Airlines. Says Benson:

> "We had workers from all over the world. But rather than making us a global workforce, we were a chaotic amalgamation of different forces working against each other."

This was not helped by the fact that, rather incredibly, employee's work numbers started with a different number, for example, 1, 2 or 3, to designate the previous company the employee belonged to. Says Campbell:

> "As you can imagine this was very divisive and it was difficult to pull these forces together.

> "However we largely achieved this through the Go Forward Plan which set out common goals and common bonuses. This led to the 'different airlines' now pulling together. Instead of working to beat each other we now work together for the same team which is focused on beating the competition."

Importantly Campbell adds:

> "Many employees felt a personal sense of injustice over the way past mergers were handled. We were honest and said there was a lot of things from the past that were indeed wrong but that we couldn't fix them. All we could do was focus on creating a better future.

> "Gordon Bethune likes to say 'you're on your third marriage and we can't fix problems associated with your first marriage.'"

Building Commitment

Building commitment within Continental Airlines was largely through:

*   communication
*   rewards
*   recognition
*   trust.

For internal communication, Campbell, as with all practitioners interviewed for this Report, stresses that to succeed with a culture change programme you cannot communicate enough. He also states that for a global company it is important to use a variety of communication mechanisms:

> "No one communication mechanism will work on its own. We have, as examples, a daily one-page newspaper, weekly voicemail messages from Gordon Bethune, a corporate intranet, monthly and quarterly magazines, monthly meetings in Houston where people are invited to talk with Gordon, e-mail, and Go Forward bulletin boards.

> "Moreover, all executive officers are assigned cities that they have to visit on a quarterly basis. And when we release quarterly earnings, all employees can dial a toll-free number and listen to a taped conversation between a market analyst and a senior executive.

> "On top of this, all leaders are responsible for internal communication to their own people, and are measured on this within the leadership survey."

In his *Harvard Business Review* article, Greg Brenneman outlined the critical importance of communication when first launching the Go Forward Plan. He said:[19]

> "We [Bethune and Brenneman] got out there in the airports and on the planes. We loaded bags, we stood alongside the agents at ticket counters. We just talked at every opportunity about our plans for the airline and how we were going to accomplish them. In general, our communication policy changed from 'don't tell anybody anything unless absolutely required' to 'tell everybody everything'.

> "We also told our employees we believed in them. They knew how to treat customers right, and we moved quickly to let them do just that. In the past, any time an employee provided a benefit for a customer that was considered unacceptable, the bankers and lawyers running Continental would write a rule documenting the proper action. Over the years these rules were accumulated into a book about nine inches thick known as the Thou Shalt Not book. Employees couldn't possibly know the entire contents of the book. When in doubt, everyone knew it was advised just to let the customers fend for themselves. In early 1995, we took the Thou Shalt Not book to a company parking lot. We got a 55-gallon drum, tossed the book inside, and poured gasoline all over it. In front of a crowd of employees, we lit a match to it. Our message was this, 'Continental is your company to make great. Go do it – now'."

A particularly innovative mechanism for building commitment is the company's 'perfect attendance programme', through which the company, twice yearly, awards fully-loaded Ford Explorer vehicles to three or four employees. To be eligible for entry to the award draw, all an employee has to do is attend work without a sickness break for six months.

Bethune and Brenneman personally telephone the winners to inform them of their good fortune, a special lunch is given to the recipients and the car presentation is made outside the winning employees' own office.

In the six months period to the end of 1998, 14,000 (35 per cent) employees were eligible for the draw. And if awarding cars for full attendance sounds like an extravagance, Messner points out:

> "The programme costs us about $700,000 a year and our loss-time is down 25 per cent. It more than paid for itself in the first year of its implementation."

The company also has a profit sharing scheme, which for 1998 paid out about 6.7 per cent of an employee's annual salary. Since inception in 1996 more than $270 million has been distributed as profit share.

Clearly such incentive programmes go some way to achieving the fourth of Continental Airlines employee performance dimensions, building employee participation.

Building Employee Participation

Within Continental Airlines, building employee participation is largely based on the company's belief in creating an atmosphere of honesty, trust, dignity and respect, key values that now underpin the culture of the company. As Campbell says, "it's really about treating each other like adults".

One mechanism employed to build participation is a toll-free hotline to handle employees' suggestions, which is managed by a cross-section of the employee-base, as examples, pilots, flight attendants, mechanics and gate agents. These employees are required to research each submitted suggestion and get back to the sender within 48 hours with one of three responses:

1. We fixed it.

2. We are not going to fix it, and here is why.

3. We need to study it a little more, and will get back to you by such and such a date.

In its first three years of implementation the hotline received, on average, more than 200 calls per week.

However, to treat employees in accordance with the values also meant the company had to communicate openly when messages were tough. As Brenneman said:[20]

> "Let me tell you, for instance, about the day I had to shut down our operations in Greensboro, North Carolina.
>
> "The historical norm for delivering bad news at Continental was for a senior manager to dump the news on the local airport manager's lap and then hide in our corporate office building. But I decided to go to Greensboro myself, make the announcement to the employees and take my punches publicly."

Measuring Success

So how does the company measure the success of its change programme? This can be done by looking at both hard and soft performance measures.

For a company who, just a few years ago, was facing liquidation, financial measures of success are critical. And here success has been dramatic. The 1998 pre-tax profit of $770 million was the fourth year of record pre-tax profits returned by the organization, and indeed has shown the greatest ever improvement in any Fortune 500 company, with stocks changing hands at $48 at the close of 1997 against just $4.58 in 1994.

Additionally, employee turnover has reduced dramatically as has workers compensation claims. Moreover, against the crucial Department of Transport metrics of the top ten airlines the company is constantly at or near the top for on-time performance, the lowest number of customer complaints and least mishandled bags.

External recognition of the turnaround success has not been slow to follow. In 1996 Continental was voted Airline of the Year by the US-based Transport Association. And in both 1995 and 1996 it won prestigious US-based JD Power awards for customer service on long haul flights (500 miles or more). In 1996 it was also voted *Fortune* magazine's 'comeback kid' and in 1997 was voted *Business Week*'s 'Stock of the Year'.

When it comes to employee satisfaction, perhaps the most telling measure of all has been that sales of merchandise, such as caps, T-shirts, etc, rose 400 per cent in a four year period – purchases made largely by the same employees who once tore their logos of their lapels so nobody externally would know they worked for Continental Airlines.

But this is not the end of the story for Continental Airlines and Campbell recognizes that there's no place for complacency. He says:

> "We have to work hard to maintain momentum. Managing success is our next challenge after successfully managing turnaround.

> "To achieve this we have to stay focused on the business plan, continue to reinvent ourselves, keep on communicating, and constantly find ways that keep up energy generated during the turnaround."

Conclusion

Culture change success at Continental Airlines has been achieved because it believed a simple truth of business success. As Brenneman said:[21]

> "When the employees are happy, everyone is happy, from the customers to the shareholders.

> "When I look back now, I realize the biggest factor in our favour was momentum. The rallying cry of our turnaround was, "do it fast, do it right away, do it all at once. Do it now!' We lit a fire of urgency beneath

Continental, we rotated quickly and picked up speed as we climbed to 41,000 feet. Pretty soon, we were unstoppable.

"Saving Continental wasn't brain surgery. The actions required to revive a moribund company usually aren't. In Continental's case we simply needed to fly to places people wanted to go, when they wanted to go, in clean, attractive aeroplanes; get them there on time with their bags; and serve food at mealtimes. The tough part – like in most turnarounds – was getting all that done fast, right away, and all at once.

"The fact is, you can't afford to think too much during a turnaround. Time is tight, money is tighter. If you sit around devising elegant strategies and then try to execute them through a series of flawless decisions, you're doomed. We saved Continental because we acted and we never looked back."

According to Campbell the three keys to transforming Continental's culture were:

1. **A strong business strategy**: "The people part has to be a substantial part of that".

2. **Strong leadership**: "It is leadership that drives culture change".

3. **Communication**: "Make this a substantial part of the change strategy".

Key Learning Points

The dramatic success of Continental Airlines has been due to getting a number of fundamentals right. These include:

1. The appointment of a new chairman and CEO, Gordon Bethune, and a new president and COO, Greg Brenneman, provided the catalyst and leadership required to succeed with culture change.

2. Culture change within Continental Airlines was focused on a simple requirement – corporate survival.

3. The leadership team refocused the company's competitive position from one based on cost to one based on reliability and service.

4. A new strategy to support this competitive position, the Go Forward Plan, was robust and easily devolved throughout the organization.

5. The company recognized that leadership at all levels would be critical to success.

6. Similarly, the company recognized that success depended on the buy-in of all employees. To achieve this the company needed to invest a considerable amount of time and resource.

7. Continental Airlines recognized the absolute importance of internal communications in driving strategic change and that a mix of communication approaches would work best.

8. Innovative compensation and reward mechanisms have played a significant role in moving the change effort forward.

2

CORPORATE CULTURE – THE KEY TO SUCCESSFUL BUSINESS TRANSFORMATION

Executive Summary

1. Culture change initiatives, research for this Report finds, have to support strategic objectives. Conversely, it is difficult to implement strategies successfully without accounting for cultural attributes.

2. Research from both the USA and the UK finds that corporate cultures have a powerful impact on bottom-line performance.

3. Culture change experts Senn-Delaney Leadership Consulting Group provide a useful template for calculating an organization's 'cost of culture'.

4. Creating a 'winning' culture means shaping an adaptive culture; one that is capable of constant alignment with changing customer and market-place requirements.

5. Linked to the above, culture change exemplars focus squarely on the cause-and-effect linkages from employee satisfaction, through customer satisfaction to business results.

6. Creating an adaptive culture goes hand in hand with fashioning a 'high performance' culture.

7. Exemplary organizations do not just manage culture but orchestrate the culture they require.

8. A case study on the UK's Inland Revenue Accounts Office, Cumbernauld, Scotland, demonstrates best practice in creating a new corporate culture.

Section A: Context

The introductory Chapter explained why corporate culture has become an agenda item for senior management teams. This Chapter focuses on why corporate culture change must be aligned to wider strategic or organizational change initiatives. For as Luca Mortara, managing director of the UK arm of ASI, says:

> "A culture change programme makes sense only if it contributes to a shift in strategy and planning. Culture change *per se* means nothing."

Therefore, this Chapter shows how exemplary change organizations are indeed ensuring that culture change is not a stand-alone initiative, devoid from wider organizational issues, but rather is clearly focused on business imperatives aimed at delivering competitive advantage.

The Chapter will then show why, in undergoing a cultural change programme, organizations must work to ensure that rather than just creating a new culture for the business, they build capabilities into the corporate mind-set that enables the culture to be adaptive to evolving market and customer requirements. As the renowned US-based management guru Rosabeth Moss Kanter said in her 1985 book, *The Change Masters: Innovation and Entrepreneurship in the American Corporation*:[1]

> "Cultures... will need to change over time as the tasks change, as the organization grows, or as people change. Much trouble in organizations comes from the attempt to go on doing things as they used to be done, from a reluctance to change the culture when it needs to be changed."

So it is critical to stress that creating a 'winning' culture is not a one-off exercise, but rather an ongoing process of alignment.

Finally this Chapter will explain why cultures must be managed with the same level of attention as paid to any other aspect of organizational activity. Indeed it will show that exemplary organization actually orchestrate the cultures they want.

First, however, this Chapter looks at research evidence that shows the bottom-line power of proactively managing corporate cultures, and, importantly, the cost of not doing so.

Section B: Research Findings

'Culture and Change Management' Survey Findings

The 'Culture and Change Management' survey, exclusively commissioned for this Report, of 236, mainly large, organizations in Europe, USA and the Rest of the World, discovered a correlation between a well-defined culture and business success.[2]

Of the responding organizations, 11.53 per cent claimed to have an 'extremely well defined' culture. The same number stated their culture was 'very poorly defined'.

To the question, 'how well does your current culture support your strategic objectives?', 11.58 per cent replied 'extremely well' against 6 per cent who said 'not at all'. Tellingly, however, those organizations who claimed to possess an 'extremely well defined' culture achieved a mean score of 1.76 (with 1 equalling 'extremely well and 5 'not at all') against a mean of 3.64 for those with 'very poorly defined' cultures.

Of the 236 responding organizations, 58.79 per cent have attempted to change their corporate culture. Taking this percentage as a 100 per cent, 58.94 per cent were thus far able to assess the impact of the culture change process, with 51.25 per cent of respondents claiming the culture change process had achieved its goals, 15 per cent stating that it had exceeded its goals, whereas 33.75 per cent said it had failed to meet its goals.

However, a comparison of the answers from those with 'extremely well defined' cultures and those with 'very poorly defined' cultures is telling. A full 50 per cent of those with 'extremely well defined' cultures had achieved the culture change goals and 14.28 per cent had exceeded its goals, whereas 28.74 per cent had failed to meet its goals.

Conversely, only 20 per cent of companies with 'very poorly defined' cultures had achieved the culture change goals, 10 per cent had exceeded the goals and 60 per cent had failed to meet the goals. (Note that the above figures do not add up to 100 per cent because some companies stated they cannot yet tell.)

These findings suggest at least a link between a well defined culture and success against the business goals that underpinned the culture change effort. The findings for the 'Culture and Change Management' survey are analysed in detail within Chapter 3.

Harvard Research

Probably the best known piece of analysis into the efficacy of corporate culture in driving sustainable and superior financial performance was carried out by the Harvard Business School Professors John P Kotter and James L Heskett in the late 1980s and early 1990s, and published in their seminal work *Corporate Culture and Performance*.[3]

The following extract was reported within 'The Inclusive Approach and Business Success: The Research Evidence. An Interim Report' by the UK-based Centre for Tomorrow's Company.[4]

"Kotter and Heskett... studied 207 firms drawn from 22 different industries. Using a simple questionnaire they constructed a 'Culture Strength Index' for each company. The questionnaire [invited] top management... to rate the firms in their own industry on the degree to which they believed that their managers had been influenced by having a strong corporate culture – for example to what extent did they speak of their company's distinctive style or way of doing things, to what extent were the values explicit and to what extent had the firms been managed according to long-standing policies and practices, not just those of the current CEO.

"They then calculated measures of economic performance for these companies, using three methods:

1. Average yearly increase in net income.

2. Average yearly return on investment.

3. Average yearly increase in share price.

"There was a slight tendency for firms with strong cultures to have outperformed those with weak cultures over the previous decade.

"[However] a study of 20 of the firms with strong cultures but weak performance... indicated that they were companies which had done unusually well in the past but which had held onto cultures which no longer were functional in the face of changed market conditions.

"Twenty-two companies from ten industries were selected for further study. All had strong cultures. They included such firms as Hewlett-Packard, American Airlines, Wal-Mart, Pepsi Co, Xerox, Texaco and Citicorp. Comparing them on an industry basis, 12 were classified as high performers and 10 as low performers. None of the low performers did badly in an absolute sense – they just did not do so well as others.

"... Industry experts were invited to rate all 22 companies on how much value they placed on leadership and on relationships with customers, employees and shareholders [see Table 2.1].

Value Placed on Relationships	High Performers	Low Performers
	(average performance score out of 7)	
1. Leadership	6.0	3.9
2. Customers	6.0	4.6
3. Employees	5.8	4.1
4. Shareholders	5.7	3.9
Share price increases (1977–88)	400%+	100%
Return on invested capital	11.3%	7.7%

Table 2.1: Value Placed on Relationships by Industry Experts

"Finally, the researchers compared the performance of the 12 companies which placed strong emphasis on stakeholder relations with the performance of the group of companies, 20 in number, identified as having 'problem' cultures, ie, ones which were strong, but not performance-enhancing and not adapted to current conditions. The figures relate to the years 1977–1988 and are shown in [Table 2.2].

	Average for 12 firms with performance-enhancing cultures	Average for 20 firms without performance-enhancing cultures
Revenue Growth	682%	166%
Employment Growth	282%	36%
Stock Price Growth	901%	74%
Tax Base (Net Income) Growth	756%	1%

Table 2.2: The Economic and Social Costs of Low-performance Cultures (1977–1988)

Within *Corporate Culture and Performance*, Kotter and Heskett conclude that:[5]

1. "**Corporate culture can have a significant impact on a firm's long-term economic performance.** We found that firms with cultures than emphasized all the key managerial constituencies (customers, stockholders and employees) and leadership from managers at all levels outperformed firms that did not have those cultural traits by a huge margin.

2. "**Corporate culture will probably be an even more important factor in determining the success or failure of firms in the next decade.** Performance-degrading cultures have a negative financial impact for a number of reasons, the most significant being their tendency to inhibit firms from adopting needed strategic or tactical changes. In a world that is changing at an increasing rate, one would predict that unadaptive cultures will have an even larger negative financial impact in the coming decade.

3. "**Corporate cultures that inhibit strong long-term financial performance are not rare; they develop easily, even in firms that are full of reasonable and intelligent people.** Cultures that encourage inappropriate behaviour and inhibit change to more appropriate strategies tend to emerge slowly and quietly over a period of years, usually when firms are performing well. Once these cultures exist, they can be enormously difficult to change because they are often invisible to the people involved, because they help support the existing power structure in the firm, and for many other reasons.

4. "**Although tough to change, corporate cultures can be made more performance enhancing.** Such change is complex, takes time and requires leadership, which is something quite different from even excellent management. That leadership must be guided by a realistic vision of what kinds of cultures enhance performance."

Kotter and Heskett's research suggests that culture has a powerful impact on financial performance (for better or worse). But to be a winning culture they must be adaptive and must, it suggests, be sympathetic to wider stakeholder concerns. (Frameworks such as the Balanced Scorecard and the European Foundation for Quality Management's (EFQM) Business Excellence Model – see Chapter 6, Section F – are being used by many organizations to capture and measure stakeholder-facing performance.)

So a key learning from both the Business Intelligence survey and the Kotter and Heskett research is that corporate culture has a powerful influence on what happens within organizations. However, this is not necessarily a positive influence. After all, the Business Intelligence survey found that almost 30 per cent of companies with 'extremely well defined' cultures who had undergone a culture change programme had failed to meet the business goals of the culture change effort. Due to the format of this survey it is impossible to tell whether that having an 'extremely well defined' culture was in itself a barrier to change. However, research for this Report, and outlined in the following Chapters (in particular Chapter 5), suggests that a strong culture can prove a potent barrier to change. As John Childress, chief executive officer, and Larry Senn, chairman of the culture change specialists Senn-Delaney Leadership Consulting Group, state in their 1995 book *In the Eye of the Storm: Reengineering Corporate Culture*:[6]

> "Very often, the culture that brought the organization success in its early years may be the very cause of a company's demise. The trick is to recognize this problem and look for ways to shift the culture. All too often the temptation to work harder with old cultural behaviours can lead the organization down a path from which it is difficult to return."

Indeed, it can be argued that many of the problems faced by Western companies first trying to contend with the Japanese competitive challenge were due to an unwillingness to change traditional Western approaches to work. It was only when faced with extinction that many organizations decided that had to change their working methods, and therefore their corporate cultures, in order to compete successfully. Quality exemplars Motorola and Xerox being two of the better known cases.

The Financial Impact of Employee Satisfaction

Interestingly, all of the companies profiled as case studies within this Report firmly believed that to align corporate culture successfully to strategic objectives required a firm focus on employee satisfaction. And given the fact that the high failure rates of change programmes of the early to mid 1990s (such as corporate restructuring and business process re-engineering) are now seen as due to massive damage to employee morale, recognizing the importance of maintaining employee commitment during any change effort is judicious.

An important piece of analysis that measured the relationship between the satisfaction of employees and an organization's productivity and profitability, was carried out by researchers from the UK's Sheffield University and London School of Economics.

The researchers tracked 42 UK companies over a ten-year period from 1988 to 1997. Their findings showed that overall job satisfaction was a better predictor of the company's economic performance than competitive strategy, market share or spend on research and development. Having looked at a range of cultural factors which could contribute to productivity, they concluded that what contributes most to differences in productivity was the extent to which employees felt valued and trusted.

Writing about the research in the UK's *The Guardian* newspaper in December 1998, managing consultant Carole Pemberton said:[7]

> "And the impact of feeling valued went beyond the individual and impacted on teamworking. Where co-ordination of effort was needed the highly satisfied employee was more likely to put in extra effort to support others.

> "It prompted them to do things which were not part of their job. Much of what they contributed made a significant difference to productivity. Looked at from a different angle the 'jobsworth' mentality which blights many organizations is not the result of the attraction of small-minded people to petty bureaucracy, but an internally logical response to feeling that one's contribution does not matter."

As examples of how the case study companies emphasized the value of their employees, Hyundai Car (UK) Ltd (the case study to accompany Chapter 7), focused its culture change programme through the well-known Harvard Business School performance improvement framework, the Service-Profit Chain, which has four key links. Link one, profit and growth, is driven by link two, customer satisfaction and loyalty. This is a result of link three, service value, which in turn is determined and enhanced by link four, employee satisfaction and loyalty (see Figure 2.1).

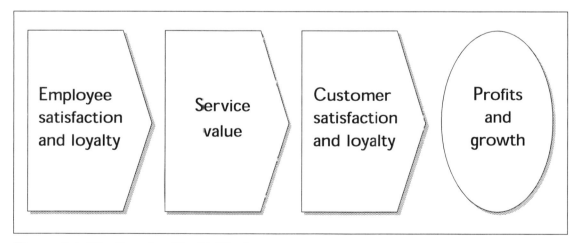

Figure 2.1: The Service-Profit Chain

Consequently, according to this theory, a breakdown in employee satisfaction and loyalty will break the links of the Service-Profit Chain and therefore seriously damage corporate performance.

Strategic implementation frameworks such as the Balanced Scorecard and the EFQM Business Excellence Model contain the same core belief. Exponents of the Balanced Scorecard believe that it is a cause and effect relationship in the three 'non-financial' perspectives of learning and growth (which normally includes employee satisfaction measures), processes and customers that drive financial success. The EFQM framework states that people management is a key enabler of people satisfaction which is a key driver of business results. The increasing number of companies using one or both of these frameworks suggests that senior managers are taking such notions seriously.

At the Inland Revenue Accounts Office in Cumbernauld, Scotland (the case study that accompanies this Chapter, and an exemplary user of the EFQM framework), the company's management eventually realized that key to delivering business results, and indeed surviving, was to transform the distinctly negative employee morale into a positive. As did Continental Airlines (the case study to accompany Chapter 1) which uses a strategic management framework bearing a striking resemblance to the Balanced Scorecard, and has a people plan (called 'working together') as one of its four key strategic thrusts. Both organizations realized, like others in this Report, that the cost of a debilitating culture on the organization was significant in both performance and financial terms.

The Cost of Culture

Calculating, or at least recognizing, the financial implications of the cost of poor performance has been a central tenet of performance improvement initiatives since the principles of Total Quality Management (TQM) started to grab senior management attention in the US and Europe during the late 1970s and early 1980s. The Japanese had shown that concepts such as 'getting it right first time', eliminating rework and implementing teamworking approaches had a powerful effect on driving down costs and gaining competitive advantage. Concepts such as the 'cost of quality' (or more accurately the 'cost of non-quality') became popular focuses for organizations travelling down the total quality road.

An interesting spin on the 'cost of' calculation appears in the book *In the Eye of the Storm: Reengineering Corporate Culture*. The authors, Childress and Senn, provided a template for calculating how much an organization's current corporate culture is costing in terms of lost dollars. This 'cost of culture' calculation, therefore, helps put a tangible financial number on so-called intangible cultural attributes. The authors write:[8]

1. "Assemble your senior management team and ask them each to write down an estimate of the percentage of the work day that is 'lost' to such cultural issues as: complaining about other people, talking about management or other departments' actions, blaming others, finding excuses or fault, complaining about lack of direction, etc. Ask them to write down a percentage (usually it is between 5–25 per cent) representing the time that is wasted and lost.

2. "Add up everyone's estimate and get an average:

    _____ Average percentage of time lost.

3. "Next determine the total number of employees in your company (or group):

    _____ Number of employees.

4. "What is the average yearly salary including benefits:

    $_____

5. "Multiply step 3 (number of employees) and step 4 (average salary plus benefits):

    $_____   Total yearly payroll cost.

6. "Multiply step 2 (average percentage of time lost) and step 5 (total yearly payroll cost):

    $_____   Estimate of lost payroll $ = cost."

Within their book, Childress and Senn reported a study of Fortune 1000 companies by US-based Accountemps which estimated that 20 per cent of peoples' time in an organization is wasted on issues related to the corporate culture.

This calculation, supported by academic research, suggests that the 'cost of culture' is a heavy burden to organizations and indeed national economies. Therefore, there appears to be a real bottom-line benefit in driving down the cost of culture.

Section C: Aligning Corporate Culture with Strategic Goals

So if we accept the premise, and it appears injudicious not to, that there is a tangible bottom-line value in managing organizational cultures, then we need to turn our attention to the task of managing cultural change. Just how does a company begin the process of creating a winning corporate culture?

First, and critically, culture change must be aligned to strategic goals or to organizational change objectives (which themselves should be aligned to strategic goals). Otherwise, the research shows, employees will not see the point of culture change and so will not commit to it, and just as importantly, any culture change initiative will quickly be forgotten as 'more important' issues demand attention.

However, if culture change must support business imperatives, then conversely it is extremely difficult to implement strategies successfully without taking into account cultural factors and ensuring they are in alignment with these long-term corporate objectives.

So culture and strategy become mutually dependent. As an example, research for the Business Intelligence report, *Building and Implementing a Balanced Scorecard*, found that rolling out such a framework causes a huge amount of culture change and that the prevailing culture is one of the biggest barriers to success.[9]

Within their 1998 book, *21st Century Leadership: Dialogues with 100 Top Leaders*, Lynne Joy McFarland, Larry Senn and John Childress provide support for this finding:[10]

> "The leaders we interviewed agree that an organization's culture can be its greatest strength when consistent with its vision, values and strategies. But a culture that prevents an organization from meeting global competition, or adapting to changing economic and social environments, can threaten the organization's very existence.
>
> "Many companies are establishing new operational strategies and altering their organizational structure to improve their competitiveness. But our research and experience [suggests] that unless an organization's culture is properly aligned with those new strategies and structures, they cannot be fully implemented."

Case Study Examples

Evidence from the case study companies supports this view. For example, at Continental Airlines, chairman and CEO Gordon Bethune and president and COO Greg Brenneman devised a brand new strategy called the Go Forward Plan to transform a near-bankrupt organization into a winning company. Despite creating four robust strategic elements (Fly to Win, Fund the Future, Making Reliability a Reality, Working Together), the company's leaders realized that just creating a new strategy would not in itself guarantee success. As Brenneman says:[11]

> "[Gordon Bethune and I] knew that the two of us could not save Continental on our own. But if we could get every employee headed in the same direction, we had a chance."

Indeed new strategies had been rolled-out so often in the decade preceding Bethune and Brenneman joining the company in 1994 that employees had stopped taking notice. So implementing the Go Forward Plan was significantly dependent on a major programme of cultural re-engineering.

At KFC, the case study to accompany Chapter 4, the new CEO David Novak realized that to deliver a customer-focused strategy to significantly improve shareholder value, the company had to tackle the 'sick' corporate culture and get people enthused by the strategy. Explaining why he was so determined to change the company's culture, Novak says:

> "The fundamental reason was a deep down belief that companies grow through people working better together. So whatever we could do to create a better working environment would, I believed, pay off in superior results."

This employee, customer, shareholder value concept is similar to the Service-Profit Chain used by Hyundai Car (UK) Ltd, which is described in Section B of this Chapter.

At Siemens KWU (a case study to support Chapter 6), the culture change programme was to support the organization's strategic move from being a predominantly designer, manufacturer and servicer of power generation plants and components for the nuclear industry to a fossil-based focus, and also to support the change from operating in a competitive rather than essentially monopolistic environment.

As Childress concludes:

> "There is no greater role for senior management during a culture change programme than to ensure that the process is driven by the overall corporate strategy." (Much more on the role of senior management can be found in Chapter 4).

Where Culture Fits with Strategic or Change Objectives

The performance measurement and change consultancy Organizational Dynamics Incorporated (ODI), provides this outline of how changing corporate culture fits in with wider change management and strategic initiatives.[12]

Change management

"Corporations, their environments, and employees' and customers' expectations are changing constantly. These changes must be met with corresponding changes in a firm's strategic focus to maintain competitive advantage, brand equity and/or value propositions. The corresponding new organizational and operational strategies need to incorporate human behaviour.... Real life operational implementation programmes are only successful when culture is considered. This includes focusing on the symbols, rituals and myths that exist within organizations. These existing 'mental models' or mental paradigms must be revealed, discussed and incorporated into any change programme.

"From the macro perspective, all change initiatives would have the following four components:

"**Direction**: Any change programme, whether global, divisional, by business unit or by product line – must have a strategic focus, integrated into the overall company-wide principles, vision and goals. The creation of a clear direction is key to creating a focus with which to anchor the project and to measure progress/results. In addition, without a clear direction, communication of the change initiative suffers.

"**Structure**:   The initiative must follow a common approach – using endorsed methodologies, tools, attitudes and values.... It is only with a consistent approach (a deployment structure) that employee confidence and trust is built. The results are improved teamwork and empowerment and a belief that the change programme is under control and not chaotic. Always remember that... your employees will be implementing the change initiative – their co-operation, enthusiasm, discipline and accountability is critical.

"**Behaviour**:   Culture change is driven both by action teams and by management. Both are working to open communications and with practical experience become role models. This exemplary behaviour becomes reinforced through success and can easily be transferred from employee to employee. Key concepts include Living with Ambiguity; Culture – passenger, navigator or architect; Alignment – creating a shared reality; Commitment – franchising high performance; Integration – helping people.

"**Systems**:   Successful change is only known if measured... measurement [must] link directly into a firm's strategy... and also link into the financial reporting and budgeting processes."

The latter point is important in that measurement is critical when implementing a culture change programme. As Dr George Labovitz, chairman of ODI, says, "measures drive behaviour and behaviour creates culture".

All of ODI's points are addressed in more detail in subsequent Chapters, but this outline does serve to stress how culture change has to be aligned with corporate strategy and how it has to be a key component of any change programme. Culture change is not be taken lightly, because if implemented properly it will impact every aspect of organization performance and activities. As Labovitz succinctly states, "the management of culture change is not for weak people".

Section D: Culture and Change Objectives

It is clear from the research for this Report that a fact of business life today is that change is ever-present, and is becoming more a case of initiative laid on top of initiative rather than a series of discrete programmes with significant periods of rest in-between.

The almost overwhelming nature of this change was outlined at the Business Intelligence conference *Corporate Agility 97* by Daryl Conner, founder and president of Organizational Development Resources (ODR) and widely accepted as a leading thinker in the fields of organizational and cultural change.

In his presentation, Conner outlined ODR research which found that there are three key factors why change has become so challenging for so many organizations:[13]

1. **Volume**: "The number of times companies are facing significant disruptions in the workplace has grown dramatically".

2. **Momentum**: "The momentum of change is certainly higher. We measure momentum in two ways. How long were you given in-between requests for change and how long do you have to execute each initiative you are asked to deal with. When you decrease those two variables you are increasing velocity".

3. **Complexity**: "Our parents and grandparents may have been asked to reorganize but we are asked to re-engineer while we bring in technology as we introduce new markets to the workforce, while we have a new CEO and while we empower the workforce. We take various complex changes and we stack them".

He states that you need that level of complexity of change simply to be able to compete today, and goes on to say:

> "When you combine these three variables – volume, momentum and complexity – in our environments you end up with the turbulence that many organizations are contending with.

> "[Therefore] the ability to anticipate what's going to happen is much less than it used to be."

He adds that he believes that there is a dangerous myth within organizations that they are just one re-engineering project away from tranquillity, when the truth is that in the future organizations are going to spend more time 'between' than 'in' familiar territory.

If this sounds a frightening prospect to some (although it probably sounds familiar to most readers), Conner goes on to say:

> "Despite all this there are organizations that are successfully managing this turmoil and achieving prosperity in the midst of all this chaos."

What they do, he says, is strive to become a nimble organization. And the importance of becoming a nimble or 'adaptive' culture is explored within the next section. Indeed the emergence of concepts such as knowledge management and the Balanced Scorecard has been essentially the outcome of a need to share knowledge quickly in order to be nimble in the face of dramatic market-place and customer change and to contend with ever intensifying competitive pressures.

Section E: Creating an Adaptive Culture

This brings us to the crucial importance of creating adaptive cultures. According to Conner the nimble organization consistently succeeds in unpredictable, competitive environments by quickly and thoroughly modifying its operations. He says that a nimble organization:[14]

- Displays alertness, agility and responsiveness when dealing with constant irregularity and disorder.

- Demonstrates speed, grace, dexterity and resourcefulness when adjusting to unfamiliar pressures.

- Is able to move through the 'assimilation' process more efficiently and effectively than its competitors.

- Is malleable within existing boundaries of operation and capable of redefining these boundaries to shift its entire paradigm, if necessary.

- Maintains a workforce that does not simply bounce back from the demands of change, it springs forward with an expanded capacity to absorb even more disruption.

Conner concludes:

> "Every organization has its own unique success factors and if you can align those with your market-place then the market-place will reward you with prosperity. The trouble is that once you are aligned you're operating in a very turbulent environment so you're constantly having to make adjustments. Some of those are small, some are large."

This last point is extremely important. Aligning the culture with the market-place is a never-ending process. As Labovitz says, "companies do not stay in alignment for long".

Quite simply, as markets transform so must strategy, change initiatives and the organization's culture. Although a culture may develop a powerful set of values by which it defines itself over a long time (this is explored in more detail in Chapter 4) the expression of those values in everyday performance should constantly be re-evaluated to ensure they are being focused in such a way as to contend with competitive demands.

As Dr David Clutterbuck, chairman of the UK-based internal communications consultancy The ITEM Group, comments:

> "There's a distinction between core beliefs – the ultimate philosophy of the organization – and the way that they are expressing those. The core beliefs will not change but ways of expressing them will."

As an example he points to the leading UK headquartered organization The Body Shop, which became renowned and successful as a retailer of environmentally friendly products. He says:

> "The Body Shop is now being copied so it is having to go back to its core beliefs to find a new way to differentiate itself."

Case Report: Bulgari

A good example of a company that recognized that it had to significantly change the way it expressed its core beliefs, is the watch and jewellery division of the Rome, Italy headquartered luxury-goods retailer Bulgari. As Labovitz (ODI had been working with Bulgari on the company's culture change programme) says:

> "The Bulgari story is interesting because they had a culture that was no longer appropriate to their needs. Until recently they serviced very rich people who made appointments. The stores were locked and only opened when a customer requested a personal viewing. But because of increased competition the senior management team realized that they needed to go out and be a different type of retail company; one where people were invited into the stores from the street to buy. Obviously the old rules of behaviour, when you had three customers a day who made appointments, became dysfunctional with the strategy."

Imagine

To align the culture with the new strategy, the division launched a culture change programme entitled Imagine. The aims were to support a total customer focus strategy that would:

1. Instil in all employees – whether in Bulgari stores around the world, in watch manufacturing operations in Switzerland, or in the company's headquarters in Rome – the fundamental principles of total customer focus.

2. Adopt a more disciplined and coherent approach to managing the business.

3. Align all of its employees around a common management approach and culture.

Following an assessment of the prevailing culture in 1996, the company spent 18 months creating awareness of the importance of customer focus, training employees in basic customer focus techniques and launching customer-focused improvement teams.

The company also developed 19 key performance indicators which would be tracked and measured, with targets set, to drive up customer-facing performance. These indicators were grouped into three scorecard perspectives of 'customer relationships', with indicators such as customer satisfaction and loyalty; 'work processes', with indicators such as on-time delivery and time to market for new products; and 'organizational support', with indicators such as motivation and energy, and teamwork (see Figure 2.2).

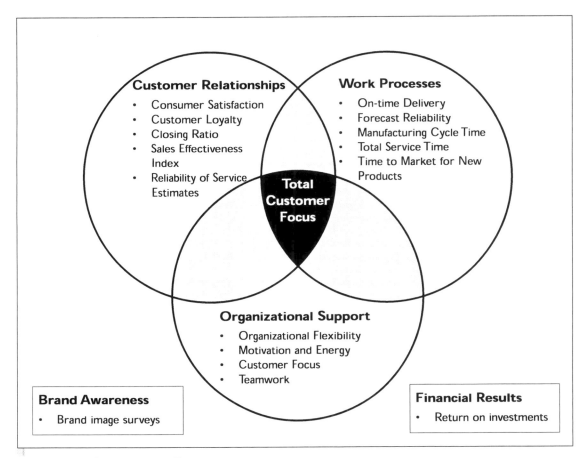

Figure 2.2: Imaginator Compass

By linking together these perspectives, Bulgari intends that employees will also gain an understanding of how to manage, measure and improve their own work processes, and in doing so increase customer retention and therefore the bottom-line. Note again how similar this concept is to concepts such as the Service-Profit Chain.

Importantly, Bulgari realized that paying personal attention to its customers was central to its success. Through its Imagine culture change programme, this was kept as the key corporate differentiator despite a significant widening of its customer base. Therefore Bulgari did not alter in any way its belief in paying personal attention to its wealthy clientele, just they way this belief was expressed and operationalized.

It is clear that Bulgari's senior managers went out with the aim to adapt their culture to new commercial needs, thus ensuring that an organization launched as a single shop in the late 19th century is in a good position to compete as a multinational concern as we enter the 21st. If the senior management team had determinedly held onto the old ways of working, its future may well have been bleak.

Comparing Adaptive and Unadaptive Cultures

Based on their research for their book *Corporate Culture and Performance*, Kotter and Heskett provided an outline, shown in Table 2.3, of the differences between an adaptive and unadaptive culture:[15]

	Adaptive Corporate Cultures	Unadaptive Corporate Cultures
Core Values	Most managers care deeply about customers, stockholders, and employees. They also strongly value people and processes that can create useful change (eg, leadership up and down the management hierarchy).	Most managers care mainly about themselves, their immediate work group, or some product (or technology) associated with that work group. They value the orderly and risk-reducing management process much more than leadership initiatives.
Common Behaviour	Managers pay close attention to all their constituencies, especially customers, and initiate change where needed to serve their legitimate interests, even if that entails taking some risks.	Managers tend to behave somewhat insularly, politically and bureaucratically. As a result, they do not change their strategies quickly to adjust to or take advantage of changes in their business environments.

Table 2.3: Adaptive vs Unadaptive Corporate Cultures

As this shows, adaptive cultures possess a corporate personality and mind that are clearly willing to embrace change and is continually focused on the key stakeholder groups of employees, customers and shareholders.

Fashioning a 'High-performance' Culture

Creating an adaptive culture, research for this Report finds, goes hand in hand with fashioning a high-performance culture. Indeed there is little point in creating an adaptive culture if the goal is not to fashion a high-performing culture.

In their book, *In the Eye of the Storm: Reengineering Corporate Culture*, Childress and Senn state that during a number of senior executive retreats in the USA, they asked corporate leaders to describe what a high-performance culture would look like. They write:[16]

"Remarkably, they all tended to come up with a similar feeling and even some of the same words. Many described a high-performance culture this way.

"It would be flexible and highly adaptive... where employees display a 'can-do' attitude, a contagious sense of optimism and belief in themselves and their products and services, and where people at all levels feel energized, motivated, and find that they are growing both personally and professionally by being a part of the company. A high-performance culture sees business and people problems as part of the game and tend to keep a healthy perspective and balance between numbers, results, people and relationships. Everyone has a focus on the customer, knows what is important, where the company is going, and can't wait to beat the pants off the competition."

Section F: Orchestrating Culture

But such cultures do not just happen, they must be orchestrated. The companies profiled for this Report did not sit back and let the culture evolve, rather they worked hard to create such a high-performing, adaptive culture. All of the case study companies had well thought out plans for creating the intended culture.

As examples, Ernst & Young (the case study to accompany Chapter 8), spent between three and four years launching initiatives that would move the somewhat staid culture to one that was clearly client-focused. The Inland Revenue Accounts Office, Cumbernauld, Scotland, first identified that they wanted to create a culture that focused on business success through employee involvement and then spent around ten years launching initiatives to create that culture. The Office director Andrew Geddes says this process was painful, but in the end worth it.

These examples reinforce the key learning point that culture change is a lengthy, and more often than not a difficult exercise. Writing in the Business Intelligence report, *Managing and Sustaining Radical Change*, the authors Carol Kennedy and David Harvey stressed:[17]

> "What [exemplary] companies share in common is the conscious intention to develop a culture that is in line with its business objectives. The trouble for most organizations is that their cultures have not been moulded or developed to reflect a set of values and beliefs but have developed by default."

They go on to report research by ODR that shows that evolutionary cultures rarely drive new strategic initiatives successfully but are more likely to demonstrate hit-or-miss results. This, they explain, is often through a lack of cohesion across the company, rivalry between subcultures within the organization and a tendency to be backward rather than forward-looking. They also state that beliefs and assumptions are more likely to be implicit rather than explicit. They go on to say:

> "By contrast, cultures that have been purposefully orchestrated to foster particular values, beliefs and behaviour... tend to be more in tune with present and future strategies, to support multiple but consistent beliefs, and to have diverse but compatible subcultures. Also, because values and beliefs tend to be stated and shared, their cultures are more manageable. Culture's importance derives from the fact that it establishes a unique set of formal and informal ground rules for how members of an organization think, behave and assume to be true. There is always diversity within an organization, but culture generates a collective viewpoint that serves as a common bond."

ODR has created a profile of evolutionary and architecturally designed cultures. This is shown in Table 2.4.

Evolutionary	Architectural
Reactive	Proactive
Reinforces past beliefs and behaviours	Reinforces beliefs and behaviours to support present and future strategy
Allows for inconsistent, multiple beliefs and behaviours	Establishes multiple, but consistent beliefs and behaviours
Subcultures form, possibly contradictory beliefs, behaviours, etc	Subcultures form with different but synergistically supporting agendas
Unconscious assumptions are strongest influence	Conscious beliefs and behaviours become dominant
Culture is difficult to manage and composed of covert assumptions	Culture more manageable and composed of overt beliefs and behaviours

Table 2.4: The Features of Evolved and Designed Cultures

Section G: Conclusion

The research for this Chapter has identified the crucial role that an understanding of corporate culture has in the successful implementation of strategic goals and change management initiatives. The evidence of the effect cultural factors have on corporate bottom-line performance shows that it is unsafe for organizations to view culture as a 'woolly intangible'. Indeed, those companies who pay significant attention to cultural factors and create adaptive, or nimble, cultures constantly aligning with customer and market-place needs, are likely to find themselves in a much stronger competitive position than those who do not.

Importantly, successful culture change demands a clear focus on the links between employee performance, customer satisfaction and business results. Time after time, the research finds, exemplary organizations recognize the power of these linkages and seek to create mechanisms for leveraging them.

However, critical before rolling out programmes to leverage these links, is the commitment to the beliefs that underpin culture change by the CEO and the rest of the senior management team, which is the subject of Chapter 4. Without it culture change, no matter how appealing, will not happen.

Key Learning Points

1. As commentators and best practice companies have shown in this Chapter, changing corporate culture must be to support strategic or change management goals.

2. Corporate cultures should be viewed as 'amoeba like' insomuch as they should be capable of incremental, or indeed dramatic, alterations if required.

3. Linked to the above, a strong culture does not necessarily correlate with excellent and lasting financial performance. It is adaptive cultures that provide the foundation for sustainable bottom-line success. Indeed, strong cultures may just as easily lead a company to ruin as to prosperity.

4. Companies with winning cultures demonstrate commitment to all an organization's stakeholders, especially employees, customers and shareholders.

5. Cultures should not be allowed to 'evolve' but rather must be managed and indeed orchestrated to ensure that the company develops a high performing culture. Otherwise, as Dr George Labovitz states, "you'll get a culture anyway, but it may not be the culture you want".

CASE STUDY: INLAND REVENUE ACCOUNTS OFFICE, CUMBERNAULD, SCOTLAND

Summary

An employee involvement initiative has transformed the Inland Revenue Accounts Office, Cumbernauld, Scotland, from a bureaucratic, poor performing organization to a benchmark of excellent public service. A focus on process measurement and improvement and total commitment from senior management have proved crucial to effecting the massive culture change required to achieve this turnaround.

Introduction

The Inland Revenue Accounts Office in Cumbernauld, Scotland, is one of two offices set up by the UK government in 1978 to deal with the UK's tax and National Insurance payments. Previously the work had been handled by a network of small local offices.

With about 1100 employees, and an annual operating budget of around £31 million, the Accounts Office, Cumbernauld, maintains about 26 million taxpayer accounts; banks and accounts for £82,000 million of tax and National Insurance contributions annually; and handles an average of £272 million in payments each day. The Office is also responsible for the registration and administration of Profit Related Pay Schemes for the whole of the UK.

Vision

The Accounts Office vision statement says that 'by the year 2000 to be recognized as the leading public sector organization in the UK'. Recent plaudits suggest this to be an attainable goal. For example, in 1996 the Office achieved Chartermark status, which is awarded to organizations which provide excellent public service. In that same year it was the winner of the Quality Scotland Business Excellence Award for the Public Sector.

The latter is based on the European Foundation for Quality Management's Business Excellence Framework. The framework assesses performance against nine criteria, split into the two performance dimensions of enablers and results. With each criteria assigned a percentage weighting to denote relative importance, the enablers are leadership, people management, policy and strategy, resources, and processes. The results criteria are people satisfaction, customer satisfaction, impact on society, and business results. In 1998 the Accounts Office was one of the first two public sector prize winners in the prestigious European Quality Awards.

However, such accolades would have seemed an impossible dream in the early to mid 1980s, when the culture of the Office could, according to the director of the Office, Andrew Geddes OBE, be described in one word, "awful".

Cultural Challenges

Geddes elucidates on the significant business and cultural challenges that the Office would, in 1985, start to tackle through an employee involvement initiative. This would, in time, bring revolutionary changes to the culture and the way people thought and behaved. Geddes explains:

> "In 1985 we had a typical civil service culture. It was traditionally command and control, bureaucratic and status counted for everything.

> "The Office had been designed as a clerical, factory process system, so people were doing a routine job and had no idea of the business objectives they contributed to. Employees had low morale and little job satisfaction. As one member of staff put it at the start of the change programme, 'the skills required for this job are an ability to count to 50 (the number of cheques in a processing batch) and an abiding love of boredom'.

> "And employee morale was further weakened by the fact that we were facing possible job losses and/or closure. Job losses because we were investing heavily in new information technology (IT) systems, which had to be paid from cost savings, and closure because we were seen by the then government as an obvious target for market testing and therefore outsourcing to the private sector."

The Need for Change

Recognizing the need for change within the Office was not through a blinding flash of inspiration, explains Geddes, but rather through a slow acceptance that there had to be a better way to manage the business. He recalls:

> "We thought we were good managers, in fact we were convinced of that. As managers we reviewed the business on an on-going basis and kept coming up with same three findings:
> 1. We were good managers – we knew that because we'd all done the training programmes and read the text books.
> 2. The processes and procedures were exceptionally good – we knew this because we as managers had designed them.
> 3. Our staff were working hard – we knew that because we were standing over them. We got the full 7 hours 25 minutes out of the staff every day. And a good manager was one that got 7 hours 30 minutes without the staff noticing.

> "Therefore, we concluded that if we were not delivering our business results then it had to be a resource problem.
>
> "So we got additional resources. But the more resources we got the worse our business results became. We just could not improve our business output, which in 1985 was a purely volume measure.
>
> "Then one day the then director said in exasperation, 'there must be a better way of doing this'."

This near desperate plea meant that for the first time in its history the Office had recognized the need for radical changes to the way it operated. As the Office managers had no real idea at this time how to change they decided to sit down and talk to staff about how managers and staff together could drive the business forward.

Resistance

Although an everyday approach to business improvement today, this was still relatively rare in any UK organization in the mid 1980s, especially within the public sector. And just talking to staff caused great consternation within the Office. Geddes explains that concern emanated from three key groups:

> "We initially met a brick wall in terms of resistance from the trade unions, suspicion from staff and unbelievable confusion from our line managers.
>
> "The trades unions saw it as threatening that we were talking directly to their members. At that time there was the notion that all communication with the staff had to go through the appropriate trades union or Whitley channels [a local avenue through which employee concerns were taken up by the trades union for discussion with management].
>
> "Second, the staff themselves believed that management had created this communications mechanism as a smoke-screen to keep the staff happy while the managers got on with their real goal of closing the business.
>
> "And finally, line managers believed that if we were going to involve staff in running and improving the business then their role would change beyond recognition, if not be wiped out completely."

However, if there were any positives, believes Geddes, then at least the term 'employee involvement' was introduced into the Office and the need to change was on the organization's agenda.

Pilot

With such a huge task of organizational change ahead, the Office first decided to run an employee involvement initiative within its 200 employee-strong banking area, one of the key parts of its business. Banking was seen as an ideal pilot candidate as new integrative IT systems offered the opportunity for multi-skilling within the area, thus moving away from the routine single-skilled way of working.

According to Geddes, key goals of the pilot were to convince employees of senior management's commitment to the tenet of employee involvement and to secure business benefits that would prove invaluable in rolling out the initiative company-wide.

The banking process essentially consists of the receipt, processing and banking of taxpayer cheques. The pilot ran for two years from 1985 to 1987, at the end of which dramatic improvements had been made to the process. In short, cheques were now smoothly going through the process rather than being continually delayed for, as an example, rework purposes. Geddes says:

> "We had effectively moved from a production-line process to one in which the group handled the whole job.

> "The one overriding contributor to the pilot's success was that we had taken all the ideas for improvement from the staff and honoured our commitment to implement them and to allow their ideas to feed into the decision-making process."

Employee Involvement Roll-out

The next stage in the employee involvement initiative was company-wide roll-out. To launch the programme the Office held a number of discussions groups, each consisting of 25 employees from all grades, to explain the initiative and to solicit honest views on how staff viewed the organization. The forthright responses, recalls Geddes, "pinned us to the wall". He continues:

> "The staff told us some incredible home truths that, on looking back more than ten years later we can say that as managers we were incredibly naive not to have recognized.

> "We started by asking people to name three things that made them proud to work for this organization and then we asked them for three negatives. It was almost impossible to get any prouds, and in fact some people had difficulty substituting the word 'like' for 'pride'. The negatives, however, seemed never-ending."

The catalogue of damning indictments included the fact that few, if any Cumbernauld employees, enjoyed working for the organization. A great number of employees felt the Office had hit rock bottom. Senior managers were seen as being remote, uncaring and with no real knowledge of what life was like on the shop floor. And employees said that, despite what managers believed, staff did not come to work to do a bad job.

Additionally, the staff had no real sense of who their customers were. Says Geddes:

> "When we first mentioned the word 'customers' to our staff they didn't really know what we were talking about. They saw our seven million taxpayers not as customers but as people who gave them problems and got in the way of them doing their work."

The primary reasons for this view was that in 1987 staff were measured on one performance indicator only. Says Geddes:

> "It was actually announced as a creed, 'thou shalt not have anything over 14 days old'."

Staff were measured once a month on the number of unanswered pieces of correspondence on their desk. Effectively, they were not measured on what they had done, but on what they had not done. So employees felt at risk of not hitting their all-important performance measure if they had to 'stop work' to deal with a tax-payer's enquiry.

With such an unambiguous expression of employee discontent and without any customer focus to speak of, the Office's senior management realized that to turn this situation around would necessitate a massive focus on culture change. It was also recognized that if people were going to deliver to the performance standards that senior management wanted, then it was up to management to create a high-performing environment and to equip people with the requisite skills.

Employee Involvement Aims

A crucial early decision was to articulate a set of aims for the employee involvement initiative. This was largely an output from the early discussion groups which generated 125 'ambitions' from the staff on how they would like to see the Office develop. These were crystallized to three key themes – communication and morale, quality versus quantity, and, importantly, employee involvement.

The purpose of the employee involvement aims were to act as an endorsement that all staff would indeed be involved in the decision-making process and create an 'employees charter' that all could relate to, and which would underpin the future behaviour of the organization. Seven aims were chosen to:

1. *Generate* commitment from all staff to the successful operation of the Accounts Office, Cumbernauld.

2. *Improve* job satisfaction.

3. *Provide* all staff with the opportunity to influence decisions.

4. *Enhance* customer service.

5. *Increase* performance and productivity.

6. *Encourage* the adoption of new working methods.

7. *Help* the office manage change.

Says Geddes, "no initiative is green-lighted unless it maps onto this charter".

Additionally, the Office senior management drew up a very brief and simple management creed, which they accepted as their core management aims:

> '[To] replace authority and control with involvement, commitment and ownership.
>
> 'The sum of which = business improvement and corporate pride.'

Geddes recalls:

> "We started to move away from a bureaucratic regime based heavily on status and authority to one based on shared values that encompassed a very high level of customer service."

These values were based on three main elements:

- relationships (creating an environment of trust and openness)
- work (a commitment to team-working and getting individuals to take a pride in what they are doing)
- management (which must provide leadership which gives a clear direction to the Office's people and must give them visible support and training).

An early decision was to also set in stone two key changes that would have to be made if the Office was to prove successful. These were:

- To set out to make the Inland Revenue Accounts Office, Cumbernauld, synonymous with quality.
- To continue to uphold the public sector ethos while removing the civil service mentality.

Geddes recalls that a very simple question was posed to managers and staff alike:

> "With every single one of our seven million taxpayers, ask yourself this question, 'if our customers did have a choice, why would they bring their business back to us?'."

Developing Customer Awareness

The Office realized that it had to develop a real sense of customer awareness and that the service it offered its customers had to be better than could be provided by a private sector organization. The threat of outsourcing was an ever-present reality and could only be effectively repelled if the Cumbernauld Office delivered exceptional customer service.

Driven by the principles of employee involvement, the Office set about this challenge by launching a 'task team' charged with introducing an action plan for quality improvement. The team was given three interrelated key objectives:

1. Develop customer awareness.
2. Develop quality improvement measures.
3. Develop and enhance people skills.

For the objective of customer awareness a programme was launched with the simple title 'Going for Quality'. All 1100 employees attended a one-day customer awareness workshop. Importantly, employees attended in natural work teams as a strong element of team-building was built into the workshop.

In total it took about six months for this workshop to be delivered to all employees. But, according to Geddes, it was well worth the time and effort:

> "The main objective of the workshop was for our people to begin to believe, think and talk customer service, and there's no doubt that when we measured staff post-workshop, there was a noticeable improvement in attitude and approach to our external customers. There was even a change of language, staff were beginning to really see taxpayers as customers and not interruptions to their work."

Post-workshop, employees were also beginning to behave differently towards 'internal' customers, a concept that had been hitherto unknown within the Office. Previously, blame had been the main focus of the relationship between internal groups and sections.

Process Measurement and Improvement

Following on from the success of the workshops, the Office took another important step towards its hoped-for customer service culture by introducing customer service improvement groups (CSIGs) throughout the organization.

A CSIG, which comprises volunteer managers and staff, exists in each of the Office's 18 business units, meaning that a total of 150 people are involved in these Groups.

The purpose of CSIGs is to identify core business processes, develop, implement and refine quality improvement measures and build quality into the business process. This approach marked a significant change to the process and purpose of quality measurement within the Office. Explains Geddes:

> "Previously, sampling was done on work that had been done months earlier and was a large exercise conducted on an infrequent basis. Managers developed and carried out the exercise and used the results to criticize staff performance."

Through CSIGs, the focus is on sampling work 'in flight' and on a frequent basis, thus enabling errors to be identified and corrected before they affect the customer. Managers and staff develop and carry out the measurement together and, importantly use the results to identify training needs and process improvements.

The CSIGs have a set of criteria to follow when designing the quality improvement measures, but they are allowed to design their own measures and targets. Says Geddes:

> "To improve performance it's vital to remove the blame culture, and let staff own their work and be responsible for the quality of their output."

Devolving responsibility for quality measurement to self-directing CSIGs brought the office into conflict with its internal auditors, who were alarmed to discover that nobody was responsible for 'checking the checkers'. It took the Office a full six years to convince the internal auditors of the wisdom of this approach. However, the auditors are now clearly won over, evidenced by this extract from a recent internal audit of the Office's quality measurement programme:

'[Accounts Office, Cumbernauld's] quality philosophy is centred on the shop floor and the trust of senior management in conducting that is implicit....We believe the overall approach adopted has been extremely successful and has resulted in a strong quality culture being firmly embedded at all staff levels. The commitment to quality has been reinforced by every single person we have spoken to.'

Job Commitment

Creating a culture conducive to process improvement required one important commitment at the outset. That all saving accrued as a result of improvements would be reinvested into the business. Geddes explains why this was crucial:

"Historically our work was subject to considerable amounts of rework. And so, not surprisingly, employees feared that if rework was eliminated, so would be their jobs. So this commitment to reinvest was a signal that jobs would be safe."

This commitment was born out in 1992 when a quality improvement group of five people was launched within the Office, as was a customer service group of seven people. These groups came from other parts of the business and were fully funded through cost savings resulting from process improvements. A communications group has also subsequently been set up, again financed from cost savings.

Investor In People (IIP)

The third element of the original task team objectives was developing and harnessing people skills. And this, says Geddes, underpins the previous two elements.

Focusing on this element led the Office to committing to the UK's Investor In People (IIP) standard. Essentially, IIP is a framework which ties individual training and development to business goals, and it has four key components:

1. Senior management has to publicly commit to the standard and either self-assess against the standard or receive a 'health check' from the local Training and Enterprise Council (TEC).

2. Training needs are then reviewed for all employees against business goals, leading to action plans which address identified gaps.

3. The launch of training and development action plans for employees.

4. The training is assessed for effectiveness.

External assessment against the IIP standard is based on completion of the action plan, and submission of a portfolio of evidence to the TEC, who validates this by site visits and interviews with employees.

The Accounts Office, Cumbernauld, committed to IIP in 1993 and was awarded IIP status in 1994, the first department of the Inland Revenue to achieve this and indeed one of the first in the public sector.

According to Geddes (who is now a director of IIP Scotland) IIP provided the right focus for training and development to meet the Office's business objectives. Central to this has been the creation of a personal development review system and individually focused personal development plans. Through this a dialogue between manager and job holder identifies individual skills requirements and how these are aligned to business priorities.

And employees do seem to be satisfied with how they are treated and their skills developed. Staff surveys carried out over the past four years show that people's overall satisfaction level has risen from 65 per cent to 78 per cent. Over the same period the response rate to the survey has gone up from 69 per cent to 84 per cent. In the latest survey 82 per cent of staff confirmed that they find their work satisfying.

EFQM Business Excellence Framework

By 1994, the Office had developed a real sense of customer awareness – process measurement and improvement was well established and IIP was enabling the Office to develop and enhance its people skills. So the next challenge for its senior management team was to decide what would be the next focus for continuous improvement. Says Geddes:

> "Although we had already come a long way and were certainly getting results, there still seemed to be a sense that all these initiatives were somehow separate from each other and we needed a mechanism to bring these three main elements together."

And this brought the Office to the EFQM Business Excellence Framework. Geddes recalls:

> "We began looking at how other organizations were assessing their organizational effectiveness and we found that many were using the EFQM framework. This did seem to be an effective tool but we were a little hesitant about using it because in the mid 1990s the framework was still very much focused on big private businesses and not on public sector organizations."

However, after adapting the model's assessment elements for its own needs (but still within the nine criteria areas) the Office decided to pilot the framework within one of its business units during 1995.

Importantly, responsibility for the pilot was devolved to business unit CSIGs, with additional support provided to help the CSIG understand how to use the framework to:

- identify strengths and weaknesses

- identify the vital few areas for improvement to build into the business units business improvement plan

- to customize it to the business unit's own requirements.

The Office believes that delegating responsibility for assessment to the CSIGs means that the people doing the jobs themselves work out exactly what needs to be fixed, what results are being achieved and how the unit compares to business excellence benchmarks. Says Geddes:

> "Armed with that information, the CSIGs can then focus on the excellence gap and put into place the measures to improve quality. This fits perfectly with our philosophy of employee involvement and for units themselves to be responsible for their own process measurement and improvement."

Following the success of the pilot, all business units now self-assess against the framework's criteria on a rolling two-year cycle. According to Geddes the framework provides a systematic view of the organizational activities, is a robust benchmark of best-in-class performance and provides a consensus view of quality improvement. He says:

> "We are confident that continued use of the framework will take our organization beyond leading public sector organization status and towards world class."

However, the Office is itself being recognized externally as a benchmark organization, as its Quality Scotland Foundation and European Quality Awards testify.

It is noteworthy that these accolades were received while the Office was dealing with the biggest change to the UK taxation process in 50 years. The new system involves taxpayers completing an individual assessment form to calculate their own liability. The first of the new 'self assessment' taxation forms began arriving at the Office in January 1998. Training staff in the new process began three years earlier and, Geddes believes, was made significantly easier thanks to the spirit of employee involvement and customer focus that had by then been embedded into the organization.

Succeeding with Change

According to Geddes there are two key elements to a successful culture change programme – leadership and communication. And these are interconnected. He says:

> "In times of change there's a natural uncertainty among staff. They want to be told the bad news as well as the good and they want managers to be open and to share a genuine two-way dialogue about the business. And it's my job as director to ensure that this two-way dialogue takes place."

To help achieve this, a communications department was set up and charged with developing and implementing a communications strategy. Each work area has a communications representative, who acts as a gateway from the communications group to the management board.

Also, a personal copy of the strategy goes to every member of staff and an annual communications plan sets out how the Office is going to improve communications over the next 12 months.

In addition, the Office has launched management update meetings (MUMs). These quarterly events review the progress of the business and includes all managers, CSIG and Trade Union representatives. Also, focus group meetings of about 100 people are held to further inform staff of business direction and gain useful feedback. Geddes adds:

> "We've also introduced a team listening system that feeds information down to the workplace in a structured way and allows teams to discuss issues and feedback."

The Office has also introduced an information help line which anybody in the organization can use to ask questions. Impressively, they are guaranteed they will have at least a holding answer within three hours and a full response within 24 hours.

However, Geddes firmly believes that by far the most effective communications mechanism is face-to-face:

> "Sit down with people on their own patch and talk to them about their work. That's how you get the best information about what's going on in the business."

Conclusion

In conclusion, Geddes believes that, based on the experience of Accounts Office, Cumbernauld, there are three stages of change:

1. Overcoming the fear of change.

2. Creating an attraction to change (here people have lost the fear and are starting to see that there may be benefits to them in being part of a change process).

3. Sharing the ownership of change (change is no longer coming solely from the top of the organization but also from the bottom, becoming effectively a two-way process).

According to Geddes, going through these three stages may be painful but will be worth it when the pay-off comes. He says:

> "Today we have very high levels of customer and employee satisfaction and our financial performance has improved beyond recognition. We now deliver well within our budget on an annual basis and our unit costs show a year-on-year improvement in real terms.

> "We've moved from being a relatively obscure part of the Inland Revenue, and a poor performer at that, to a highly respected executive unit within the public sector and are recognized as a quality performer by much of the private sector."

Key Learning Points

1. Launching a culture change programme was not a blinding flash of inspiration but rather a recognition that with possible closure and/or job losses compounded by poor performance and low employee morale, there had to be a better way to manage the business. Essentially, senior management took responsibility for its own failings.

2. Management decided to involve all staff in the change programme through an employee involvement initiative. Although early resistance was met, management knew that this was the way to drive the business forward.

3. The Office first piloted the initiative in its banking section. This was valuable in demonstrating management's commitment to the principles of employee involvement.

4. Management set up discussion groups to outline the initiative's goals and for soliciting honest feedback on how employees viewed the organization. The feedback was exceptionally painful but a valuable mechanism for understanding the cultural challenges ahead.

5. The Office articulated a set of aims for the employee involvement initiative, which became an employees' charter. This formed the basis for all subsequent improvement initiatives.

6. A Task Team was launched and charged with responsibility for developing customer awareness, quality improvement measures and developing and enhancing people skills.

7. The Office devolved responsibility for quality improvement measures to Customer Service Improvement Groups (CSIGs) within each business unit. This ensured that people doing the work owned the work.

8. The UK's Investor in People (IIP) standard had proved a powerful mechanism for developing and enhancing people skills.

9. The Office self-assesses performance against the EFQM Business Excellence Framework, responsibility for which also resides within the CSIGs, before being rolled up to an organization-wide level. This has proved an exceptional integrating framework.

10. A proactive approach to internal communication has been critical to the success of the culture change programme.

3

CULTURE AND CHANGE MANAGEMENT – EXCLUSIVE RESEARCH

Executive Summary

1. Entitled 'Culture and Change Management', this survey set out to discover what importance organizations give corporate culture, how well managed culture is and the key cultural change enablers.

2. A total 236 organizations, 159 from Europe and 79 from USA/Rest of the World, responded to the survey.

3. Almost 12 per cent of respondents claimed they had an 'extremely well defined' culture, and the same percentage claimed a 'very poorly defined' culture. Tellingly, the former group performed better in virtually all subsequent questions.

4. Over a third of organizations scored 3 (on a scale of 1, change resistant, to 5, highly adaptable). This suggests that most organizations have some way to go before they create adaptive cultures. Even those with 'extremely well defined' cultures only scored a mean of 3.32.

5. Companies with 'extremely well defined' cultures are much more likely to discuss culture formally than those with 'very poorly defined' cultures.

6. A total of 72 per cent of companies with 'extremely well defined' cultures claimed that responsibility for culture resided at a senior level, against just 40 per cent of companies with 'very poorly defined' cultures.

7. Interestingly, 50 per cent of companies with 'very poorly defined' cultures devolve responsibility for culture to the HR function.

8. Well-defined corporate values play a key role in building successful cultures.

9. Companies with 'extremely well defined' cultures are far more likely to possess cultures that support strategic objectives than those with 'very poorly defined' cultures.

10. Forty per cent of organizations claim to actively manage corporate culture.

11. Almost 60 per cent of respondents have attempted to change their corporate culture.

12. Communication mechanisms played an important role in changing the corporate culture.

13. Respondents seems fairly, but not overly, satisfied with the role played by consultants in the change effort.

14. Senior management role modeling new behaviours was by the most important enabler of successful culture change.

15. Companies with 'extremely well defined' cultures were massively more likely to succeed against their change goals than those with 'very poorly defined' cultures. Indeed, just 10 per cent of the latter group claimed to have exceeded their goals.

16. The importance of culture change has grown significantly over the past five years and is set to increase further over the next five.

Section A: Ten Key Findings from the 'Culture and Change Management' Survey

Corporate cultures are not well defined

Just 11.53 per cent of all organizations claim to possess an 'extremely well defined' corporate culture. The exact same percentage reported a 'very poorly defined' culture. Just 40 per cent of respondents claim to actively manage corporate culture within their organizations against 49.36 per cent who do not. A further 10.63 per cent were unsure.

These findings strongly suggest that organizations have some way to go before they are really managing culture as a corporate asset.

Companies with 'extremely well defined' cultures are more likely to possess 'positive' cultural attributes

As a mean finding, companies with 'extremely well defined' cultures were significantly more inclined to demonstrate 'positive' cultural attributes (such as being 'empowered', 'open', 'highly ethical' and 'accountable') than the rest of the respondents. Tellingly, however, those with 'extremely well defined' cultures were only slightly less 'change resistant' than the mean for the whole survey, and only marginally more likely to be 'elitist' than 'single status'.

This suggests that resistance to change is still a problem for most organizations, irrespective of how well defined their culture.

Senior management likely to be responsible for corporate culture, except in companies with 'very poorly defined' cultures

Senior management in over 60 per cent of organizations hold formal responsibility for the corporate culture. However, this is true in just 40 per cent of organizations with 'very poorly defined' cultures. In addition, 50 per cent of organizations with 'very poorly defined' cultures devolve responsibility to HR, compared to 19.54 per cent of the total responses and just 12 per cent of organizations with 'extremely well defined' cultures.

This suggests that most companies realize that senior management should own corporate culture.

Senior management support is the key to culture change success

A massive 98.66 per cent of respondents stated that senior executives role modeling new behaviours is key to enabling culture to be changed.

This finding suggests that if senior management are not enthused by and leading cultural change then lasting success will not be achieved.

Corporate values are extremely important

Just 8.47 per cent of respondents stated that their corporate values were totally understood within the organizations. The vast majority of companies, 77.11 per cent, proffered a score of 2 or 3 (on a rating of 1, 'totally understood' to 5 'not at all understood'). However, 12.65 per cent of US and the Rest of the World respondents said their values were totally understood against just 6.36 per cent of European companies. Moreover 87.47 per cent of all respondents believe that gaining buy-in to shared values across the organization is essential to their future.

These findings suggest that organizations recognize the pivotal importance of corporate values but have a long way to go to make them totally understood within the company.

Culture not yet clearly supporting strategic goals

Just 11.58 per cent of responding organizations believe their current cultures supports their strategic objectives. However, with a mean score of 1.76 (with 1 being 'extremely well' and 5 'not at all') those with 'extremely well defined' cultures showed a stronger culture/strategy alignment than the average of 2.70. Those with 'very poorly defined' cultures scored a mean of just 3.64.

These findings show that companies still have a lot of work to do in creating a culture/strategy alignment.

Cultures just about enabling critical performance-enhancing capabilities

In general, organizations felt their current culture were slightly above adequate in enabling critical performance-enhancing capabilities such as being 'responsiveness to market and customer needs', 'successful implementation of performance improvement programmes', the adoption of new information technologies' and the 'development of knowledge sharing practices'. However, the mean score for those with 'very poorly defined' cultures showed that their cultures are not adequate for these purposes. Tellingly, these organizations had a scored a mean of 4.10 (with 1 being 'extremely well' and 5 'not at all') for their cultural abilities to develop knowledge-sharing practices.

This finding suggests that companies can still improve their cultures impact on developing performance-enhancing capabilities.

Subcultures pose threat to cultural unity

A total of 47.22 per cent of respondents gave a score of 1 or 2 (on a rating of 1, 'completely agree', to 5, 'strongly disagree') to the statement, 'subcultures within our organization pose a major barrier to gaining a unified culture'. Interestingly, those companies who actively manage their culture reported a mean score of 3.2.

This finding suggests that organizations have a lot to learn about managing subcultural pressures on corporate culture.

Internal communications are critical to successfully driving culture change

Just 11.48 per cent of respondents completely agreed with the statement, 'internal communications are well managed to communicate corporate priorities and cultural values'. Another 12.34 per cent of companies strongly disagreed with it. However, 88.75 per cent of companies believe internal communication programmes are important or extremely important in enabling culture to be changed.

These findings suggest that although aware of the absolute importance of internal communications organizations are not satisfied with its present performance.

Most companies achieve their corporate culture goals

A total of 66.25 per cent of respondents claimed their culture change programme achieved or exceeded its goals. For companies with 'extremely well defined' cultures, the figure was slightly lower at 64.28 per cent, and for companies with 'very poorly defined' cultures a much lower figure of 30 per cent was reported.

These findings suggest that culture change programmes may be more effective than generally thought, although those with 'very poorly defined' cultures were likely to fail with change objectives. However, these success ratings do not take into account the scope and difficulty of the culture change programmes or whether respondents were claiming success too early as, to be meaningful, culture change success has to be measured over the long-term.

Section B: Context

'Culture and Change Management' was a survey commissioned by Business Intelligence to discover how organizations view the importance of corporate culture, the key levers of successful culture change initiatives, and whether there is a correlation between the active management of cultural characteristics and success against change objectives.

The prime targets for the questionnaire were companies struggling to reform themselves, recently privatized organizations, industries subject to global competition, and those subject to rapid change and innovation.

The questionnaire was sent to key personnel within these organizations, including those responsible for performance improvement projects involving major change, innovation and corporate wide transformation, human resource managers, change managers, line managers, and information technology managers.

The survey was sent to organizations in the UK and Europe and separately to companies in the USA. A few companies from other geographical regions responded to the survey, and their results have been integrated into the USA responses under the heading 'USA and the Rest of the World'. Indeed, Millennium Inorganic Chemicals, the case study to support this Chapter, responded via their Bunbury, Western Australia plant. This is a valuable case study as they have additional plants in the USA (where they are headquartered), South America and Europe. Other best practice case studies identified from this survey are Superdrug (a case study to accompany Chapter 5) and Ernst & Young (the case study to support Chapter 8).

Representatives from a total of 236 organizations responded to the survey; 159 came from European organizations (or European operating locations) and 77 from the USA and the Rest of the World. In analysing the results this Chapter looks first at the combined responses and, where appropriate, compares the European results with the USA and the Rest of the World in order to discover whether there any obvious differences in approaches to dealing with cultural issues.

We shall also, for many of the questions, look at how the replies of companies with 'extremely well defined' cultures compares with those companies whose culture is 'very poorly defined'.

Questionnaire Format

First though, here is an explanation of how the questionnaire was formatted. The questionnaire required the respondent to answer 22 questions, many broken down into subsections. The replies are generally on a five point scale, requiring the respondent to tick the most appropriate box that is representative of their organization. In some cases the respondent may be asked to reply a 'yes', 'no' or 'unsure' answer, or to rate a list of characteristics or factors of corporate cultural activities that most apply to their company. Many of the questions also carry a subsection that allows the respondent to answer with words or sentences to give a much more varied picture of current corporate culture and the change process.

The questionnaire is broken down into the following three sections:

Section 1: Rating your corporate culture

This set out to discover how well defined the culture was, its key characteristics, how widely it was understood, who was responsible for the culture and how well it supported the current corporate strategy.

Section 2: Managing corporate culture in your organization

This set out to discover how well the culture was managed, whether it was assessed and the difficulties in managing discrete cultural elements.

Section 3: Changing corporate culture

This set out to discover whether organizations had attempted to change their culture, how effective the culture change programme had been and the key enablers of successful cultural transformation.

Subjectivity

First some words of warning. It is important to bear in mind that, due to the nature of such a survey, the replies are going to be, to some extent, subjective. The responses will largely be the individual respondent's own perception of their corporate culture, and therefore may not necessarily reflect the view of the whole employee-base. Indeed a diametrically opposite set of answers may be proffered by another organizational representative.

Section C: Rating Your Current Corporate Culture

Section one of the survey was entitled 'Rating your Current Corporate Culture' and the first question, on a scale of 1 to 5, with 1 being the most positive answer, asked respondents the question 'how well-defined is corporate culture in your organization?' An 'extremely well defined' culture was claimed by 11.53 per cent of all respondents and the same percentage claimed a 'very poorly defined' culture. The mean score was 2.94. Therefore, as Table 3.1 shows, most companies proffered a 'quite well defined' culture.

Mean	Extremely well defined		Quite well defined		Very poorly defined
2.94	11.53%	22.64%	37.17%%	17.09%	11.53%

Table 3.1: How well defined is corporate culture in your organization? – all respondents

As a mean score, the USA and the Rest of the World did slightly better than Europe with a score of 2.86 against 2.98. Also, whereas only 8.38 per cent of European companies claimed an 'extremely well defined' culture, this rose to 17.72 per cent in the USA and the Rest of the World. Conversely, whereas 9.67 per cent of European companies claimed a 'very poorly defined' culture, this ballooned to 15.18 per cent in the USA and the Rest of the World.

Cultural Characteristics

The second question of section one provided respondents with a list of 13 cultural characteristics against which they had to rate their organizations on a scale of 1 to 5, as shown in Table 3.2. A score of 1 relates to replies on the left of the table (eg, Autocratic) whereas 5 relates to the right (eg, Empowered).

As a key part of this analysis is to compare the responses to many subsequent questions of those who claimed an 'extremely well defined' culture with those who claim one that is 'very poorly defined', the mean scores for each are listed to the far right of the table.

An interesting finding here is that on a score of 1 'change resistant' to 5 'highly adaptive', almost a third of respondents proffered a 3 score. Only 13.79 per cent claimed a 5 score. Given the importance stressed in the previous Chapter about the importance of developing adaptive cultures, this is somewhat worrying.

Companies with 'extremely well defined' cultures at 3.32 did better than those with 'very poorly defined' cultures at 2.35. But a score of 3.32 is not an uplifting finding.

However, those with 'extremely well defined' cultures scored better than those with 'very poorly defined' cultures in all categories, and the scores were

Mean						Extremely well defined mean	Very poorly defined mean
	Autocratic		shares both characteristics		Empowered		
3.12	7.69%	17.52%	42.73%	18.80%	13.24%	3.76	2.32
	Risk averse		shares both characteristics		Entrepreneurial		
2.94	14.10%	23.50%	29.05%	20.51%	12.82%	3.42	2.57
	Suspicious		shares both characteristics		Trusting		
3.125	10.77%	19.82%	31.03%	22.84%	15.51%	3.36	2.28
	Functionally-based		shares both characteristics		Process-based		
2.78	16.95%	19.13%	40%	13.47%	10.43%	3.23	2.22
	Centrally controlled		shares both characteristics		Devolved		
2.93	14.16%	20.60%	36.19%	18.02%	12.01%	3.16	2.71
	Hierarchical		shares both characteristics		Team-based		
3.00	14.10%	23.07%	26.92%	19.65%	16.23%	3.73	2.00
	Defensive		shares both characteristics		Open		
3.06	12.5%	20.68%	28.01%	25.43%	13.36%	3.60	2.03
	Bureaucratic		shares both characteristics		Collaborative		
3.00	14.10%	22.64%	26.06%	23.07%	14.10%	3.53	2.03
	Internally focused		shares both characteristics		Customer-focused		
3.27	10.3%	13.73%	34.76%	21.03%	20.17%	3.80	2.67
	Unprincipled		shares both characteristics		Highly ethical		
3.95	2.13%	5.98%	23.07%	32.05%	36.75%	4.46	3.28
	Faceless		shares both characteristics		Accountable		
3.57	15%	10.72%	31.33%	24.46%	25.32%	4.23	2.96
	Elitist		shares both characteristics		Single status		
3.05	12.33%	16.29%	37%	22.02%	12.33%	3.04	2.42
	Change resistant		shares both characteristics		Highly adaptable		
3.10	11.63%	18.13%	31.46%	24.13%	13.79%	3.32	2.35

Table 3.2: How would you describe corporate culture in your organization in relation to the following pairs of contrasting characteristics (please tick one box per pair)

significantly different in a couple of instances. As examples, a score of 3.73 against 2.00 were given for the characteristics 'hierarchical' and 'team-based', and a score of 4.23 against 3.28 for 'unprincipled' and 'highly ethical'. The latter is a telling finding given that our research finds, and indeed our case studies demonstrate, the importance of shaping corporate values as part of a culture change programme (more on this can be found in Chapter 4).

Overall the USA and the Rest of the World respondents scored slightly better (if better equals scores to the right) than Europe. Two notable exceptions being that more USA and Rest of the World respondents claimed they were 'elitist' rather than 'single status' and, importantly, with a mean score of 2.96, more saw themselves as 'change resistant' than 'highly adaptive'. The Europeans scored 3.17 on this. Indeed only 0.32 per cent of European organizations believed themselves to be 'change resistant' (ie, proffering a 1 score) against 14.28 per cent from the USA and the Rest of the World.

A supplementary question to question two asked respondents, 'what are the dominant features of your corporate culture?'. For Europe, the highest, with 12 responses was 'client/customer focused'. Ten claimed to be 'risk adverse'. Next, at four replies each, came 'highly ethical', 'empowerment', 'open' and 'hierarchical'. Other replies included 'fear management', 'old colonial style', 'defensive senior management', 'devolved' and 'passionate'.

With three replies each, the highest from the USA and the Rest of the World respondents were 'bureaucratic' and 'hierarchical', followed by 'change resistant' with two replies. Other comments included 'fast paced', 'collaborative', 'competitive' and 'customer-focused'. However, there were a number of 'negative replies such as 'brutal fear is persuasive', 'stifling' and 'stupidity'.

Discussing Culture

Question three of this section asked, 'to what extent is corporate culture a matter of discussion as an issue relevant to day-to-day performance?'. The responses from all respondents are shown in Table 3.3. Again responses from those organizations with 'extremely well defined' and 'very poorly defined' cultures are shown. Also, a score of 1 equals 'widely and regularly discussed' and 5 'rarely discussed.'

Mean	Widely and regularly discussed		Occasionally discussed		Rarely discussed	Extremely well defined mean	Very poorly defined mean
	a) Formally, in board, management and other staff meetings						
2.65	21.27%	25.95%	31.06%	9.78%	11.91%	1.84	3.71
	b) Informally						
2.10	30.56%	36.24%	26.63%	4.8%	1.74%	1.42	2.21

Table 3.3: To what extent is corporate culture a matter of discussion as an issue relevant to day-to-day performance?

What is interesting from this finding is that culture seems to be discussed widely on an informal level (although what this means may be open to question). Similarly, culture does seem to be well discussed on a formal level, in board meetings and other staff meetings.

Tellingly, however, companies with 'extremely well defined' cultures performed better than those with 'very poorly defined' cultures, especially when it came to formal discussions with a mean score of 1.84 against 3.71.

The responses from European organizations were essentially the same as those from the USA and the Rest of the World.

Owning the Culture

Question four of section one asked respondents, 'does any person, or group, have formal responsibility for corporate culture in your organization?'. The total replies were:

Yes: 44.39 per cent

No: 38.79 per cent

Proposed: 8.62 per cent

Unsure: 6.89 per cent.

1.29 per cent of respondents ticked more than one box.

At 46.75 per cent, more European organization answered yes to this question than from the USA and The Rest of the World, at 39.74 per cent.

However, for companies with 'extremely well defined' cultures the overall replies were:

Yes: 76.92 per cent

No: 11.53 per cent

Proposed: 3.84 per cent

Unsure: 7.69 per cent.

This is substantially different from those with 'very poorly defined' cultures, the answers being:

Yes: 21.42 per cent

No: 57.14 per cent

Proposed: 3.57 per cent

Unsure: 17.85 per cent.

A supplementary question to question four asked, 'if yes, or proposed, please indicate who is responsible (tick one box only)'. The total replies are shown in Table 3.4:

The interesting finding here is that a total of 72 per cent of companies with 'extremely well defined' cultures claimed that responsibility for culture

	Overall response	Extremely well defined	Very poorly defined
The CEO	22.55%	20%	10%
The board	18.79%	20%	0%
Senior management team	24.81%	32%	30%
HR	19.54%	12%	50%
Other	14.28%	16%	10%

Table 3.4: People/Departments Responsible for Corporate Culture

resided at a senior level, against just 40 per cent of companies with 'very poorly defined' cultures. As Chapter 4 will show, research for this Report finds that it is critical during a cultural change effort that responsibility for corporate culture is held at the top of the organization.

Also telling here is that whereas just 12 per cent of those with 'extremely well defined' cultures devolved responsibility for the culture to the Human Resources (HR) function, this ballooned to 50 per cent in those with 'very poorly defined' cultures. As Chapter 7 will show, although HR can be play an crucial enabling role in driving corporate change efforts, as was the case at Continental Airlines (the case study to accompany Chapter 2) and Hyundai Car (UK) Ltd (the case study to accompany Chapter 7), it is normally a mistake to devolve responsibility to this, or indeed any other function.

Corporate Values

Question five of section one asked respondents, 'are the values of your organization well understood?'. The results are shown in Table 3.5.

Mean	Totally		Partially		Not at all	Extremely well defined mean	Very poorly defined mean
2.62	8.47%	37.71%	39.40%	1.86%	2.54%	1.67	3.57

Table 3.5: Are the values of your organization well understood?

With a mean score of 2.62 (with 1 equalling 'totally' and 5 'not at all') values do seem to be at least understood within most responding organizations. However, the big difference is between those with 'extremely well defined' cultures, who scored a mean of 1.67, and those with 'very poorly defined' cultures who scored 3.57.

With a mean score of 2.36, USA and the Rest of the World firms did slightly better than Europe, who scored 2.75. And although 3.82 per cent of European companies said that their values were not understood at all, this fell to 0 per cent for USA and the Rest of the World respondents.

The supplementary question to question five asked responding organizations whether the values were 'explicitly stated', 'implicit in the way we do things here', or 'both' of these. The total replies are shown in Table 3.6.

		Extremely well defined	Very poorly defined
(i) Explicitly stated	58.26%	69.23%	22.22%
(ii) implicit in the way we do things here	32.60%	11.53%	70.37%
(iii) other	1.73%		
Both (i) and (ii)	7.39%	19.23%	7.4%

Table 3.6: How the values of respondents organizations are stated

These are difficult replies to analyse, because whereas 69.23 per cent of companies with 'extremely well defined' cultures said their values were 'explicitly stated' against 22.22 per cent of those with 'very poorly defined' cultures, the corresponding scores to the statement '[values are] implicit in the way we do things here' was 11.53 per cent against 70.37 per cent. Therefore, those with 'extremely well defined' cultures may be looking at how well their 'explicitly stated' values are implied, whereas those with 'very poorly defined' cultures may be saying how the informal cultural rules by which they work are implied.

Cultural Alignment to Strategic Objectives

Question six of section one gets to the heart of a central theme of this Report. Respondents were asked, 'how well does your current culture support your strategic objectives?'. The total replies are shown in Table 3.7.

Mean	Extremely well		Partially		Not at all	Extremely well defined mean	Very poorly defined mean
2.70	11.58%	33.90%	32.61%	15.87%	6%	1.76	3.64

Table 3.7: How well does your current culture support your strategic objectives?

With a mean score of 2.70 it seems slightly more likely that an organization's culture will support strategic objectives than not. However, just over one in ten said the culture supports strategic objectives 'extremely well'. Tellingly, though with a mean score of 1.76 companies with 'extremely well defined' cultures performed much better than those with 'very poorly defined' cultures at 3.80.

Responses from Europe were largely the same as those from the USA and the Rest of the World, a notable exception being that whereas just 2.53 per cent of USA/Rest of the World respondents said their current culture supported the strategic objectives 'not at all' this rose to 7.79 per cent of European companies.

Supporting Key Activities

Question seven of section one asked respondents, 'how well does your current culture support [a specified activity]?', on a scale of 1, 'extremely well', to 5, 'not at all'. The total replies are shown in Table 3.8.

Mean	Extremely well		Partially		Not at all	Extremely well defined mean	Very poorly defined mean
The ability to attract and retain high quality managers and staff							
2.67	13.13%	32.20%	33.89%	15.25%	5.50%	2.2	3.42
Responsiveness to market and customer needs							
2.51	16%	35.59%	30.50%	16.10%	1.69%	1.92	3.17
Successful implementation of performance improvement programmes and initiatives							
2.80	10.63%	27.65%	33.20%	19.14%	5.10%	2.15	3.64
Adoption of new information technologies, working practices and procedures							
2.63	12.6%	32.76%	35.31%	16.17%	2.97%	2.00	3.17
The development of knowledge-sharing practices							
3.02	9.36%	20.42%	37.87%	23.48%	8.93%	2.15	4.10

Table 3.8: How well does your current culture support the following activities?

With the highest mean of 2.51, 'responsiveness to market and customer needs' scored best across all respondents. The worst mean, at 3.02, was proffered for 'the development of knowledge-sharing practices'.

Unsurprisingly, given the scores in the survey thus far, those with 'extremely well defined' cultures scored much better than those with 'very poorly defined' cultures. Most notably, with a mean of 2.15 against 4.10 in the area of 'developing knowledge-sharing practices'. Interestingly, a number of our case study companies, such as Ernst & Young, Millennium Inorganic Chemicals and Superdrug believe this to be a critical ability.

Again there were only slight differences in responses from European and USA/Rest of the World respondents.

Change Mechanisms

Question eight asked respondents, 'how important are the following mechanisms for bringing about change in the way your organization operates and performs? (please state the following in order of importance, one being most important)'. The results are shown in Table 3.9.

Interestingly, there was very little difference in ranking from companies with 'extremely well defined' and those with 'very poorly defined' cultures, or either from European and USA/Rest of the World responses.

	Ranking	Mean
New roles and responsibilities	1st	2.67
Organizational restructuring	2nd	2.93
Culture change	3rd	3.35
Information technology	4th	3.82
Retraining	5th	4.02
Reward system redesign	6th	4.12

Table 3.9: Ranked importance of various mechanisms for bringing about a change in how respondents organizations operate and perform

What is particularly interesting here is that 'reward system redesign' was ranked last out of the six options. This is somewhat surprising given that commentators repeatedly stated during the research for this Report the absolute importance of redesigning reward systems to support culture change objectives (this is covered in detail in Chapter 7).

Section D: Managing Corporate Culture

Section two of the questionnaire, 'Managing Corporate Culture in Your Organization' started with question nine, 'is corporate culture actively managed in your organization?'. The total replies were:

Yes: 40 per cent
No: 49.36 per cent
Unsure: 10.63 per cent.

Again results were largely similar for European and USA/Rest of the World respondents.

Respondents who answered 'yes' to question nine were then asked question 10a, 'do you have a method for assessing the alignment of corporate culture with your strategy?'. So the 40 per cent who replied 'yes' should be seen as a 100 per cent for this question. The replies were:

Yes: 44.68 per cent
No: 43.82 per cent
Unsure: 10.63 per cent.

Question 10b asked, 'if yes (to question 10a) what is the method based on (please tick one or more)?'. Therefore, the 44.68 per cent should now be seen as 100 per cent. The replies were:

Staff surveys: 22.32 per cent
Customer surveys: 6.25 per cent
Other: 6.25 per cent
Both staff and customer surveys: 65.17 per cent.

Staff surveys and customer surveys were seen as vital culture enhancing tools in many of our case study companies such as Ernst & Young (the case study to accompany Chapter 8) and Siemens KWU (a case study to Chapter 6). Such tools enable the organizations to track progress against cultural goals and to ensure that employees are aligned behind strategic and cultural goals and, crucially, that customers are reaping the benefits of the change effort.

Cultural Statements

All respondents were then asked question 11, 'in relation to your own organization, please indicate your level of agreement with [a series of statements]'. The total replies are shown in Table 3.10. Also shown is the mean figure for those who answered 'yes' to question nine. Note that 'completely agree' equals a 1 score and 'strongly disagree' a 5 score.

Mean	Completely agree		Partially agree		Strongly disagree	Mean of yes to Q9
	Our corporate culture is the product of too many factors which we cannot control					
3.73	2.56%	5.38%	31.19%	36.32%	23.93%	4.06
	Our corporate culture is managed as a corporate asset					
3.23	10.72%	19.31%	26.18%	23.17%	20.60%	2.35
	Our corporate culture is largely determined by the senior management team					
2.54	17.02%	35.31%	29.36%	12.34%	5.95%	2.42
	Subcultures within our organization pose a major barrier to gaining a unified culture					
2.66	23.82%	23.40%	24.68%	18.29%	9.78%	3.20
	Gaining buy-in to shared values across our organization is essential to our future					
1.60	57.69%	29.78%	8.97%	1.28%	2.13%	1.39
	There will always be tensions between different subcultures within our organization					
2.73	10.68%	34.18%	32.90%	15.81%	6.41%	2.83
	Internal communications are well managed to communicate corporate priorities and cultural values					
2.92	11.48%	27.65%	30.21%	18.29%	12.34%	2.39

Table 3.10: Please indicate your level of agreement with the following statements

What is interesting here is that companies who answered 'yes' to question nine proffered a more positive response in all categories than the mean for all respondents, but not by a significant margin. However, what must be borne in mind is that the scores from those who answered 'yes' to question nine are also included in the answers from all respondents, making it difficult to gain from this table a comparison between companies with managed and non-managed cultures.

Again there was little significant difference in the mean scores of European against the mean for USA/Rest of the World respondents.

Section E: Changing Corporate Culture

Section three of the questionnaire, 'Changing Corporate Culture', sought to discover how many organizations had indeed attempted to change corporate culture, what mechanisms were used, and how successful the change programme had proven to be.

Note that for the purpose of this survey, 'changing corporate culture' was defined as fundamentally altering values, beliefs and behaviour in all or significant sections of the organization to bring about radically new ways of working and operating.

The first question in this section, question 12, asked 'has your organization attempted to change corporate culture?'. The total replies being:

Yes: 58.79 per cent

No: 23.60 per cent

Proposed: 17.59 per cent.

This was broken down for European companies into:

Yes: 60 per cent

No: 20 per cent

Proposed: 20 per cent.

For USA/Rest of the World respondents the replies were:

Yes: 56.41 per cent

No: 30.76 per cent

Proposed: 12.82 per cent.

Actions to Change Corporate Culture

Question 13 asked, 'which of [a specified selection of] actions has your organization taken to change corporate culture?'. The answers of all respondents are shown in Table 3.11.

Ranking		Percentage
1st	Development of new organizational structures	81.03%
2nd	Changes in roles and responsibilities	74.71%
3rd	Redefining of corporate values	71.83%
4th	Changes in leadership practices	70.68%
5th	Redesign of reward systems	57.47%
6th	Involvement of staff in prioritizing new values	55.74%
7th	Introduction of new skills	52.87%
	Other	20.11%

Table 3.11: Which of the following action has your organization taken to change corporate culture?

The results were again similar from Europe and USA/Rest of the World, an exception being 'redefining corporate values' which received a percentage rating of 78.83 per cent in Europe, against 62.96 per cent in USA/Rest of the World.

It is also interesting here to note the relative poor performance of redesigning reward systems.

Communications

The survey then went on to look at the use of communication mechanisms during the culture change effort. It is worth saying that every commentator interviewed during the research for this Report, stressed the fundamental importance of communication during a culture change effort. Communication mechanisms are covered in detail in Chapter 8

Respondents were asked in question 14, 'what type of communications did you use in the culture change process? (please tick more than one)'. The total responses are shown in Table 3.12.

Ranking		Percentage
1st	Newsletters and other published materials	81.03%
2nd	Cascade briefings	75.28%
3rd	Mass meetings	65.51%
4th	Redefinition of corporate values	60.34%
5th	Intranet	35.63%
6th	Videos	35.63%
	Other	

Table 3.12: What type of communications did you use in the culture change process?

Significant differences between European and USA/Rest of the World responses were that in the USA/Rest of the World 'mass meetings' came second with a percentage score of 75.92 per cent whereas they were fourth in Europe, scoring 60.83 per cent. And at 44.44 per cent more USA/Rest of the World companies were using an 'intranet' than their European counterparts, at 31.66 per cent.

Timetabling Cultural Change

Question 15 asked whether the culture change programme had been timetabled. The total responses being:

Yes: 34.10 per cent

No: 49.71 per cent

Proposed: 16.18 per cent.

Question 16 asked, 'how long has/will the culture change process take?'. The mean score was 3.42 (3 years 6 months). The total responses are shown in Table 3.13.

Mean	<1 year	<2 years	<3 years	<4 years	<5 years	>5 years
3.42 (or 3 years, 6 months)	8.97%	24.35%	27.56%	9.61%	13.46%	16.02%

Table 3.13: How long has/will the culture change process take?

The Use of Consultants

Question 17a asked respondents whether they had used external consultants to help with the culture change process. The total replies were:

Yes: 62.06 per cent

No: 32.18 per cent

Proposed: 5.74 per cent.

At 63.86 per cent against 58.18 per cent, European companies were slightly more likely to have used external consultants than USA/Rest of the World companies.

Question 17b then asked respondents to rate the contribution of the consultants to the change effort. With a mean score of 2.80 (with 1 being 'extremely valuable' and 5 being 'of no value'), the total results are shown in Table 3.14.

Mean	Extremely valuable		Quite valuable		Of no value
2.80	14.54%	16.36%	48.18%	15.45%	5.45%

Table 3.14: How do you rate the contribution of the consultants?

Both European and USA/Rest of the World replies were broadly similar. But what is interesting is that just under half of all respondents believed the consultants were 'quite valuable'. Although just under 15 per cent said they were 'extremely valuable', only 5.45 per cent said they were 'of no value'. So the performance of consultants gets a measured endorsement from survey respondents.

Cultural Change Enablers

Question 18 asked respondents to rate a specified list of factors according to how they enabled the culture to be changed. The total responses are shown in Table 3.15.

Interestingly, and endorsed by the research for this Report, 'senior executives role modeling new behaviour – 'walking the talk', was seen as by far the most

Mean	Extremely important		Quite important		Totally unimportant
	Vision statements				
2.32	32.02%	23.59%	28.08%	12.35%	3.93%
	Senior executives role modeling new behaviour - walking the talk				
1.15	88.62%	8.37%	1.67%	0%	0%
	Aligning organization structure with strategy				
1.53	60.33%	28.49%	9.49%	1.11%	0.55%
	Involving staff in defining new corporate values and standards				
1.67	52.80%	29.21%	15.16%	2.80%	0%
	Internal communication programme				
1.50	61.79%	26.96%	10.11%	1.72%	0%

Table 3.15: How do you rate the following factors in enabling culture to be changed?

important factor, scoring a mean of 1.15. A total of 88.62 per cent of respondents claimed this factor to be 'extremely important'. Not one company gave it a score of 4 or 5 (with 5 equaling 'totally unimportant'). Only 1.67 per cent proffered a 'quite important score' score of 3.

Also no company proffered a 'totally unimportant' score for 'involving staff in defining new corporate values and standards' and 'internal communication programmes'.

Culture Change Results

Question 19a focused on the critical question, 'are you able to assess the impact of the 'culture change process?'. The total replies were:

Yes: 58.94 per cent

No: 40.39 per cent.

However, and importantly, this changed dramatically between companies who claimed to possess 'extremely well defined' cultures and those with 'very poorly defined' cultures. The actual replies being:

'Extremely well defined' cultures:

Yes: 77.77 per cent

No: 22.22 per cent.

'Very poorly defined' cultures:

Yes: 50 per cent

No: 50 per cent.

If the gap is wide here, it is wider still to question 19b, 'if yes, has the culture change process achieved its goals, exceeded its goals, failed to meet its goals?'. The total replies were:

Achieved its goals: 51.25 per cent

Exceeded its goals: 15.00 per cent

Failed to meet its goals: 33.75 per cent.

In companies with 'extremely well defined' cultures, the results were:

Achieved its goals: 50 per cent

Exceeded its goals: 14.28 per cent

Failed to meet its goals: 28.57 per cent.

Whereas in companies with 'very poorly defined' cultures, the results were:

Achieved its goals: 20 per cent

Exceeded its goals: 10 per cent

Failed to meet its goals: 60 per cent.

So just 10 per cent of companies with a 'very poorly defined' culture 'exceeded the goals' of the change programme, and only one in five 'achieved the goals'. Half of those companies with 'extremely well defined' cultures 'achieved its goals' and a further 14.28 per cent 'exceeded the goals'.

However, according to these findings, those companies with 'extremely well defined' cultures performed slightly below the average for both 'achieved' and 'exceeded' its goals. Also, although overall these results do show that a company with a 'extremely well defined' culture is significantly more likely to succeed against change objectives than those with 'very poorly defined' cultures, it is clear that 'defining' the culture is not the whole story. Indeed a quarter of companies with 'extremely well defined' cultures failed to meet the goals. Therefore, these statistics seemingly reinforce comments made in the preceding Chapter that just having a strong culture will not in itself lead a company to business success.

Maybe a statistic from an earlier part of the survey (section 1, question 2) has an impact here. On a score of 1 to 5 (with 1 equaling 'change resistant' and 5 equaling 'highly adaptable') companies with 'extremely well defined' cultures scored 3.32, which was only slightly above the overall mean of 3.10. This may suggest that there are a significant number of companies with 'extremely well defined' cultures who still have a long way to go before their *strong* culture becomes a *winning* one. And indeed, as Chapter 2 suggested, this strong culture may itself be a hindrance to success.

Interestingly, a total of 79.32 per cent believe culture change to be currently a more important issue within their organization than five years ago (question 20a). And 74.44 per cent believed it would become more important over the next five years (question 20b). This seems to suggest that companies are beginning to realize the power that corporate culture has on performance, and will therefore ensure that it is aligned to organizational needs.

Key Problems and Lessons

The final two questions of the survey, 21 and 22, asked, 'what are the three main problems you encountered in culture change' and 'what are the three main lessons encountered in culture change?'.

To the former question, European respondents highlighted problems around the behaviour of corporate leaders such as 'senior management attention', 'insufficient walking the talk', 'no senior management role modeling'. Another key problem identified was 'poor communications'.

USA/Rest of the World respondents also complained of senior management being unwilling to 'walk the talk', but also highlighted 'resistance to change from various levels and subgroups' as being areas of difficulty.

As for the key lessons, both European and USA/Rest of the World respondents stressed the importance of 'leadership', 'involving everyone', 'being consistent', 'having a compelling case for change' and 'communication'.

Therefore, difficulties around senior management commitment and communications seem to head the list of problems faced in a culture change programme, a fact reinforced by both the survey data and other research for this Report.

Section F: Conclusion

Although not an exact science, due to the subjective nature of such a survey, these findings so seem to suggest a correlation between how well defined and managed, a corporate culture is and success against change objectives. It also suggests that the better defined a culture is, the more likely it will support strategic objectives (and as research for this Report has shown, culture change efforts should be in support of strategic objectives).

What has come out strongly is that a number of key themes of this Report were seen as critical in a culture change programme, such as the importance of senior managers being role models, of involving everyone in the change effort and of internal communication.

The survey also suggests that the better defined the culture, the more likely organizations are to secure benefits such as the ability to attract and retain high quality managers and staff, to be responsive to market and customer needs and to successfully implement performance improvement programmes and initiatives.

Overall, the evidence suggests that defining and managing corporate culture has clear benefits to an organization, its staff and its customers. As other research evidence has shown, such as that in the preceding Chapter, successfully satisfying these two key stakeholder groups will go some way to securing benefits for shareholders. Many of the case study companies, such as Hyundai Car (UK) Ltd and Continental Airlines, have made this belief central to their transformational efforts. This is equally true of Millennium Inorganic Chemicals, the case study that now follows.

Key Learning Points

1. Companies with well defined and managed corporate cultures are more likely to succeed against change objectives than those with poorly defined cultures.

2. Organizations with well defined cultures are more likely than those with poorly defined cultures to be responsive to customer needs and to attract and retain high quality staff.

3. Similarly, companies with well defined cultures are more likely to successfully implement performance improvement initiatives.

4. Companies with 'extremely well defined' cultures are more inclined to place ownership of the culture with the senior management team than those with 'very poorly defined' cultures, who were more likely to devolve responsibility to the HR function.

5. The better defined the culture, the more likely it is that the corporate values are understood organization-wide.

6. Staff and customer surveys are both used extensively to track progress against culture change objectives.

7. The importance of senior management role modeling new behaviours is by far the most important enabler of successful cultural change. This is followed in importance by internal communication programmes and aligning organizational structure with strategy.

8. Managing corporate culture seems set to remain a critical issue well into the future, thus supporting the view of many commentators interviewed for this Report that senior management is waking up to the importance of managing culture as a corporate asset.

CASE STUDY: MILLENNIUM INORGANIC CHEMICALS

Summary

Millennium Inorganic Chemicals has restructured its organization from one that is regional in focus to one that takes a truly global perspective. Key to this has been creating a culture focused on sharing best practices across the organization. Taking out unnecessary costs and driving up Economic Value Added (EVA) have also been key goals, which support its parent company's approach to profitable global growth.

Introduction

Heaquartered in Hunt Valley, Maryland, USA, Millennium Inorganic Chemicals is the world's second largest provider of titanium dioxide, used as a white pigment in coatings, paints, plastics, paper, rubber and other applications. It is also the largest merchant seller of titanium tetrachloride, which is used as the raw material in titanium metal production and in other manufacturing processes.

With more than 3800 employees, the company has eight manufacturing plants – two in the US, France and Brazil, and one each in Australia and the UK. It also has 17 sales and marketing locations in the three global regions of North America, Europe and Asia/Pacific.

Millennium Inorganic Chemicals is the largest manufacturing company of US-headquartered Millenn_um Chemicals Inc, the other companies being Millennium Speciality Chemicals and Millennium Petrochemicals Inc. The parent company also has a 29.5 per cent ownership of Equistar Chemicals and a 26 per cent ownership of Suburban Propanethe.

Millennium Chemicals Inc has over 4400 employees and achieved net sales of over $3 billion in 1997 and reported an Economic Value Added (EVA) figure of $104 million. As this case study will explain, improving EVA has been central to the corporate change, and indeed cultural change, efforts within the group.

Change Goals

Change within the Millennium group began in October 1996 when it demerged from the global conglomerate Hanson Industries plc. Millennium's senior management knew that survival in a fiercely competitive market-place would require a focus on growth. This would be achieved both organically and by strategic global acquisitions.

With a growing global presence, the sharing of best practices and creating global strategic, process and behavioural consistency would be pivotal to achieving a winning and unified corporate culture. Ian Hampton, human resources director at Millennium Inorganic Chemicals' plant in Bunbury, Western Australia, says:

> "We set out to educate our employees to pit their considerable skills against the opposition and to work as one global team. To achieve this we had to quickly move away from our regionalized structures and thinking and put in processes to share best practices across the organization and convince people that this was the way to secure competitive advantage."

However, Hampton does stress that moving from a regionalized to a global approach does not mean dismantling local cultures but rather gaining corporate consistency while still recognizing the importance of micro cultural characteristics, which is, "a significant challenge in the change programme".

Capturing Hearts and Minds

Another challenge within Millennium Inorganic Chemicals was uncovered via a mid 1990s employee survey within its Asia/Pacific sites. Hampton explains:

> "We knew that our employees were happy with the company, as we are known for our excellence in safety and environmental performance and for our compensation policies. We are known as an employer of choice. Therefore, people tend to stay with the organization for a long time and express a high level of commitment. However, we discovered that this commitment was passive. We benefited from their expertise but we didn't really have their hearts and minds."

Millennium Inorganic's management recognized that to succeed globally it had to activate this feeling of commitment and pride. Moreover, it would need to change both its operations and culture from being manufacturing to market driven, thus aligning activities with the needs of its customers.

Fortunately for the company, the 1996 demerger had in itself created a feeling of pride in the organization, a pride in being 'out on their own', that fuelled a desire to really make things happen both within Millennium corporately and Inorganic Chemicals specifically.

Corporate Restructuring

Significant change within Millennium Inorganic Chemicals started in 1997 with corporate restructuring. A matrix organization was created by replacing the regional structure with new functional links throughout its worldwide organization. This is headed by a Global Executive Team of nine senior managers under the leadership of then recently appointed chief executive officer (CEO) Robert E Lee.

This group was created to envision the company's future, devise global strategies and establish strong, productive and personal communications with all employees around the world.

In an article that appeared on the group's website, Millennium Inorganic Chemicals explained the primary purpose of this shift:[1]

> "Behind all the talk about globalization in the business world, you'll often find companies that have international facilities and markets lack a true global perspective. To go global, a company must go through profound changes – re-examining and reshaping ways of doing business, breaking old habits, devising new models of success, discarding obsolete thinking and adopting an empowering new attitude."

One significant outcome of this matrix organization would be that best practices could be easily gathered and spread around the world.

According to Hampton, the appointment of Lee (who was transferred from corporate headquarters) was significant in driving the new culture within the company. He says:

> "Bob Lee and the executive team have really taken charge of rolling the cultural change programme out throughout the organization. I wouldn't say the team manage the culture change programme, rather they lead it actively and passionately."

Better Ways

The culture change programme within Millennium Inorganic Chemicals is branded 'Better Ways'. Better Ways is a global initiative to enable the company to achieve its vision of being 'the most respected, value-creating company in the world'.

Supporting the vision, and also communicated as part of Better Ways, are the company's mission statement and operating principles. The mission is:

> 'To maximize value creation in our global chemicals business by continually improving our technology and business processes to provide products and services which exceed our customers' expectations.'

While the operating principles (essentially the organizations' value statements) are:

> 'We will conduct our business so as to protect the health and safety of our employees, the public and the environment. We will treat each other with respect, trust and openness; provide opportunities for personal and professional growth; and recognize and reward superior performance and teamwork.'

According to Hampton, coining these statements of strategic intent would prove a powerful mechanism for securing a sense of cultural and operational congruence within this globally diverse organization.

The Better Ways documentation also includes a set of global strategy guidelines and tactics to help focus local decision-making and operational processes. And these are critical components of the company's change programme.

Responsible Care

At the top of the guidelines, is how to use 'responsible care' (a charter of environmental and safety commitments) to guide decision-making. As Hampton says:

> "The safety of our employees and our commitment to environmental excellence has always been, and always will be, our number one priority."

Indeed, Millennium Chemicals has launched a Responsible Care Team which operates with the full authority of the board of directors. The Team seeks to identify and encourage best practices, both within and outside Millennium, which will ensure continuous improvement in Responsible Care performance throughout the company.

Building EVA

Also within Millennium Inorganic Chemicals' strategic guidelines are the company's commitment to the principles of Economic Value Added (EVA),[2] which supports Millennium Chemicals Inc's focus on EVA as the primary mechanism for gauging how it creates shareholder value. For Millennium Inorganic Chemicals, EVA is built and delivered by focusing on value-creating businesses and technologies, and is used to measure success.

Within Millennium Chemicals, EVA principles are used as the basis for all capital projects and acquisition activities. However, EVA had to become real and meaningful for all the group's employees if it was indeed to prove a powerful mechanism for driving performance. Therefore, key to this was communicating to all the group's employees the benefit to them, as well as the organization, of EVA. As Bill Landuyt, chairman and CEO of Millennium Chemicals Inc has said:[3]

> "We're asking employees to act like owners, so we're planning to treat [them] like owners, too. [In] 1998, Millennium [instituted] a new incentive plan based on our EVA improvement."

Through this bonuses are paid and corporate stock allocated to employees based on EVA performance. So the better the company does, the greater individual rewards. As Landuyt aims to quadruple the corporate stock price in a couple of years, then this stock could prove a valuable benefit to employees. Additionally, top management within Millennium are mandated to take a significant equity stake in the corporation.

To further instil the EVA spirit, Millennium has initiated at group level a Chairman's Award for Excellence Programme. Importantly, in creating a 'unified' culture, this was the first time all Millennium employees, from all companies and countries, were eligible for the same award programme.

The award was designed to recognize and reward employees for embracing the value-creative spirit. Employees could nominate themselves or their team, or another individual or team. At group level this was also sending a clear signal that the group's senior management recognizes the important role that the employee-base plays in creating shareholder value.

Within Millennium Inorganic Chemicals' Hunt Valley, Maryland facility, EVA-building ideas are enabled through a Best Practices Support Team. Every month employees submit their ideas to the team. An executive team then reviews the ideas, and the 'bright ideas' winning suggestion is announced and published along with the runner up. The winner gets special parking for a month, and the Best Practices Support Team then determines how to implement the ideas. The Best Practices Support Team has a photograph of Albert Einstein as its mascot.

The Hunt Valley-based programme began in early 1998 and has inspired similar programmes throughout the Millennium Group, thus fulfilling a Group goal of sharing best practices within each company and across companies.

According to Hampton, employees have certainly been inspired by the EVA incentives. He says:

> "EVA has really focused performance. People are now passionately interested in how we perform as a business as this has a financial implication for them. And the Millennium share price is published on walls on an weekly basis."

Cost Reduction

EVA is further enhanced within Millennium Inorganic Chemicals, and indeed other Millennium companies, through other strategic guidelines to 'reduce costs to maximize profits through the business cycle' and 'standardizing best practices'. The latter is proving a powerful mechanism for success against the former. For example, Millennium Inorganic Chemicals has put together Manufacturing Technology Teams, drawn from across locations, to find internal best practices to evaluate for usage within other sites.

Manufacturing Technology has eight teams that will identify, recommend and implement those practices. Each team will focus on one of seven areas; chloride, sulphate, finishing, quality, reliability and maintenance, energy, process control and process engineering.

Team members will brainstorm ideas for improvement and then prioritize those ideas according to impact they could have on the company. A Manufacturing Steering Committee will then review the opportunities and designate some as best practices for sites to emulate.

The ten-member strong Reliability and Maintenance Manufacturing Technology Team, for example, began meeting in May 1998 and has so far identified more than ten projects that will address reliability and cost reduction issues.

Within year one it is estimated that Manufacturing Technology Teams would reduce costs in the company by about $50 million. Says Hampton:

> "These teams are proving outstanding at making change happen quickly. We are really starting to work in global teams and understand the competitive advantage secured through this approach to multi-site collaborative working."

SAP

Taking costs out of the business, the company believes, will also be effected through a global SAP implementation programme.[4]

In the first half of 1999, SAP went live for Millennium Inorganic Chemicals sites in Asia/Pacific, US, UK and France. The SAP modules installed were for Sales and Distribution, Materials Management, Production Planning, Business Planning and Financials/Controlling, Plant Maintenance, Quality Management, and Human Resources.

Importantly, SAP is a group-wide initiative and Millennium Chemicals' companies hold bi-weekly integration meetings to share experiences – whether successes or difficulties – that each Millennium organization has had during its respective SAP implementations. This, therefore, is proving another example of cross-company knowledge sharing.

Within Millennium Inorganic Chemicals, the first Millennium company to go live with SAP, a change management team focused on change readiness and getting people up-to-speed with using the new computer systems.

Additionally, Millennium Inorganic Chemicals also aims to foster innovation, share experiences and get new products to market quicker through a new $18 million technical centre near Baltimore, Maryland, construction of which commenced in 1998.

The People Policy

The other key strategic guideline included within the Better Ways documentation is to 'invest in our people to realize their full potential'. Says Hampton:

> "Millennium Chemicals as a group recognizes that people are a strategic advantage. Therefore, the group has put together a 'people policy' document which communicates our commitment to developing our people. This states clearly that it is people, as individuals and through teams, who will make us the most value-creative chemical company in the world."

The people policy, which was explained group-wide within small teams during the final months of 1998, states that:

'We will enable our people to excel by:

- creating a safe, innovative work environment, which responds to human needs for support at the workplace and at home
- designing and delivering competitive compensation and people support programmes
- meeting strategic business needs for knowledge and skills and our people's needs for growth, mobility and team-building
- communicating openly to promote respect and trust
- building an increasingly productive, multi-cultural and diverse workforce
- developing fair and consistent human resource policies and services
- sharing responsibility for people management between all Millennium managers and human resources.'

According to Dick Lamond, Millennium Chemicals' vice president of human resources:[5]

"Investing in our people is smart business. We want to create value for Millennium in every way possible. We believe that investing in people just as we invest in equipment and technology will pay off in very tangible ways as our people begin the bankroll knowledge, skill and global savvy. Building a confident, creative and can-do workforce is one of the key ways we will grow and improve this business."

To make the people policy meaningful, throughout 1999 Millennium will launch new initiatives, processes and policies, some championed by HR and some by line management. All of these will be based on the foundations of the people policy and will be measured by how they add value to people and the company.

Internal Communication

Within Millennium Inorganic Chemicals, reaching out to people has been a primary focus for Lee and his global executive team. And this has been notable in the early days of the Better Ways programme. Says Hampton:

"Our executive team has been at the forefront of announcing, leading and explaining the change process. They've been travelling all round the world to present the Better Ways programme. That sort of approach would not have happened previously in the company."

Indeed senior management communications have been proactive and exhaustive.

With the goal of replacing detached, hierarchical communication processes with an open, direct and lively exchange of ideas and opinions, the members of the global executive committee spent the whole of October 1997 travelling the world and holding meetings to talk about the future with Millennium employees. Impressively, in nine meetings, over 60 per cent of the company's people got to meet the executive committee face-to-face and hear them describe the new global vision, mission and the search for Better Ways. This also enabled the executive team to hear the thoughts, ideas and concerns of front-line employees.

In addition to these face-to-face meetings, the company is employing a number of other internal communications mechanisms to deliver the 'Better Ways' message. These include:

- **Monthly Executive Committee Meetings**: This is where information and ideas from all functional areas and all regions come together to be fitted into the global matrix. It is also the origin of strategic direction and the clearing house for information needed in the field.

- **Employee Briefings**: After the monthly Executive Committee Meeting, results are reported – along with more localized information – in briefings held in every Millennium Inorganic Chemicals facility around the world.

- **Semi-annual Organizational Briefings**: Members of the executive committee hold update meetings with employees in their specific areas of responsibility, discussing how their activities relate to the company-wide vision and strategic plan.

- **Ongoing Executive Committee Visits**: Individually and in groups, the executives will continue to travel to Millennium Inorganic facilities around the world.

Other communications mechanisms include newsletters, e-mail bulletin-boards, and, from early 1999, a company-wide intranet. There is also an annual global conference for all employees.

Acquisitions

These proactive communications have been going on while the company has been pursuing an aggressive acquisition programme, making three major purchases during 1998, one in Brazil and two in France. Says Hampton:

"Before these acquisitions, we were an exclusively English speaking company, but we now have to take into account two other languages. However, we've been successful in getting Better Ways to all employees in different languages, and taking into account subtle differences in meaning."

He adds that recognizing the language differences also focused the company's attention onto different cultural approaches to work:

"It was really about being sensitive to local cultural nuances, and leveraging those benefits while we focused the geographical sites onto the global Better Ways programme."

Scorecard

To measure progress against strategic goals, and to communicate this to the employee-base, Millennium Inorganic Chemicals has introduced a scorecard, which tracks performance against seven key factors:

- Worldwide TiO2 Selling Price.
- Economic Value Added (EVA).
- Cost Savings.
- Millennium Chemicals Share Price.
- Safety.
- Lost Workday Incidents.
- TiO2 Sales Volume.
- Customer Complaints.

The scorecards are distributed quarterly and posted in all locations and reviewed with employees in departmental meetings. These measures were chosen because they affect the organization globally, thus further encouraging a synergized global culture focused on performance improvement.

So how has Millennium Chemicals Inc generally and Millennium Inorganic Chemicals specifically, been performing since demerger? Writing in 'Creating Value: Millennium Chemicals Inc. Report to Shareholders 1997', Landuyt stated:[6]

> "Value creation is our guiding principle, one that we will not compromise and one that is sweeping through the organization in these formative years.

> "Economic Value Added... crossed firmly into positive territory in 1997, totalling $104 million versus a proforma negative $30 million in 1996 [and] basic earnings per share from on-going operations was $2.60 versus $1.56 the year before.

> "For 1997, [we] targeted opportunities to generate an annualized $100 million of savings in cost-cutting and productivity improvements.

> "We exceeded that target by a substantial margin. Led by programmes at [Millennium Inorganic Chemicals], we reduced actual costs by an estimated $110 million during the year, which would equate to an annualized figure well above that."

Additionally, Millennium Chemicals net debt (a key strategic goal) reduced from about $2300 million in October 1996 to $1000 million in September 1998.

Conclusion

In conclusion, Hampton says that the company is well on the way to becoming an organization that really works as a global team, and that people are focused on discovering and sharing best practices and in striving to cut unnecessary costs and thus drive up EVA. This cultural change from a company that was exclusively regional in its approach has, Hampton states, been achieved by focusing on three key success factors:

1. Constant and consistent messages.
2. Ensuing that support systems are in place to drive behaviours and an EVA focus.
3. Demonstrable commitment from the executive team.

Key Learning Points

1. Millennium Inorganic Chemicals' strategic goals are clearly linked to those of Millennium Chemicals Inc. This enables a direct line of sight from group to company strategies.

2. Change goals within Millennium Inorganic Chemicals were primarily focused around moving from a regional to a global approach to business.

3. Linked to the above, the company restructured from a regionalized to a matrix organization.

4. The appointment of a new CEO, Robert E Lee, was crucial to driving change throughout the organization.

5. Millennium Inorganic Chemicals branded its change programme Better Ways, and this was actively communicated to all employees. Lee and the global executive team passionately led the communication programme.

6. Better Ways clearly aligned cultural and operational goals with strategic goals.

7. Millennium Inorganic Chemicals, and Millennium as a group, have focused employee performance on building EVA. The use of incentive programmes has been critical for this.

8. Global teams have been launched by Millennium Inorganic Chemicals to find best practices to evaluate for sharing company-wide.

9. A Millennium Inc people policy clearly demonstrates the value the group places on the contribution of employees.

10. A Millennium Inorganic Chemicals scorecard has been introduced to track performance against key strategic measures.

4

LEADING CULTURE CHANGE – THE ROLE OF THE CEO AND SENIOR MANAGEMENT TEAM

Executive Summary

1. The leadership of the CEO and senior management team, the research for this Report finds, is the single most important success factor in culture change programmes.

2. The senior management team must understand the need for, and business benefits of, culture change, otherwise lasting change will not occur.

3. The research also finds that culture change roll-out requires corporate leaders to invest a significant amount of time and effort.

4. Linked to the above, senior management must take an active lead in communicating the need for change throughout the organization.

5. The importance of senior managers role-modeling desired new behaviours cannot be overstated.

6. According to one theory, organizations are 'shadows of their leaders'. So a company's behaviour tends to be congruent with that of its leaders.

7. Changing senior management behaviour can, our research shows, be difficult, but is vital if the rest of the employee-base is to be asked to change its behaviour.

8. Corporate value statements can be powerful tools for aligning behaviour with the new cultural ethos. But such statements are often not effectively implemented within the organization and, crucially, too many senior managers do not align their own behaviours with these new values.

9. Vision and mission statements can be powerful tools for aligning behaviour with strategic goals, but suffer from the same shortcomings in design and implementation as values.

10. Culture change specialists Senn-Delaney Leadership Consulting Group provide a useful model of 21st Century Leadership. This shows how winning behaviours in the future will be diametrically opposite to behaviours valued in this century.

11. A case study on KFC demonstrates best practice.

Section A: Context

In virtually every case of organizational change, the leadership of the senior management team, and especially the chief executive officer (CEO), is the single most important factor in its success or failure. Without support from the top, change efforts – be they process re-engineering, implementing a balanced scorecard, etc – are doomed to failure, or at best, partial and rarely lasting success. When it comes to changing a corporate culture the leadership of the CEO and the senior management team is an absolute pre-requisite for success. Quite simply, a culture will not change unless this leadership is visible, active and determined.

As Dr George Labovitz, chairman of the US-headquartered performance measurement and organizational change specialists Organizational Dynamics Inc (ODI), says:

> "Senior managers are the key to success in almost every case of culture change I know."

Such is the power of a well established corporate culture that only top management has the remit and clout to kick-start the process of cultural renewal. The senior management team, advisers comment, must be the keepers of the culture, must nurture it and fuel its growth and development. As John Childress, chief executive of the culture change specialists Senn-Delaney Leadership Consulting Group, comments:

> "The organization's culture and corporate values must be centrally controlled by the senior management team. You can devolve decision-making powers etc, but you must keep central control over the culture."

And Robin Cammish, presently the managing director of the change consultancy QPA and previously one of the key architects of a major cultural change programme during the merger that created pharmaceutical giant SmithKline Beecham, states that the single most important consideration at the start of a culture change programme is that senior management has to recognize and understand the need. He says:

> "If they are deaf, dumb or blind it's a waste of time. They need to agree that they have to do things differently."

This, our research finds, is a crucial observation. Why an organization needs to change the culture has to be understood first by the senior management team. Not least because it will be they who must lead and drive the cultural change effort, but also because they will need to clearly articulate compelling reasons for undertaking what can be painful change to each layer within the enterprise.

Case Study Examples

Such an explicit recognition by senior management was evident in most of our case study companies. For example, at the Inland Revenue Accounts Office, Cumbernauld, Scotland (the case study to accompany Chapter 2), the culture change programme sprang from a simple recognition by the then Office director that there had to be a better way of running the business. He knew that if his Office was to survive then a participative style of management had to replace the traditional public sector command and control approach then in operation.

At Ernst and Young, the case study to support Chapter 8, the culture change effort was the result of the now chairman Nick Land realizing that recession coupled with permanent changes in customer and market demands dictated that the firm had to develop a new entrepreneurial and client-focused cultural ethos.

At Continental Airlines, the case study to accompany Chapter 1, a new chief executive officer (CEO), Gordon Bethune, and chief operating officer (COO), Greg Brenneman, knew that nothing short of massive cultural transformation powered by a well articulated and devolvable corporate strategy would save the organization from extinction.

While at KFC (the case study to accompany this Chapter), David Novak knew, on becoming CEO of the company in July 1994, that he had to change the dreadful corporate culture if he was going to revitalize the organization's sluggish growth and poor financial performance. As he says, "the soft stuff drives hard results".

Section B: Research Findings

'Culture and Change Management' Survey Findings

The important role of the senior management team in driving culture change initiatives was shown in exclusive research for this Report by Business Intelligence into 236, mainly large companies from Europe, USA and the Rest of the World (the results are analysed in-depth in the Chapter 3).[1]

The research found that in companies which claimed to possess 'extremely well defined' corporate cultures, 72 per cent stated that members of the senior management team, board, or indeed the CEO had formal responsibility for the corporate culture, against just 40 per cent in companies which possessed 'very poorly defined' cultures.

Tellingly, 64.28 per cent of companies with 'extremely well defined' cultures met or exceeded their cultural change goals against just 30 per cent of companies with 'very poorly defined' cultures. This strongly suggests that where senior management recognize that corporate culture is as much an asset as anything 'tangible' and manage it as such, then positive business benefits are a much more likely outcome.

Harvard Research

The crucial importance of leadership was also emphasized strongly within Harvard Business School professors John Kotter and James Heskett's research for their seminal work, *Corporate Culture and Performance*. The authors firmly conclude that competent leadership from the top is the single most visible factor that distinguishes successful from unsuccessful cultural change initiatives. They write:[2]

> "Effective leaders changed strategies and cultures to make their firms more competitive despite the natural tendency of cultures to resist change, despite the large size and mature environments found in most of these cases [that they studied], despite everything. And in the process, these individuals demonstrated how closely interrelated are five topics of great interest in managerial circles today: competition, leadership, change, strategy and culture."

They make the observation that leadership from one or two people at the very top of an organization seems to be an absolutely essential ingredient when major cultural change occurs. A finding echoed within many of the case studies for this Report.

Statistical validation of Kotter and Heskett's unambiguous conclusion was provided through the authors asking a series of culturally related questions to industry analysts about a sample of 22 of the original 207 companies studied. All of the companies in this sample were categorized as having strong cultures. However, based on their relative economic performance in the period 1977 to 1988, 12 were further categorized as higher performing and the remaining 10 as lower performing.

A specific question on leadership was, 'how much does the culture (at some specific firm) value excellent leadership from its managers on a scale of 1 (doesn't value leadership) to 7 (highly values leadership)?'. The research found that the higher performing firms received scores averaging 6.0. Indeed all but two of the 12 scored higher than 5.5 and 4.8 was the lowest score from this group.

Conversely, the lower-performing firms did much worse. On average they scored 3.9, with only two of these companies scoring higher than 4.8.

More on Professor Kotter's and Heskett's findings can be found in Chapters 2 and 7.

Section C: The Role of the Senior Management Team

Given the premise that the CEO and the rest of the senior management team are the primary drivers of culture change efforts, then it is important to take a closer look at their role.

Mark Krueger, managing director for the US-headquartered Answerthink Consulting Group, articulates four primary roles for the senior management team, especially the CEO and four behaviours that underpin these roles. The four roles are:

- They must be visionary and lay out the organization's future direction.
- They must prioritize what must be done to achieve that vision.
- They must be the resource provider – taking resources, including key people, and redirecting that to achieve the change goals. The more visible that resource the more credibility it will have in the organization and thereby substantially increasing the likelihood of success.
- They must be champions of change, articulating what needs to be done and why – but not necessarily how.

The four key behaviours that support the above are:
1. Walking the talk.
2. Casting a long shadow in the organization.
3. Being with people at the front line of change.
4. Visibly empowering other people.

Case Study Examples

These key leadership roles and behaviours were evident in all the case study companies. As examples, at Millennium Inorganic Chemicals (the case study to support Chapter 3), the appointment of CEO Robert E Lee was, according to Ian Hampton, human resources director at Millennium Inorganic Chemicals' Bunbury, Western Australia plant, critical in driving the new culture within the company. He says:

> "Bob Lee and the executive team have really taken charge of rolling the cultural change programme out throughout the organization. I wouldn't say the team manage the culture change programme, rather they lead it actively and passionately.

> "Our executive team has been at the forefront of announcing, leading and explaining the change process. They've been travelling all round the world to present the Better Ways programme [Millennium Inorganic Chemicals culture change initiative]."

Indeed the team spent the whole of October 1997 on global travels, holding meetings to talk about the organization's future with Millennium employees. Impressively over 60 per cent of the company's people got to meet the executive committee face-to-face and hear them describe the new global vision, mission and the search for Better Ways.

At Continental Airlines, CEO Gorton Bethune and president and COO Greg Brenneman personally went to airports and visited planes where they helped load bags and stood alongside the agents at ticket counters. Said Brenneman:[3]

> "We just talked at every opportunity about our plans for the airline and how we were going to accomplish them."

At BT Northern Ireland (a case study to accompany Chapter 6), CEO Lucy Woods conducts non-management breakfast meetings throughout the province where she discusses with the employee-base subjects such as improvement plans, public image, etc.

These are powerful examples of leaders taking the message direct to the employee-base. Crucially such practical demonstrations of 'walking the talk' goes some way to overcoming cynicism within the organization and for the leaders to 'cast their shadow' deep inside the company.

Independent UK-based consultant Garrey Melville, states that a key role of the CEO is to ensure that the culture is geared to high performance. To achieve this he says:

> "The CEO is a catalyst, a leader, a mentor. He or she has to ensure that the staff are happy, want to satisfy customers and enjoy life in the organization. It's about creating a happy family."

And he makes this valuable point:

> "People related issues are essentially about making sure the organization makes money and outperforms competitors in the market-place."

Melville's observation supports a theme running through this Report that satisfied employees equals satisfied customers, who are more likely to remain loyal and therefore drive financial success. As KFC's CEO David Novak says:

> "I hope that the results that we generate over time will demonstrate that a value-based work environment is powerful, but I think it is too early to claim victory. The proof will be in the pudding, but I'm betting my job that it will work."

Case Report: Western Provident Association

An exemplary case of how excellent leadership can transform the culture of an organization, is shown by the role played by chief executive officer Julian Stainton and his senior management team in dramatically altering the culture of the UK-based specialist private health insurer Western Provident Association (WPA).

WPA achieves over a £100 million a year in premiums, and has about 500,000 customers served by 150 staff. WPA is recognized as an exemplary customer-facing organization. As examples of the many plaudits given to the company, it was selected as a UK southern regional winner in the 1998 Arthur Andersen Best Practices Awards for the category 'Exceeding Customer Expectations'. In an independent survey in July 1998 of customer views on major health insurers by the National Opinion Poll Research Group, WPA was the highest in all the categories examined, these being: recommend own insurer, satisfaction with claims, helpfulness of personnel, efficiency of service, value for money, overall quality of service, and happiness with insurer.

However, this would not have been the findings of a similar survey when Stainton joined the company as CEO in November 1987. He explains the difficulties he found:

> "When I arrived as CEO, nobody seemed to know I was coming and it was more of a surprise to them than to me to find me on the premises. I couldn't make a phone call. The lines were always busy. Despite the fact that we had 400,000 customers we only had four phone lines. Our switchboard opened at 9.30 and closed at 4.30."

And in 1987 the company only had one personal computer, which was on Stainton's desk. Culturally the company at the time put greater value on manual endeavour than it did on technology. As another indicator of the existing culture, every employee received a pencil on joining the organization as only managers were allowed to write in ink.

As examples of the company's performance problems, shortly after arriving, Stainton was receiving 50 written complaints a day, and its renewal rate was around 80 per cent against an industry average of between 90 per cent and 95 per cent.

Satisfying customers

Stainton therefore realized that to transform organizational performance would require a radical change programme, which he focused on one simple goal – to satisfy customers.

However, the initial attempt at change failed to meet expectations, as Stainton explains:

> "I thought the problem would be fixed if we invested in technology. But this was a mistake and most of the money was wasted. The people who had been employed in the company had been so for their manual efforts and no other reason, so the more we tried to modernize the worse things got."

Stainton, as with many leaders who have attempted to change culture, came face-to-face with the power of a deeply ingrained culture. Consequently, he realized that he had to change the culture from one that valued manual endeavour to one that would value the customer. An important step on the road was to articulate a vision 'to be wholly consistent and wholly reliable and to provide the best service of any insurance company in the UK'.

To achieve this, Stainton reorganized WPA into self-managed customer-facing teams. But possibly more importantly, he supported this restructuring by rolling-out the philosophy that the people who serve the customers are the most important members of the organization. Consequently, the fundamental role of management is to support these customer-facing staff. (A similar philosophy is used at KFC, where CEO David Novak launched the concept of the restaurant general manager as the number 1 leader, and that all support functions exist to support than leader). Says Stainton:

> "Our business today is run by people with an average age of 22. The role of leadership is to say 'don't worry, we'll invest in you, we'll support you. You run the business and we'll worry about the other things'."

All the goals for the self-managed teams are self-set and derived from a laid down set of criteria focused on satisfying customers. Additionally, measurement plays a crucial role in communicating the importance of customer-facing behaviour (measurement as a driver of behaviour is dealt with in more detail in Chapter 6). Stainton says:

> "Basically our clients want claims to be paid quickly and accurately, so we have a measure of paying all claims in seven days and measures around telephone calls, correspondence etc. These all come together as value and financial goals, and each team buys into those goals and sets its own goals and measures from these."

Key leadership roles

Stainton believes that in a culture change programme the CEO has one key role, having a vision and making sure it is well articulated. He says:

> "Leaders have to be enthusiastic and committed in selling the vision. You need obsessive people who are wholly committed to the enterprise and its customers. If the leaders demonstrate this it will rub off on all of the people. It's really about leaders 'walking the talk'."

According to Stainton, and somewhat surprising considering the often quoted remark to the contrary, large-scale culture change is relatively straightforward. He says:

> "People can recognize and understand big change. An analogy would be a mountain. If we say we have to climb this mountain if we are to survive and prosper then its tangible and employees can, with management support and direction, figure out what they will need to do to achieve this. However, if you tell people there are a 1000 foothills and they have to change incrementally then this is much more difficult."

Involving non-executive directors

Changing the culture at WPA has also involved the non-executive directors, who have to work one day a quarter in the business serving customers. If they fail to do so, they cannot sit on the board. Says Stainton:

"One day a quarter will not make them experts but it will give them an insight into the everyday stresses and strains of the young people running the business. And it is tough. But if leaders forget how tough it is serving customers then they will lose touch with the business."

Key to culture change at WPA has also been changes to human resource practices and procedures, which are explained in Chapter 7.

Role Models

A key component of successfully focusing on people is senior management understanding the crucial part played by their role modeling desired new behaviours. They must, as commentators interviewed for this Report repeatedly stressed, show through their own example, that they themselves are willing to 'live' these new behaviours.

If, for example, senior management states that a desired new behaviour is to put the customer first, then they must show examples of how they themselves are doing this. A powerful instance of this is Alan Jones, CEO of TNT (UK), which won the 1998 European Quality Award. Jones explains:

> "Answering the telephone is an example. If somebody wants to ring me then they get straight through to me, there's no screening. We don't ask who you are, you're put straight through to the person you want to speak to. The telephone is an important instrument of communications with our customers. If we as leaders don't show that we are willing to talk to customers ourselves then you would get double values."

Also, if the senior management team states that an openness to learning is a hoped for new behaviour, then they must show, and indeed communicate examples of how they themselves are learning on an ongoing basis. For the latter, being brave enough to show how they as leaders made mistakes and how they have learnt from these mistakes will go a long way to embedding this cultural ethos.

As an example, Siemens KWU, a case study to accompany Chapter 6, mandates, in a formal statement, that leaders admitting their mistakes is a vital attribute of outstanding leadership and a key component of role modeling. It states that:

> 'All leaders must act as role models. Therefore our leaders must:
>
> * discuss mistakes openly, including their own
>
> * acknowledge excellent employee performance promptly
>
> * promote the establishment and improvement of relations with internal and external suppliers.'

Shadow of the leader

A central philosophy of the culture change approach of Senn-Delaney Leadership Consulting Group is the concept of the organization as a 'shadow of the leader', in that culture flows from the behaviour of the top team.

Senn-Delaney CEO John Childress states that an important aspect of working with senior management teams to change their cultures and to understand how their 'shadow' influences that culture, is to get them to recognize what the culture means in terms of hard data such as profits, productivity, new product development, etc. He says:

> "If they can understand that linkage they can start to understand the power of a culture and the influence of their behaviours on that culture."

In his book, *In the Eye of the Storm: Reengineering Corporate Culture*, Childress and his co-author, Senn-Delaney's chairman Larry Senn, explained the cultural implications of the 'shadow of the leader':[4]

> "One of the most common mistakes we hear throughout organizations is that the senior team is 'not walking the talk'. Whenever a company begins to make statements about desired behaviours and people don't see those behaviours being modeled at the top, there is a sense of a lack of integrity."

Senn-Delaney provides four examples of how this this lack of integrity is manifested:

1. The organization is asking people to be more open to change and the top leaders are not themselves changing.

2. Increased teamwork and cross-organizational collaboration is preached and the senior team itself is not a good team.

3. The organization is seen to cut back on expenses and the senior team does not change any of its special perks.

4. People are being asked to be accountable for results while the senior team members continue to subtly blame one another for lack of results.

Consequently, Childress and Senn believe strongly that the fastest way to create a positive, self-fulfilling prophecy about culture change is to have the leaders individually and collectively shift their own behaviours.

Research evidence

Tellingly, the 'Culture and Change Management' survey,[5] found that no less than 88.62 per cent of respondents believed that senior executives role modeling new behaviours was an extremely important factor in enabling culture change. And on a score of 1 to 5 (with 1 being extremely important and 5 being not important at all) not one respondent proffered a score of 4 or 5, and only 1.67 per cent gave it a score of 3, which equaled 'somewhat important'.

In answer to the question, 'what are [the] three main problems encountered in the culture change?', respondents repeatedly stated difficulties such as 'no senior management role modeling and insufficient 'walking the walk'.

So it is evident that if senior management lives by the old adage 'do as I say, not as I do', then no matter how much investment there is in the culture change effort, nothing will change. Johan Van der Hel, human resources manager for DSM Resins' Coating Resins Business Unit (DSM Resins is a case study to accompany Chapter 5) serves this useful warning:

"No matter how much internal communication you do via newsletters etc... all that expense will be wasted if management does not display the [correct] behaviours."

Section D: Senior Managers as Communicators

The role of communication is critical, and although in a hierarchy of importance it is safe to say that behaviour takes precedence over communication, this does not imply that the efficacy of communication in driving cultural change should in any way be devalued. Indeed, effective communication plays a central role in driving the new culture, with its values and behaviours, deep inside the organization. This subject is dealt with exclusively within Chapter 8. However, such is the importance of senior management communication that it must also be touched on within this Chapter.

Every advisor and practitioner interviewed for this Report stressed the absolute importance of senior management leading the communication effort behind the culture change initiative. For example, BT Northern Ireland's CEO, Lucy Woods, makes the following statement, sentiments of which were echoed by many of the practitioners interviewed:

"The aims of the [culture change] programme have to be communicated over and over and over again, until you are sick of saying it. We have 3000 people. I haven't met them all yet, so I may be tired of saying the same things but they aren't tired of me saying it."

According to Andrew Geddes, director of the Inland Revenue Accounts Office, Cumbernauld, there are two key elements of a successful culture change programme – leadership and communication. And these are interconnected. He says:

"In times of change there's a natural uncertainty among staff. They want to be told the bad news as well as the good and they want managers to be open and to share a genuine two-way dialogue about the business."

He stresses that one of his key responsibilities as the Office director is to ensure that this two-way dialogue takes place.

Nancy Blodgett, president of the US-based consultancy Performance Excellence Inc, comments that communicating the need for culture change is not just about words, but also backing up the words with practical action around changes to procedures and policies that will directly impact behaviour. She says:

"The key roles of the senior management team is communication and reinforcement of the new messages in a variety of ways, not only by actions but by modification of an organization's compensation, recognition and reward systems. You can talk to employees about the necessity for change all you want but as long as you keep rewarding the old behaviours and senior managers still act as they always have then long-lasting, effective change will not occur." (Rewarding new behaviour is dealt with in detail within Chapter 7).

ODI's Labovitz succinctly sums up the above points:

> "In cultural change the kiss of death is for the senior management to espouse one thing and recognize and practice another."

Section E: Changing Senior Management Behaviour

However, as the research finds, changing senior management behaviour can be difficult. This is not surprising as most people reach the top by being excellent at demonstrating the behaviours that were valued in the existing culture, and these behaviours may be diametrically opposite to those that the organization now needs to demonstrate.

Garrey Melville points out some of the core difficulties in changing these often deeply ingrained behaviours:

> "For example, in a high tech industry there are a lot of senior managers who are essentially excellent salesmen, so there is often a strong sales culture or there may be a strong technology culture.

> "The same applies to every industry. In banking, for example, some people at the top went through the banking career path so are risk adverse. That type of individual and the values they have in terms of decision-making may not be right for a more entrepreneurial or customer-focused organization. So their behaviours and mind-sets have to change radically, which is not easy."

Melville believes that coaching can play a powerful role in changing these behaviours. Childress believes that the use of an outside consultancy to 'gently' show how the behaviour of the senior management team may have been right for the past but is now hurting the company, can be useful. He also believes that senior managers are much more receptive to these messages than people tend to think, as leaders often really want to do what is best for the company.

However, there is no escaping the fact that certain ways of working may be so deeply ingrained within senior managers that they will need to be replaced by new leaders. For example, at Hyundai Car (UK) Ltd (the case study to accompany Chapter 7), director of customer satisfaction Sue Stoneman admits that changing some of the leaders released a lot of energy within the organization.

At Continental Airlines, within a couple of months of launching the corporate turnaround, the organization replaced 50 of its top 61 officers with about 20 new individuals. How this was done speaks volumes for the new cultural values of dignity and respect that would be pivotal to the change effort. Says president and COO Greg Brenneman:[6]

> "If you fire people inhumanely, you'll be left with a bunch of employees who don't trust the company or their co-workers. We needed to create a culture in Continental where people liked coming to work. We couldn't afford to have people hoarding ideas or sapping enthusiasm as we built our new organization.

So when we let people go we went out of our way to be fair by honouring their contracts and letting them resign with dignity."

This is powerful example of how, even in difficult situations, senior management behaviour has to aligned with how they say the organization must behave.

Case Report: BT Northern Ireland

Changing the behaviour of the senior management team was a critical challenge in CEO Lucy Woods' effort to transform the culture of BT Northern Ireland.

To start the process of changing behaviour at the top, the organization rolled out to all of BT Northern Ireland's 300 managers, a series of one-day workshops. The aim was to show them that a coaching, participative style of leadership is much more effective than the command and control style they were used to.

The managers were taken through a series of role-playing exercises that demonstrated the difference in outputs and experience from the two opposing management styles. One exercise comprised a situation where there was one boss and a number of subordinates. This group would be given a task to complete, but all directions had to come from the boss and the subordinates could not make any suggestions, as their role was to be told what to to do. So they would just stand around waiting for the boss to direct. In another exercise, the group would be given a task and everybody was encouraged to contribute suggestions on effective task completion.

According to Woods, this workshop clearly demonstrated that the latter approach was much more effective and enjoyable than the first. She provides this useful advice:

> "As a chief executive it's important to show the leadership team how taking a new approach to managing is beneficial to them and to the organization, and to support them in this development."

Case Report: KFC

Changing leadership behaviours through the use of workshops was also key to cultural transformation at KFC. Explains Senn-Delaney Leadership Consulting Group consultant Mike Birtwistle:

> "Through the workshop everyone [took] a look in the mirror at their own leadership style. People become reflective and introspective of their own behaviours."

Birtwistle describes some of the important aspects of the KFC senior management workshop:

> "Creating a sense of accountability for individual actions within the team was important; personal accountability for coaching, feedback and support. For this it's important to start asking the question, 'how can I support people so that they can perform better?' – essentially helping people succeed rather than just giving them directions."

Important here was to challenge any tendency to finger-point or blame when problems arise. Says Birtwistle:

> "Rather than falling back into this conflict mentality, the team looked to proactively build relationships with each other focused on self and team improvement."

It is therefore critical for the leaders to recognize that they can improve. Birtwistle recounts a Senn-Delaney facilitated workshop for 600 lower-level managers where the CEO David Novak stood up and asked for feedback on how he himself could improve as a leader:

> "This sent a powerful message to all these managers that Novak valued people who recognized that they could improve."

Statements of Leadership Behaviour

Increasingly, the research reveals, organizations are viewing the role of leadership in creating a high performing culture so seriously that they are formulating statements that set down the leadership behaviours an organization expects from its managers. For example, DSM Resins has articulated a set of key behaviours for the whole organization, which are:

- capable
- reliable
- empowered
- responsive.

Importantly, the group recognized that to instil these into the employee-base would require the instigation of a more coaching style of management throughout the organization. Therefore, DSM has articulated a set of required managerial responses to the employee behaviours:

- For a *responsive* employee a manager has to be *accessible.*
- For a *reliable* employee a manager has to give *confidence.*
- For a *capable* employee a manager has to *coach.*
- For an *empowered* employee a manager has to *delegate.*

Says Johan Van der Hel, human resources manager for DSM Resins' Coating Resins Business Unit:

> "[The change initiative] has to be a partnership between management and the employee-base. And for [this] to succeed, management has to provide

every employee with a more challenging and satisfying working environment. Through this business success will follow."

As explained in Section C, Siemens KWU has a written, formal policy on leadership behaviour. This supports a key message which is proactively rolled-out company-wide:

'*Our company is built on a foundation of good leadership.* We demand and promote good leadership. Ultimately, our success is dependent on the extent that we integrate good leadership into our vision for KWU.'

Therefore, the research shows that changing leadership behaviours can be difficult, and indeed is possibly the most difficult challenge in a culture change effort. But if this does not happen then any culture change effort will almost certainly falter. It is not, however, impossible. Case study companies such as Inland Revenue Accounts Office, Cumbernauld, KFC, BT Northern Ireland and Lehigh Portland Cement Company (the latter following a merger; see the case study to accompany Chapter 9) all successfully moved from command and control management styles to more open, participative styles. Each was successful because it was clearly communicated to the senior management team and then to the rest of the employee-base *why* a change in behaviour was critical for business success. This was then followed by a careful and concerted process for shifting these behaviours.

A New Model for 21st Century Leadership

In their book, *In the Eye of the Storm: Reengineering Corporate Culture*, Childress and Senn, provided this useful model for 21st century leadership shown in Table 4.1.[7]

From earlier paradigm	To current and future paradigm
Being a manager	Being a leader
Being a boss	Being a coach and facilitator
Controlling people	Empowering people
Holding onto authority	Delegating authority
Micro-managing	Leading with vision and values
Directing with rules and regulations	Guiding with winning shared values
Relying on 'position power' and hierarchy	Building 'relationship power' and networked teams
Demanding compliance	Gaining commitment
Focusing only on tasks	Focusing on quality, service and the customer
Confronting and combating	Collaborating and unifying
Going it alone	Utilizing the team
Judging others	Respecting, honouring and leveraging diversity and differences
Changing by necessity and crisis	Commitment to continuous learning
Being internally competitive – win/lose	Being internally collaborative – win/win
Having a narrow focus 'me and my area'	Having a broader focus 'my team, my organization'

Table 4.1: A New Model for 21st Century Leadership

As this makes clear, leaders in the future will need a diametrically opposite set of skills and behavioural traits than have been valued in this century. Indeed, as Kotter and Heskett put it:[8]

> "The implications here are powerful… if our economic organizations are going to live up to their potential, we must find, develop and encourage more people to lead in the service of others. Without leadership, firms cannot adapt to a fast moving world. But if leaders do not have the hearts of servants, there is only the potential for tyranny."

Developing such leaders within many companies has seen the introduction of new leadership evaluation techniques such as 360 degree or upwards appraisal. This is the case in a number of our case study companies such as Hyundai Car (UK) Ltd, BT Northern Ireland, Siemens KWU and Ernst & Young. This subject is covered in detail in Chapter 7.

Section F: Value Statements

For many organizations, creating lasting behavioural change throughout the organization has led to the articulation of a set of corporate value statements through which the expected standards of behaviour are formally documented. This is an important role for the senior management team, as it will be they who will, through their own behaviours, lead the cultural transformation by living these new values.

However, the efficacy of values, the research finds, is questionable. Dr David Chaudron, managing partner of the US-based Organized Change Consultancy, dismisses such statements with the damning comment:

> "I haven't seen too many value statements that are different to each other. A consultancy could do a mail-merge and provide an essentially same set of values whether for the Red Cross or for an oppressive military regime."

Robin Cammish, managing director of the change consultancy QPA, summarizes the views of many advisers and practitioners interviewed for this Report when he says that more often than not values are formulated and then hung on a wall and basically forgotten about.

Just as common, the research shows, is for the senior management team itself to coin the new values, espouse their importance, and then not change their own behaviours to align with these values. Such an attitude will make the statements essentially 'valueless' as subordinates will almost certainly continue to ape the 'real' values of their leaders.

However, corporate value statements can be extremely powerful in shaping behaviour if they are made tangible, real and meaningful to each level of the organization, if they are supported by measurement and indeed if they influence the decision-making process.

SmithKline Beecham leaders took its values to 35,000 people in a 12 months timescale. Cammish states that this was essentially about the leaders going out to the company and saying, "this is what the values mean and this how we can all apply them in our workplaces".

David Miller, managing director, ODR Europe, offers American Express as a powerful example of 'living the values' that he has witnessed in recent years. He says:

> "People would go to the then CEO with a proposal, say for a new business, and he would say, 'I'm going to assume you've got a good financial case for this, now how does is it align with our values'. And if it wasn't aligned the proposal would not be taken further."

He adds:

> "It's useful to look at an organization 12 months following the articulation of the values set and measure what's in place within the organization to reach those values. For example, what rewards are in place for people who live by them and, importantly, what are the punishments for people who do not. And if you're not willing to make these reinforcements, then don't do it in the first place."

Research on Values

Interestingly, the 'Culture and Change Management' survey,[9] found that values were explicitly stated 'in the way we do things here' within almost 70 per cent of companies with extremely well defined' cultures against just over 22 per cent in companies with 'very poorly defined' cultures.

Redefining corporate values was, with a percentage rating of 71.83 per cent, ranked third out of seven in the list of actions taking by organizations to change corporate culture, behind the top-ranked development of new organizational structures and second ranked changes in roles and responsibilities.

Moreover, on a scale of 1 to 5, 87.47 per cent of companies gave a score of 1 or 2 (with 1 being completely agree and 5 being strongly disagree) to the statement, 'gaining buy-in to shared values across our organization is essential to our future'. Only 3.41 per cent proferred a score from 4 to 5.

Case Report: General Electric

Probably the best known example of a leader who has made corporate values central to the way he runs his business is Jack Welch, chairman and CEO of the US-headquartered global organization General Electric (GE).

While being interviewed for the book *21st Century Leadership: Dialogues with 100 Top Leaders*,[10] Welch outlined the importance of the organization's seven core values. He said:

"Our first value for GE is to 'create a clear, simple, reality-based, customer-focused vision and be able to communicate it straightforwardly to all constituencies'. This puts our customers first. It ensures that we all say the same things to everyone.

"[Our] second statement [is] about aggressive targets with unyielding integrity.... You are not going to get an honest culture by lowering standards.... We really beat this value in. We are going to set the bar high. We are going to go after the targets, and always with unyielding integrity.

"In the third statement, we use the words 'hate bureaucracy', and 'all the nonsense that comes with it'. Values are great but bureaucracy can defeat them, so you have to continually fight it.

"The fourth value – [the first part of this value is] 'to have the self confidence to empower others and behave in a boundaryless fashion', – is a big issue.... We use the word 'boundaryless' to break down the turf issues.

"The second part of the value is 'being open to ideas from anywhere'. This is important to us. It's been a big breakthrough at GE. In the past, unfortunately, we pretended that we knew it all. Our engineers all knew it. They wouldn't go to Honda, they wouldn't go to Bell Atlantic or Wal-Mart. Now openness [and getting better ideas] is a way of life.

"Our fifth value is to have the capacity to develop diverse and global teams.

"Our sixth value is a big one for us – 'we stimulate and relish change... are not frightened or paralysed by it [and] see change as an opportunity not a threat'.... The question really comes down to leadership. It's not a matter of reshuffling the pack – the deck is now up for grabs so opportunities exist. We talk a lot about dealing with change, and the fact that every time you see a change, it's an opportunity to change the deck. So don't get scared and don't get paralysed – but redo it all....

"[The first part of] our last value is 'having enormous energy and the ability to invigorate others'. It's easy to be a high energy bully... but it doesn't leverage the game. Rallying teams and invigorating others are other aspects of leadership needed to leverage this game.

"The last element in our seventh value statement has to do with the concept of speed. This is a world we live with.... You can't have speed and bad quality, because bad quality will stop the process. You can't have fast receivable service without high quality billing, or you'll be stopped. So speed just serves you all the time. Speed is something you can't say is bad. The forces of resistance can't mount themselves against speed. So as a value, speed becomes a very important driver."

GE leadership types

Famously, Welch has also articulated a model describing four types of leaders and how their performance is evaluated. The model is designed to emphasize expected cultural behaviours that must underpin the achievement of positive financial results. In the book, *In the Eye of the Storm: Reengineering Corporate Culture*, he described these leadership types:[11]

"The **Type 1** leader has the values and meets the numbers. That leader is brilliant. We would like a zillion of these. For them it is onward and upward.

"The **Type 2** leader is also easy – that is the leader who does not meet the commitment and does not share our values. While not as pleasant a call, it is just as easy to evaluate.

"The **Type 3** leader who has the values and does not meet the numbers. That person gets a second chance. You have to keep coaching and hoping. And we have some great success stories about this kind of leader changing, although nowhere near the amount we would like. It is well known that we do give people who live the values a second chance.

"The **Type 4** leader is one who meets the numbers but does not share the values we believe we must have. For years we looked the other way – today we do not believe the person will make it over a sustained period of time."

Case Study Value Examples

An approach similar to that of GE is now being used by Superdrug, a case study to accompany Chapter 5. The company, as with GE, believes that if people are achieving good financial results but not living the values then this will cause long-term damage to the reputation and, therefore, financial success of the organization. Superdrug's values have been defined as:

- Delighting the customer.
- Winning.
- Generosity of spirit.
- Constructive rigour.
- Being straightforward.
- Diversity.
- Involvement, Ownership, Pride, Excellence of Execution (IOPE).

Other value statements have been coined by case study companies. At Lehigh Portland Cement Company, for example, the value statement reads:

'Our companies are totally committed to:
- providing superior quality products and services to our customers
- maintaining the highest level of integrity, ethics and excellence in all aspects of our business

- providing a safe, challenging and rewarding work environment for our employees

- fulfilling our responsibilities to our industry, to our communities and the protection of the environment

- continuously improving our people, our products, our services and our profitability.'

Hyundai Car (UK) Ltd, takes an interesting approach to values in that its organizational values are exactly the same as those that customers ascribe to Hyundai cars – confidence, value, warmth, reliability, style and honesty. These values have been distilled into ten key performance criteria:

- Be willing to make significant change in the way we do things now in order to create greater value for customers.

- Make only those commitments you honestly expect to be able to meet; genuinely try to deliver as promised.

- Review both success and mistakes to find ways to improve for the future.

- Provide/seek out appropriate training, guidance and support.

- Keep abreast of customer/clients needs and priorities.

- Organize activities and timescales to achieve objectives on schedule.

- Let people know that their efforts are appreciated and valued.

- Seek feedback from customers on individual and departmental activities/contribution.

- Suggest ways to improve the way we do things.

- Support and co-operate with other departments.

What is important in these examples is that the organizations set their stalls out to ensure that their values are real and alive deep in the organization and are not just pieces of paper hanging decoratively on walls.

Values Questionnaire

In their book *21st Century Leadership: Dialogues with 100 Top Leaders*, the authors set a simple questionnaire with which people could evaluate their organization's commitment to value statements and the individual's own role in shaping those behaviours.[12]

This, in itself, can be a powerful tool for assessing a gap analysis from the current to intended culture at the start of a culture change effort, (which is dealt with in more detail in the following Chapter) and for appraising progress towards the new cultural ethos. The questions are:

1. Has my organization established a meaningful set of shared values or guiding principles to define and shape our culture? To what extent are people 'living the values'?

2. What are some of the winning shared values I see?

3. How well am I role modeling these values? Is the most senior team role modeling them?

4. What cultural barriers or counter-productive habits do I see in the organization (ie, lack of teamwork, boss-driven behaviour, lack of openness and trust, resistance to change, etc)?

5. In what way could I cast a better shadow to influence the culture around me?

6. Does our culture support the current needs and strategies of our organization?

7. What cultural qualities would I like to see strengthened?

As a final word on values, and how this dovetails with senior management behaviour, Kotter and Heskett state in their book *Corporate Culture and Performance*:[13]

> "The values and practices [leaders of high performing companies] wanted infused into their firms were usually on display in their daily behaviour: in the questions they asked at meetings, in how they spent their time, in the decisions they made. These actions seem to have given critical credibility to their words. The behaviour made it clear to others that their speeches were serious. And successes, which seemed to result from that behaviour, made it clear that the speeches were sensible."

Section G: Vision and Mission Statements

Of course, within many organizations value statements are articulated in support of corporate vision and/or mission statements. Creating vision and mission statements is a crucial role of the senior management team in setting and articulating strategic direction.

Unfortunately, the weakness of such statements of strategic intent are, the research finds, identical to those of value statements. Indeed many of the experts interviewed for this Report were quite damning in their appraisal of these statements of strategic intent. For example, Dr David Clutterbuck, chairman of the UK-based internal communications consultancy The ITEM Group, says:

> "Such statements led to a lot of euphoria in the 1980s. Nowadays, however, mostly no-one cares. The statements are primarily aspirational, but if people can't see how to achieve the aspiration then they won't take them seriously."

Alison Rankin-Frost, head of the UK-based Context Consulting, comments that within organizations there is often too much effort in writing them and not enough in communicating and embedding them in an organization. She says:

> "I know organizations that have taken eight months to write the statements and then they stick them on the wall, think they're finished with the work and can't understand why people aren't interested. So it should be 20 per cent of the time on writing them and 80 per cent on embedding them."

However, as with value statements, visions and missions can be powerful performance motivators. And can, if framed and implemented properly, be effective in aligning behaviour with strategic goals. As Robin Cammish says:

> "What you're looking for is a compelling statement that people can relate to and say 'I want to be part of that vision'."

BT Northern Ireland's Lucy Woods makes the excellent point that too many CEOs are eager to publish such missives without thinking through whether they themselves are willing to act in accordance with the words. Although agreeing that statements of strategic intent can be powerful motivators and intrinsic to changing corporate cultures, Woods does feel that they are too often overdone:

> "You've got to define what you want to be but visions can be overly complex and therefore meaningless. My vision for BT Northern Ireland is 'to be the best'. By which I mean the best at how you define the work. The best typist, the best engineer, the best company in Europe. So I tell my people to work to be the best, find benchmarks for this and drive performance upwards."

She adds that in the 30 seconds it takes to explain 'be the best' people can get quite excited:

> "Its clear, understandable and it's possible to make it measurable. Much better than a whole lot of management mumbo-jumbo that nobody reads or understands."

Woods also stresses that you can write a vision for your boss, or write one that is compelling to your people:

> "Remember, most people come to work to do a job not with dreams of running FTSE 100 companies. Good leadership is about knowing what motivates ordinary people."

A Good Vision

Visions, of course, should be individual to each company but, according to our research, there are some general rules about vision creation and testing that can be followed.

Within his paper, 'Leadership In Tomorrow's Company', Philip Sadler, chairman of the UK-based Centre for the Tomorrow's Company, quoted the five conditions which, according to management guru Charles Handy, need to be met if visionary leadership is to be effective:[14]

- First the vision has to be different: "A vision has to 'reframe' the known scene, to re-conceptualize the obvious, connect the previously unconnected, to dream a dream".

- Second the vision must make sense to others. It should be seen as challenging, but capable of achievement.

- Third it must be understandable and capable of sticking in people's minds.

- Fourth, the leader must exemplify the vision by his or her own behaviour and evident commitment.

- Finally, the leader must remember that if the vision is to be implemented, it must be one that is shared.

And when it comes to testing the efficacy of the vision, Dr Andy Neely, a research fellow with the business performance management group at the Judge Institute of Management, University of Cambridge, offers this three-step process:

1. Replace your company's name with another and see if this makes any difference. A good vision statement should be unique to your own organization.

2. Ask a sample of senior managers what the vision is and then see how many different answers you get.

3. If they do know what the vision statement is, ask what they have personally done over the past week to move the organization forward towards achieving its vision.

If a culture change programme is to successfully align behaviours to strategic direction then it is, the research shows, critical that employees can see how their performance and their behaviours will support movement towards achieving the organizational vision.

Case Report: Ernst & Young

Ernst & Young provides a powerful example of how a vision statement can be actively managed and developed within the firm. The company had invested a considerable amount of time detailing exactly what the vision is, why the vision is important and articulating a set of seven building blocks that together would drive the organization to achieving its vision.

This success model has been visualized in a form that, because of its shape, has become know within the firm as 'the rocket'. This shows how the vision derives from the firm's characteristics, supported by the competitive advantage, and driven by the seven building blocks (see Figure 4.1). The firms vision is:

> 'Being recognized as the leading firm which contributes most to its clients' success'.

Ernst & Young defines its competitive advantage as:

> 'harnessing the skills and talents of all our people better than our competitors can or will – learning faster and sharing more.'

In the rocket model, Ernst & Young then goes on to define its characteristics as:

- Truly Client Driven.
- Totally Integrated with No Barriers.
- Fast, Flexible, Agile and Market Driven.
- Committed to Continuous Improvement.

The firm's seven building blocks are:

- demonstrating value
- excellence at client service
- growing our people

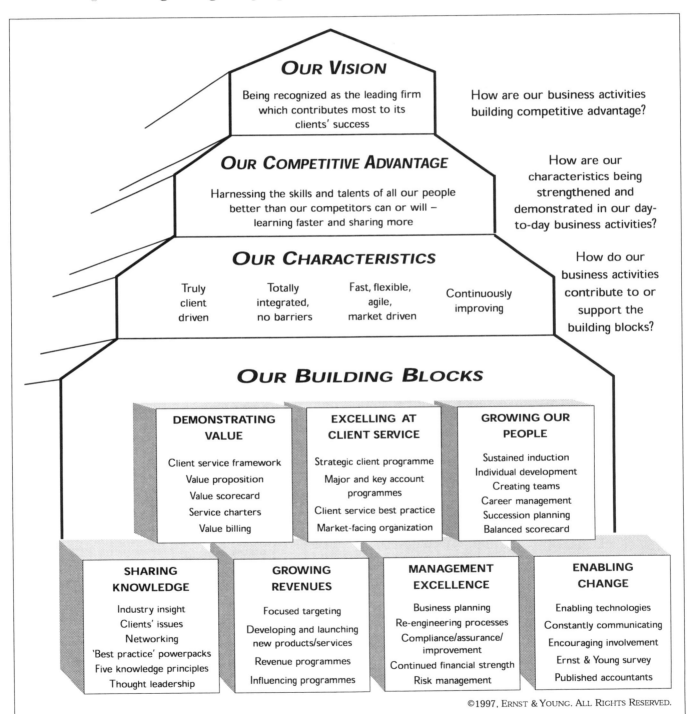

Figure 4.1: Ernst & Young Success Model – Living Our Vision

- sharing knowledge
- growing revenues
- management excellence
- enabling change.

As Figure 4.1 shows, each block contains specific supporting business activities.

Devolving statements of strategic intent and indeed driving culture deep into the organization requires the active participation of change agents at each level of the company. This is explored in further detail in Chapter 6.

Section H: Conclusion

The leadership and behaviour of the CEO and the senior management team is, this Chapter has shown, crucial for successful cultural change. So corporate leaders must realize that if they seriously want to drive cultural change deep inside their organizations they must first look at and challenge their own behaviours, and ask the simple question, 'are we demonstrating the style of leadership and behaviour which is congruent with the new cultural ethos we wish to create?'.

According to research for this Report, the simple truth is that if senior managers are not willing to change then lasting cultural change will not take hold within the company. Similarly, senior management has to constantly communicate the need for culture change and the new values that will underpin corporate performance, and this, as several of the case study companies have shown, can mean a considerable investment in time and effort.

KFC, the case study to accompany this Chapter, provides a best practice example of how committed leadership from the top can transform the culture of an organization. But, as the study will show this required the leadership team to look in the mirror at, and change, their own behaviour before asking the rest of the organization to accept the cultural and behaviour change.

Key Learning Points

1. The CEO and the senior management team must lead and direct the culture change effort. Without this leadership, culture change will not succeed.

2. The senior management team must analyse their own behaviours and ensure that these are aligned to the desired cultural ethos.

3. Senior management must be cultural role models.

4. The CEO has a vital role in driving behavioural change within his or her own executive team. Ideally, this change should happen before rolling culture change out to the rest of the organization.

5. Communicating the need for change throughout the organization is a vital role for the senior management team.

6. When devising vision, mission or value statements, senior managers may benefit from the advice of one adviser who said they should spend, "20 per cent of the time on writing them and 80 per cent on embedding them".

7. Value statements will only prove powerful change levers if senior management personally 'live the values'.

8. About vision and mission statements, and indeed leadership generally, Lucy Woods, CEO of BT Northern Ireland, provided a valuable piece of advice:

   "Remember, most people come to work to do a job not with dreams of running FTSE 100 companies. Good leadership is about knowing what motivates ordinary people."

CASE STUDY: KFC

Summary

Cultural transformation within KFC was achieved by the appointment of a new CEO, David Novak, who absolutely believed that a winning organization was one wholly focused on supporting the interaction between front-line employees and the customer.

Introduction

KFC, the retailer of the famous chicken meals, operates through about 10,000 wholly-owned and franchised restaurants in around 80 countries worldwide. The company accounts for about 55 per cent of restaurant-based chicken sales in the US alone, where its system sales are around $4 billion per year.

KFC is one of four operating divisions of Louisville, Kentucky headquartered Tricon Global Restaurants. The others are Pizza Hut, Taco Bell and Tricon Restaurants International, the latter essentially being the consolidation of the international operations of the first three. Tricon has about 30,000 outlets around the world and a global workforce of around 650,000, making it the world's largest restaurant chain.

Tricon Global Restaurants is itself a new organization, being born in October 1997 when the global conglomerate PepsiCo sold Tricon its three restaurant businesses. And thus far, Tricon is proving itself financially successful. For 1998, the organization reported an operating profit of $768 million. Operating earnings were at $236 million, up 32 per cent on the previous year.

The Appointment of David Novak

The start of the Tricon success story, however, can be traced back to July 1994 and the appointment of Novak as president and chief executive officer (CEO) of KFC North America Coming from within the PepsiCo organization, Novak is now president and vice-chairman of Tricon.

When Novak took over the KFC reins the company was an ailing giant. It had experienced several years without growth and had significant cultural problems which affected internal relationships and relationships with its franchisees. Mike Birtwistle, a senior consultant with Senn-Delaney Leadership Consulting Group, which played a facilitative role in the cultural turnaround, describes the then KFC culture:

"It was top-down and authoritarian. The role of the boss was to tell people what to do.

"It was also inwardly focused. The key requirement of restaurant managers was to please people within the organization's headquarters. Consequently, the restaurant managers were so busy responding to upper management that they simply did not have time to pay attention to their employees or customers."

Birtwistle adds that one of KFC's strengths has always been its business processes. Although this has not changed, at the time it was adding to the cultural problems:

"The product is fresh and therefore it is not like taking it from the freezer and heating it up. So food preparation and inventory management are complex.

"However, the focus was on the process and not on servicing customers, which of course is the point of the process. The culture was inward and upward. The customer and the employee were simply not in the business formula."

Employee retention rates provide a powerful example of the damage caused by such a culture. In the restaurant business employee turnover rates are, by nature of a primarily young workforce, high; within KFC at the time turnover was in the region of 150–180 per cent per year. Now it is down to around 120–130 per cent and falling. This in itself represents an enormous cost saving to the business.

Novak himself explained the central tenet that drove his decision to transform KFC's culture:[15]

"The fundamental reason was a deep down belief that companies grow through people working better together. So whatever we could do to create a better working environment would, I believed, pay off in superior results."

People working together would also have to reach out to the company's many franchisees. Says Birtwistle:

"The company had gone through a series of different owners and their relationship with their franchisees was terrible. It was a contentious win/lose relationship which had reached the point where the company and the franchisees would not talk to one another except through their lawyers."

The Culture Today

So how does the culture within KFC look now, five years on from Novak's appointment? Says Birtwistle:

"It's a people-focused, customer-focused culture. The hallmark of the culture is recognition and appreciation. And it was Novak, with committed support from his senior management team, that relentlessly drove this cultural shift."

Said Novak:[16]

> "The big thing is that people usually don't leave a company because they are underpaid. They are not motivated primarily by salary, although you have to be competitive on that front. They leave because they are under-nourished and under-recognized.

> "So what we are trying to do in our organization is to put a higher premium on people recognition because we think that 'soft stuff' drives hard results."

This seems self evident given that KFC has experienced four successive years of growth under Novak's leadership. He added:

> "We are tied very much to accountability, feeling good, getting results, and being a great company."

It is worth looking at how Novak drove the cultural transformation. First, he recognized the importance of the people in the business processes. Says Birtwistle:

> "Novak said 'take people out of the process and the process doesn't run, the chicken doesn't fry itself and the inventory doesn't manage itself, so you need people'."

Recognizing that people's output and attitudes are primarily driven by the culture in which they operate, Novak began a root and branch transformation of KFC's culture.

According to Birtwistle, one positive factor at the start of the journey was that there were very few barriers to cultural change. He says:

> "The culture needed to change and people were desperate to change as the corporation had been unsuccessful for so long. So people were ready and, indeed, hungry for change.

> "And Novak proved himself a fanatical leader of the culture change."

Leadership Workshop

An early step on the road to change saw Novak and his executive team attend a three-day off-site workshop in September 1995, facilitated by Larry Senn, chairman of Senn-Delaney Leadership Consulting Group. Novak and his senior team knew that in order to create real and lasting change, the transformation had to start at the very top. According to Novak:[17]

> "The Senn-Delaney exercises show you more about yourself as an individual and how you impact other people. The process seeks inputs, gets people involved and gets ownership"

For the leadership team, understanding yourself as an individual rested on accepting a fundamental tenet of the Senn-Delaney process that the organization is the 'shadow of the leader', meaning that how the organization operates is essentially dependent on the values, behaviours and attitudes demonstrated by the leadership team. Novak states that an important element of his role is to build the team that casts a positive shadow. Says Birtwistle:

> "Through the workshop everyone takes a look in the mirror at their own leadership style. People become reflective and introspective of their own behaviours."

Birtwistle describes some of the important aspects of the KFC senior management workshop:

> "Creating a sense of accountability for individual actions within the team was important. Personal accountability for coaching, feedback and support. For this it's important to start asking the question, 'how can I support people so that they can perform better', essentially helping people succeed rather than just given them direction."

Important here was to challenge any tendency to finger-point or blame when problems arose. Says Birtwistle:

> "Rather than falling back into this conflict mentality, the team looked to proactively build relationships with each other focused on self and team improvement."

It is therefore critical for the leaders to recognize that they can improve. Birtwistle recounts a Senn-Delaney workshop for 600 lower-level managers where Novak stood up and asked for feedback on how he himself could improve as a leader:

> "This sent a powerful message to all these managers that Novak valued people who recognized that they could improve."

Another key element of the senior leadership workshop was for leaders to buy-in to the concept of 'assumed innocence'. Explains Birtwistle:

> "Often if you go into the workplace and see things that aren't right, there's an assumption from management that their people are incompetent.

> "However, with the principle of 'assumed innocence' you give people the benefit of doubt and believe that they really are doing their best, but, for whatever reason, today they're doing something wrong. So instead of a typical 'blame' situation, the leader sees this as an opportunity for positive interaction and asks the employee questions and provides guidance, that helps them get back on the right track. This is much more effective at creating a performance improving culture than telling somebody off."

Key Values

Also critically important to creating a performance improvement culture within KFC were the articulation of the three key KFC values of 'teamwork, friendliness and pride'.

Friendliness is about creating a family-like atmosphere (indeed many franchisees are family-owned). Being friendly to each other and to the customer. Teamworking means also working with the customer to continually improve the KFC experience as well as teamworking within the restaurants and throughout the KFC organization. And pride is about being proud of the product, the company and the work, a feeling that was clearly lacking at the start of the culture change programme. For example, Birtwistle explains that even in the 'bad years' the KFC brand was still one of the most recognizable in the world, but employees had no real sense of pride in that.

Crucial to identifying these three key values, Novak and his senior team travelled throughout North America holding meetings with both employee groups and customer groups. The purpose was to uncover views on KFC, both good and bad, in order to pinpoint the key cultural drivers of change at where it mattered most, the front-line employee-customer interface.

According to Birtwistle, each member of the senior management team overtly demonstrated and role modeled these values when interacting with employees or customers. He says:

> "Novak holds himself accountable to these values and holds others accountable too – this proves a massive momentum factor."

These values also support the mission of Tricon:

> 'To put a yum on people's faces around the world with:
>
> • crave and rave food
>
> • comeback value and customer-focused teams.'

'Mega' Workshops

With the top team clear as to the culture they wished to create, and indeed the shadow they wished to cast, the process began to devolve the Senn-Delaney workshops to all managers within the organization – regional, district and restaurant. This proved to be a challenge, due to the sheer number and dispersed geographic locations of KFC restaurants.

To resolve this, the workshops below senior management level were 'mega' sessions. Birtwistle explains:

> "The outline and content of these sessions were still three day and similar to the off-site senior management workshop in that they still explored the fundamental principles such as accountability, feedback, support and shadow the leader. However, these sessions were delivered to a much larger audience, often around 500 at a time. In fact, in March 1996 we had a session in Louisville, Kentucky with 2800 people – corporate-owned restaurant managers and all support function managers.
>
> "The structure of this workshop ensured it remained interactive. For the general assembly, we installed three image magnifying cameras, 40 foot and 15 foot screens and an excellent sound system. These general meetings were supported by breakout sessions for regional teams, and then further breakout sessions for people who worked with each other. This meant the messages from the top were devolved and debated at regional and local levels."

Importantly, trained facilitators ensured a successful devolution of message and debate. A lot of these were regional managers who had each attended up to ten previous Senn-Delaney training sessions, thus demonstrating another key KFC belief – do it over and over again until it becomes second nature.

According to Birtwistle, another important reason for the success of these mega sessions was the presence of senior management to listen to proceedings and answer questions. He says:

> "For example, Chuck Rawley, then chief operating officer and now president of KFC, attended all three days of each workshop held. This was an incredible time commitment but an important signal of just how seriously senior management took cultural change.

Said Novak:[18]

> "There hasn't been a single group who haven't been passionate about the workshops and the underlying principles being something very positive, productive and a great way to run our business and their lives."

Change at the Front-line

Following these 'mega' sessions, videos and work-based programmes were developed and delivered to all front-line people. And each restaurant holds monthly staff sessions to discuss performance improvement ideas such as 'pay attention to the customer'.

An innovative tool used throughout KFC are 'mood elevator' posters. Essentially these describe different moods on a higher and lower mood scale (see Figures 4.2 and 4.3).

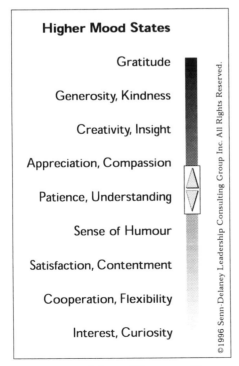

Figure 4.2: Mood Elevator Poster – Higher Mood States

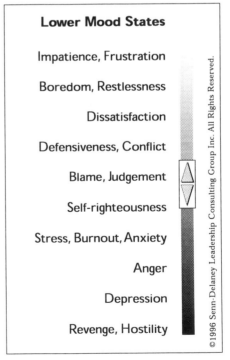

Figure 4.3: Mood Elevator Poster – Lower Mood States

The purpose of these Mood Elevator posters are to help people identify their mood, understand the mood's impact on performance and help the individual, often with the team's or leader's help, drive the mood to a higher and more positive level. Says Birtwistle:

> "At KFC front-line employees need to be in a higher mood to deliver an excellent service experience to the customer, so managers have to manage the restaurant and lead the team from a higher mood.

> "A service business that can run from a higher mood will make more money because customers will enjoy the experience and so keep coming back. That's why the mood elevator is such an important tool for KFC, and indeed for the whole of Tricon."

RGMs as the No. 1 Leader

Another critical change in the cultural mind-set of KFC was achieved by its decision to recognize the restaurant general manager (RGM) as the company's No. 1 leader. It recognized that although executive teams set strategy and allocate resources, it is the RGM who builds the team at the restaurant level that will satisfy the customer and therefore make the money.

Consequently the whole structure of KFC, and now Tricon, has focused support functions onto delivering value and services to the RGMs (a complete cultural turnaround from the days pre-transformation).

Importantly, outward symbolism of this change in focus has been renaming corporate headquarters 'Restaurant Support Centres', and uniquely placing RGMs on stock certificates. Said Novak, "everything we do above our own restaurants is designed to support our RGMs".[19]

Franchisee Change

Changes at KFC corporately and in its owned-restaurants instigated changes within the previously disgruntled franchisee base. According to Birtwistle, franchisees had started to personally experience the change in attitude emanating from corporate headquarters:

> "They were beginning to feel that KFC cared about them and were willing to support them in their businesses, rather than just demanding more and more and offering little in exchange. Therefore franchisees wanted to be a part of this culture change process."

So in April 1997 Novak and Don Parkinson, senior vice-president, franchise, sponsored a programme for key franchisee leadership at corporate level and about 150 of the top franchisee leaders. The aim was to begin the process of healing the fractured KFC-franchisee relationship. Says Birtwistle:

> "We called this the KFC Franchisee Leadership Council. And during this session there was a noticeable change in the relationship. By exploring their attitudes, both sides decided to let go of the negative attitudes of the past and to build a positive future."

Subsequent franchisee programmes were delivered throughout the KFC regions and in general, says Birtwistle, franchisees now have a wonderful relationship with KFC.

According to Birtwistle, the role of Novak was central to the change in attitude of franchisees. He says:

> "Franchisees could trust him. They knew he was honest, open and didn't promise what he couldn't deliver. When they asked for information he gave it to them and they recognized that he cared for them and their business."

An interesting outcome of mending the relationship with franchisees was the impact on new product development and introduction, a key success driver in the restaurant business. When the relationship was poor, independent franchisees did not pass on new product suggestions to KFC corporately, so a huge amount of valuable ideas lay un-harvested within the franchisee system. Now new product ideas continually flow in from KFC's franchisee base.

Birtwistle says that this has been a critical contributor to the financial turnaround of KFC:

> "New products came out, customers liked them and the service experience and they keep coming back. This has led to double digit growth and a massive improvement in the bottom line."

Rewards and Recognition

Another important contributor to KFC and Tricon's success has been the significant attention the senior management has paid to rewards and recognition. For example, Tricon has launched 'Yumbucks', an innovative programme that grants each RGM an initial $20,000 in stock options, with the likelihood of more based on the annual performance of his or her restaurant. Therefore, RGM performance is directly tied to restaurant performance.

Additionally each senior manager has to purchase Tricon stock, thus demonstrating their commitment to, and belief in, Tricon performance and growth.

Front-line employees have the option of buying stock at a highly discounted price. Often, of course, these employees are young and so this is part of a wider programme to teach them to manage their own money and invest in their future.

Tricon has also launched a 'YUM' Award for staff who put a 'yum on customers' faces'. This award is a six-inch tall set of smiling, talking teeth on legs. Press a button on top and you can watch teeth walk and talk the Tricon mission. It also comes with a $300 gift certificate; $100 for each of the company's three brands.

For KFC there is also a prestigious Floppy Chicken award that rewards individuals for outstanding performance, and comes with a $100 gift certificate. Interestingly, Senn-Delaney was the first external organization to win this award.

Internal Communications

KFC also recognized from the start, the absolute importance of internal communications. For example, in the mega workshops, during day two, attendees would receive photographs and articles detailing the events of day one.

Importantly the company has also started to tell success stories and create new heroes. For example at the Louisville, Kentucky, headquarters there is an underground tunnel that connects two buildings. This has been transformed into a 'walk of leaders', containing photographs of outstanding performers throughout the restaurant system. Some people have even been taken to Kentucky to see their photographs.

But despite its success KFC is not standing still. According to Novak, "[we have to] keep the pedal to the metal, the job is never done".[20]

Tricon Roll-out

Indeed part of the forward momentum has been transferring the KFC learning throughout the Tricon system. Each of the operating divisions has a common language and a common approach to doing business – essentially recognizing that the most important interface is between the employee and the customer, and therefore all operations must be to make that interaction as positive as possible.

To help ensure the culture remains focused on the values of the corporation, every manager or prospective manager in North America, for all three chains, undergoes a one-week course at corporate headquarters. In addition to teaching these managers the business skills of restaurant management, they are also taught about the importance of culture and leadership. A similar programme is being rolled-out to locations outside North America. Said Novak:[21]

> "It has been very gratifying to be able to help and show people how great a leader they themselves can be and for them to want to do it for themselves and for the company.

> "So for me it has been a great process and very satisfying to see people elevate their performance because you invest in them. I've also learned how to be a better leader by learning more about myself.

> "I hope that the results that we generate over time will demonstrate that a value-based work environment is powerful, but I think it is too early to claim victory. The proof will be in the pudding, but I'm betting my job that it will work."

Conclusion

According to Birtwistle, the three key things that KFC did right to succeed with its culture change programme, can be summed up as:

*   Focus on people.

*   Focus on people.

*   Focus on people.

He adds:

> "David Novak understood that business processes could not be executed without the people and that people were critical to KFC performance.
>
> "In fact he has said, 'at KFC we are not in the chicken business, we are in the people business'."

Key Learning Points

The culture change success within KFC was based on a number of important factors, such as:

1. The appointment of David Novak as president and CEO of KFC North America was the primary catalyst for culture change.

2. Under Novak's leadership the culture transformed from one that was hierarchically- and inwardly-focused to one that is people- and customer-focused.

3. Novak recognized that it is employees who create a positive customer experience and therefore a successful organization.

4. Culture change within KFC started at the top with a three-day workshop for the senior management team. The workshop was then rolled out to other management levels

5. A key component of the change workshop was recognizing that an organization is a 'shadow of the leader' and so operates in accordance with the values, beliefs and attitudes of its leaders.

6. The values of teamwork, friendliness and pride were identified as key guides for the cultural transformation.

7. An important structural change was re-focusing the KFC operation around restaurant general managers (RGMs) by recognizing the RGM as the No. 1 leader.

8. Outward symbols such as renaming corporate headquarters 'Restaurant Support Systems' played a crucial role in creating this new corporate mind-set.

9. Franchisees too have been brought into the change process. In doing so, a previously fractured relationship has been mended, which has created value for customers and the organization alike.

10. Innovative recognition and reward mechanisms have been important in creating the new culture.

11. The organization has also begun to create new corporate heroes, model performers that are customer- and people-focused.

5

ASSESSING THE CULTURAL CHALLENGES

Executive Summary

1. Assessing, and understanding the existing corporate culture prior to launching a change effort substantially increases the prospects of success.

2. Undertaking the assessment will help senior managers decide how far they want the culture to shift and to visualize the considerable challenges ahead.

3. An employee opinion survey can be a powerful mechanism for assessing, and measuring changes to, the corporate culture. But, the research for this Report finds, survey results must lead to improvement initiatives.

4. Several cultural assessment tools are profiled within this Chapter, one being the Normative Systems Culture Change Process devised by the US-based Human Resource Institute Inc. This provides a significant number of questions to ask when planning and rolling out the cultural elements of a change project.

5. Understanding the power of organizational subcultures is vital for succeeding with a change effort.

6. Similarly, understanding the 'unwritten rules' of the organization is critical for driving change forward.

7. Resistance to change, the research shows, is a natural reaction by many people. Understanding the reasons for this is also an important lever of change.

8. Case studies on Superdrug and DSM Resins, demonstrate best practice.

Section A: Context

The preceding Chapter detailed the paramount importance of gaining senior management leadership of a culture change effort. But, according to research for this Report, before embarking on a programme to roll-out cultural change, it is judicious to understand the existing culture of the organization. One key reason is that there are typically numerous challenges within a culture change effort, and early warning signs of these can normally be found through a rigorous assessment of the culture as it is at the start of the initiative.

As this Chapter will show, such warning signals may be found by understanding the differing agendas of the many subcultures which exist within an organization. In addition, a great deal of the most powerful and influential characteristics of a corporate culture may be hidden within the 'unwritten rules' of the organization.

Another reason for cultural assessment is quite simply that, as several advisers interviewed for this Report stated, if you do not know where you are at the start of the culture change journey, it is virtually impossible to successfully navigate to the new cultural destination. As John Childress, chief executive of the culture change specialists Senn-Delaney Leadership Consulting Group, says:

> "Senior managers must have a starting point for change, a place where they have undertaken the required analysis to understand the current strengths and weakness of the culture. This will provide a gap analysis from where they are today to where they want to be in the future."

Undertaking such an exercise will provide management with a good overview of some of the key cultural elements that will need to be changed. Techniques for how to do this will be explored later in the Chapter.

Such an assessment will also pose some important questions for management to contemplate and answer before they embark on cultural change. For example, Dr David Clutterbuck, chairman of the UK-based internal communication specialists The ITEM Group, says that if the cultural assessment reports that the organization operates under a lot of secrecy and distrust, then management must ask themselves how far they want to shift the culture to one that is open and honest. And they must, he continues, understand that if secrecy and distrust are deeply embedded cultural traits, then changing these will require a huge amount of investment of senior management time and significant changes in organizational structure, policies and reporting procedures.

Therefore, the research finds, senior management must beware the danger of lofty aspirational statements. Words that may take seconds to articulate may require huge amounts of energy to make alive within the company.

In his web-published working paper, *Creating an Energized Organization: Aligning Strategy and Culture*, US-based consultant John Burns states the importance of thinking through the cultural challenges ahead. He makes the useful observation that:[1]

> "In any change effort you need to know early on whether what you want in the future matches what you have to work with and what you have to work against."

He states that that this involves having a deep understanding of movements within markets, customers, service offerings and competition, but also an excellent understanding of the internal cultural elements that the organization has to work with and against. He continues:

> "The degree of change required in your organization's course or direction will indicate how much energy has to be invested in reshaping the culture and making the change successful. The road that leads organizations to be something they have never been or for people to do things they haven't been able to do before is a hard journey.

> "Change requires choosing among risk-taking courses of action. While it is impossible to eliminate all risk and uncertainty, the risks that are taken must be the right ones, and they must avoid stepping off into an abyss of uncertainty on the basis of wishful thinking. Actions necessary for future success are likely to take the organization outside of present cultural boundaries and increase the level of challenge and risk. Understanding these cultural boundaries and what's involved in reframing them provides invaluable insight for the development of the improvement strategy."

As Clutterbuck succinctly puts it:

> "Senior mangers tend to write a wish list of the cultural factors they want, but this doesn't change culture."

Such statements reinforce the research finding that cultural change is a huge undertaking, comprising many changes to organizational structures and thinking and therefore a myriad of potential challenges.

Section B: Assessment Tools

Organizations can use a range of techniques to understand, and plan changes to their present culture. Within this section we will look in detail at several approaches. These include generic techniques such as employee opinion surveys, and also consultancy approaches such as an Alignment Diagnostic Software tool created by the global change and performance measurement consultancy Organizational Dynamics Inc (ODI), Senn-Delaney's cultural profile, and a Normative Systems Culture Change System designed by the US-based Human Resource Institute Inc.

However, before outlining the frameworks, it is important to stress that many frameworks assess existing culture *and* are used to implement and drive cultural change. For the sake of simplicity, such frameworks have not been split between this Chapter and the next. Similarly, areas such as leadership, human resource management and communication systems normally appear in such frameworks. Neither have these been removed and placed in other specific Chapters.

Employee Opinion Surveys

Employee opinion surveys are the most widely used approach to assessing corporate culture (and indeed for measuring the success of culture change programmes).

Within the Business Intelligence research survey, 'Culture and Change Management',[2] 40 per cent of the 236 responding organizations from Europe, the US, and the Rest of the World said that corporate culture was actively managed in their companies. Taking this 40 per cent as a 100 per cent, 81.3 per cent said they had a method for assessing the alignment of corporate culture with their strategy. And taking this 81.3 per cent as a 100 per cent, 65.17 per cent used both staff and customer surveys, 22.32 per cent used staff surveys only and 6.25 per cent customer surveys only.

Case study examples

Employee surveys are used extensively within the case study companies. As examples, Ernst & Young (the case study to accompany Chapter 8), Siemens KWU and BT Northern Ireland (both case studies to accompany Chapter 6), Hyundai Car (UK) Ltd (the case study to accompany Chapter 7) and Superdrug (a case study to accompany this Chapter) all use employee surveys.

At Hyundai Car (UK) Ltd, the company's initial employee opinion survey was seen a key first step on the road to cultural change. The results told senior management that about 40 per cent of the workforce were afraid to openly say what they thought, and that employees felt undervalued. Although the feedback was somewhat negative, this did give the senior management team unambiguous data with which to plan the change programme. Therefore it gave them a feel for some of the key cultural challenges ahead.

At Superdrug, the primary mechanism used to ascertain the company's cultural characteristics is an organization culture survey carried out by the UK-based Anglia Polytechnic University. The first survey was undertaken in 1996, and then yearly in 1997 and, with some amendments, 1998. Such is Superdrug's belief in the value of the survey data that the intention was to survey employees twice during 1999.

The Superdrug survey is organized into two sections. The first to be completed by all employees, and the second just by those who had been with the company for more that 12 months. The latter section being an additional mechanism to track progress towards the customer-focused total quality culture envisioned by Superdrug.

At Siemens KWU there is a strong belief in the efficacy of employee opinion surveys to create and measure a culture of continuous improvement. Board members and top executives even stood at the factory and headquarters gates together with representatives of the workers' council to motivate employees to fill out their questionnaires.

CARE

A well-established employee survey is used by BT Northern Ireland, and indeed has been by the whole of the BT organization since 1989. Called CARE (Communications and Attitude Research for Employees), the survey asks employees up to 100 questions relating to their experience of working for BT. These are structured under the following headings:

1. **Job**: measures such as motivation, level of responsibility and enjoyment.

2. **Performance management:** measures the quality of the feedback each employee receives about their performance.

3. **Development and training:** measures how the employees view their opportunities for skills development.

4. **Reward and recognition:** considers employees' views on informal and formal recognition schemes.

5. **Managers:** considers how approachable the employee feels managers are and how committed they are to BT's corporate values.

6. **Communications:** how information is devolved throughout the company.

7. **Working environment:** considers issues such as safety and how pleasant the working environment is.

8. **Customers:** how employees feel about the quality of service provided to their customers.

9. **The company:** how proud employees are to work for BT, and whether they believe the company will attain its vision.

Results against CARE provide meaningful comparisons across BT's business units and divisions, and can easily roll up into a corporate level employee satisfaction metric.

Continuous improvement

At Ernst & Young employee surveys have been used since 1994 and have grown to become an invaluable mechanism for tracking both employee satisfaction and the firm's success in creating a client-focused culture. It also, says Edmund White, national head of internal communication, provides a tremendous opportunity to learn and to prioritize action. He says:

> "[Our employee survey results] show we're doing the right things in engaging people. But we know we must still improve. For example, we haven't got our measurement system right. Reward and recognition performed relatively poorly on the survey, so we now know where we have to prioritize."

This is an important point, for as White says (and this was echoed by other advisers and practitioners interviewed for this Report):

> "When you publish results, the only point is to use the findings for continuous improvement and then to communicate these changes."

Senn-Delaney Corporate Culture Profile

The US-headquartered Senn-Delaney Leadership Consulting Group is a leading consultancy in the culture change arena. One assessment tool it uses is a corporate culture profile. Through this, a sample of employees (which can be as small as the executive team or as wide as the whole company) assesses each of 18 cultural traits on a scale such as the one shown in Figure 5.1. The traits are paired into contrasting statements such as:

1. [there is a] clear alignment/common focus of leadership at the top versus [there is an] obvious lack of alignment at the top

2. people take responsibility for their actions versus [people] find excuses, blame others, feel victimized

3. [the organization is] open to change versus resistant to change.

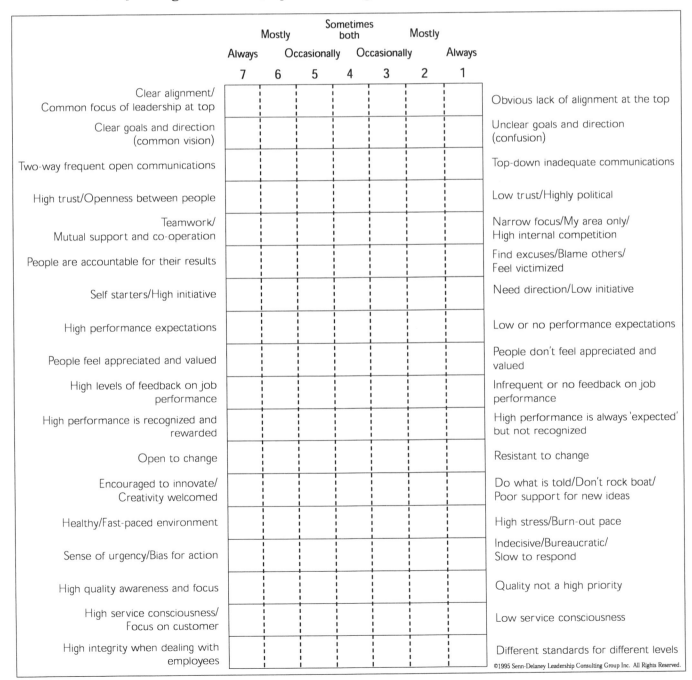

Figure 5.1: Senn-Delaney Corporate Culture℠ Profile Output

© BUSINESS INTELLIGENCE 1999

Subjective interviews

According to Childress such a qualitative questionnaire can help management prioritize cultural change efforts. He also believes that such an approach to assessing corporate culture is best supported by subjective interviews with employees from each level of the organization.

Key 'subjective' questions, the consultancy believes, are:[3]

1. What are the major strengths of the company?
2. How well is the company prepared for the future?
3. In what ways is the company vulnerable?
4. Which areas in the company co-operate, and which ones do not?
5. Is more effort spent on internal competition or external?
6. When a goal or deadline is missed, or a result not accomplished, do people tend to make excuses and blame others or are they highly accountable?
7. Is it OK to make a mistake around here?
8. Does the organization tend to be hierarchical and level conscious?
9. Do people tend to have a strong work ethic?
10. What is our customer service really like?
11. Does the culture tend to encourage new ideas or shoot them down?
12. Are issues discussed openly in meetings or afterwards in the hall?
13. What is the current levels or trust or openness in the organization?

Of course organizations should choose the questions that will give them the most accurate picture of the gap between their existing culture and the one they wish to create.

ODI Alignment Diagnostic

Another interesting assessment method is an Alignment Diagnostic Software tool recently developed by Organizational Dynamics Inc (ODI). This is an electronic application which enables a computer-based graphical analysis of how well the organization is aligned. It allows for an analysis and comparison of alignment by, as examples, region, work function, employee-type or length of service. The actual level of alignment is displayed visually against an indicator of optimal alignment. Through the Diagnostic, an organization can, the consultancy claims, quickly pinpoint where misalignment is occurring.

Cultural misalignment

According to ODI it also provides for a powerful snapshot of the corporate culture and where cultural misalignment exists. Lawrence Brink, ODI's vice president for marketing/product development, and instrumental in designing the Diagnostic Software, sees this as an important point. He says:

> "Too many organizations try to change a culture without understanding what their people are thinking. The Diagnostic is a way to assess the current reality. For example, are the roles and responsibilities right, is the

organization designed to share information, do employees think the organization has a bright future, are managers passionate about goals, and are employee values consistent with the values of the organization. All critical questions in any change programme."

The Diagnostic, which can be either a Windows or Internet-based application poses a series of statements, which employees have to rate from 'strongly agree' to 'strongly disagree' within the criteria areas of strategic excellence, organizational readiness and value chain advantage. These three areas are split into sub-categories. As examples, the strategic excellence category includes external focus, future customer orientation and competitiveness. The organizational readiness category includes distributed leadership, motivational energy and knowledge management. And the value chain advantage category includes customer focus, IT integration and process orientation (see Figure 5.2).

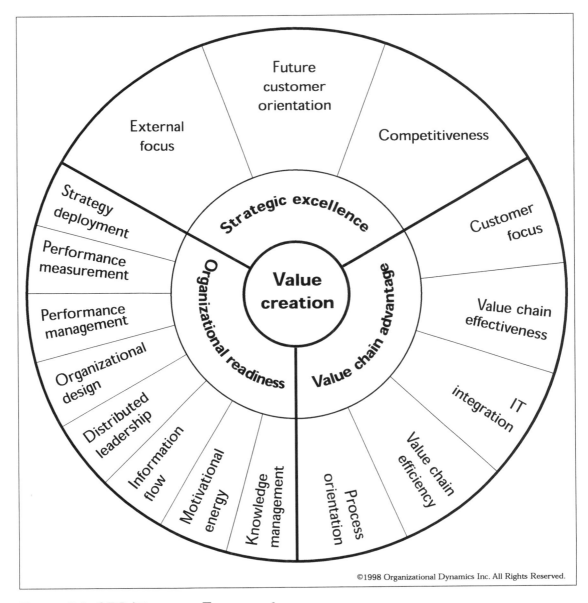

Figure 5.2: ODI Alignment Framework

A *phased approach*

Using this tool requires a phased approach to alignment implementation. In the first phase the consultancy, along with the client, define the population the Diagnostic will study including the make-up, size and demographic categories of that sample For example, it may study different divisional units, job functions, seniority levels, age and length of service.

The next step involves the input modes. These can be pen and paper which are scanned into a database, telephone interviews or face-to-face. The answers are then collected and analysed. Following this is an alignment workshop, which is a half-day, graphics-based presentation of the key findings to the senior management team.

The next phase is typically a three-day off-site workshop involving consultants and up to ten people from the client organization. The purpose here is to look more in-depth at the diagnostic results. Comments Brink:

> "In this session we will do a series of exercises where we facilitate conversations with clients to help them take what we've found and what their experts know about the business and look at the relationship between the expert knowledge and the data findings. From this we can determine the intervention actions which are needed immediately to get the organization into alignment and the short-term and long-term needs.

> "Then we present the findings to senior management and say 'here's our deliverables with a prioritized list of needs'."

Brink goes on to explain that this is followed by a solution implementation phase, which is essentially the responsibility of the client, although ODI consultants may be involved if they have the requisite expertise. Importantly, according to Brink, the Diagnostic Software enables targeted interventions:

> "For example, if the misalignment is within hourly paid employees or those with over, say, five years service, or within a particular function, then intervention strategies can be developed just for these groups."

He continues:

> "The final phase is ongoing assessment of progress. This may be done quarterly, twice-yearly or annually. Here we would re-deploy the Diagnostic to find out if the intervention initiatives are working."

Case Report: DSM Resins

DSM Resins, a case study to accompany this Chapter, has used another ODI tool, the Working Climate Analysis, as a critical performance-enhancing mechanism within its culture change programme.

The Working Climate Analysis is an employee questionnaire that aims to discover their perceptions of six areas that directly influence the environment in which they work and therefore their performance. The areas are:

- Goals and Follow-up on Results.

- Change.

- Organization/Flexibility.

- Motivation/Energy.

- Management.

- Specific Local Focus Area Concerns.

Tailored to DSM Resins' own requirements, these are divided into further subheadings. As examples, for Goals and Follow-up on Results, subheadings include 'attention to goals and 'management encouragement'. For Change they include 'innovation' and 'attitudes', while for Motivation/Energy, subheadings include 'trust' and 'working relations'.

Employees rate each of the 80 statements that make up these six categories from 1 (disagree entirely) to 7 (agree entirely). Statements include:

1. 'in our department most people have a good knowledge of the goals of the organization'

2. 'we have a systematic follow-up to all our goals'

3. 'we have the freedom to organize our own work'

4. 'you get support and encouragement when you contribute new ideas'

5. 'our unit is customer-oriented'.

Johan Van der Hel, human resources manager for DSM Resins Coating Resins' business unit, explains why DSM Resins embraced the Working Climate Analysis approach and how it fits with the company's wider culture change programme called VITA:

> "VITA as a concept only sets down a framework for managers and employees to develop themselves and the business. To really make it work we chose the Working Climate Analysis as the implementation tool. It is primarily a bottom-up process where improvement takes place within [employees'] own work area. Therefore, the Working Climate Analysis enables us to quantify where we were today in relation to the VITA objectives, but also lends itself to the identification of future improvement opportunities."

Essentially the Working Climate Analysis process entails sending the questionnaire to all employees in each strategic business unit work area. Once the data is processed, trained facilitators present the survey findings to local management and feedback work groups. The purpose of these feedback sessions is to understand the results, study trends and to highlight improvement opportunities on the basis of a fundamental group discussion.

All actionable ideas are, if necessary, reviewed by managers who have to provide the budget for the project and any resources required. They also have to clearly explain their reasons for turning down any submitted suggestions.

Internal measurements ensure that local management is indeed playing a proactive role in ensuing that the Working Climate Analysis process is used to drive continuous improvement within the work areas.

Therefore, the Working Climate Analysis, as with the Alignment Diagnostic tool and more common employee attitude surveys, is of value within a culture change programme when it is assessing the present culture, and is used to define improvement opportunities and to measure the progress towards cultural goals and therefore the efficacy of intervention initiatives.

Normative Systems Culture Change Process

A comprehensive framework for assessing, and indeed changing corporate culture, is the Normative Systems Culture Change Process[4] devised by the US-based Human Resource Institute Inc. This is an ever-evolving approach and, indeed, a version was first used in the US during the 1960s.

The Normative Systems Culture Change Process consists of four phases, each of which is broken down into further categories which contain a number of critical questions to ask as part of the culture change effort. These four phases are:

1. Analysis, Objective Setting and Leadership Commitment.

2. Systems Introduction.

3. Systems Integration.

4. Evaluation, Renewal and Extension.

Phase I: Analysis, objective setting and leadership commitment

The purpose of this phase is to establish a clear picture of the existing culture, set specific measurable objectives and commit leaders to a vision for change. This covers the three critical success factors which the research has found to be central to succeeding with a cultural change effort.

According to the system designers, analysis in this phase covers three broad categories of information – A) performance, B) programmatic and C) cultural.

A) Performance Analysis

Performance data encompass both financial and behavioural measures. Key questions to ask here include:

1. What are the human and economic costs of the current behaviour?

2. What new behaviours are likely to produce the largest human benefit and economic returns?

3. How will the economic and human impact be measured?

4. How will behaviour be measured?

B) Programmatic Analysis

This sub-phase examines how change efforts should be organized to maximize the likelihood of success. Key questions to ask here include:

- How will the past influence the change process?

- Who will need to be involved in the change process?

- Who should play a leadership role in steering the change process?

- What is the best strategy for introducing the change process?

C) Cultural Analysis

This sub-phase is broken down into five component parts:

C.1 Value statements.

C.2 Norms.

C.3 Organizational support systems.

C.4 Peer support.

C.5 Climate.

C.1 Value Statements

As explained in the previous Chapter, value statements, if deployed correctly, can play a powerful role in driving cultural change. According to this system, key questions to ask here include:

- What are the current core values or belief systems that are related to project goals?

- How might current value systems get in the way of adopting cultural solutions?

- What core project values (or themes) might inspire collective action?

- What differences exist in the ways subcultures view potential project values?

C.2 Norms

A norm is an expected and accepted behaviour, 'it's the way we do things around here'. Key questions to ask here include:

- What norms stand in the way of project goals?

- What norms support project goals?

- How well do current norms reflect individual and cultural values?

C.3 Organizational Support Systems

According to the Human Resource Institute there are a variety of mechanisms that define and perpetuate the culture. Formal structures such as laws, rules and policies play an important role, and informal structures such as the 'grapevine' are also powerful. Information about organizational support can be organized into the following ten broad categories:

- Modeling.
- Recruitment and selection.
- Orientation.
- Training.
- Rewards and recognition.
- Confrontation.
- Communication systems.
- Relationships and interactions.
- Symbols, myths and rituals.
- Allocation of resources.

According to this system, strengths and opportunities for improvement should be identified for each of the ten organizational support systems. Key questions to ask here include:

- How are project-related behaviours being modeled? What can be done to increase the modeling of desired behaviour and/or to reduce the modeling of behaviours that run counter to programme goals?
- Are key behaviours rewarded and recognized? What will increase the positive impact of rewards and recognition?
- How are inappropriate behaviours being rewarded and recognized? How can these rewards and recognition systems be modified?
- How are rituals, myths and symbols linked to project-related behaviour?

C.4 Peer Support

Key questions to ask here include:

1. Who will support the change (eg, family, friends, co-workers, boss, etc)?
2. What forms of support are given (eg, help with goal setting, modeling, eliminating barriers, locating supportive environments, working through relapse, and celebrating success)? What gaps exist?
3. Are members of the culture receptive to support being offered?
4. Do members of the culture ask for the support needed to accomplish project goals?

C.5 Climate

This sub-phase us made up of four categories; sense of community, shared vision, positive outlook and leadership commitment.

- **Sense of Community**. A sense of community is present when people feel as if they belong and trust one another. Key questions to ask here include:
  - Do members of the culture really get to know one another (eg, special interests, history, etc)?
  - Do people support each other in times of need?
  - Do people feel as if they belong and are welcomed?

- **Shared Vision**. A shared vision exists when people recognize that they hold similar value systems. Key questions to ask here include:
  - Do people recognize that they share common values (or at the very least can be enthusiastic about each other's values)?
  - Can people describe shared goals and strategies for achieving those goals?
  - Do people find their shared goals and strategies inspirational?

- **Positive Outlook**. With a positive outlook, the designers state, people look for opportunities rather than obstacles and for strengths rather than weaknesses in one another. Key questions here include:
  - Do people have faith that constructive change is possible?
  - Do people recognize individual and organizational strengths or do they focus on what is wrong?
  - Do people view needed change as an opportunity for improvement, or do they view change as a problem?
  - Do people make use of individual and organizational strengths in addressing needed change?

- **Leadership Commitment**. Obtaining leadership commitment is a key element in Phase I. Key questions here include:
  - How should leaders state the intended benefits of the culture change effort?
  - How will leaders get an opportunity to experience the desired culture?
  - What is the best way to teach leaders skills and concepts that will make them useful in the culture change process?
  - How will leaders link their personal values and vision to the project?

Much more on this subject is covered in Chapter 4.

Phase II: Systems introduction

The second phase of the Normative Systems introduces members of the culture to the project vision and invites participation in the change process. Phase II efforts also teach skills in creating a climate that supports change, ie, one with a sense of community, a shared vision and a positive outlook.

Although printed materials and visual media can, the designers state, be useful in getting the word out, Phase II efforts tend to be organized around a workshop. The workshop provides a forum for relating project goals to personal values and experiences. Introductory workshops tend to cover three broad subject areas – A) understanding, B) identifying, and C) changing.

A) Understanding

Members of the culture, state the designers, should become familiar with the key lessons of the Analysis and Objective Setting phase.

It is also useful, they continue, to review the history of past change attempts that did not succeed and ask questions such as 'what were their strengths and why did they fall short?'.

Participants, the designers state, would also benefit from an understanding of the power of culture. This issue is sometimes addressed by discussing the impact of cultural norms. The discussion can also be instrumental in helping people to realize that they will need to work together to bring about meaningful results.

Finally, the designers state, it can be beneficial to develop an understanding of the building blocks of culture – values, norms, organizational support systems, peer support and climate. Feedback from the cultural analysis helps build such a conceptual framework. Key questions to ask here include:

- How will the economic and human costs of the current culture be shared?

- What will be said about the impact on the individual? What will be said about the impact on the group, organization or society?

- How will past change attempts be explained? What lessons about culture change can be integrated into this explanation?

- What is the best mechanism to teach about the power of culture? Will some cultural norms reveal this power? Can the discussion of culture be summarized in such a way that people will understand the futility of negative blame-placing and realize the importance of joining together in finding a lasting solution?

B) Identifying

Project participants need to identify meaningful goals. Such goal-setting activity should be done at both individual and collective levels. Goals may be organized by short- and long-term objectives and/or around the degree of difficulty. Key questions to ask here include:

- How will participants assess their own behaviour?

- How will individual goals be set? Will they be organized around degree of difficulty? Will they be organized around a timeline?

- How will groups be given feedback on current behaviour?

- How will groups establish behavioural goals? Will these goals be organized around degree of difficulty? Will they be organized around a timeline?

C) Changing

Members of the culture, the designers state, should be given an opportunity to develop a change plan. Key questions to ask here include:

- What format will individual action plans take? Will specific action steps be recommended?

- What format will group level action plans take? Will specific action steps be recommended?

- How will people be informed about the availability of support programmes and materials?

- How will new ideas and suggested changes in current plans be shared?

Phase III: Systems Integration

To assure success, the designers say, change should take place on multiple levels. The Systems Integration phase focuses on A) individual self-help, B) peer support, C) organizational support, and D) leadership development.

A) Individual-level Integration

Activities here include; attending seminars, watching videos, reading books and pamphlets, and using computer programmes. Most self-help activities combine some form of personal assessment with an action plan.

Problem behaviour is addressed by focusing attention on the needs, history and skills of the individual. Key questions to ask here include:

- What format(s) should self-help material and support take (eg, counselling, videos, pamphlets, newsletter, etc)?

- How will those involved in self-help activities be given opportunities to share their experiences?

- How will self-help programmes include a role for cultural support?

B) Peer-level Integration

Key questions to ask here include:

- What support groups, if any, should be organized? How long and how often will they meet?

- How will family members or housemates be involved in the change process? What training might these people receive?

- How will co-workers support each other? How often should co-workers discuss their change efforts? What training in peer support will co-workers need?

C) Organization-level Integration

Organizational support systems are composed of formal and informal policies and procedures. Although organizational supports take many forms, they can, according to this model, be organized into the following eight broad and overlapping categories:

1. Recruitment and selection.
2. Orientation.
3. Training.
4. Rewards and recognition.
5. Confrontation.
6. Communication systems.
7. Symbols, myths and rituals.
8. Allocation of resources.

Key questions to ask here include:
- Who will lead changes in recruitment, selection and orientation processes? What support will be needed to bring about such changes?

- Who will lead changes in rewards and recognition (eg, awards, promotions, pay, work team bonuses)? What support will be needed to bring about such changes?

- Who will lead changes in the allocation of resources (eg, money, time, information)? What support will be needed to bring about such changes?

- Who will lead changes in myths, rituals and symbols (eg, organizational stories, celebrations, rites-of-passage)? What support will be needed to bring about such changes?

D) Leadership Development

Leaders (as explained in the previous Chapter) play important roles in consistently articulating a vision of success. Leaders are also instrumental in inspiring commitment, recognizing contributions, delegating needed resources and making sure that plans are followed through to completion.

Key questions to ask here include:

- What skills will leaders need in order to successfully model their commitment to desired change?

- What new leadership roles might be necessary to bring about desired change? How will these new leaders be trained?

- How will leaders foster a climate that supports change?

Phase IV: Ongoing evaluation, renewal and extension

The fourth phase is both an ending and a beginning. An ending because Phase I performance, programmatic and cultural measures are repeated for evaluation purposes. And an ending because successes are celebrated. Phase IV also represents a beginning in that new performance, programmatic and cultural objectives are established.

Phase IV efforts, state the designers, must provide sufficient opportunity to celebrate accomplishments. There is, they say, a tendency in many cultures to focus on what has not been achieved.

Key questions to ask here include:

- What performance, programmatic and cultural goals were achieved?

- What new goals, if any, should be set?

- How can lessons from this experience be shared with other groups, organizations or communities?

- How can lessons from this experience be applied to other cultural problems?

The Normative Systems Culture Change Process is clearly a comprehensive approach to assessing and rolling out cultural change. The key questions asked within each phase do indeed tally with the type of questions posed as critical by the advisers and practitioners interviewed for this Report. However, such an approach has to be firmly focused to meet defined, and business-enhancing, project goals.

An obvious criticism of the Normative Systems is that the word 'customer' does not appear anywhere in the list of questions, although the designers would claim that customer-facing improvements would be implicit in the project goals set at the start of the cultural change process. However, companies should beware that in the excitement of changing themselves, they do not lose sight of why they are changing.

Section C: Involving Stakeholder Groups

To understand the present culture, and of course to ensure that the culture change process is aligned with business needs, it is important to look at the needs of stakeholder groups wider than just the employee-base, for example, customers, suppliers, shareholders and even the community. However, according to the research, there is conflicting advice as to how widely stakeholder views should be sought.

Dr George Labovitz, chairman of Organizational Dynamics Inc (ODI), states that although it is important to listen to all stakeholder groups, the primary stakeholders to focus on as part of a culture change programme are employees and customers. He says:

> "As a general rule those organizations that focus primarily on the customer and each other as the major components of the change process are the ones that provide the greatest return to the shareholders."

This view is clearly shared by case study companies such as Hyundai Car (UK) Ltd (the case study to accompany Chapter 7), and KFC (the case study to Chapter 4).

Dr David Clutterbuck, chairman of the UK-based internal communication specialists The ITEM Group, says that, based on ITEM's experience of managing stakeholder relationships, the time to talk about culture to stakeholders wider than employees and customers, is when you have determined what the new values are. He says:

> "For example, if a company decides to move the culture to having a much stronger focus on environmental management then suppliers may have to change what they're doing to suit these new values."

However, Mark Krueger, managing director of the US-based Answerthink Consulting Group, believes that it is extremely important to involve all stakeholders at the start of the cultural change effort but he stresses that customers can be the biggest tool for up-ending a staid culture. He says:

> "We're finding that involving customers is an excellent way to help build winning and lasting relationships. Surveying and involving customers brings home how the culture is developing. As an example one of our clients found that they were beginning to build walls between them and their customers.

> "Suppliers and partners also provide insight, particularly from the stand-point of identifying how difficult it is to do business with the organization. This will also help show if there's a consistency of thought in strategy and

whether that is being communicated well and also if empowerment is really happening – suppliers can see that clearly."

According to Philip Sadler, chairman of the UK-based Centre for the Tomorrow's Company (which stresses the importance of taking an inclusive approach to management, ie, involving all stakeholder groups) it is also important during a change programme to keep in mind the needs of shareholders. He says:

> "Shareholders need to be told, or rather the analysts and fund managers who act on behalf of the shareholders."

Understanding the needs of the community may also be important, especially if the organization is a primary employer in the community and if the change will lead to (or if people fear it will lead to) job cuts.

Customer Surveys

It is clear from the above that involving customers early in the culture change process is important, as this will help ensure that the new cultural values and behaviours of the organizations are aligned with customer needs. Similarly, and the research supports this, customers should be surveyed both to ensure this alignment is perpetuating and to measure progress of cultural change goals.

This is the case at Ernst & Young and at Siemens KWU. At both these organizations, results from customer surveys are used to create improvement plans, progress against which is measured through the next survey.

For example, Ernst & Young has designed a client satisfaction engagement questionnaire. This comprises about 20 questions measured on a scale from 1 (extremely dissatisfied) to 5 (extremely satisfied). Questions include how satisfied are you that Ernst & Young:

- understood and helped you identify the issues key to your success

- demonstrated a good understanding of your business

- shared knowledge with you and your team

- provided fresh insights, ideas and suggestions

- demonstrated the value they added to your business.

There is also room for additional comments. Reinforcing the firm's belief in delivering exceptional customer value, Edmund White, the firm's national head of internal communications, says:

> "Client handlers know that anything below five means they have to do something about it."

And at Siemens KWU, customer opinion surveys ask questions about, for example, the customer's willingness to recommend KWU to other companies, the customer's intention to continue the business relationship with KWU and the customer's satisfaction with marketing and project management. The company also tracks customer satisfaction through a scorecard that measures performance against the key success factors of quality, reliability and delivery.

Through using a methodology designed by the German-based Institute of Infratest, KWU uses client surveys to identify high leverage customer-facing improvement opportunities. Again closing the loop is crucial here. Improvement action plans are created and the customer asked to rate the improvement through the next survey.

Importantly, therefore, as with employee surveys, our research finds that customer surveys are essentially useless unless they are used as springboards to measurable performance improvements. Indeed, if they do not lead to improvement in customers' eyes they can be extremely damaging, as all they will do is frustrate customers who will believe that their suppliers are ignoring their views.

Section D: Geographical and Subcultural Considerations

National Cultures

For a geographically dispersed organization an important consideration before rolling-out a cultural change programme is the relationship between national cultures and organizational cultures. As Alison Rankin-Frost, head of the UK-based Context Consulting, says:

> "The geographic question is interesting. In the future, cultures may merge at national levels as countries become increasingly westernized. This will be driven by global brand advertising for products such as Coca Cola, Levi jeans, etc.

> "In the meantime, however, globalized companies too often get culture change wrong with their staff. They try to impose corporate culture onto local regions that will be diametrically opposite to the values of the local culture. An example of this is that a company may launch an employee of the month award as a way to encourage and reward individuals who focus on a new cultural characteristic. This is fine in the UK and the US, but in Korea would be seen as an insult. They don't want to be singled out. They want to be seen as part of a team."

Labovitz states that change concepts such as total quality management can be rolled out globally, but *how* the programme is implemented has to be up to local management. As Ian Hampton, human resources director at Millennium Inorganic Chemicals' Bunbury, Western Australia plant (the case study to support Chapter 3), states:

> "We set out to educate our [increasingly globally based] employees to pit their considerable skills against the opposition and to work as one global team. To achieve this we had to quickly move away from our regionalized structures and thinking and put in processes to share best practices across the organization and convince people that this was the way to secure competitive advantage."

Hampton stresses that moving from a regionalized to global approach does not mean dismantling local cultures but rather gaining corporate consistency while still recognizing the importance of micro cultural characteristics, which he stresses is "a significant challenge in the change programme".

So, as the research finds, it is important to implement culture change programmes with a full understanding of, and reference to, distinct local cultural characteristics.

Subcultures

Another significant challenge in a culture change effort, and one that is wise for organizations to recognize at the start of the programme, is that posed by the fact that many subcultures may exist within one company. These may be functionally based (eg, in manufacturing, IT, etc), geographically based, professionally based (eg, in finance), or even hierarchically based (eg, operator, middle and senior management).

The Business Intelligence research survey, 'Culture and Change Management',[5] of 236 companies in Europe, USA and the Rest of the World found that on a scale of 1 to 5 (with 1 meaning the respondent 'strongly agreed' with the statement and 5 they 'strongly disagreed'), just under 50 per cent of companies gave a score of 1 or 2 to the statement, 'subcultures within our organization pose a major barrier to gaining a unified culture'. Just under 10 per cent scored a 5 and the mean score was 2.66. However, in companies who claimed to actively manage their culture this rose to 3.20, again demonstrating why the proactive management of corporate cultures should be a key organizational requirement.

Three 'super' subcultures

In his autumn 1996 article for *Sloan Management Review*,[6] leading culture change expert Edgar Schein claimed that organizational learning (a key corporate focus for the knowledge era) is being undermined within organizations because, in his view, three distinct subcultures exist who speak different languages and fail to understand each other. These, he claimed, were executives, engineers and operators. Schein states that:

> "Getting cross-functional project teams to work well together is difficult because the members bring their functional cultures into a project, so they have difficulty communicating with one another, reaching consensus, and implementing decisions effectively. Moreover, the functional groups have different meanings for the same word."

As an example, he said that the word 'marketing' will mean product development to the engineer, studying customers through market research to the product manager, merchandising to the salesperson, and constant change in design to the manufacturing manager.

He goes on to say 'occupational communities' also arise that generate cultures that cut across organizations. For example, he says, fishermen around the world develop similar world views, as do miners and members of a particular industry based on a particular technology.

Schein outlined the key differences between the three 'super' subcultures:

> "The operator culture is based on human interaction, and most line units learn that high levels of communication, trust and teamwork are essential to getting the work done efficiently."

Operators also, he goes on to say, learn that no matter how clearly the rules are specified for different operational conditions, the world is unpredictable and so they must be prepared to use their own innovative skills. Rules and hierarchy, Schein claims, often get in the way of coping with unpredicted conditions.

About an engineering culture Schein says:

> "In all organizations, one group represents the basic design elements of the technology underlying the work of the organization and has the knowledge of how the technology is to be utilized. This occupational community cuts across nations and industries and can be labelled the 'engineering culture'."

This culture, he says, is also evident among the designers and implementers of all kinds of technologies – information technology, market research, financial systems, etc. Engineers, Schein claims, are stimulated by puzzles and problems and are pragmatic perfectionists who prefer 'people free' solutions.

And finally, he says that the 'executive culture' is the set of tacit assumptions that CEOs and their immediate subordinates share worldwide:

> "This executive world view is built around the necessity to maintain an organization's financial health and is preoccupied with boards, investors and capital markets."

Schein says that as managers rise in the hierarchy, two factors cause them to become more 'impersonal':

> "First, they are no longer managing operators but other managers who think like they do. Second, as they rise, the units they manage grow larger until it becomes impossible to personally know everyone who works for them."

Therefore, he says that this 'subculture' increasingly sees people as 'human resources' to be treated as a cost rather than a capital investment.

So he claims that both the executive culture and the engineering culture see people as impersonal resources that generate problems rather than solutions.

According to Schein, organizations will not learn effectively until they recognize and confront the implications of the three occupational cultures. Essentially, executives, engineers and operators need to acknowledge that different cultures, languages and assumptions exist and they must learn to treat the other cultures as valid and normal, or otherwise organizational learning efforts will continue to fail. Schein comments:

"First, we must take the concept of culture more seriously than we have. Second, we must acknowledge that as a consequence of technological complexity and globalization, some of the old assumptions no longer work. Third, we must create communication across the cultural boundaries by learning how to conduct cross-cultural dialogues."

Why not homogenize subcultures

Recognizing how different cultures operate was also stressed by Labovitz, who makes the observation that different groups within organizations spin at different speeds, and that this must be recognized and appreciated as part of a change effort. He says:

"For example, if you ask a production guy making trousers for his idea of heaven, he'll say 'one size, one colour, one fabric'. So he wants to spin at 5 rpm. Any change causes him incredible pain, through retooling, etc. So production people crave stability.

"Then you go and talk to a sales guy. His idea of heaven is 'every size, every colour'. He wants to spin at 500 rpm, because he lives in a world of 18 year old kids who change their mind every Tuesday about what colour they want. Sales guys want change and get frustrated because change doesn't happen quicker.

"Then you go to headquarters where everything spins at 250 rpm.

"The challenge is not to homogenize and get everyone to spin at 250 but to recognize the legitimacy of the different cultures that are caused by very rational reasoning."

And he concludes:

"In my view when we talk about changing culture we're talking about a super-ordinate culture – a culture for the organization that's based on values and vision and mission. Whether I'm spinning at 5 or 500 rpm there's nevertheless a super-ordinate culture that we all belong to, that's our company's way of doing things – it's commitment to its customers, to each other, etc."

This is an important point in unifying subcultures. For according to our research, trying to create 'one culture' is certainly not about forcing every department, function, site or even country location to think in exactly the same terms. As Childress says:

"An organization needs subcultures because they reflect the different requirements, functions or geographic regions. It's a big mistake to try to homogenize everything. But you should have a universal set of core values, so wherever you are in the world you have a shared experience of working for that company and customers recognize that you work for that company."

As an example, he refers to the fast food chain McDonalds, because wherever you go in the world you will get a consistency of product, service, packaging, etc. So you will always get the 'McDonalds experience'.

And the same can be said about numerous other successful organizations. At global carrier Federal Express, for example, every employee, from the chairman down and across every function and geographic location, knows that 'absolutely reliable service' is the key to the company's success. And therefore every subculture shares that one overriding cultural value. So IT people are still IT people and marketing people are still marketing people, but they all revolve around the cultural prerequisite of 'absolutely reliable service'.

Philip Sadler, who until recently was head of Ashridge Management College, one of the UK's leading management schools, echoes this view:

> "I don't think subcultures pose a difficult problem. You only have to look at companies such as HP and Johnson & Johnson. These are companies with strong cultures. Certainly there will be differences between guys in marketing and manufacturing in, for example, Johnson & Johnson, but overall the Johnson & Johnson culture is the dominant thing."

He adds:

> "It's by focusing people's attention onto the corporate goals as a whole that helps creates the focus on the culture."

He provides this example, from his own experience, of bringing together two diverse cultural mindsets:

> "While I was at Ashridge we had the two cultures of the academic staff and the hotel and catering staff. We were the biggest hotel in the county of Hertfordshire. If you're running a 180 bedroom hotel and you're running an academic institution providing MBA degrees you've got two totally different cultures, but there's no doubt that people thought there was a very strong Ashridge culture. This reflected the fact that we deliberately set out to do that because we saw it as a competitive strength."

And he concludes:

> "Subcultures are only a problem if the perceived rewards and recognition for the different groups are inappropriate for their contribution. If, for example, you have an organization where the salespeople are rewarded disproportionately to the manufacturing people then there could be difficulties."

Section E: The Unwritten Rules of the Organization

Sadler's final statement leads to another key area to address at the start of a culture change effort, and one that can prove difficult to penetrate – the company's unwritten rules. Essentially these are the tacit and unconscious rules that really shape the culture of the organization. Companies tend, advisers comment, to have difficulty articulating what these unwritten rules are, but when somebody breaks these rules they are often ostracized or fired.

In the Business Intelligence report, *Re-engineering: The Critical Success Factors*, the author David Harvey states that unwritten rules are the product of both formal cultural aspects (such as management control methods, reward and promotional policies) and equally powerful informal signals. He writes:[7]

> "What senior managers say, evidence of behaviour which has traditionally

been rewarded or punished, and the influence exerted by movers and shakers within the organization all contribute to the formation of the unwritten rules. The effect is to confirm what behaviour is acceptable and what is strictly off-limits.

> "This includes the eradication of below-the-surface assumptions and beliefs – the rules of the game which deter people from adopting behaviour and practices which run counter to the way things have always been done in the past."

Importantly, the research shows, internalizing the unwritten rules starts immediately an employee joins the organization. Therefore, and quite naturally, these rules can quickly take hold within the conscious and unconscious mind of the new recruit. These rules may, if the employee stays with the company a long time, and indeed climb the corporate ladder, become the 'way we do things around here'. Of course, if there are lots of people indoctrinated with these rules then it is clear how difficult it can prove to unearth and change them. Childress explains:

> "The first thing you want to do is understand how to work in the company and to be accepted. So rather than read all the brochures you watch how people behave. The manager does it that way so I guess it's OK. How we treat each other and relate to other departments is watched. Manufacturing may always be blaming sales so you naturally think, if you're hired into manufacturing, that the problems lie in sales. It's the insidious way that we train people in culture. It's bound to affect them, it's a virus."

David Miller, managing director of ODR Europe, explains that the best way to make unwritten rules explicit is by getting people to identify what these rules are and then, through process change and leadership behaviour begin to systematically deal with them. As an example of how to effect this change, he says:

> "You have to look at who the heroes are around here. In some companies it may be research, sales or whatever. So you've got to take actions to reward the people who you see as driving the culture you want. As an example at IBM a new CEO said 'why am I hearing all this stuff about research, whose making the money around here, why don't I see these people?"

Mark Krueger summarizes much of the statements in this section when he says that the best way to start to understand the unwritten rules is through a two-pronged process:

1. A round table discussion, led by individuals who have been in the organization for a long time, should be used to share, and make explicit, experiences of living with unwritten corporate rules.

2. The use of a mentor programme: as new recruits are susceptible to cultural influences on joining the company, a mentor, who understands what the new culture should be, can help shape the new recruits thinking.

However, it should be stressed that the latter approach will only work if the individual sees that such things as rewards, promotion, etc, are indeed aligned to the new cultural ethos (this is dealt with in Chapter 8).

Section F: Resistance to Change

Finally on resistance we will take a general look at why people resist change. Of course a common cause for resistance is when the change effort may lead to job losses. How this is handled and communicated early in the process will play a big part in determining the level of resistance to the change effort, and this is dealt with in Chapter 8. It is also crucial in mergers and acquisitions as is explained in Chapter 9.

Resisting change is, for a lot of people, a quite natural response, as most people do not like change. Indeed culture change exemplary leaders such as Jack Welch at GE Electric (see the case report in Chapter 4) admits that resistance to change within the organization was incredible. And resistance can happen at any level of the hierarchy. Some managers, senior and middle, may resist change, especially cultural change, because they have got to their present position by being good at leveraging personal benefits from the existing way of doing things. As UK-based independent consultant Garrey Melville says:

> "Introducing a new culture allows most people to blossom, but it will clearly expose others such as bully boys, control freaks, etc. These two types will resist change. Managers who are insecure will resist change as this will show how they behave and treat people. Remember that some people get to the top through devious routes and culture change programmes will find them out."

Melville adds that some people, say those who have been doing the same job for 30 years, may resist change because they are happy with their lot, do not want to change, and do not see the value to them of learning a new way or working, or new skills sets.

Alison Rankin-Frost, head of Context Consulting, said in a article published in *Focus on Change Management* that people really come into their own when it comes to thinking up strategies to avoid changing what they do. She wrote:[8]

> "Individuals, or even teams, can conjure up tremendous resources when faced with what is perceived as a common enemy, ie, change, enforced from the outside. Preventative strategies can include objections, criticism of how the change is being managed, delaying tactics, eg, failing to meet timescales due to pressure of existing work, gossip or general undermining tactics."

Pro-change and Anti-change Forces

Rankin-Frost's colleague, Phil Hodges, outlined in another *Focus on Change Management* article differing group responses to change. He explained that there were two general groups. The first is pro-change – the force pulling the group towards a new position. The second is anti-change – the force pulling the group back towards its existing position. He warns that the relative strengths of these two forces control the final nature and success of the change.[9]

Hodges identified that within a change effort the are three key constituencies

– the promoters, the resistors and the fence-sitters. He explained that 'the promoters' are people who support a change initiative and therefore create the pro-change force:

> "A change agent should use these people to promote the change among the unit at large. To do this promoters must understand and appreciate the position of the other two groups.... The promoters play an important part in pushing change through, but if they have an aggressive relationship with the other groups they may indirectly increase the anti-change force."

The resistors, he said, are the people who are against a change initiative and create the anti-change force. He says:

> "This is an important group for a change agent, because successful change happens by harnessing the forces for keeping the status quo. By working with these people and addressing their concerns, you will not only secure the long-term survival of change, but you will also uncover issues that will shape the change initiative itself."

The fence-sitters, he writes, are indifferent about the change and so contribute to neither force. Importantly, he says that this group is, in many respects, the greatest enemy of the change agent as they do not provide support, nor do they offer constructive opposition that can be approached in the development of the initiative. He explains:

> "This places a change agent in a difficult position. He or she does not have the support of this group but has no real way of addressing their concerns. This is particularly problematic because fence-sitters will often become an anti-change force by default when a change initiative reaches its climax. By this time it's difficult for the change agent to address their concerns and build solutions into the programme."

According to Hodges, surveys and facilitated meetings should be used in change projects in order to deal with the resistors grievances, enabling possible solutions to be built into the change project, stating that process will bring to light new issues and ideas which may not have been considered in the initial change proposal. Such issues and ideas, he says, might not just help build support for a project, but might also improve the quality of the project itself.

In their book, *In Eye of the Storm: Reengineering Corporate Culture*, Senn-Delaney's chief executive John Childress and chairman Larry Senn stated that the primary reasons behind resistance to change are:[10]

- **Fear**: Change means doing things differently and results in risk and the loss of a person's comfort zone. People's imagination work overtime creating 'fear of the imagined'.

- **Scepticism:** Some change initiatives lack clear and obvious management commitment. No one wants to get geared up for a new way of working only to find out that management changed its mind or that it was just a passing fad.

- **No perceived need**: Why are we doing this? We're doing just fine. What's the need? What are the benefits?

Basically, according to the authors, the entire change management process revolves around two activities:

> "Stimulating enthusiasm and commitment, while at the same time minimizing the threat and fear involved with change."

The role of change agents, which Hodges and other advisers interviewed for this Report see as crucial to successfully managing change, is dealt with in the following Chapter. But in overcoming resistance it is important, our research finds, to identify, as early as possible, change champions at each level of the organization, promoting the benefits of the change, both to the organization and the individuals. Such people should have excellent communication and facilitation skills, should be respected by their peers and, importantly, must demonstrate the new cultural values in the way they work day-to-day. Indeed, Sue Stoneman, director of customer satisfaction at Hyundai Car (UK) Ltd, states that one of the keys to success in a culture change programme is to "put champions and advocates in place early on".

Resistance was faced by some of the case study companies (though much less than anticipated). For example, at Siemens KWU, senior manager Dr Horst Kayser said:[11]

> "There are some people who are sceptical of change, some who welcome it and a small percentage who will never change the way they work. If you can convert the first group then they become very enthusiastic advocates and influence others. The last category may include some people who are very good at what they do but do not wish to participate in management decisions. Our organization can cope with them also, providing they are adding value. But increasingly, our group-wide culture is to see employee added value as coming from positive suggestions for process improvement. Our task is to encourage this thinking and let natural selection take its course."

And his colleague, Dr Christian Forstner, director of business excellence, adds:

> "Some of our key engineers had been with us for 25–30 years. They had experienced the good old times when there was no need for change. Some of these people resisted change as they tended to think back to the glorious, and easy, days. So communication and constant reinforcement of the need for change and how they and the company would benefit, was pivotal to getting these people to buy into change."

At Superdrug, head of total quality Peter Raine says the main barriers come not from the front-line, to whom change can be obvious, nor at senior management level, who may think it is logical, but at middle management level. Raine says that people at this level must be shown the benefits of change, both to themselves and to the organization.

Therefore, the powers that can be summoned to resist change should not be under-estimated. Senior managers should, through a detailed assessment of the existing culture and creating a gap analysis against the intended culture, understand as early as possible where this resistance may come from and develop strategies to deal with this resistance. Hoping it will just 'go away' is clearly a mistaken approach.

Section G: Conclusion

It is clear from the research that gaining a thorough understanding of the current cultural situation is paramount to driving successful cultural change.

There are a number of assessment tools for conducting this analysis, of which only a sample have been analysed within this Chapter. To get a clear understanding of the culture, and therefore of the challenges ahead, the organization must dig deep to find the unwritten rules that tend to govern the way the organization really operates.

They must also understand that there are a number of subcultures working within any one organization. Rather than make these culturally exactly the same which is impossible it is better, the research shows, to recognize the differences and allow cultural diversity within one 'super-ordained' culture which is usually found in the vision, mission and, possibly most importantly, in the values of the organization.

Key Learning Points

1. An assessment of the current culture is important at the start of a culture change programme. This will provide a gap analysis between present and desired cultural states and will therefore help organizations develop a road-map for reaching their goals.

2. Exemplary organizations use assessment tools, such as employee opinion surveys, to drive performance improvement and not to just take a snapshot of the present culture.

3. According to one adviser, quantitative surveys should be supported by qualitative interviews, thus providing a richer and deeper understanding of the cultural challenges.

4. The most important stakeholder groups to involve at the start of the change process are employees and customers. However, wider stakeholder groups need to be informed of culture changes at some stage.

5. When launching a culture change programme across geographically dispersed units, companies must be sensitive to local cultural nuances.

6. The power, and concerns, of subcultures must be factored into the change effort.

---

7. Similarly, organizations must work to unearth the 'unwritten rules' that govern behaviour within the company, and work to ensure that unwritten and written rules work in congruence to inform and shape the new culture.

8. Pro- and anti-change forces will naturally emerge in any change effort. The mindsets of both forces need to be understood and addressed for a cohesive and successful change to occur.

CASE STUDY: DSM RESINS

Summary

Netherlands headquartered DSM Resins is undergoing a culture change programme called VITA. With the goal of revitalizing the organization following the early 1990s recession, four key behaviours are used to guide the initiative. Supporting VITA has been a questionnaire-based Working Climate Analysis that gauges employee perceptions of the working environment and organization performance. The results are being used as a mechanism to drive bottom-up continuous improvement.

Introduction

Headquartered in Zwolle, The Netherlands, DSM Resins is one of the world's leading producers of synthetic resins for the coating and plastics industry. With about 1850 employees and annual revenues of about NLG 1.5 billion, DSM Resins, which operates in Europe, the United States and Asia, comprises two strategic business groups, Coating Resins and Industrial Resins & Compounds, and one strategic business unit, Radcure Products.

DSM Resins is one of the largest business groups within DSM, a highly integrated international chemicals and materials group with annual sales of over NLG 14 billion and a workforce of about 22,000. The group's main products are plastics, resins, rubbers, fibre intermediates, fine chemicals, plastic consumer products and fertilisers. DSM is also involved in the exploration and extraction of oil and natural gas. In addition it recently took over the Dutch-based company Gist Brocades, whose main products are pharmaceutical intermediates, food specialities and bakery ingredients.

VITA

Culture change within DSM Resins is part of a group-wide change initiative called VITA, short for revitalization. Johan Van der Hel, human resources manager for DSM Resins' Coating Resins Business Unit, provides the background:

> "The recession of the early 1990s proved a very difficult time for DSM and the industry generally. To cut costs the group underwent considerable restructuring and downsizing and little attention was paid to developing human resource capabilities. Survival was the name of the game during that time for DSM and its competitors.

"Consequently, in 1995 we realized that to gain a competitive edge for the economic upturn we had to focus the minds of all employees on to continuous business improvement. But importantly, we did not want to just implement a top-down initiative, but rather find a mechanism for encouraging all employees to actively seek opportunities for continuous improvement, and a change in management and employee style was also needed. And the concept for doing this we called VITA."

Four Behaviours

Thinking on the VITA concept was first conducted at a corporate level in the mid 1990s. Understanding that enthusing the employee-base would necessitate a significant effort to revitalize the culture, the group decided not to spend huge amounts of time debating the meaning of culture, but rather create a guiding set of behaviours that would define what the group had to focus on to gain a competitive edge. Van der Hel explains:

"In an internationally diverse company such as DSM there are as many cultures as there are departments, companies and countries. Often a problem in a culture change process is to first understand what the culture is and therefore what you want to change. This can prove a fruitless process. Therefore, we devised VITA as an umbrella which said to all business units that if we want to succeed as an organization, meet customer demands and be the best-in-class we have to comply to four behaviours."

These behaviours are:

- capable

- reliable

- empowered

- responsive.

Importantly, to instil these into the employee-base, the group recognized that this would require the instigation of a more coaching style of management throughout the organization. Therefore, DSM has articulated a set of required managerial responses to the employee behaviours. These are:

- For a *responsive* employee a manager has to be *accessible.*

- For a *reliable* employee a manager has to give *confidence.*

- For a *capable* employee a manager has to *coach.*

- For an *empowered* employee a manager has to *delegate.*

Says Van der Hel:

"VITA has to be a partnership between management and the employee-base. And for VITA to succeed, management has to provide every employee with a more challenging and satisfying working environment. Through this business success will follow."

Guiding Principles

A fundamental tenet of the VITA approach is that, with the four behaviours as a guide, implementation is the responsibility of each of DSM's business groups. Within DSM Resins a key implementation tool is the so-called Working Climate Analysis. However, it is important to first note that there are powerful connectors from the VITA concept and the Working Climate Analysis which are the guiding principles of DSM Resins, headed by its vision and value statements on human resource management.

Vision:

"Our *team-members* will be highly energetic, entrepreneurial and internationally oriented and will work as a *team* to achieve joint goals."

Values:

"Our *people* are our most valuable asset"

These are supported by the following statements:

- Create a *working environment* that motivates and inspires our employees.

- *Develop* and *train* our team-members.

- Establish a *transparent organization* with clearly defined tasks, powers and responsibilities.

- Adopt a *coaching* management style.

Working Climate Analysis

The Working Climate Analysis is developed by the change management consultancy, Organizational Dynamics Inc (ODI). It is an employee questionnaire that aims to discover their perceptions of six areas that directly influence the environment in which they work – departments, strategic business units (SBUs) and the corporation – and therefore the performance of the employee-base. These six areas are:

1. Goals and Follow-up on Results.
2. Change.
3. Organization/Flexibility.
4. Motivation/Energy.
5. Management.
6. Specific Local Focus Area Concerns.

Tailored to DSM Resins own requirements (which defines 'working climate' as the employees' subjective and qualitative perception of the performance conditions within the organization) these are further divided into the following sub-headings:

1. Goals and follow-up on results:
   - DSM Resins Ambitions.
   - Attention to Goals.
   - Demand for Performance.
   - Result-orientation.
   - Consequence.
   - Mutual Self-confidence.
   - Management Encouragement.

2. Change:
   - Innovation.
   - Support for Ideas.
   - Attitudes.
   - Encouragement.

3. Organization/Flexibility:
   - Freedom of Action.
   - Co-operation within our Department.
   - Co-operation between our Departments.
   - Decentralization.
   - Encouragement.

4. Motivation/Energy:
   - Possibilities for Development.
   - Freedom on Job-situation.
   - Trust.
   - Liveliness.
   - Working Relations.
   - Encouragement.

5. Management:
   - The Influence of our Management.
   - Management as Model.

6. DSM Resins Local Attention Areas:
   - Customer Satisfaction.
   - Specific Local Issues.

Employees rate each of the 80 statements that make up these six categories from 1 (disagree entirely) to 7 (agree entirely). Statements include:

- 'in our department most people have a good knowledge of the goals of the organization'
- 'we have a systematic follow-up to all our goals'

- 'we have the freedom to organize our own work'
- 'you get support and encouragement when you contribute new ideas'
- 'our unit is customer-oriented'
- 'we are encouraged to develop our own potential'
- 'people feel the management inspires'.

Van der Hel explains why DSM Resins embraced the Working Climate Analysis approach:

"VITA as a concept only sets down a framework for managers and employees to develop themselves and the business. To really make it work we chose the Working Climate Analysis as the implementation tool. It is primarily a bottom-up process where improvement takes place within their own work area. Therefore, the Working Climate Analysis enables us to quantify where we are today in relation to the VITA objectives, but also lends itself to the identification of future improvement opportunities."

According to Van der Hel, the Working Climate Analysis also dovetailed perfectly with VITA initiatives already under way within DSM Resins. He says:

"We had already been working hard on a range of VITA projects to do with, as examples, management style, coaching, customer excellence, continuous improvement teams and delegating responsibilities further down the line."

Van der Hel was also impressed by the ODI attitude that, although the consultancy would train the facilitators and process the questionnaire data, the more responsibility DSM Resins itself took for the process the more likely lasting success would be. He says:

"This fits perfectly with our culture of self-responsibility and ownership for the process and results."

Essentially, the Working Climate Analysis process entails sending the questionnaire to all employees in each strategic business unit work area. Once the data is processed, trained facilitators present the survey findings to local management and feedback work groups. The purpose of these feedback sessions is to understand the results, study trends and highlight improvement opportunities on the basis of a fundamental group discussion.

Following this, a list of possible action plans is generated by the employees, who then develop their own implementation plans, comprising ideas for their own department, for interaction between departments and suggestions for top management.

All actionable ideas are, if necessary, reviewed by managers who, if the idea is worth implementing, have to provide the budget for the project and any resources required. They also have to clearly explain their reasons for turning down any submitted suggestions.

Internal measurements ensure that local management is indeed playing a proactive role in ensuing that the Working Climate Analysis process is used to drive continuous improvement within the work areas. Says Van der Hel:

> "It is straightforward to track local management commitment. We can look at the questionnaire and feedback process and see how many identified actions have led to continuous improvement projects, how much budget and resources has been allocated to these projects and the percentage of operational employees working in continuous improvement teams.

> "And it's made crystal clear to local management that the senior management team within DSM Resins is absolutely committed to the Working Climate Analysis process. And local management will be provided with support from the top through the allocation of additional resources if required."

Measuring Success

The senior management team states that the success of the Working Climate Analysis process is *not* measured by the absolute score of the questionnaire (which is seen as an indication for site management of cultural challenges and improvement opportunities), but rather that success *is* measured by the commitment of local management to enhance the working climate. This is based on an input measure of the quality of the action plans, process measures of the management of the implementation process and the communication of improvements, and the output measure of actual performance improvement. Says Van der Hel:

> "This ensures that the Working Climate Analysis fulfils a key organizational tenet that the VITA process has to be a two-way dialogue between management and employees, with both actively involved in the constant pursuit of continuous improvement."

Pilots

Before rolling-out the Working Climate Analysis to all DSM Resins business units and sites, pilot projects were launched at the end of 1997 within three sites at Landskrona in Sweden, Meppen in Germany, and Augusta in the US.

From sending out the questionnaires, analysing data, holding feedback sessions and generating action plans to launching actual continuous improvement projects took a total of just three months. Says Van der Hel:

> "This was a very intense period and a key learning for the company was that for the second wave of roll-out we would take longer over the process, say between five to six months."

Despite the intensity, Van der Hel firmly believes that the pilot sites did demonstrate that the Working Climate Analysis does indeed inspire employees to focus on concrete improvement programmes, and that it has led to a more open culture in which managers are coaches and employees take responsibility for their own actions, as these statements from managers and staff from the Landskrona site in Sweden testify. Personnel officer Inger Wittfjord says:

"I'm enthusiastic about the method. It gives people the chance to come up with improvements. It is important that these ideas be followed up well, though. We, the management, should, for example, improve our internal communication by publishing results in a way that everybody understands and we intend to publish the minutes of our meetings. We plan to hold appraisals more often and not keep on postponing them."

Shift leader, Rolf Stomblad says:

"I want to be proud of DSM Resins. I have to confess that we didn't think much of [the Working Climate Analysis] at the start. We had to meet with the shift one free evening We sat slouched in our chairs; I felt almost guilty towards our facilitator. Our attitude was, 'let's see what the man has got to say'. But bit by bit our enthusiasm picked up.... Instead of having only a few minutes to talk about something with each other, we now had a few hours. And that threw up a lot of surprises."

And accountant Par Johnsson adds:

"Before that analysis we already had open communication, but this process can encourage even more. I'd like to say to my colleagues, 'be motivated and don't let critical questions about the management spoil the discussion'. After all... I'd rather take a look at myself and ask, 'what can I, with my colleagues, improve?'."

Other Landskrona improvement suggestions included:
- Better description of roles and responsibilities throughout the organization.
- Improving the effectiveness of meetings throughout the site.
- Improving the external communication process (despite being one of the largest local employees, the plant was not very well known in the town).

As examples of improvement ideas that came out of other pilot sites, in Augusta, initiatives focused on better management guidance/leadership and better team-building. And in Meppen, initiatives focused on, as examples, setting up an improvement-idea generation system and developing a more coaching style of management.

According to Van der Hel, a positive finding from the pilots was that about 80 per cent of actionable ideas were improvements that employees could implement themselves without needing to refer up to site management level:

"These are practical down to earth improvements. For example, a team cleaning up at the end of a shift. This may be a minor improvement but it may have been going on unchecked for 15 years, during which time a lot of frustration and bad feeling would have been created. Just rectifying this problem plays a part in instilling a teamworking culture within the organization."

Another benefit from the first phase of the Working Climate Analysis roll-out was that it generated internal benchmarks and examples of results that were valuable during the second roll-out phase to sites in Holland, Spain and the UK. Says Van der Hel, "this was extremely useful for quickly securing buy-in within those plants".

Management Commitment

According to Van der Hel, possibly the greatest learning was that the vast majority of employees really do want to be empowered to take responsibility to implement continuous improvement ideas. He says:

> "This means that management must show wholehearted commitment to the process, because once employee energy is unleashed it would prove terribly demotivating if this was held back again."

And Van der Hel warns that if management is serious about unleashing this energy, it has to recognize that fully involved staff will be more critical of both the change programme and management. He says:

> "When people feel empowered they want to see things happen and make things happen. Any slowness to respond by managers can be frustrating."

A particular danger, according to Van der Hel, is cynicism setting in once the process slows down after the initial, and intense, roll-out period. He says:

> "This is where you may face resistance. As the first wave of enthusiasm wanes, employees may start to think that the programme was no more than management espousing the latest hot topic which they really had no intention of implementing. And if organizations don't deal with this, they will soon find themselves in a valley of despair, which will be very hard to climb out from."

Displaying the Behaviours

To counter this the company has spent a considerable amount of time communicating to managers the critical importance of displaying the VITA behaviours at all times and being seen to 'walk the talk', constantly interacting with employees and jointly working on improvements every day. Van der Hel says:

> "No matter how much internal communication you do via newsletters, etc, and we have invested significantly here, all that expense will be wasted if management does not display the VITA behaviours."

A key mechanism for ensuring that managers do indeed display these behaviours is that the appraisal system, which is the basis for remuneration, includes assessments against both professional and behavioural competencies.

Also, the company's management development systems has skills such as coaching and mentoring as compulsory elements. Proving yourself a competent coach is a prerequisite for advancement through the DSM Resins' ranks.

In relation to the Working Climate Analysis, Van der Hel believes that, given that there may be a time-lapse of several months between collecting employee data and the employee feedback sessions, it is important for management to keep informing employees of the progress of the analysis in order to create a positive anticipation about the feedback sessions.

Internal Facilitators

Van der Hel also stresses the critical role of the internal facilitators during the feedback stage. For the first phase these were either ODI consultants or trained staff from DSM Resins. For the second roll-out phase they were all DSM Resins people. He says:

> "We have learnt that facilitators can make or break this process. They have to be committed and enthusiastic as it is they who, during the feedback session, have to enthuse the employees. And we also benefited from an unintended, but welcome, effect. Facilitators are often asked afterwards to facilitate the follow-up process."

Conclusion

DSM is due to complete the first round of plant analyses by the end of 1999, and it will recommence the process during 2000, at the start of which the company will, says Van der Hel, be able to learn from the lessons learned during the first roll-out.

However, Van der Hel says there have been four key lessons so far:

- **Senior management commitment**: "This is a prerequisite, you need constant commitment from top managers and if that's not there, then you may as well forget it".

- **Choose projects/processes that can really enhance the culture you want to achieve**: "It s extremely important that you first choose projects/processes that convince people change can be initiated and carried out by themselves".

- **It is crucial to follow-up, focus and prioritize**: "Make one thing happen rather than promise ten and deliver nothing. This is important otherwise employees become sceptical".

- **Ensure honesty**: "Management and employees have to do what they say they will, when they say they will. This will generate mutual trust".

Finally Van der Hel says:

> "The real test of the company's commitment to the Working Climate Analysis, and indeed the overarching VITA project, will come when there's another economic dip.

> "We will see whether employee empowerment and development remains a management priority. But I am sure it will because, these days, those companies that manage to get all their employees focused on improving customer-facing performance will gain and maintain a competitive edge. And it is to that end that we initiated both VITA and the Working Climate Analysis."

Key Learning Points

1. The VITA project was launched to meet specific corporate objectives – revitalize the employee-base following a deep and painful recession, and gain a competitive edge by focusing the minds of all employees on to continuous business improvement.

2. Creating a partnership between managers and employees was also a key goal of VITA.

3. Realizing that DSM had an internationally diverse culture, the group chose four key behaviours that would guide the change programme.

4. DSM Resins implemented the Working Climate Analysis as way to further implement the VITA objectives.

5. Senior management was totally committed to the Working Climate Analysis and local management were equally committed to the process. A measurement system tracks how many ideas are implemented within the manager's sphere of responsibility.

6. Appraisal and management development systems ensure that coaching competencies develop within DSM managers.

7. DSM Resins piloted the Working Climate Analysis in three sites prior to full company roll-out. This provided powerful learning points, not least that such an approach does indeed inspire employees to continuously improve.

8. The company recognized the key role of facilitators in enthusing the employee-base.

CASE STUDY: SUPERDRUG

Summary

Health and beauty retailer Superdrug is transforming its culture through a business transformation programme called Living the Mission. Key to this has been the education and training of all employees in total quality management (TQM) tools and techniques and using a cultural survey to track progress against cultural objectives.

Introduction

Headquartered in London, United Kingdom, Superdrug Stores, is a retailer of a wide variety of health and beauty products. It employs 12,000 people and has more than 700 stores throughout the UK.

The company is owned by Kingfisher plc, one of Europe's premier non-food retailers. Other Kingfisher-owned businesses include leading high street and out-of-town store brand names such as Woolworth's, B&Q and Comet.

The Case for Change

Superdrug's culture change programme can be traced back to late 1995, when the then managing director decided to instigate a business transformation programme based on the principles of total quality management (TQM). Peter Raine, Superdrug's head of total quality, recalls:

> "Within a previous company our managing director had experienced the positive effects of a successful customer-driven total quality management programme. Such an approach was totally congruous with how Superdrug wanted to progress with established initiatives."

For example, Superdrug had already started the process of creating a customer-focused culture by deciding how it wanted to be perceived by its customers. The innovative way the company created a mission statement to capture this perception showed that the concept of total employee involvement, an essential ingredient of a successful total quality programme, was not completely unknown in the business. Explains Raine:

> "Prior to 1995, our executive team had identified the seven core characteristics that would summarize the type of retailer Superdrug wanted to be."

Those seven core characteristics are:

1. Superdrug's primary market focus will be on health and beauty.
2. Superdrug goes the last mile for its customers.

3. Superdrug has its finger on the pulse.

4. Superdrug offers superior value.

5. Superdrug offers superior choice.

6. Superdrug is friendly and fun.

7. Superdrug creates winning teams.

Raine continues:

> "Based on these characteristics, which we called 'stands', we launched a company-wide competition to distil them into a single mission statement. From the 1300 entries received came three submissions which, when fused together, created the statement, 'to be the customer's favourite, up-to-the-minute health and beauty shop, 'loved' for its value, choice, friendliness and fun'."

Living the Mission

By 1995 the company had recognized that, although a powerful statement of strategic intent, the mission was essentially aspirational, and that as an intrinsic element of creating a customer-focused culture the organization had to devise a road map for making the mission come alive in the company.

Consequently, in 1996 the company launched a business transformation programme branded Living the Mission. It also created a diagrammatic road map, containing 14 interrelated elements, explaining what the programme was all about and how every employee could contribute to delivering the mission. The 14 elements are:

1. What's it all about?

2. Aim of the Living the Mission programme.

3. The Stands – a reminder.

4. The Superdrug triangle.

5. Achieving the mission through TQM.

6. How can we 'Live the Mission'?

7. How people will be involved.

8. Store Living the Mission Contracts.

9. Customer service standards.

10. Head office and distribution service improvements.

11. Improvement through IOPE ('through Involvement comes Ownership, giving Pride, leading to Excellence of Execution').

12. Continuous improvement action plans.

13. Improvement groups.

14. Individual action plans.

Before analysing some of these 14 elements in detail, and indeed how the organization trained and empowered the employee-base to deliver according to this programme, it should be pointed out that the mission serves as one of three elements of the Superdrug vision. The second element is Brand Benefits, which are:

1. Great value.

2. New ideas.

3. Easy shopping.

4. Fun and friendly.

The third element is the company values, which are:

- Delighting the customer.

- Winning.

- Generosity of spirit.

- Constructive rigour.

- Being straightforward.

- Diversity.

- Involvement, Ownership, Pride, Excellence of Execution (IOPE).

Says Raine:

> "We believe that our vision is a combination of our mission, brand and values. Therefore we decided not to create a separate vision statement."

Cultural Vision

Raine explains how Superdrug focused on the roll-out of the Living the Mission programme:

> "On launching the programme in February 1996 we created a three year vision of what a customer-focused, total quality management culture would look like. Essentially, this was about getting to a point where employees were actively involved in the business, making decisions closer to the customer based on a clear understanding of what the customer wanted. To do this employees had to understand and continuously improve the processes by which they would deliver ever increasing value to the customer."

To achieve that vision, the company drew up a three-year transformation plan:

- Year 1: planning.

- Year 2: education and awareness.

- Year 3: transformation through understanding.

From the outset the company knew that it wanted to use TQM principles as the overriding framework and management by project as the rigorous approach to programme implementation.

Wisely, Superdrug also recognized that before rolling the programme out company-wide, it first had to gain a clearer understanding of its present culture. This, according to Raine, was critical to gaining a detailed overview of the cultural challenges ahead and for identifying parts of the business more amenable to early roll-out.

Cultural Survey

To assist in this cultural audit, Superdrug appointed a consultancy team from The Centre for Business Transformation, Anglia Polytechnic University in the UK. One of the reasons why they were chosen, explains Raine, was that they were willing to fund their initial fees from cost savings accrued during Year 1 of the programme (in fact, thanks to early company-wide projects, Superdrug realized a three-fold return on investment during the planning year).

The primary mechanism used to ascertain Superdrug's cultural characteristics was, and still is, an organization culture survey carried out by Anglia Polytechnic University. The first survey was undertaken in 1996, and then yearly in 1997 and, with some amendments, 1998. Such is Superdrug's belief in the value of the survey data that the intention is to survey employees twice during 1999.

In 1997 the survey was organized into two sections. The first section was to be completed by all employees, and the second just by those who had been with the company for more that 12 months. The latter section is an additional mechanism to track progress towards the customer-focused total quality culture envisioned by Superdrug.

An important feature of the survey is that its 'clients' are line managers, not senior managers and directors. Results are used by line managers to improve, not by senior managers to punish.

The first survey section comprises of 31 questions under the heading, 'if you were a *fly on the wall*, what would be typical about the way we do things at Superdrug?'. All questions are scored from 0 (lowest) to 8 (highest). To help guide staff, definitions are provided for scores from 0–3 and 5–8. Therefore, 4 represents an average score.

The employees are asked how Superdrug does things in relation to, as examples, its 'paying' customers and suppliers, its attitude to quality and internal communication, the behaviour of leaders, employee attitudes, career development and standards of internal service. Table 5.1 provides examples of the actual questions.

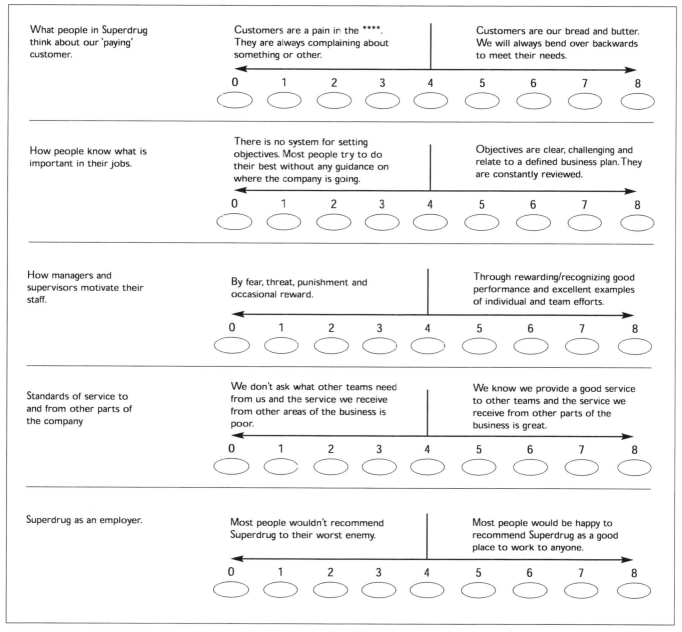

Table 5.1: Example of the First Section of Superdrug Survey (reproduced with kind permission of Barnes Associates/UCT, ©1999)

So how has Superdrug's performance fared against these 31 questions from the survey's launch in 1996 through to 1998? Impressively, all scores show an upward trend from 1996 except 'what people in Superdrug think about suppliers of our products and services', which remained stationary. However, this is still the second highest behind 'what people in Superdrug think about 'paying' customers'. And two further questions, 'attitude towards quality' and 'physical working conditions', were, as of 1998, in the 'very good' results category. Only one, 'use of recognition' scored less than 4, and this just marginally so. However, even this shows an improvement of about 0.5 from the 1996 base figure.

The second section of the survey comprises a further 22 questions, testing whether there has been an overall improvement in culture in the last 12 months, therefore tracking the impact of the Living the Mission programme on the Superdrug culture.

Each question is scored for 1 (much worse) to 5 (much better). A score of 3 equals no change. Questions include:

- The way we deal with customers has got...
- The attitude in Superdrug towards quality has got...
- Teamwork within my store/department has got...
- Involvement of employees in decision-making has got...
- The way managers try to motivate people has got...
- The number of new or different ideas being tried out by people in Superdrug has got...

The 1998 results showed that only one question has a score less than 4, this being 'use of recognition'. The highest scores, on an ascending scale, were 'physical working conditions', 'attitude towards quality', 'attitude towards suppliers' and 'orientation towards customer'.

Overall, performance shows an upward trend against the 1996 base figure and further shows that employees perceive key areas such as customer orientation and attitude towards quality as moving towards a state of excellence.

A further value of the second section of the survey, according to Raine, is that it helps overcome a problem with statistical evaluation and comparison. He provides this example:

> "A new recruit will have little knowledge of what constitutes excellent customer service and may score us very highly. If, in the following year, we make major changes to benefit customers and things get better, how does he or she raise the score? Therefore these additional questions measure perceived *change*."

Stores Roll-out

Returning to one of the original aims of the first cultural survey, to identify parts of the business more amenable to early roll-out, the survey results showed that there were at least three discrete cultures in the business – one each in stores, distribution and head office. Indeed, according to Raine, there were probably seven subcultures within head office alone. However, the survey results showed the company that it could launch a Living the Mission roll-out in stores. Says Raine:

> "A culture of employee involvement was already evident in the stores, and so would, we believed, prove less problematic in shifting to a culture of total quality. Our distribution arm was some way away from an 'involving' culture whereas head office was placed somewhere between the two."

So following on from the first survey, and for the rest of the 1996 planning year, the big issue for Raine and his team was how to roll this programme out to 12,000 people in 700 locations. Roll-out, the education and awareness year of the Living the Mission implementation plan, commenced in February 1997.

To assist in the preparation, a project management team was set up to focus on the culture change element of the overall Living the Mission programme. The teams included senior managers that fed information to the executive team. However, the challenges of roll-out to so many places was nowhere near as daunting as Raine first thought. He says:

> "Actually, it was relatively straightforward. We found that a store is a store is a store. They've all got similar objectives such as sales, cost of sales, etc, staff are all used to working together and in each store staff are close to the customer."

Living the Mission roll-out was a top-down initiative. First, as a workshop to regional managers and their area managers, and second, for area managers with their store managers. Finally, facilitators trained in presentation skills delivered a workshop to all staff in geographical areas. Says Raine:

> "Through a two-day course we trained 120 presenters. These were all volunteers and were drawn from store management teams. Crucially each had expressed a desire to develop presentation skills. Additionally, each area appointed a Living the Mission co-ordinator to schedule the workshops on an ongoing basis.

Each store workshop lasted for four hours and outlined the Living the Mission programme.

Living the Mission Definitions

Each of the 14 elements of the Living the Mission programme included a clear definition of meaning. For example, element 6, 'how we can Live the Mission', is explained under the headings 'by', and 'this means':

> '[by] harnessing everyone's commitment and potential through Involvement, Ownership, Pride and Excellence of Execution (IOPE)' and '[this means] using IOPE... training everyone in TQM values and TQM principles/ improvement tools and techniques.'

About the latter point Raine stresses:

> "We'd been down the empowerment track before. At that time we said go away and do it but we hadn't trained anybody, so Living the Mission had to be underpinned by training." ·

An interesting aspect of Living the Mission is element 8, 'store Living the Mission contract'. Essentially this is a simplified balanced scorecard,[12] and Superdrug has indeed used the balanced scorecard approach for three years and has developed scorecards for each business function.

Superdrug's Living the Mission Contract consists of three performance perspectives – Service, People, Productivity. These directly support the company's mission statement. The reason for each perspective is clearly explained and stores have to set annual performance targets for each perspective (hence the 'contract').

These contracts are delivered through continuous improvement action plans, made up of the five performance improvement steps – plan, do, measure, improve and share. Says Raine:

> "This process is a way of encouraging teams to use total quality tools and display our values in their everyday work. The five step process includes questions such as 'are you involving the right people', 'do you understand the customers' requirements', 'who are you doing this for', 'how will you share your learning' and 'have you agreed what performance measures to use'."

Starfish.net

What is new to Superdrug is the focus on sharing information and knowledge. And as part of its focus on continuous improvement, the company has put a process in place to capture and share ideas that are within the business – Starfish.net, which is basically an 'Ideas Management System'. Teams forward improvement ideas to a central co-ordinating office. The ideas are generated during the company's 'team time'. Raine explains:

> "All teams hold a 'team time' ten times per year. This is a one and a half hour session broken down into three sections. The first part is about improving business awareness, the second is about Living the Mission – basically what did we say we'd do at the last team time and how are we progressing against those objectives. The final section is called Talkback, which focuses on what ideas do we have for improving things for our customers and this is where Starfish.net comes in."

During Talkback the team considers all improvement ideas that had been previously listed on a 'bright ideas' internal bulletin board and provide a yes/no decision on the validity of each suggestion.

If the decision is 'yes, we want to proceed with this suggestion', then the team decides whether to categorize it as a 'quick win' or a 'big idea'. A quick win is a good idea that the team can Plan, Do, Measure, Improve, and, if it works, Share with the rest of the organization via Starfish.net.

A 'big idea' is a suggestion that the team needs further help in developing and implementing. The idea is captured and sent in to Starfish.net for further investigation. Importantly, the team has to consider key questions prior to forwarding the idea, such as who does the idea benefit, what are the benefits to the customer and what would it cost to do? On receiving the 'big idea', a central team acknowledges idea receipt, researches its viability and communicates to the team whether the idea will be progressed.

Raine provides a interesting learning point for companies considering such an approach. He says:

"We tried something similar a number of years ago, but it quickly failed. The reason being that employees generated a lot of excellent ideas but there was no infrastructure to deal with the suggestions."

To help overcome this, Superdrug has appointed a number of 'champions' from each area of the business, such as buying, marketing, pharmacy, etc. Their role is to act as a bridge between the Starfish.net team and people within Superdrug with the skills to properly evaluate and progress ideas.

Thus far, Starfish.net suggestions have led to improvement groups being set up for areas such as product knowledge training, improving communication to and from head office, and promotions implementation.

Customer Service Standards

With improving customer service and satisfaction being the number one strategic and tactical focus within Superdrug, it is not surprising to find that the company has invested a considerable amount of time and effort into articulating clear customer service standards.

These best practice standards are visualized as a starfish (the Superdrug logo, see Figure 5.3) and each is articulated from a customer's viewpoint against five general observations.

WHEN I LOOK AROUND THE SHOP
- I don't see any litter on the floor.
- There is no dust or dirt on the shelves.
- I don't find leaking, dusty, out-of-date or damaged products.
- I can find the things I want to buy within 2 minutes.
- I can get my double buggy around.
- I can get what I want without moving anything.

WHEN I'M DECIDING WHAT I WANT
- You can tell me about the products and help me to make the right choice.
- You take me to a product if I can't find it.
- You check in the Warehouse if the product is not on the shelf.
- If you haven't got what I want and you can't get it quickly enough, you tell me where I can get it.

WHEN I SEE YOU
- I can tell that you work here and what your name is.
- You are clean, smart and look the part.
- You look me in the eye and smile.

WHEN I PAY
- I'm given a receipt and the right change.
- My bags are packed with care and easy to carry.
- You offer to gift wrap my perfume.
- Tills are never dirty or cluttered.

WHEN I NEED EXTRA HELP
- I'm never embarrassed if I have to ask something personal.
- When I need more help than most you give it to me.
- When I have an accident in your shop, it's never a problem.
- When I bring things back I'm treated the same way as when I bought them.
- You answer the phone with hello, the shop name and your name.
- If you promise to call me back you always do.

© Superdrug Stores plc

Figure 5.3: Superdrug Customer Service Standards

As examples, under the observation 'when I look around the shop', are best practice standards which include:

- I don't see any litter on the floor.

- I can get my double buggy around.

- I can find the things I want to buy within two minutes.

The observation 'when I'm deciding what I want' includes the best practice standards:

- You can tell me about the products and help me to make the right choice.

- If you haven't got what I want and you can't get it quickly enough, you tell me where I can get it.

The other observations are 'when I see you', 'when I pay' and 'when I need extra help'. Thus, the total customer experience is contained in this starfish of standards.

Importantly, and in keeping with the company's commitment to total quality, these standards are not just measurable but form the basis for continuous improvement. Raine explains:

> "Take as an easy example the customer service standard 'I don't see litter on the floor'. If an employee sees litter on the floor they may pick it up. So an easy measure is 'how many times do I pick up litter in, say, a day'. However, the next stage is 'improving on the measure' which is about the employee thinking through ways to prevent littering in the first place."

Within Superdrug, customer perceptions are further measured through a Mystery Shopping Programme, through which representatives from a specialist company visit a store and, posing as different customer types, test the customer service experienced.

Importantly, the clients for the results from these mystery shopping exercises are the Store Teams themselves. Explains Raine:

> "These results are used by store teams for continuous improvement purposes and are not seen as a big stick to be used against them."

Service Level Agreements (SLAs)

Superdrug is also continuously improving performance in the eyes of internal customers (primarily other teams), through the use of Service Level Agreements (SLAs).

An initiative launched to progress SLAs is called 'Keep Improving Customer Service' (KICS). The purpose being to help teams identify the services and products it provides to other teams and so add value to the business.

The KICS process includes a session through which the team identifies its customers, followed by time spent talking to its customers about the service delivered and key service elements or information requirements. Once the SLA is agreed between the team and its customers, it is incorporated into the service element of team's Living the Mission Contract. The SLA is delivered through the company's continuous improvement action plans.

The company is setting up service level agreements within head office and the education and awareness stage of the Living the Mission programme has now generally been rolled-out to head office. So far the programme has not been rolled out to distribution, although team time has recently, and successfully, been introduced and projects set up which include devising and agreeing SLAs between distribution and stores.

Cultural Barriers

Despite Superdrug's undoubted success with its Living the Mission programme, it has not been without obstacles. Not least sustaining the programme through a changing population of senior managers. Says Raine:

> "A high percentage of senior managers who were here at the start of the programme have since moved on, primarily to other positions within the Kingfisher Group. Fortunately, new senior managers coming on board quickly become enthusiastic."

One way new directors are won over is by their role as judges in the company's annual 'Premier Crew' store competition. This is about getting the stores ready for Christmas and is also one way the company demonstrates its somewhat intangible 'fun' value. Says Raine:

> "This programme energizes new directors and senior managers as they go out to stores and see how employees are living the mission."

Another barrier is that traditionally, and common for this type of business, there has been competition between stores and between regions. According to Raine, the challenge here has been getting people to focus on beating the competition rather than beating each other. To address this Superdrug has launched a number of cross-functional, cross-regional improvement groups.

Similarly, the company is much more organized around processes than previously, and has taken the somewhat unusual step of integrating the HR and IT functions led by an organizational capability director. Raine explains why:

> "Historically we'd been recruiting premier quality people and given them third division systems and processes. This clearly wasn't acceptable so we gave one person responsibility for ensuring that the system capabilities were aligned with the people capabilities."

Another barrier, according to Raine was at middle management level. He says:

> "The people at the front-line think living the mission is obvious. The people at the top think it's logical. However, those in the middle have to be shown the benefits."

Internal Communication

Showing the benefits to middle management, and indeed reinforcing the benefits to the other levels, has required a significant investment in internal communications.

For instance, the company has found videos ideal for delivering consistent messages to 700 discrete stores, while the team talk sessions have proved invaluable communication mechanisms.

Additionally, Superdrug has recently established an employee representative body, called Xchange. Raine cites the following as an example of reasons people have given for wanting to be elected:

> 'I believe in the company vision, I'm involved in the company roll-out and want to take part in its continued success'.

Raine says:

> "If we'd asked for nominations three years ago we wouldn't have got replies like this. People now clearly understand the mission and want to be involved in the business."

Recruitment and Performance Management

Changes in the recruitment process have also helped to induce into people the Living the Mission concept prior to their joining the company. As part of the interview process, applicants have to go into the stores and find out about the mission, brands and products Superdrug sells. Adds Raine:

> "As a key staff competency is about approaching customers and being friendly as they do this, then it is sensible to include that in the recruitment programme. And it also means that the store team, who interviewees approach with questions, get involved in the selection of future colleagues."

Raine also hopes this will help reduce attrition levels, as the company may be able to better pinpoint appropriate candidates.

Within the company, managers are now measured through 360 degree feedback (which includes the views of direct reports as well as line managers). And here Raine stresses an important Superdrug tenet:

> "This feedback takes great account of how the manager's behaviour aligns with the Superdrug values. If people are achieving good financial results but not living the values then it's not good enough. The values impact the brand benefits which in turn impacts the customer and our mission. If a manager's behaviour is not aligned with the values then it is our belief that even if they are producing good results, the damage will be such that this can't be sustained over the long-term and indeed will damage the reputation of Superdrug."

Future Improvements

Raine admits, as the culture survey testifies, that the company has not shifted reward and recognition to support the new culture quickly enough.

However, a group has been set up to drive up this aspect of company performance and a new recognition scheme called GEM (Going the Extra Mile) has just been launched. This will recognize employees who demonstrate the company's values through a range of rewards.

Continuous improvement will also continue in other performance spheres, with the company targeting 2000 measurable improvements for customers during 1999 alone.

Another Superdrug challenge is that it recognizes that it has stores that deliver primarily to one of its three customer groups. So a key challenge here is to identify what this means for the type of staff and management recruited and for customer-facing and internal performance measures.

As for measuring the success of the Living the Mission programme, and progress towards its vision of a customer-obsessed total quality culture, Raine says:

> "Where we wanted to get to was the achievement of excellent results against the culture survey. Quite simply, total the scores up and what does the data tell us about performance. The results tell us that we are well on the way to reaching our cultural objectives."

Conclusion

At the time of writing, Superdrug had, in stores at least, entered the 'understanding and transformation' year of its three-year Living the Mission implementation plan. This is the year when the programme should start to become 'the way we do things around here'.

According to Raine, thus far there are four key lessons from the Superdrug success story:

- **Communication**: "This is around understanding that you have to deliver messages via a range of communication mechanisms again and again and again. Not everybody receives information in the same way or at the same time".

- **Integration of the change programme within the fabric of the business**: "It has to support the strategic goals of the business and link with for example the training and development agenda and performance management processes".

- **Sustaining the momentum**: "We previously tended to move from initiative to initiative which soon dropped off the agenda. However, when people say to me, what are you doing next year, I'll say the same as last year, but better – and we have allocated resources to make sure it 'sticks'".

- **Support (ie deciding when to take the support structure away)**: "For example we are now considering removing definitions of total quality management from our internal literature as people now understand, and indeed, live this. However, we have taken some other support away too early and have learned from this".

Key Learning Points

1. The business transformation programme was launched by the then CEO and senior management support has been evident throughout the programme roll-out.

2. Before launching the business transformation Living the Mission programme, the company already knew what type of retailer it wanted to be, articulating this through seven core characteristics and a mission statement.

3. The Living the Mission programme is clearly outlined as 14 interrelated elements. This explains what the programme is about and how employees can contribute to its success.

4. As part of the programmes planning year, the first year of the three-year implementation plan, a cultural survey was undertaken to assess the state of the culture and identify areas of the business amenable to early roll-out.

5. The cultural survey is now undertaken as a regular event. Data is invaluable for tracking progress towards Superdrug's programme objectives.

6. All employees are being trained in total quality management tools and techniques and teamworking. This is proving crucial to moving Superdrug towards its desired culture.

7. Starfish.net, an innovative mechanism for driving continuous improvement company-wide, is proving invaluable for generating, capturing and sharing best practice ideas.

8. 360 degree appraisals are being used to ensure that the company's managers are displaying behaviours that support Superdrug's values.

6

FRAMEWORKS FOR IMPLEMENTING AND DRIVING CULTURE CHANGE

Executive Summary

1. A crucial element of rolling-out a new cultural model is to unfreeze the existing culture and 'refreeze' the new. Measurement, rewards and incentives play a critical role in the 'refreezing' process.

2. According to research for this Report it is vitally important to involve the whole employee-base in implementing the new cultural model. This is the most effective way to gain buy-in and ownership of the culture change effort.

3. Some organizations find it beneficial to pilot a culture change programme prior to full company-wide roll-out. This can be a powerful way of showing the efficacy of the change programme.

4. Cultural change agents and facilitators play a vital role in embedding culture change deep inside an organization.

5. Altering an organization's measurement system is central to effecting lasting cultural change. Indeed as one adviser comments, "measures drive behaviour and behaviour creates culture".

6. Many organizations are using strategic implementation frameworks such as the EFQM Business Excellence Model and the Balanced Scorecard to align individual performance and behaviour with cultural and strategic goals.

7. Case studies on BT Northern Ireland and Siemens KWU and case reports on Transco, Anglian Water Services, Siemens Nixdorf Information Systems and Whirlpool Europe demonstrate best practice.

Section A: Context

The preceding Chapter explored the critical issues around assessing the existing corporate culture at the start of a culture change effort. This Chapter analyses tools and techniques used in implementing a culture change programme. It will show the importance of 'unfreezing' the existing culture, and then 'refreezing' the new, and will explain the absolute importance of involving employees at each level of the organization in the culture change effort and the need for culture change champions deep inside the company.

The Chapter will also consider the crucial role that performance measurement plays in aligning behaviour with the new culture and through to strategic goals, and will look at the use of the strategic implementation tools the Balanced Scorecard and the EFQM Business Excellence Framework in effecting this alignment.

Section B: Unfreezing and Refreezing Cultures

According to research for this Report, a critical aspect of rolling-out a cultural change programme is to unfreeze the existing culture, and once the new cultural attributes are in place to refreeze the new.

Dr George Labovitz, chairman of the US-headquartered Organizational Dynamics Inc (ODI), believes that the key to unfreezing the old ways of doing things is to use participative management to permit people to influence the design of the new ways of working. He says:

> "This is not necessarily discarding the old way of doing things, simply unfreezing the old ways so they can be reshaped to be more appropriate for new management imperatives."

This is an important point. Although it is essentially senior management's responsibility to decide on the 'new imperatives' and the cultural ethos that will drive the company towards these goals, simply imposing a new culture onto a company will not succeed. Indeed, forcing a new set of cultural rules may have the effect of galvanizing employees to cling on to the old ways of behaving and working.

Therefore, the research finds, effective cultural change requires buy-in throughout the company and the most effective way to achieve this is to put the responsibility for change in the hands of the employee-base. So essentially, culture change requires a 'partnership' between the leaders at the top and the rest of the organization. As Labovitz says:

> "It's so basic. The key to culture change is senior management leadership and employee involvement."

About refreezing, Labovitz comments:

> "Refreezing also requires involvement. You're trying out and experimenting

with new approaches. This is an organic period of time. The whole process of culture change moves from a dynamic of unfreezing to a stabilizing of how we want to do things and refreezing."

He warns that if you do not refreeze you will stay shifting. According to John Childress, chief executive of the culture change specialists Senn-Delaney Leadership Consulting Group, the three most important elements in the successful implementation of a culture change programme are:

1. Transformation training (the 'unfreezing' piece).

2. Revised human resource systems (the behaviour 'shift' piece).

3. Corporate communications (the overall reinforcement and 'refreezing' piece).

Revising human resource systems is dealt with in the following Chapter, while corporate communications is the subject of Chapter 8.

Section C: Involving the Whole Employee-base

The importance of involving the wider employee-base in driving culture change was identified by all the advisers and practitioners interviewed for this Report as a critical success factor in the change effort. Alison Rankin-Frost, head of the London, UK-based Context Consulting, comments:

> "It's vitally important to involve staff. One reason being that you can't enforce a culture that's counter to the underlying values of the workforce. As an example we have a client that wants to become more customer-facing. Their history is of a service business, a type of government department. The employees see themselves as being there to provide a service, not to sell to their customers."

She goes on to say that the management wants the employees to be more sales-focused, but the employees believe that their customers will not like this. She comments:

> "This can be overcome by getting some messages together that says that the customer relies on the company for information and therefore reframing it as information provision rather than sales. This would be more effective than saying 'you are going to be sales-focused, so just do it'. So it comes back to language. Language is very important in embedding culture."

Indeed, simple changes of language can have a powerful bearing on how the culture shifts. For example, at the Inland Revenue Accounts Office in Cumbernauld, Scotland (the case study to accompany Chapter 2), simply changing 'tax-payers' into 'customers' had a dramatic effect on implementing a new customer-focused culture.

Warning

However, for any company considering, or in the midst of culture change, Dr David Chaudron, managing partner of the US-based Organized Change Consultancy, gives this timely warning:

> "I've seen companies spend a lot of time involving employees in the creation of, for example, new organizational values, and then doing nothing with that information."

The important point here being that if you start the process of involving employees in the culture change process then you have to see it through, otherwise the damage can be considerable. As Johan Van der Hel, human resources manager at DSM Resins Coating business unit (DSM Resins is a case study to support Chapter 5), says:

> "This means that management must show wholehearted commitment to the process, because once employee energy is unleashed it would prove terribly demotivating if this was held back again."

Again this stresses the importance of senior management really thinking through whether they do indeed intend to commit to the huge transformation that a culture change process will bring to the 'way things are done around here'.

Case Study Examples

The case study companies show how the employee-base was involved in implementing cultural change. At BT Northern Ireland (a case study to accompany this Chapter), its A Better Life culture change programme was launched with the goals to:

1. Create a sense of energy/excitement within the company.

2. Build an understanding that people are fundamental to the success of the company and make a huge difference to the results.

3. Give everyone a role in, and sense of ownership of, that success.

4. Encourage considered risk-taking and innovative thinking.

Explains chief executive officer Lucy Woods:

> "The programme is very simple. The concepts are that you encourage people to own their work area, to find what needs doing and do it. To take that considered risk, take a chance and do it. Not to ask for permission all the time but to have the courage and confidence to do the job, the right thing for the customer. Most people are fully capable to understand an esoteric statement like a 'considered risk'."

Key mechanisms used to roll-out the company's culture change programme included work-out sessions where managers (who had previously, and crucially, been on their own culture change workshop) took their teams through culture change exercises, and a '31 days in May' programme through which competitions were used to encourage employees to think wider that their everyday job and suggest continuous improvement ideas.

At Hyundai Car (UK) Ltd, the whole organization, over a two day period, went through team-building exercises under the titles customer loyalty, employee loyalty and profit. The question was posed, 'what are the key

behaviours that everyone has to display if we are to meet these objectives?'
Says customer satisfaction director, Sue Stoneman:

> "The consistency was amazing, with about 98 per cent correlation on what
> people perceived as critical behaviours."

Consequently these were distilled into the ten key performance criteria,
examples being:

- Be willing to make significant change in the way we do things now in
  order to create greater value for customers.

- Make only those commitments you honestly expect to be able to meet;
  genuinely try to deliver as promised.

- Organize activities and timescales to achieve objectives on schedule.

- Seek feedback from customers on individual and departmental
  activities/contribution.

A key learning from the Hyundai Car case study is that it was the senior
management team that decided on its new competitive strategy and the key
cultural traits it wanted within the organization, but the supporting
behaviours were largely shaped by the employee-base. Therefore, having the
behaviours decided on by the employee-base significantly improved the
chances of their being adopted.

The power of pilots

Pilot programmes can be powerful learning tools when launching any change
or business-wide improvement effort. Two of the case study companies
believed fully in the efficacy of piloting the new cultural approach before full-
scale organizational roll-out

At DSM Resins, for instance, the use of its Working Climate Analysis to drive
culture change and performance improvement was piloted within three sites
before full roll-out. This gave the company key learning points before
devolution to the whole company; not least that the approach did work and
that employees really wanted to be involved in driving change and continuous improvement.

At the Inland Revenue Accounts Office, Cumbernauld, a successful pilot was
first run in the 200 employee strong banking area. According to the Office's
director Andrew Geddes, key goals of the pilot were to convince employees
of senior management's commitment to the tenet of employee involvement
and to secure business benefits that would prove invaluable in rolling-out the
initiative company-wide. Says Geddes:

> "The one overriding contributor to the pilot's success was that we had taken
> all the ideas for improvement from the staff and honoured our commitment
> to implement them and to allow their ideas to feed into the decision-making
> process."

So, in short, pilots can be a powerful way of building irrefutable evidence to
convince cynics in both the management and general employee-base that cultural change can happen and that it can have a positive effect on performance.

Case Report: Anglian Water Services

An interesting example of a company that has successfully rolled-out a far-reaching, and somewhat unconventional, culture change programme, is the UK-based water and sewerage utility, Anglian Water Services.

Called a 'transformation journey', Anglian's culture change programme can be traced back to 1994 when the then recently privatized organization moved from a geographic to a process orientation and significantly flattened its structure. The senior management team also realized that to compete effectively in the new business world, it had to become a learning organization and shake off the constraining behavioural shackles then typical of a public sector organization.

Essentially, the transformation journey is an action-centred learning process where employees work in action learning sets on a series of projects. These projects are concerned with improving business processes or some aspect of an employee's own or their team's work. It evolved from an 'executive stretch' programme for senior executives. The managing director believed that all employees should experience the type of 'away from it all' event traditionally reserved for managers.

The team of 'travellers', as journey participants are called, received support from a facilitator (an external guide) and their journey comprises a three phase process. The company refers to these as:

- Phase 1: 'Toe in the Water'.
- Phase 2: 'White Water Rafting'.
- Phase 3: 'New Horizons'.

Phase 1: Toe in the water

This is a two-day off-site workshop called 'The Traveller's Brief'. This is devoted to employees learning more about themselves and their relationship to others. This included getting participants (and about 60 per cent of the organization's 4500 employees took part) to learn to be more open about themselves in order to reduce the gap between their own and others perception of them. According to Dr Sudhanshu Palsule, the company's head of knowledge and learning, it helped people 'learn how to learn' for the first time.[1]

Four stages of growth

A key component of this new way of learning was using Palsule's concept of there being four stages of organizational and personal growth. Using a geographical representation he has the concept of the hunter-manager in the West, the herder in the North, the gardener in the East and the steward in the South.

In the West, hunter-manager stage, believes Palsule, people and organizations are youthful, pioneering, competing and go-getting. In the North, herder stage, people and organizations enter adulthood where there is a need for consolidation, for finding their niche and coming to terms with their strengths and weaknesses. According to Palsule's model, as we enter mid-life, the gardener phase, there is a need to revisit the life we have been living thus far. He says:

> "There are questions that we ask about what we will leave behind. If these questions are not addressed by an organization both in terms of its people and its own life-cycle then you have a schizophrenic organization."

Finally, you have the South, steward stage. According to Palsule, this is where people and organizations want to transfer, share and give away all the knowledge that they have built up over their lifetime, in order to create a better world. He comments:

> "This was my cast of characters at Anglian. People and the organization learnt concurrently what it meant to be at these four different stages. As a consequence we began unravelling and uncovering knowledge pathways and networks that we did not know existed."

He says that as a result of this new approach to openness and learning, an incredible amount of knowledge began to leak out of the woodwork of the organization:

> "The place turned alive. For the first time we had the feeling that we were not looking at a building or an organization, but an organism which grows and evolves and where knowledge could be accessed quicker than ever before."

He provides this interesting view of how understanding where the individual is within their own life cycle pays dividends to the organization. He says:

> "Put a 55 year old into an aspect of a culture change programme that is not befitting him and you'll get sabotage. Allow a 55 year old to feel worth, dignity and a sense of participation and you will get miracles."

Phase 2: White water rafting

During this phase employees embark on 'the expedition', typically lasting six to nine months, where employee teams tackled specific action-learning projects. And this has led to some 'expeditions' in the true sense of the word. For example, one team created a well in an Ivory Coast Village to provide better drinking water for the local inhabitants.

Essentially this phase is about moving from individual learning to team-based learning and for exploring how teams can find creative ways to work together and to share knowledge. Important here is the use of the expedition 'guides' who help individuals and teams to 'think outside the box' and to realize that though change is uncomfortable, it is possible achieve a great deal. Indeed much more that employees may at first have thought.

Speaking at the Business Intelligence conference, *Corporate Agility 97*, then head of knowledge creation, Dr David Wilkinson said about this stage:[2]

> "The big mistake we made early on was that we didn't really understand the importance of defining empowerment. You have to give people clear direction and guidance."

Phase 3: New Horizons

This is the final phase and is a journey review comprising a one-day self-appraisal of achievements, from both a task and learning perspective. Following this, the focus is on teams and individuals flourishing on their own, with continuous learning and transferring new learning into workplace improvements.

A university of water

Also key to developing this culture of learning has been the creation of a University of Water (AQUA Universitas) to encompass all aspects of learning, development and knowledge-creation.

Cambridge University is assisting the company and Anglian Water Services aims to make formal training and personal development recognized outside the business by accreditation. A main thrust of the concept is to increase the benefit to the business of individual learning by increasing the value to the employee and aligning training and development with business needs.

Interestingly a recent employee opinion survey showed a clear difference in attitude between those who had participated in the transformation process and those who had not. Those who had were much warmer to the business and were much more willing to accept change. Wilkinson explains:[3]

> "The transformation journey was about changing the hearts and minds of our people. It was a big culture shock. It took a long time for people to fully recognize the changes that were being imposed on our business, the changes in demands from customers and the threats of other companies."

Case Report: Siemens Nixdorf

Another successful, and more conventional, culture change programme was undertaken in the mid 1990s by the German-headquartered Siemens Nixdorf Information Systems (SNI), and was reported as a full case study within the Business Intelligence Report, *Managing and Sustaining Radical Change.*[4]

The SNI change process can be traced back to 1994 and the appointment of a new CEO, Gerhard Schulmeyer. At that time the organization was in deep trouble and was losing significant amounts of money. This echoes several of the case study examples where a new leader faced with pressing business challenges was a catalyst for the culture change effort.

In addition to operationally building the company around customer-facing processes, Schulmeyer wanted to create an entrepreneurial culture that was innovative and fast moving. And he wanted to do this within 24 months (see Figure 6.1).

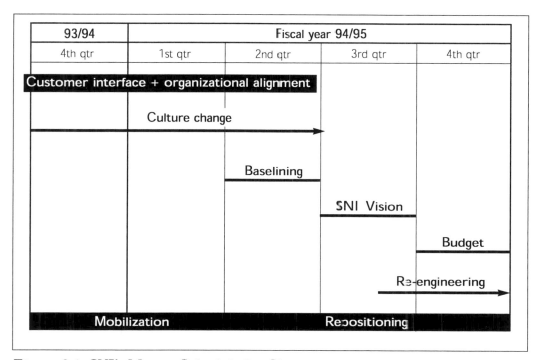

Figure 6.1: SNI's Master Schedule for Change

Importantly, central to the Siemens Nixdorf Culture Change Programme, was that staff involvement, ownership and responsibility for the change effort was built in to the whole process from the start. However, a core team, headed by the leading change consultant Mark Maletz, was responsible for designing the initial framework and the timetable for the programme. The authors write:

"The sheer scale of such an undertaking presented the company with a logistical challenge; reaching 37,000 people working in a worldwide business. This was answered by the plan to cascade the culture change programme throughout the organization in a structured way that linked ideas and precepts to action."

Agenda for change

Extensive corporate-wide consultation using surveys, meetings and workshops were used to set the agenda for change. The outcome was a 19-point agenda of topics for change that fell into three main categories:

1. Changes in the behaviour of managers and employees with a view to achieving dramatic improvement in performance and results.

2. Changing work systems to foster a culture of operational excellence.

3. Changing processes to emphasize the customer and to ensure a culture of customer excellence.

The next step was to involve the organization as widely as possible in driving this change. To do this there were a series of four, four-day interactive workshops held in Hanover, Germany. These events became known as Hanover one, two, three and four.

Importantly, given the organization's commitment to involving the employee-base, the output from these four-day events were projects that were taken back into the business where more people were involved in putting the proposals into action.

Hanover one

Hanover one was staged in December 1994. For this event the company chose 300 people who were sufficiently motivated and capable of jump-starting the process of change. These people were recognized as opinion leaders within the workplace who could be counted on to drive the programme. Therefore, demonstrating the point made by many of the commentators interviewed for this Report of the importance of identifying, and deploying the skills of, change champions early in the process.

Sixty actions related to the 19-point agenda were identified and taken back into the business where staff were enrolled by project leaders to implement the improvement ideas.

To communicate the successes a 'results fair' was held in Munich, Germany, in May 1995. This showcased the achievements of about 1000 employees who had participated in action projects.

Hanover two

Customer focus was the theme of Hanover two, which was attended by a newly identified batch of 300 opinion leaders. This time, selection was based on evidence of active commitment to the change programme. Also, 54 customer representatives were involved in defining further action initiatives.

As before, the follow-through involved the definition of projects with the results showcased at results fairs in Paderborn, Germany, and in Belgium.

Hanover three

Hanover three, held in December 1995, was dedicated to giving SNI's business partners a voice in defining the new culture.

Twenty action projects were defined by the end of the event. These ranged from the development of turnkey solutions for self-service banking and development of a value-added services business for desktop video and worldwide partner connection.

Hanover four

Hanover four was designed to mark the transition point when SNI moved from learning new values and behaviours to making them part of the day-to-day business. Key themes for this event were:

- embedding change leadership in the business

- activating the network of the 2000 opinion leaders and project members in the business (which had been identified globally)

- creation a self-sustaining process

- deploying the change toolkit – facilitation, process redesign and other techniques for bringing about performance improvement.

The first three Hanover events had developed a change leadership infrastructure working variously in customer interface, culture change and innovation. To support this it had also created subgroups in the form of action teams, project implementors, and change facilitators.

So SNI had built a powerful network of change leaders throughout the company with direct experience of managing projects. Hanover four set out to leverage ongoing benefits from this network. The authors write:

> "Communities of practice are where most of the learning occurs in businesses. SNI identified 19 geographically-based communities throughout the group, each based in a primary geographical area and operating on a cross-functional basis using a common set of change management tools and linked to a secondary area. People from the two areas meet regularly to learn from each other how to embed new ideas and practices in their own organizations, each supported by a number of opinion leaders."

And they added:

> "The nurturing of opinion leaders helped to disseminate some of the change management skills that the company needed throughout the organization. Siemens Nixdorf also put together a programme to develop change agents whose job was to stimulate business and performance improvement initiatives in different parts of the business. These were mainly young managers, marketing and professional people who were sent on a specially designed course in the US that included a mini-MBA, visits to leading US companies that had transformed their business as Nixdorf intended, and exposure to Silicon Valley, the hothouse of information technology innovation."

It is noteworthy that through this change process, Siemens Nixdorf had staunched its crippling losses by 1995 and so was in a strong position to drive the business forward.

Siemes Nixdorf: Ten Key Lessons

Since this case study was first published, one of the authors, David Harvey, and the SNI change architect, Mark Maletz (now a principal in the consultancy McKinsey & Company's Organization Practice, and a virtual associate professor of management at Babson College, USA), have put together these ten corporate transformation lessons. They are based on SNI's experiences and those from other change programmes that were used to design the SNI transformation programme.

- **Lesson 1: Achieving dynamic balance is essential to successful transformation**. Transformation is a paradoxical process. One of the biggest challenges is to find a way to balance what seem to be contradictory or incompatible objectives. For example:

  - Developing ideas and implementing actions or achieving a balance between reflecting and doing.

  - Leading and empowering others or achieving a balance between top-down and bottom-up change management.

  It is essential to understand that empowerment does not mean abdication – those who empower others must continue to coach and intervene when necessary, set clear direction and leverage improvisation. Too much focus or control and the change is viewed as being mandated and is therefore rejected. Too much experimentation can result in chaos and failure.

  Consuming and conserving energy is important as enough activity must be initiated to achieve a 'critical mass' in the change programme while not causing the programme to 'burn out'. Equally important is the creation of a safe envelope within which to change and ensure business relevance to change activities (which tends to result in less safety).

  There is a tendency for change leaders to focus on only one dimension of these polarities by asking 'which is better?'. This is entirely the wrong question. Those leading change must learn to dynamically balance the two dimensions. It is like learning to breath in and out – they are complementary aspects of a single process.

In terms of the first balance dimension, doing is intrinsically easier than reflecting because, by its very nature, doing seems purposeful and productive. By contrast, taking a step outside to reflect on the lessons and results achieved can seem like a diversion. Without reflecting on the experience and lessons, though, there is a strong risk that you will not reach the optimum destination.

Another related problem is losing sight of the fact that it is not just the specific action that is important, but its use as a vehicle for mobilizing other people to absorb the lessons of the transformation. There is always a risk that people will ignore the multiple objectives inherent in any transformation activities.

- **Lesson 2: Dealing with the 'will-nots'.** There will always be a distribution within the organization of people who subscribe immediately to the new cultural principles, those who will subscribe eventually, those who might, and those who never will. Those who never will fall into two groups: people who refuse to subscribe and people who are incapable of doing so. The 'will nots' should be a relatively small percentage of all employees or the overall transformation challenge may be too great for the organization. It is important to have strategies for working with each of these four groups.

  For the first group of early adopters of the new culture, there should be mechanisms to enroll them early in the change programme. For those who will accept the change later, it is important to find ways of ensuring that they do so as quickly as possible. Those who might subscribe should be provided with learning experiences and opportunities so that they can make an informed choice, and, when all else fails, a little cajoling will not hurt.

  There has to be ways of helping those who will not change because they are incapable of doing so to leave the company as painlessly and humanely as possible. Those who simply refuse to accept the message are more worrisome. If these people are in positions of leadership, they have to be moved out of the system fairly aggressively. Those who are less visible in the organization need to understand there is no place for them in the new organization and they should be advised to leave.

  Failure to deal with the 'will nots' is a serious mistake in many change programmes. While it may seem more humane to let them remain until they choose to leave or retire, it can cause considerable damage to the change programme and the company. Others who see the 'will nots' remaining may conclude that management is not really serious about change. To counter this at SNI, the more visible resistors to change were asked to leave the company within the first several months of the transformation journey. Rather than doing this quietly (which would have been the traditional approach), it was done publicly at large management meetings and were essentially symbolic executions.

The challenge of dealing with resistors is further complicated because their elimination can be seen as stifling debate and killing open communication. It is therefore important to encourage open communication and conflict, work to achieve consensus, and only after all this work to eliminate resistors.

- **Lesson 3: Change leaders at all levels should be linked with one another and with the top of the organization.** This 'rewiring the organization' by creating new channels of communication and new relationships that cut across the traditional hierarchy is vital. Siemens Nixdorf worked hard at linking people lower down in the organization with senior management. For example, it invited front-line opinion leaders and senior business leaders to the Hanover meetings. However, too little attention was paid to the middle managers, who found themselves sandwiched between the top and bottom of the organization at the beginning of the change programme. As a result, top management and front-line employees began to think, and talk, about middle management as barriers in the change process. It should not be surprising, therefore, to discover that they did, in fact, resist the change.

  To overcome this impasse, middle managers were invited to attend Hanover as both opinion leaders, in the case of the less senior of the middle managers, and business leaders where they were the more senior. This gave middle management a role in the programme and allowed them to choose to support it. Ironically, it also symbolically eliminated middle management.

- **Lesson 4: Leverage the old to create the new**. SNI's programme showed that it is sometimes better to use the old organization's strengths and energy to drive change, rather than directly assaulting the old system. For example, at SNI employees were used to taking orders and, in some ways, the SNI change programme began by ordering people to try new things.

  Conventional wisdom holds that management cannot order employees to become empowered. This is true over the long-term, but it is possible to begin the process of empowerment by issuing orders, as long as the experience generated by these orders becomes self-sustaining over time.

- **Lesson 5: Avoid being misled by cultural stereotypes**. One of the greatest dangers of culture change is allowing cultural stereotypes to lead you in the wrong direction. If you asked most people, including Germans, how many latent entrepreneurs could be found in a German company, the answer would be very few. In fact this question was asked numerous times at SNI and the answer was always a very small number. However, once entrepreneurial conditions were created, many aspiring entrepreneurs within the company were discovered. In other words, question your assumptions.

- **Lesson 6: Think out of the box**. One of the biggest constraints on innovative thinking is the acceptance of limits to creativity and possible solutions. These constraints are normally the product of custom and effectively box people in when they are looking for new ideas. Yet innovative solutions are likely to come from thinking beyond these limits. Once the box is visualized, it is often easier to break out of the constraints that it imposes.

  For example, in the early 1990s, SNI was a leader in the mainframe market and relied on this highly profitable business and its rich talent base. The impending death of the mainframe, however, demoralized the entire mainframe organization within SNI and stifled creativity. Engineers essentially waited for the business to collapse and hoped that they would be able to retire before this happened. One change agent from the mainframe business refused to accept this 'box' and recognized that many of the mainframe engineering skills could also be used to develop high-end servers that could be introduced into the growing client/server market. The change agent conceived a new server product that would run the same award winning operating system as the mainframe products and then launched the product using engineering talent from the mainframe organization – and in record time.

- **Lesson 7: Achieving milestones maintains momentum**. Having well-spaced milestones throughout a change programme is an important means of maintaining momentum. Without incremental results and business impact, any change journey becomes impossible to sustain – or just simply impossible. Milestones at SNI, such as 90-day interim results from action teams and the results fairs, helped demonstrate that new behaviours are achievable while simultaneously providing a tangible impact on corporate performance.

- **Lesson 8: Embed controls in the work system**. It is important to embed controls in the work system rather than imposing controls externally. For example, at SNI, prior to their transformation programme, any special task forces or initiatives were controlled by an independent headquarters-based 'programme office' that insisted on regular reporting and had authority over the teams doing the work. In the transformation programme, no such office existed. Instead, the sources of authority that were already in place were used to control the process.

  The important point here is that successful change programmes are designed to work with the entire work system, and are based on an understanding that organizations are complex and highly interconnected systems.

- **Lesson 9: Overcome resistance through involvement and shared responsibility**. When people have no control or influence over change, they resist it. When these same people have an authentic voice in shaping the change, they are far more likely to support the change and become cheerleaders for it. For this reason, employees were invited to self-select their own representatives as Hanover opinion leaders. Moreover, this is the reason that Hanover action teams invested so much time and energy in recruiting additional members after the events. It might have been easier for a smaller action team to simply do the work and achieve the desired results, but this would miss the opportunity to expand the base of shared responsibility and overcome resistance.

This lesson also drove the efforts to engage the workers' councils in the change programme from the very beginning. Conventional wisdom would have delayed involvement from the workers' council until some momentum had been achieved, but this would have caused suspicion and resistance. Instead, the council was invited to participate in the programme from the very beginning and in a variety of roles, including the Hanover facilitator roles (roles that had first-hand access to all the information associated with the culture change programme).

- **Lesson 10: Symbolic acts are a powerful means of signaling change**. Symbolic acts can help punctuate a change process by symbolizing some part of the change that is desired. For example, a CEO who commits a day per week to working on the change programme is symbolically signaling the importance of the change, in a way that is more compelling than simply stating that the programme is important. Similarly, actively refusing to move meetings that relate to the programme is another means of showing their priority in the corporate scheme of things.

A particularly interesting kind of symbolic act involves using symbolic contracts. For example, those working on an action can be asked to sign a 'commitment letter' describing the action and its target results. Such personal signatures can be a potent reminder of commitment to the change programme.

Another powerful symbolic act can be as simple as a change leader saying 'I don't know' rather than attempting to convey a sense of false certainty, especially in environments where management never admits to not knowing.

Section D: Change Agents and Facilitators

What comes out strongly from the Siemens Nixdorf case report is the need for change agents throughout the organization, proactively championing and driving the culture change effort forward. For although the senior management team has to lead the culture change programme, other pressures naturally curtail the amount of time they have available for this role. As UK-based independent consultant Garrey Melville says:

> "At the highest level, such a person, who we may call a change architect, may come from an outside consultancy with a lot of experience in driving culture change [eg, Mark Maletz], or they may be internal, for example a knowledge manager or an internal consultant with a strategic mindset. What's important is such a person has excellent facilitation and communication skills, and has the right value sets."

Mark Krueger, managing director of the US-headquartered Answerthink Consulting Group, adds that the real issue is how to get each staff functions to put aside their own silo-like thinking and get to think about what is best for the organization. This, he says, can prove a very difficult task:

> "It is best done with cross-functional teams of individuals from multiple staff areas, locations and from both an operating and staff-line function standpoint. The cross-functional team should be led by an individual with experience in organizational dynamics, with the facilitation skills to match the strategy of the company to the types of culture will support the achievement of the strategy."

Case Study Examples

A number of the case study companies recognized the importance of internal facilitators in driving culture change. At DSM Resins, for example, Johan Van der Hel, human resources manager at DSM Resins' Coating business unit, says:

> "We have learnt that facilitators can make or break this process. They have to be committed and enthusiastic as it is they who during the feedback session have to enthuse the employees."

At Superdrug (a case study to support Chapter 5), facilitators trained in presentation skills delivered a workshop to all staff in the company. Says head of total quality Peter Raine:

> "Through a two-day course we trained 120 presenters. These were all volunteers and were draw from store management teams. Crucially, each had expressed a desire to develop presentation skills."

Case Report: Transco

The use of facilitators also played a key role in a major culture change effort conducted by UK-based gas supplier Transco in support of major corporate restructuring as part of opening up the UK gas industry to competition. Transco has its roots in a restructuring of the then British Gas in 1993. The then BG Transco was one of five separate businesses which were born in March 1994.

Continuous change

Since its formation, Transco has experienced rapid and almost continuous change. Andersen Consulting said, before the restructuring, that the anticipated breadth and depth of change facing British Gas was greater and therefore more challenging to manage than anything previously experienced by other known corporate change programmes.

The root and branch reorganization enabled Transco to cut manpower by 40 per cent without industrial relations disputes or service disruptions, and reduce organizational tiers from 13 to 5 and the number of districts from 90 to 32.

Twin challenges

Transco faced the twin challenge of creating a culture responsive to emerging competition, while simultaneously managing a major downsizing programme. The seeds for creating the leadership style and the business culture change programme were sown during September 1993 during a benchmarking trip to the US by a six-strong team led by the then director of strategic change, John Dilks.

He came back enthused with the culture change experiences of utilities Michcon in Detroit and SoCal in Los Angeles, and the contact details for Senn-Delaney, who were to play a pivotal role in enabling Transco to change. Senn-Delaney vice president and senior consultant John Clayton says:

> "Transco realized early on that they could change the systems and the organizational structure, but if they didn't change the attitudes, mind-sets and behaviours of their people then it would be very difficult to accomplish their objectives.

> "The main thing they wanted to do was to 'wake up' a very bright, long-experienced engineering culture."

On top of proactive management communication, two other factors contributed to resistance being less than it might have been – a good redundancy package and the employee-base's readiness to embrace the culture change programme.

Workshops

Three-day workshops communicated six core values that would be required for the then Transco – trust, accountability, achievement orientation, customer-focus, coaching and feedback, and listening and explaining.

A team of 100 internal facilitators drawn from all levels of the company were trained by Senn-Delaney to deliver over 600 workshops. From those workshops Transco developed other learning mechanisms which identified areas for improvement, and ways to achieve best business performance. Engineering for value (EfV) and change laboratories were two (the latter is explained in Chapter 8).

EfV put engineers together to challenge the way things were done, discuss changes needed, and produce a robust improvement to processes.

Internal communications

Also important to the culture change was internal communication mechanisms. A five-strong 'You Make the Difference' team was launched to reinforce the programme by generating internal information and to encourage the facilitators by disseminating best practices and insights from other workshops.

Facilitators continued with their normal jobs while leading workshops (about one every six weeks). Additionally, they met once a quarter to share best practice and insights.

Culture groups also drove the culture change. These were from a cross-section of the workforce and they produced local newspapers, campaigns and local culture questionnaires. They also created team measurement systems, tailored workshops and focus groups. A buddy system through which two people met regularly to discuss personal change was also adopted.

According to Clayton, a key difference at Transco now, compared to the pre-culture changes is that it takes much less time to turn ideas into action and then results. The jewel in the crown of the performance and results culture was the delivery of full competition in gas in May 1998, ahead of schedule. This achievement and the hard work and dedication which went into it was recognized by the industry's regulator, the Office of Gas Supply, in a tribute to Transco.

The team which delivered the three-year long programme celebrated its arrival with a exhibition explaining the 13 workstreams to colleagues. They heard that in a changing business environment, the skills and techniques learned added real value to the Transco of the future. Clayton says:

> "People are now far more open to listen to one another and are willing to consider how new thoughts and ideas can apply to them. There has been a huge amount of change but it is a healthier place because there is less stress in the organization and there's less of a blaming culture. There really is an underlying desire to make it a successful organization."

It is noteworthy that during the first three years of the change process productivity per employee increased by 15 per cent while base operating costs were reduced by nine per cent a year. And customer service has been enhanced without compromising the safety and reliability of what is the safest gas network in the world.

14 Roles for a Change Agent

Within the book, *Strategic Partners for High Performance*, Marsh Campbell, vice president of human resources at the US-based Magma Copper, cited 14 key roles of a change agent based on his experience of a change programme at Magma Copper. These are:[5]

1. The change agent must have a deep conviction and commitment to the strategic reinvention of the organization and a new future – cultural change is a business necessity.

2. The change agent must be responsive to a perceived need within the organization – forcing ideas and concepts on the organization before it is ready is unlikely to be successful.

3. The change agent must be competent in theoretical knowledge of organizational development and practical experience.

4. Organizational change can only be accomplished by the change agent in relationship with others, by involving them in the reinvention process.

5. The change agent must be able to offer incentives to all the company's many constituencies.

6. Over-concern with power, control and personal credit is a change process killer.

7. Change agents must be willing to challenge their own assumptions, to accept new ideas and grow with the process.

8. The change agent intervenes when and where appropriate if variances or breakdowns occur.

9. Patience and persistence are required to overcome resistance, scepticism and cynicism over the change process.

10. Inclusion of unions is essential.

11. The role of traditional HR and union officials must shift. For the HR professional this means acquiring new skills and becoming versed in cultural change.

12. The change agent must be able to manage what Magma calls a "co-mingled reality", where variations of skill and commitment levels exist and may clash.

13. A change agent recognizes that there will be both management and union casualties in the change process. Some people are not willing or able to make the necessary behavioural changes required.

14. The power of the change process is in invention, generation and employee involvement rather than simplistic, off-the-shelf best practices which are captured, codified and suggested as answers, or methods of organizational change.

Section E: The Aligning Power of Measurement

According to the research, another critical part of a cultural change programme, and indeed one that can underpin all the other elements, is altering the organization's measurement systems. For as Labovitz succinctly puts it, "measures drive behaviour and behaviour creates culture".

Measures should be altered at the business unit, function and individual levels to align work approaches and behaviours with strategic goals and to align behaviour with the new cultural model. Thus creating a direct line-of-sight from individual behaviour, through culture, to strategic goals.

In his book, *The Power of Alignment: How Great Companies Stay Centred and Accomplish Extraordinary Things*, co-written with his ODI colleague Victor Rosansky, Labovitz explains how measurement can help an organization ensure that its culture is aligned to corporate strategy:[6]

"Every organization has a culture, and that culture – for better or worse – is largely determined by what its leaders have chosen to measure and to reinforce with incentives. This is why the choice of measurements is so important; measures eventually determine the behaviour of personnel and the culture of the organization."

Case Report: Federal Express

Labovitz and Rosansky put forward Federal Express (FedEx) as a good example of how to align culture with strategy. They explained that at FedEx strategy implementation rests on one fundamental success factor (the company's 'main thing' as Labovitz puts it) – absolutely reliable service. Everything the company thinks, plans and does supports that one 'main thing', a simple belief that drives the culture of this hugely successful organization.

As proof, each day at 10am, every Federal Express manager, from CEO Fred Smith down, gets a report on the previous days' results against a service quality index (SQI). This is a mathematical representation of every one of the three million customer transactions that took place the day before.

The index essentially tracks how the company performed against its 'main thing' on a daily basis. According to Labovitz, such a ritual sends a strong signal throughout the organization as to what is important to the company. The authors write:

> "The [SQI] of FedEx is a powerful example of the measure-to-behaviour-to-culture process. SQI is meaningful because it is hardwired to the main thing of the business. Everyone at FedEx recognizes that SQI provides a daily reminder of what is important; it is linked to rewards and recognition for FedEx employees and had clearly shaped the collective behaviour and culture of the organization."

Case Report: Motorola

Labovitz and Rosansky go on to explain how measurement dramatically altered the culture of total quality exemplar Motorola. They write:

> "Today, Motorola Corporation is recognized by people in the quality business as one of the great success stories of the last 20 years. It has a culture of product and process quality that few can match. Six Sigma Quality is the lingua franca of that culture, and every employee whether he or she is American, German or Chinese, speaks it fluently."

Six Sigma is a production rate of no more than 3.4 defects per million parts. Or put another way, Motorola wants to be perfect in everything 99.9999998 per cent of the time. The company has a well-defined and robust process for achieving this goal.

The authors go on to explain that Motorola was not always a quality leader, indeed during the 1970s it was getting beaten hands-down by its new Asian competitors.

The story of how it turned that situation around, and in doing so changed its culture, suggests how measures, training, and reward systems can transform even a globally far-flung enterprise. The authors write:

> "Chairman Bob Galvin's response [to the competitive pressures that were squeezing the company] was to issue a Herculean challenge to every unit of his worldwide company – improve the quality of your critical processes tenfold within the next five years."

However, the authors say, Galvin's challenge was at first met with inaction:

> "Ten-fold improvement seemed impossible. No-one in the company had a clue about how it could be done."

However, Galvin kept reiterating this challenge until Motorola managers recognized that he was indeed serious and, to their amazement, achieved his ten-fold improvement in every critical process in a year and a half.

Measurement played a key role in reshaping Motorola's culture. In fact, it headed the list of steps used by Motorola to focus attention and change behaviour in favour of quality. Those steps were to:

- start with measurement
- make quality a strategic goal
- tie measures to performance management
- train, train, train
- initiate senior management review
- create goals for everyone.

The authors write:

> "The behaviour of employees and the culture of Motorola today would be practically unrecognizable to a customer or employee from the 1970s. Today, quality is part of the company's DNA. This is clear from everything we've read and from a recent visit to a Motorola semiconductor plant in China. Scattered throughout the plant electronic scoreboards announce current performance in new customer orders, cycle time, defect rates and profits. Months in which goals are met or exceeded are celebrated in the plant cafeteria with shark fin soup!

> "For its Asian operations in general, Motorola now exceeds Six Sigma Quality."

Interestingly, when interviewed for this Report, Labovitz said that he initially showed surprise that employees valued a celebration with shark fin soup so highly. To which CD Tam, a Motorola senior executive, replied, "that's because you're not Chinese". And this reinforces the importance of understanding the intricacies and the power of local cultural thinking and symbols in driving cultural change.

Strategic Implementation Frameworks

The importance of measurement was recognized by most of the case study companies. Indeed many were using established performance measurement and management frameworks such as the Balanced Scorecard or the European Foundation for Quality Management's Business Excellence Model as important tools for aligning organizational focus and behaviour with strategic goals. As examples, the Balanced Scorecard is used at Ernst & Young and Superdrug. It is also being used at BT Northern Ireland, which also used the Business Excellence Model. This model is also used extensively at Siemens KWU, and the Inland Revenue Accounts Office, Cumbernauld.

The Balanced Scorecard

The classic balanced scorecard was created in the early 1990s by Dr David Norton, president of US-headquartered consultancy Renaissance Worldwide, and Robert Kaplan, professor of leadership development at Harvard Business School. It is a framework that has the overarching goal of transforming an organization's strategy into operational objectives, measures, targets and initiatives. The four dimensions of this scorecard are:

1. **Financial**: To succeed financially, how should we appear to our shareholders?

2. **Customer**: To achieve our vision, how should we appear to our customers?

3. **Internal Business Process**: To satisfy our shareholders and customers, what business processes must we excel at?

4. **Learning and Growth**: To achieve our vision, how will we sustain our ability to change and improve?

Each perspective includes a number of strategic objectives, measures and targets. The actual number depends on the organization's own requirements, but essentially should be those deemed essential for moving the organization forward (see Figure 6.2).

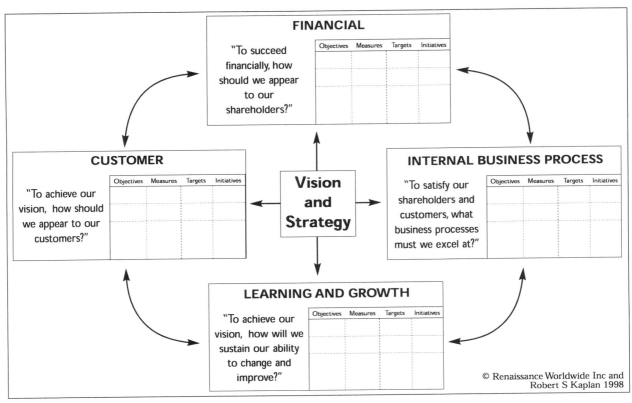

Figure 6.2: Translating Vision and Strategy – Four Perspectives

Case Report: Whirlpool Europe

Within the Business Intelligence report, *Building and Implementing a Balanced Scorecard*, a case study showed how white goods manufacturer Whirlpool Europe used the balanced scorecard to create a unified organizational culture.[7]

Whirlpool Europe, which is a part of the US-headquartered Whirlpool Corporation, has about 12,000 employees within 11 plants and has direct sales within 25 European countries and exports to 35 others. This multinational composition was one of the influences that led to Whirlpool Corporation launching its balanced scorecard in 1997. Explains Paul Kirincic, at the time vice president, human resources, Whirlpool Europe (he has since left the company):

> "As a corporation we've been expanding globally, mainly through acquisition activity, over the past decade.... In the last four years [pre 1998] alone Whirlpool has added 25,000 to its employee base. So we are using the balanced scorecard as a mechanism to manage the increased cultural diversity within the corporation."

The thinking behind the balanced scorecard was partly shaped by an employee cultural audit carried out in the first quarter of 1996, following disappointing financial results in 1995. Recalls Kirincic:

> "In 1995 we had set ourselves some tough targets which we were confident that we would hit. And we really thought we had all of our

people within the organization aligned behind them. However when we didn't perform as expected, our chairman asked 'why?'. The cultural audit clearly showed that there were significant differences in how people throughout the globe viewed the corporation, its goals and their role in attaining those goals. Our people didn't feel there was a common performance language which they could buy into. There was clearly no alignment or sense of common values within the company."

"[The cultural audit] reported conclusively that our employees felt that we had become too focused on the financials. Although as a corporation we had always said that non-financial performance dimensions such as people, customers and processes were important, the perception was that when the push came to the shove, the focus was purely on the financials."

It is important to point out that the corporation is not trying to create a standard culture throughout the globe, as it sees its cultural diversity in thinking and acting as providing its competitive advantage. Rather it is attempting to create a common sense of belonging, of purpose and direction and a common standard of behaviour.

Whirlpool Europe's balanced scorecard in 1997 is shown in Table 6.1 and consisted of three perspectives: financial (which is allocated a 50 per cent weighting), customer and employee (both allocated a 25 per cent weighting).

Measures	Weighting	Targets	Achievement	Score
Financial	**50 per cent**	**1.0**		**1.25**
EVA			102.6%	
Cash flow			120.6%	
Net Earnings			104.5%	
Total cost productivity			100.0%	
Customer	**25 per cent**	**1.0**		**1.0**
Quality			109.0%	
Market share			98.0%	
Customer satisfaction			100%	
Trade partner satisfaction			100%	
Employee	**25 per cent**	**1.0**		**1.0**
High performance culture, introduction; personal development plan, implementation			100%	
Development plan, implementation			99.0%	
Training development plan, introduction			completed	
Diversity plan, implementation			completed	
Total	**100 per cent**	**1.0**		**1.2**

Table 6.1: Whirlpool Europe's 1997 Balanced Scorecard

The percentage weighting is the same for the five scorecards that exist within Whirlpool, a master scorecard at a corporate level and one each for North America, Asia, Europe and Latin America.

Interestingly, and unlike many other companies, Whirlpool has not created scorecards at country or plant level. As Kirincic explains:

> "A danger in doing that is that managers becomes too narrowly focused on their own country or plant performance. We want all employees to feel and behave as if they belong to one global company, and so they should be looking at their performance from a local, regional, and global perspective."

The EFQM Business Excellence Framework

The EFQM Business Excellence Framework was launched in 1992 and measures performance from nine critical areas, split into the two performance dimensions of enablers and results. Enablers are leadership, people development, policy and strategy, resources and processes. Results are people satisfaction, customer satisfaction, impact on society and business results. As Figure 6.3 shows, each criteria has an importance points weighting out of a total 1000 points.

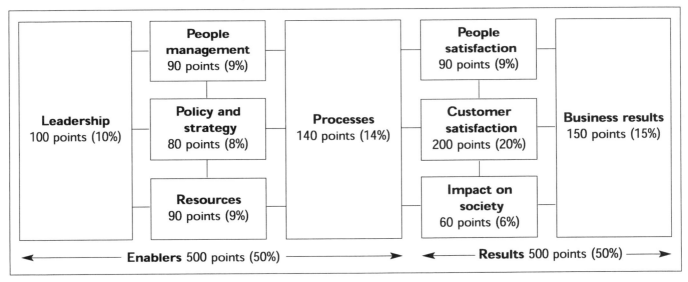

Figure 6.3: EFQM Model for Business Excellence

As this Report was being written the model had been revamped to recognize changes in business improvement strategies since the original launch. The new model is shown in Figure 6.4.

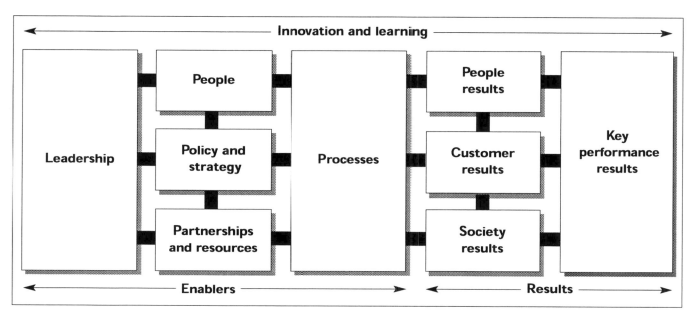

Figure 6.4: The New EFQM Excellence Framework

Case Report: Inland Revenue Accounts Office, Cumbernauld, Scotland

At the Inland Revenue Accounts Office, Cumbernauld, using the EFQM Business Excellence Model pulled together the three change objectives of:

1. Develop customer awareness.

2. Develop quality improvement measures.

3. Develop and enhance people skills.

Says Office director Andrew Geddes:

> "Although we had already come a long way and were certainly getting results, there still seemed to be a sense that all these initiatives were somehow separate from each other and we needed a mechanism to bring these three main elements together."

This brought the Office to the EFQM Business Excellence Framework. After adapting the model's assessment elements for its own needs (but still within the nine criteria areas) the Office decided to pilot the framework within one of its business units during 1995.

Importantly, responsibility for the pilot was devolved to the unit's Customer Service Improvement Group (CSIG). Additional support provided to help the CSIG understand how to use the framework to identify strengths and weaknesses, identify a few vital areas for improvement to build into the business unit's business improvement plan, and to customize it to the business unit's own requirements.

The Office believes that delegating responsibility for assessment to the CSIGs means that the people doing the jobs themselves work out exactly what needs to be fixed, what results are being achieved and how the unit compares to business excellence benchmarks. Says Geddes:

> "Armed with that information, the CSIGs can then focus on the excellence gap and put into place the measures to improve quality. This fits perfectly with our philosophy of employee involvement and for units themselves to be responsible for their own process measurement and improvement."

Employee Opinion Surveys

The most common tool for measuring culture is an employee opinion survey. The preceding Chapter explained how these are being used to both assess the existing culture and to track progress of key cultural performance factors, and it also provides examples of employee surveys used by case study organizations.

On top of new organizational measurement systems and employee surveys, the use of appraisal systems to drive home the absolute importance of the new cultural ethos and to ensure management and employee compliance is a critical measurement tool. This is considered in the following Chapter.

The value of a measurement tool

Employee surveys, or whatever mechanism is used to track cultural development, have to be unique to the organization's own needs. However, the value of having a tool to measure culture was summarized by John Childress and US-based consultants Joe Doyle and Jim Ondrus, in Chapter 19 of the multi-authored book *Lessons in Culture Change*.[8]

According to the authors, a measurement tool has three primary uses. First, they wrote, it provides a baseline of the organization's behaviour relative to the core beliefs and values of the culture and a method for objectively measuring the cultural performance over time. They write:

> "It will provide feedback on how the organization is doing in making the core beliefs and values a reality in day-to-day activities of the company."

Second, measurement sends a clear message to the entire organization that living the core beliefs and values of the culture is one of the most important things everyone needs to do, from senior through to non-management levels.

Third, it provides the opportunity for everyone to develop personalized action plans based on the report's feedback and receive continuous coaching on their performance relative to the living of the core beliefs and values. The authors write:

> "This strengthens the message of continued self-improvement for all participants utilizing the assessment tool."

Section F: Conclusion

Implementing a new culture within an organization essentially requires an active partnership between senior management (who have the power to decide on a new culture) and the whole employee-base, who through everyday actions have the power to implement the new culture. So culture change can be seen as both a top-down and bottom-up process.

Shifting from one cultural model to another requires a well thought out action-plan, usually involving facilitated workshops, to drive home the urgency of cultural change. Within these workshops new behaviours can be identified and explained and the process of learning the new cultural rules begun. Change agents and facilitators play a crucial role in explaining and rolling-out these new rules; measurements and incentives play an important role in embedding them.

Key Learning Points

1. Ensure the cultural change initiative supports the strategic aims of the organization.

2. Take time to 'unfreeze' the existing culture and to 'refreeze' the new cultural ethos. If companies do not refreeze they will keep shifting.

3. Once the senior management team has agreed upon the new culture for the organization, and how that is aligned with strategic goals, it is important to involve the whole of the employee-base in the cultural implementation. It is extremely difficult to enforce a new, and lasting, culture onto an unwilling employee-base.

4. Piloting a culture change effort prior to full organization-wide roll-out can prove a powerful way to both test the new cultural ethos and build evidence of the efficacy of change.

5. Put change agents and champions in place throughout the organization. But ensure that they have the requisite knowledge and interpersonal skills to influence their colleagues.

6. It is vital to change an organization's measurement system in support of the new cultural ethos, as measurement is a powerful lever of culture change. As one adviser said, "measures drive behaviour and behaviour creates culture".

7. Strategic implementation frameworks such as the Balanced Scorecard and the EFQM Business Excellence Model, can prove powerful mechanisms for aligning behaviour with strategic and cultural goals.

CASE STUDY: BT NORTHERN IRELAND

Summary

To create a coaching style of management and unleash the energy, contribution and creativity of the employee-base, BT Northern Ireland has launched a corporate change programme called 'A Better Life'. This builds on previously successful BT initiatives.

Introduction

Belfast-headquartered BT Northern Ireland is a business unit of BT plc, one of the world's premier suppliers of telecommunications services and products, ranging from residential services to sophisticated network solutions for global businesses. BT plc earns more than £15 billion in annual revenues and has about 130,000 employees.

BT Northern Ireland has about 3000 employees and for 1997 reported revenues of around £265 million.

A History of Change

To understand culture change within BT Northern Ireland it is important to place it within a story of continuous, and often dramatic, corporate change within BT.

Until the mid 1980s BT was state-owned and, as part of the old Post Office structure, a monopolistic supplier of UK telecommunication services. It was then subject to a high profile privatization (during which a significant percentage of the UK population became shareholders for the first time), after which BT was out on its own and being prepared to face, what would become fierce competition for the first time in its history.

As Lucy Woods, chief executive officer of BT Northern Ireland says, the corporate mentality at the time was very much that of the civil service:

> "Although employing some of the world's best telecommunications specialists the company was certainly not customer-focused."

Indeed her colleague, BT Northern Ireland's quality centre manager Norman McLarnon, has said, in pointing out the remarkable task BT has completed in transforming its corporate culture:[9]

> "In the early 1980s you could have any telephone you wanted as long as it

was black, because we told you what you could have... you could have your
phone installed when we told you – which could have meant a delay of weeks.
You could have your fault fixed when we wanted to do it. People forget that
we had to come out of that background to where we are today."

Taking the road to change within BT has comprised both quantum leaps in
the culture and in the corporate structure, and also a substantial downsizing
programme.

Structurally, the organization changed in the mid 1980s from 63 customer
service areas (each responsible for all customer requirements in their own
area) to 27 districts.

In 1991 these districts were replaced through a major restructuring carried
out under the banner Project Sovereign. Through this BT created three
discrete customer-facing divisions:

1. personal communications (largely residential phone users)

2. national business communications (UK businesses)

3. global communications (for multinational businesses).

Project Sovereign was followed by a voluntary redundancy programme which
reduced the BT headcount by around 100,000 from a peak of almost
250,000 at the start of the 1990s. This was achieved without any significant
industrial unrest, largely the result of a huge emphasis on retraining,
generous redundancy packages and carefully managing the emotional impact
on employees leaving BT and those remaining.

To drive customer focus through the new structure BT launched Project
Breakout in 1993, a wide-ranging examination and re-engineering of key
processes.

Throughout these structural and process changes BT employees had been
well-drilled in total quality management (TQM) tools and techniques such
as cause and effect diagrams and cross-functional teamworking.

Collectively, the above changes had, by the mid 1990s, largely transformed
the organization from a hierarchical, bureaucratic organization to one
focused on mobilizing its structural and human resources to delivering
world-class products and services to its customer base.

External Recognition

External recognition of BT's excellence has been widespread. For example,
BT corporately was a prize winner for the European Foundation for Quality
Management's (EFQM) European Quality Award in 1996 and both BT
Yellow Pages and BT Northern Ireland were prize winners in 1998. BT
Northern Ireland was a previous winner of both the UK Quality Award and
Northern Ireland Quality Awards.[10]

For the 1998 award, the EFQM assessors gave BT Northern Ireland a best-in-class score for customer satisfaction. In fact, BT Northern Ireland has consistently outperformed other BT business units on customer satisfaction measures over recent years. However, Woods says (and in doing so demonstrates a strong commitment to continuous improvement):

> "Although the EFQM best-in-class assessment was great news, we were concerned that in many cases the only relationship that our customers had with us is the bill they get and in seeing the odd engineering van. So we are being much more proactive at talking with them, for example describing new products, offering them reduced prices and slowly explaining the challenges and opportunities of the information age."

The Need for Cultural Change

Having reached such an exalted position of excellence, why was culture change felt to be so important within BT Northern Ireland? Woods explains:

> "When I became chief executive officer in 1997 I found an organization that was still largely based on a command and control style of management. The culture was traditional and based on obediently serving senior people.

> "Our people were very focused on their own jobs, worked hard, and fully understood that the customer was their number one priority.

However, despite this focus Woods explains that there was no real energy in the company, and that BT Northern Ireland's staff did not feel they had a right to an opinion or that they could take risks. Instead they did exactly what they were told to and were not expected to challenge the thinking of others, even if they knew they were right. As Woods says, "they did their work very well and then went home".

Woods' belief, though, is that in order to create an organization which is delivering supreme performance and continually raising the levels of excellence in the company, the full ability and energy of all the people must be unleashed on that company. She continues:

> "If you manage people you have two choices. First, you can tell them what to do and make sure they do it or, second, nurture them and get them involved. I prefer the latter approach. Basically if people are motivated and energized they will perform twice as well than if you tell them what to do, not to think and just do their job."

A Better Life

As a consequence of this, in 1997 a culture change programme called A Better Life was launched within BT Northern Ireland, the key goals being to:

1. Create a sense of energy/excitement within the company.

2. Build an understanding that people are fundamental to the success of the company and make a huge difference to the results.

3. Give everyone a role in, and sense of ownership of, that success.

4. Encourage considered risk taking and innovative thinking.

Explains Woods:

> "The programme is very simple. The concepts are that you encourage people to own their work area, to find what needs doing and do it. To take that considered risk, take a chance and do it. Not to ask for permission all the time but to have the courage and confidence to do the job, the right thing for the customer. Most people are fully capable to understand an esoteric statement like a 'considered risk'. And as for the aims of the programme that's about it.

> "We essentially set out to keep what was good from the past – the work ethic and customer focus – but build around these an open, enthusiastic culture; basically replacing the formal with the informal."

Woods stresses though, that however simple a concept may be, words are not enough:

> "People many still think 'so what', so you need to launch programmes to reinforce this new ethos."

And, as with most best practice organizations profiled for this Report, reinforcement started with management.

Management Workshop

Starting in November 1997, a one-day workshop was rolled-out to 300 of BT Northern Ireland's managers. The aim was to show them that a coaching, participative style of leadership is much more effective than command and control.

The managers were taken through a series of role-playing exercises that demonstrated the difference in outputs and experience from the two opposing management styles.

One exercise comprised a situation where there was one boss and a number of subordinates. This group would be given a task to complete but all directions had to come from the boss and the subordinates could not make any suggestions, as their role was to be told what they to do. So they would just stand around waiting for the boss to direct.

In another exercise, the group would be given a task and everybody was encouraged to contribute suggestions on effective task completion. Says Woods:

> "This workshop clearly demonstrated that the latter approach was much more effective and enjoyable than the first. And the managers found this to be fun and creative as well as educational."

Importantly, to start the process of dismantling the command and control mentality, this workshop was optional which was, according to Woods, almost unheard of within BT Northern Ireland. However, about 85 per cent of managers voluntarily attended the programme, although Woods senses that such a high turnout may well have been the result of the 'obedient' culture that existed at the time.

Also non-managers were trained to facilitate these workshops – another important step in dismantling the old cultural structure.

A Strategic Focus

A key goal of changing the behaviour and attitudes of senior management was that Woods wanted them to release their people to focus on operational matters while they concentrated on strategic issues. She says:

> "My senior management team would come to me every month with an armload of operational statistics because they thought I would go through them with a fine tooth-comb and check them for accuracy.

> "However, this doesn't help drive the business. If they tell me they're hitting targets I'll believe them, I can see the data any day. I didn't need them to prove it. Obviously if there was a problem we could talk it through. What I really wanted was for them to use their undoubted skills to work with me to grow the business.

> "When I asked for views on strategy they were always about operational objectives, which previously had been the correct answer. Then I'd ask 'and what else?'. This raising of their sights has proved a difficult, but in the end rewarding, challenge."

Central to this challenge is that changing the behaviours and attitudes of senior management is, she says, much more difficult than changing those of front-line people:

> "Senior management have got to where they are because they have been proficient in the previous way of running the business. So when somebody comes along and says 'you have to behave in a different way' it can be resisted. As a chief executive it's important to show the leadership team how taking a new approach to managing is beneficial to them and to the organization, and to support them in this development."

Part of this support has been the use of management consultants to work with the team on understanding today's role of senior managers and to also provide a significant amount of self help.

As an example, for the top 40 leaders a coaching scheme has been introduced. So if, for instance, one leader is outstanding at one aspect of leadership, say presentation, that person coaches his or her top team colleagues who need development in presentation skills. Says Woods:

> "This is informal and regular. It's about getting people to recognize and appreciate skills in each other and to being relaxed about learning from their colleagues.

> "I find that you can do lots of formal training, and we quite rightly do a lot of that, but some less formal and more innovative approaches have a more positive and lasting impact."

214

CEO Commitment

According to Woods, crucial to changing the behaviours of the top team, and indeed the whole organization, is the personal involvement of the chief executive officer (CEO), stating that if the CEO is not wholeheartedly behind the culture change effort then it's probably not worth starting in the first place. She explains:

> "If the CEO tells the organization that he or she wants it to behave in a certain way and then he or she doesn't make a big effort to change his or her own behaviours then people become very cynical, very quickly. Big organizations fall on this point all the time."

Be the Best

Woods also believes that too many CEOs fall down through their use of vision and value statements, being to eager to publish such missives without thinking through whether they themselves are willing to act in accordance with the words.

Although agreeing that statements of strategic intent can be powerful motivators and intrinsic to changing corporate cultures, Woods does feel that they are too often overdone:

> "You've got to define what you want to be, but visions can be overly complex and therefore meaningless. My vision for BT Northern Ireland is to 'be the best'. By which I mean the best at how you define the work. The best typist, the best engineer, the best company in Europe. So I tell my people to work to be the best, find benchmarks for this and drive performance upwards."

She adds that in the 30 seconds it takes to explain 'be the best' people can get quite excited:

> "It's clear, understandable and it's possible to make it measurable. Much better than a whole lot of management mumbo-jumbo that nobody reads or understands."

Woods also stresses that you can write a vision for your boss or write one that is compelling to your people:

> "Remember, most people come to work to do a job not with dreams of running FTSE 100 companies. Good leadership is about knowing what motivates ordinary people."

Upwards appraisal, through which leaders are assessed by their direct reports, plays an important role in ensuring that coaching-style leadership traits are demonstrated by managers at each level of the organization.

Workout Sessions

Devolving the A Better Life concept involved managers taking their own teams through 'workout' sessions. These sessions were designed by the managers themselves and included activities as wide ranging as orienteering, team away-days, office-based activities and car racing. Says Woods:

> "With the aim of building teamworking and strengthening the relationship between managers and teams, this workout was all about doing something unusually wonderful and purposeful for the day."

Woods explains that this caused a major stir in the organization because never had every single employee been taken through this type of programme:

> "Managers get team-building programmes like this all the time, whereas staff are rarely taken out of their workplace and treated like this for a day."

In addition, the company launched an initiative called 'Roots and Wings'. This, explains Woods, was about giving people the roots to grow and the wings to fly. Essentially, this is a mentoring programme where employees from any level would, for example, go to schools in underprivileged areas and talk to the children about what it is like going through maturity and going to work. And, as Woods described, "this proved a powerful development tool for our employees".

31 Days in May

Phase one of A Better Life was about teaching managers to let go and start the process of employees taking responsibility and considered risks. Phase two of the programme followed on from this by being about creativity and innovation and this was focused through a programme called '31 days in May', during which the activities were broken down into four weeks.

Weeks one and three consisted of daily 'light-hearted' challenges being set for all employees. Challenges for which the winning submissions would receive prizes. Challenges included 'name our new headquarters building', 'how many customers does BT Northern Ireland serve' and 'how many minutes of telecommunications traffic is handled by BT Northern Ireland each day'. The challenges were communicated over the company's intranet and other information systems. Says Woods:

> "Such questions really got people looking into what BT Northern Ireland does, and people would make comments like 'I had no idea we handled so much traffic'. So it really got people thinking wider than just their own job and so seeing how it connects to the bigger company picture."

Week two of the initiative was focused around the company's Balanced Scorecard. BT Northern Ireland, as with each business unit has a balanced scorecard to support BT divisional and corporate level scorecards. Essentially the scorecards are focused on objectives, measures and targets within the four performance perspectives of shareholder value, customer/key stakeholders, process excellence and organizational learning. Says Woods:

> "In week two people were asked to submit improvement suggestions for one or more of the scorecard perspectives."

Week four saw the company setting challenges for suppliers. For example, it challenged the recruitment agency Manpower to reduce the time it took to recruit a BT employee.

During the '31 days in May' programme there were about 12,000 calls from BT employees to a free 0800 number, around 15,000 website hits and each day there were about 300 competition entries. Every single suggestion received was assessed and responded to.

Throughout the month senior managers travelled all over Northern Ireland presenting prizes to competition winners. Indeed, the senior management team was challenged to present one of these prizes in an innovative way. Recalls Woods:

> "We made up a song and when the recipients arrived we sang this song.
>
> "And I picked up a teapot and poured the winners a cup of tea. This behaviour was communicated around the organization in about an hour. It was so opposite to the previous culture. Successful culture change is largely based on such symbols."

To further innovative thinking, the company has also launched creative thinking training programmes using the techniques, such as brainstorming, of management consultant Edward De Bono. Woods explains:

> "Innovation is important to us. We've been really good at stifling this in the past. A lot of the time people think about innovation in product terms. However, we're encouraging a culture in which innovation equally applies to services or processes. In fact, we want to get to the point where people see innovation in processes or service as a natural part of their job. If somebody wants to spend time redesigning a process then that's OK."

The company is also getting much more innovative in creating new revenue growth. As an example, BT Northern Ireland opened the Apollo Call Centre in Belfast in February 1998 in order to make the company more proactive and entrepreneurial in dealing with present and prospective customers.

The project to get the call centre up and running took just 90 working days. Starting with a workforce of more than 200 the company expects that Apollo will employ 750 by the end of 2000, providing call centre services from both BT and other companies.

Employee Challenges

Phase three of A Better Life was focused on team-building and again creativity and innovation were central to this part of the programme. For this a one-day workshop was held. In the morning delegates were taught the theory of teamworking. In the afternoon the team, which was cross-functional and cross-hierarchical, were set a challenge. This workshop was run in association with the charity Business-in-the-Community and was based on the UK television programme 'Challenge Annika', in which the programme's star, Annika Rice, was set a challenge to, for example, build a new children's swimming pool in a weekend. She would then have to muster the voluntary support and resources of local experts and businesses to make this happen by the deadline.

For BT Northern Ireland, the challenge teams were given an afternoon to, for example, organize and run a children's party in Londonderry. As with the television programme they would get no prior warning of the challenge, and therefore no time to prepare. They were given a budget of £50 and a mini-bus and driver and told that in four hours time a lot of children will be expecting to be entertained by the team. Says Woods:

> "The team had a task and it's time critical. And they had limited funds so they had to be imaginative. But the real power of the exercise was that people had to make decisions quickly, take considered risks and just do it. There was no time to wait around for direction."

Most BT Northern Ireland employees went through this exercise and in December 1998 alone over two man-years of community work was given by BT employees. It received a huge amount of local press coverage and other tasks included painting, gardening and preparing deliveries for Romania. Says Woods:

> "The feedback has been incredible both from the community and employees."

End of Year Stretch Targets

The next phase of A Better Life (which was happening while this case study was being prepared) focused on year-end results. On top of approved budgets and objectives, teams had to select another target which they would commit to hitting in a three month period. Woods explains the purpose of this phase:

> "It's about achieving business results and going that extra mile to achieve one more thing. It encourages a sense of urgency, a need for teamworking and the need for a mindset that says 'try it today'."

Again this phase is incentivized, with prizes including five £2500 holidays, five £500 holidays and 100 CD players.

Another example of the company's focus in congratulating employees for a job well done, was when BT Northern Ireland won the 1997 UK Quality Award it held a party for 6000 people (employees and partners) at the King's Hall in Belfast.

According to Woods, winning the Award and the celebratory event helped further the real sense of pride in achievement that is now pervasive within the organization.

CARE Survey

Pride in the company is also measured through BT's corporately mandated Communications and Attitude Research for Employees (CARE) survey.

In use since 1989, CARE asks employees up to 100 questions relating to their experience of working for BT. This is structured under the following headings.

- **Job**: measures such as motivation, level of responsibility and enjoyment.
- **Performance management**: measures the quality of the feedback each employee receives about their performance.
- **Development and training**: measures how the employees view their opportunities for skills development.
- **Reward and recognition**: considers employees' views on informal and formal recognition schemes.
- **Managers**: considers how approachable the employee feels managers are and how committed they are to BT's corporate values.
- **Communications**: how information is devolved throughout the company.
- **Working environment**: considers issues such as safety and how pleasant the working environment is.
- **Customers**: how employees feel about the quality of service provided to their customers.
- **The company**: how proud employees are to work for BT, and whether they believe the company will attain its vision.

Results against CARE provide meaningful comparisons across business units and divisions, and can easily roll-up into a corporate level employee satisfaction metric.

Also, each year every BT Northern Ireland employee receives a personal review by their boss against competencies required for their level (not just for their job). And development objectives are set to further improve the skills sets.

Moreover, employees receive an assessment (often anonymous) from six colleagues, and development programmes are also based on this feedback.

Internal Communications

As with other business leaders interviewed for this Report, Woods stresses the fundamental importance of internal communications in successfully driving forward a culture change programme. She says:

> "The aims of the programme have to be communicated over and over and over again, until you are sick of saying it. We have 3000 people. I haven't met them all yet, so I may be tired of saying the same things but they aren't tired of me saying it."

Woods adds that a lot of good plans fail to be implemented due to under-communication.

An example of an effective communication mechanism Woods uses is meeting every single manager for a meal once or twice a year. About 12 managers attend each meal and Woods attends about two dinners per month. She also conducts non-management breakfast meetings throughout

Northern Ireland where she discusses with the employee-base subjects such as improvement plans, public image, etc.

Additionally, two 'state of the nation' type conferences are held each year. And once a month Woods leads an audio-conference where she will speak for about ten minutes and then anybody can ask her live questions on any relevant subject. If she cannot provide the answer she will get the reply to them later.

The Culture Today

So how does the culture of BT Northern Ireland feel now compared to pre-change days. According to personnel director Mary Donnelly, the culture is now more open, enthusiastic, informed. She says, "everything is possible now instead of impossible". And Woods adds:

> "People now know that we want them to contribute, that we want them to share their ideas and that we want them to take responsibility.

> "Front-line people like this culture programme and approach a lot because, quite simply, they're being treated like adults.

> "When this culture change is complete – and of course it never will be as there will always be new challenges – my aim is that people will instinctively know how they contribute to the business and to customer delight. They will take personal ownership and responsibility for handling the customer. And they will take the appropriate actions to delight the customer without fear of censure."

Knowledge Management

So what are the challenges to BT Northern Ireland in the near future? According to Woods, knowledge management is one:

> "It would be brilliant if the knowledge in people's heads was available for others when they needed it. A lot of companies are working on computer databases accessed by everyone. I'm not sure if it will work as well as people hope."

One member of Woods' strategy team is presently gathering data on knowledge management and sharing that knowledge. Woods is particularly keen to develop knowledge on BT Northern Ireland's customers in order to understand their needs as individuals as opposed to seeing them just as customers. This would also fit in with the end-goal of all of BT Northern Ireland's efforts – to improve its customer service.

Conclusion

According to Woods, there are three things that a company must do to succeed with a culture change programme:

1. There must be a genuine desire to commit to change. It has to be real and it has to be consistent.

2. Leadership is of fundamental importance. Without it a positive culture change will not happen.

3. Recognition. People must be recognized for their achievements and their part in creating the new culture and for driving business results.

Key Learning Points

BT Northern Ireland is succeeding with culture change because it got a number of fundamentals right. These include:

1. The BT Northern Ireland culture change programme built on previously successful BT change initiatives. The positive aspects of previous approaches were kept intact and indeed built upon.

2. Although recognized as an exemplary organization, the company realized that it was still possible to further improve customer-facing performance, and that it was the behaviours and attitudes of its people that would take it to the next performance level.

3. The appointment of a new CEO, Lucy Woods, was central to launching and driving cultural change throughout the organization. She was, and is, totally committed to culture change and recognizes that she has to lead through example by changing her own behaviours.

4. The culture change programme started with the company's management. Woods realized that change must start at the top.

5. Managers were then tasked to find innovative ways to take their own teams through culture change workouts.

6. Use of innovative approaches, such as the 'Challenge Annika' type programme, were critical to building new approaches to teamworking.

7. A month long initiative called '31 days in May' helped get employees thinking about how they could suggest improvement opportunities and for understanding BT Northern Ireland wider than from just the perspective of their own jobs.

8. Woods recognized the importance of 'symbols' in driving cultural change.

9. Similarly Woods understood the absolute importance of internal communications.

10. Despite its successes, BT Northern Ireland is not standing still, and is actively considering its next business and cultural challenges.

CASE STUDY: SIEMENS KWU

Summary

Siemens KWU has transformed itself from a company primarily building nuclear power plants to one building fossil-based plants. In doing so it has had to learn to work in an open, global market-place rather than a closed German market, and to build employee awareness of the importance of price issues and continuous improvement within a competitive market-place.

Introduction

Headquartered in Erlangem, Germany, Siemens Power Generation Group (KWU) employs about 27,500 people and reported a turnover of DM 10.6 billion in 1998. KWU is part of the 400,000 employee-strong German headquartered Siemens group of companies, which is present in nearly all the world's countries and operates in fields that include energy, communications, healthcare, transport and lighting.

KWU's major operations are in the design, manufacture and servicing of power generation plants and components. About 80 per cent of the company's work is for fossil-based and hydro plants, with the remaining 20 per cent focused on nuclear plants. This signals a complete percentage turnaround from the end of the 1980s, when the company was primarily concerned with the nuclear market.

This transformation of business priorities was one of the two major catalysts for the company's change programme. The other was that KWU was also having to operate in an open market-place, where German companies could purchase power generation supplies from anywhere in the globe, rather than just from within Germany, and therefore Siemens.

Dr Christian Forstner, KWU's director of business excellence and co-ordinator of improvement initiatives according to the European Foundation for Quality Management (EFQM) Excellence Model, says:

> "At the end of the 1980s we had to accept that in the closed market for nuclear plants and fuel the order volume had declined rapidly especially for new plants and that we had to change rapidly to fossil-based products and services. And in many ways the business and cultural challenge in this transformation is obvious. In a closed market there is no real competition so you can concentrate on technical matters rather than price. However, in an open market price also becomes a critical issue, which takes time for employees to adapt to."

Forstner states that this would prove a challenge as the prevailing culture at the end of the 1980s was one of 'business as usual' and a sense among the employee-base that there was no need to change as the company had been continually successful during that decade. However, he says:

> "It was critical to our survival that they did change this mindset. Our markets were changing and there was enormous pressure on prices as increasing numbers of companies throughout the world were developing the requisite skills and resources to compete globally.

> "On top of this, of course, there was a major challenge in re-skilling the employee-base so that their expertise was appropriate for fossil-based technologies."

Another change was the need to learn foreign languages. As 80 per cent of KWU's business would now be outside Germany, there was a major investment in language skills, which had not been necessary when the company was mainly a German operation.

The Culture Today

According to Forstner, the culture today can be characterized as one of teamworking, learning, collaboration and continuous improvement. This belief is supported by KWU being a 1998 finalist for the prestigious European Quality Award.

However, teamwork has always been a dominant cultural trait within KWU, as Forstner explains:

> "When we were mainly a nuclear operation we were producing the most complex technical plants in the world. Nuclear power stations are actually even more complex to design than space rockets. Therefore our culture has always been focused on teamwork and collaboration. So this gave us a solid foundation to build from."

Resistance to Change

However, this is not to say there has been no resistance to change. As senior manager Dr Horst Kayser said in *Aspects of Excellence*, the European Quality Award's official publication:[11]

> "There are some people who are sceptical of change, some who welcome it and a small percentage who will never change the way they work. If you can convert the first group then they become very enthusiastic advocates and influence others. The last category may include some people who are very good at what they do but do not wish to participate in management decisions. Our organization can cope with them also, providing they are adding value. But increasingly, our group-wide culture is to see employee added value as coming from positive suggestions for process improvement. Our task is to encourage this thinking and let natural selection take its course."

And Forstner adds:

> "Some of our key engineers had been with us for 25–30 years. They had experienced the good old times when there was no need for change. Some of these people resisted change as they tended to think back to the glorious, and easy, days. So communication and constant reinforcement of the need for change and how they and the company would benefit was pivotal to getting these people to buy into change."

Vision and Mission Statements

Important elements of this constant reinforcement are KWU's vision and mission statements. Its vision has the simple heading 'power for generations', which, says Forstner, not only explains what the company does but also that it intends to be in business for a long time, serving successive generations of people and customers.

The vision is further explained through four subheadings:

1. We ensure a supply of electricity from environmentally friendly power plants worldwide and at reasonable prices.

2. We offer our customers optimal solutions as a partner of choice.

3. We influence the market through innovative products and business approaches.

4. We are successful in competition through openness, creativity and dedication.

Each of these subheadings is further broken down into supporting statements. For example, subheading four is made up of:

- We trust each other and are open to new ideas.

- Each of us acts in the interest of the company, oriented towards vision and corporate strategy, thereby ensuring just returns.

- We handle regional attitudes with respect and understanding and act accordingly.

This vision is supported by KWU's mission, which is:

> 'Our main goal is to become the *most competitive company* in our business by being the *most flexible and most responsive company*, a company in which every employee serves the customer best.

> 'We strive to provide all of our customers with products and services of the highest quality. Quality is achieved through processes which involve each and every employee in one function or another. We will optimize our costs, boost productivity and offer our customers the best possible services by *mastering and continuously improving our processes.*

> 'We will enter new markets and gain new satisfied customers in the nuclear sector and other KWU fields of activity. *We will continue to aggressively and relentlessly pursue current improvement projects.*'

Economic Value Added (EVA)

Critical to transforming the KWU culture into one that understands the importance of making money has been the use of Economic Value Added (EVA)[12] as both a financial measure and the end-goal of continuous improvement projects. Forstner explains why EVA was seen as so important:

> "These days all of the companies operating in our markets can offer high quality products and services, so price becomes a key competitive differentiator. And this leads to real pressure on profit margins, so we needed a mechanism for ensuring good profitability.

> "And EVA is really a simple idea with a straightforward equation. Therefore it's a valuable way to understand the contribution made to profitability by each level of the organization."

To devolve the EVA message deep within the organization, high ranking business leaders made a series of short presentations during 1998, explaining what EVA is and why it was important to the company. As an incentive, any employee who attended a presentation was eligible to enter a prize draw, for which the winner received a new car.

A further incentive for developing an EVA mindset is remuneration. During the 1999/2000 financial year, the pay of the top 500 managers of Siemens is substantially tied to EVA targets, making up 60 per cent of their annual income, excluding additional stock options. This is being broadened to include lower level managers for the following financial year, although the percentage of tied income will decrease depending on the level of the manager.

EVA objectives are also built into the company's target agreement process (see the Policy Deployment section below), therefore EVA goals are broken down to function, team and individual levels.

The Business Excellence Model

According to Forstner, an important mechanism for driving continuous EVA improvement is the European Quality Award feedback report (received by companies selected for site visits as part of the Award process):

> "Our last assessment said that we could still do more to drive up EVA, which is an element of the Award's business results criteria. Employees take seriously this external feedback, so the assessment process and feedback has proved a powerful way to communicate the importance of EVA targets."

Importantly, therefore, improving EVA is seen as the key outcome of performance against the EFQM Business Excellence Framework (on which the European Quality Award is based). The framework measures performance against nine criteria elements split into the two specific areas of 'enablers' and 'results', each carrying a 50 per cent points allocation. The enablers are leadership, people management, policy and strategy, resources, and processes. The results criteria are people satisfaction, customer satisfaction, impact on society and business results (see Figure 6.5).

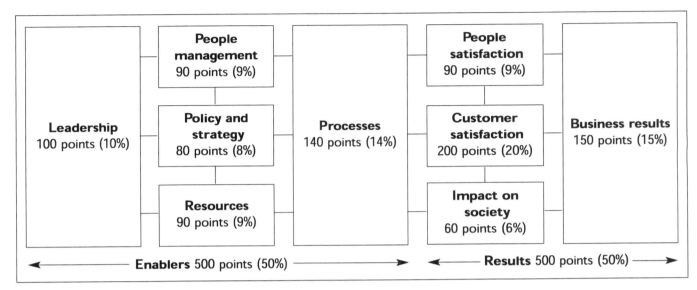

Figure 6.5: EFQM Model for Business Excellence

Within KWU the business excellence model and EVA principles are seen as working in unison to provide an overview of short-term and longer-term performance dimensions. Said KWU president Adolf Hüttl:[13]

> "I'm fully convinced that only the holistic approach of the excellence model based on self-assessment together with EVA-oriented thinking and action will bring a company into the European top group and assist it to stay at a high level of business excellence."

KWU has been using the business excellence model since 1994, and this was a natural development from the systematic implementation of total quality management tools and techniques, which had been mandated group-wide in 1991.

Importantly, how the framework is managed and devolved within KWU ensures that it remains a key focus company-wide. First, the president Adolf Hüttl is totally committed to the process. Second, each of the nine criteria areas is sponsored by a senior manager, who takes on responsibility for their criteria area in addition to their everyday work. And each main sponsor has supporting management sponsors within the nine KWU divisions, so there's a matrix of about 100 top managers with business excellence responsibilities.

Moreover, quality management people support deployment in the different business areas, and more than 250 improvement teams work in their assigned areas. Regular meetings are held to discuss results and problems, and new opportunities are examined from the context of business results, and therefore against the key EVA measures.

Interestingly, as Forstner explains, the business excellence framework was not, as is often the case, piloted within a local business unit before being rolled-out company-wide:

> "The president believed that the chances of success would be improved if all the management board and divisional leaders were totally committed and focused on improvement from the start. He said 'let's go for it and get the whole organization on the cultural path that will lead to business excellence'."

Forstner adds that absolute support from the top creates an enormous pressure on all employees to buy into the continuous improvement ethos of the framework. Indeed the president has said that all improvement programmes have to be aligned to the EFQM framework. Forstner explains:

> "KWU is one of 16 groups within Siemens. And every year five or six major improvement objectives are deployed Siemens-wide. So by tying them to the EFQM framework employees can see why these initiatives make sense and so more readily buy-in to the programmes. And improvement initiatives normally involve a cross-section of people from different levels in the organization, thus improving teamwork and collaboration.
>
> "Also, say the improvement is around customer satisfaction, then the manager in charge of that EFQM criteria takes responsibility for its alignment and devolution."

Policy Deployment

Devolution of key business excellence results areas is also facilitated through the company's policy deployment process. Detailed in the company's 'blue book', policy deployment is a process first used by the total quality exemplar, the Xerox Corporation. Within KWU each employee is given a folder that includes the company's vision and mission, the division and sub-divisions mission and strategy and the mission for the sector, department and team.

Objectives and priorities at each level are assigned for the four EFQM results areas of customer satisfaction, people satisfaction, impact on society and business results. Targets and benchmarks are assigned for each criteria. Importantly, each target has an EVA component and people are shown how to look at their work from an EVA perspective, thus keeping the organizational focus on driving up EVA. The outline is shown in Table 6.2.

The blue book also includes each employee's personal target agreements with his or her leader. Therefore, each employee can see how their work links to the company vision and strategy, thus creating a direct line of sight from employee to board-level targets.

Leadership

Successful deployment is also enabled through the company's absolute focus on proactive and demonstrable leadership practices, which has also been a critical principle of KWU's change process. Indeed leadership is the first enabler criteria within the European Business Excellence Model and internal KWU documentation states that:

This is what we in .... want to achieve		
Customer satisfaction	Parameter/Target	Benchmark
•	•	•
•	•	•
•	•	•
•	•	•
•	•	•
•	•	•
•	•	•
•	•	•
People satisfaction	Parameter/Target	Benchmark
•	•	•
•	•	•
•	•	•
•	•	•
•	•	•
•	•	•
•	•	•
•	•	•
Impact on society/image	Parameter/Target	Benchmark
•	•	•
•	•	•
•	•	•
•	•	•
•	•	•
•	•	•
•	•	•
Business results/market share	Parameter/Target	Benchmark
•	•	•
•	•	•
•	•	•
•	•	•
•	•	•
•	•	•
•	•	•

Table 6.2: Organizational Outline

'Our company is built on a foundation of good leadership We demand and promote good leadership. Ultimately, our success is dependent on the extent that we integrate good leadership into our vision for KWU.'

The company also mandates that:

'All leaders must act as role models. Therefore our leaders must:

1. Discuss mistakes openly, including their own.

2. Acknowledge excellent employee performance promptly.

3. Promote the establishment and improvement of relations with internal and external suppliers.'

Leadership Appraisal

Key to discussing their own mistakes openly, and indeed identifying improvement opportunities, is KWU's annual, and compulsory, upwards feedback process called 'Leadership Appraisal for Employees'.

For this each leader, at whichever level in the organization, has to self-analyse performance against a range of questions, measured on a 1 to 5 scale, in areas such as customer orientation, team leadership skills, team-building, analytical skills and process control. Says Forstner:

"The leader's direct reports also fill in the same questionnaire, also detailing performance on a 1 to 5 scale.

"An employee representative then collects the employees' questionnaires and compares the answers with those provided by the leader. The representative then arranges and facilitates a discussion between the leader and reports where the questionnaire findings are openly discussed."

Based on the employee feedback, the leader has to agree improvement objectives for the following year. And completion of these goals are measured in the next appraisal process.

Forstner stresses, however, that it is critical that from this feedback that the leaders' focus on three or four key improvement objectives:

"It is possible that say 15 or 20 improvement opportunities are highlighted. This will be too much to manage in a one-year period, so it's important to focus on those which will deliver the greatest benefit to the individual, team and company, while not ignoring the other improving suggestions."

Forstner says that when the company first introduced this appraisal system some employees were hesitant about being honest in their upwards assessment, because they were not sure whether they could openly criticise leaders. Therefore the survey is anonymous.

Importantly, the leaders' boss does not get to see the full survey results but does get a summary. Therefore, if a leader gets poor assessments for several years running then this will be focused on in an interview between the leader and his or her boss. Says Forstner:

"The possibility of effectively succeeding with change is much higher if the change comes from the leader based on his or her people's views rather than imposed top-down."

Failure Forgiveness

An important leadership principle within KWU is 'failure forgiveness'. As Forstner explained in *Aspects of Excellence*:[14]

"One of the central points of traditional quality management is 100 per cent conformance. This runs counter to natural laws of physics.... It is more sensible to allow for forgiveness in systems. Of course, the goal is 100 per cent, but demanding this in fluid situations is simply counter-productive. For example, in certain nuclear plants when you replace fuel rods there is a danger that a foreign body can fall in if procedures are not adhered to. One of our workers lost his dentures this way but was too scared to report the incident. While not physically dangerous, the damage was massive financially and in terms of time because we were aware of a problem but could not pinpoint the cause. If the system had allowed him the freedom to admit the error, it would have been infinitely less costly."

Employee Opinion Survey

To help create and measure a culture conducive to continuous improvement, KWU introduced an employee opinion survey in 1994. Employees are asked to rate on a scale of 1 to 5 around 150 questions such as 'the effectiveness of communication', 'contentment with remuneration systems', 'opportunities for career progression' and, importantly, 'progress against improvement action plans that followed the previous survey'.

Forstner stresses that such a survey is pointless unless the loop is closed and identified improvements are indeed acted upon. For this reason, employee surveys may not be conducted each year if improvements will take more than a year to implement.

KWU's most recent employee satisfaction survey showed a response rate of 67 per cent. To boost response, board members and top executives stood at the factory and headquarters gates together with representatives of the workers' council motivating employees to fill out their questionnaires.

Customer Opinion Surveys

KWU has also introduced customer opinion surveys which ask questions such as the customer's willingness to recommend KWU to other companies, the customer's intention to continue the business relationship with KWU and satisfaction with marketing and project management.

The company also tracks customer satisfaction through a scorecard that measures performance against the key success factors of quality, reliability and delivery.

Using a methodology designed by the German-based Institute of Infratest, KWU uses client surveys to identify high leverage customer-facing improvement opportunities.

Again closing the loop is crucial here. Improvement action plans are created and the customer asked to rate the improvement through the next survey.

KWU is also building win-win relationships with customers through launching joint improvement programmes. Specifically, the company is working with several customers on business excellence best practice initiatives.

An interesting way KWU focused on delivering value to its customers is the use of a tool, similar to a parking meter, which calculates the cost of time spent in meetings. Consequently, the cost the customer would have to pay for that meeting is made visible. The cost of such as tool is less than €2.00.

Internal Communications

As with all companies profiled for this Report, KWU has recognized the pivotal importance of internal communications. For example, the company organizes what it calls 'Monte Carlo round tables'. Through this, a high ranking leader, normally at board level or just below, selects randomly about 20 people and invites them to a round table discussion.

This discussion has no agenda so employees are free to speak openly about how they see the company progressing and any problems they are facing. The meetings are confidential and according to Forstner this is proving a powerful way to connect senior management with the concerns of the shop floor.

The company also held a major communications event called the 'KWU day' on 20 June, 1998. Forstner, who was in charge of its organization, says:

> "This was a day to celebrate our achievements and discuss our future plans. This was held on a Saturday and out of 16,000 people in Germany 10,200 attended. We hired four of the biggest conference centres in Germany and used the Newcastle, UK, plant's parking lot. These centres were connected by ISDN and our board was spread out between the sites."

According to Forstner, the day started with a presentation from the board followed by a live discussion with employees based on questions selected on-line. The event also included a live discussion with KWU's customers:

> "These were board level customers, so it helped further the culture of open communications. Everybody could hear what the customer thought we were good at and where we could improve."

Forstner believes that the event was a powerful learning experience, and at the end of it the employees were asked what they had learnt and were encouraged to create improvement action plans to take back to the workplace. He stresses, "that direct communication from the top is key and is much more powerful than a communication cascade".

Acquisitions

Communication is becoming more important as KWU grows through acquisition, recently purchasing the Newcastle-based Parsons UK Power Generation division from Rolls Royce and acquiring Westinghouse's business with fossil-fired power plants from CBS in the USA. As a result Siemens KWU is now one of the world's leading power plant suppliers. Says Forstner:

> "We are dealing with a lot of communication issues and are working hard to find out more about the people in these sites, how they feel and how we can integrate them into the KWU company.

> "Culture awareness is a big issue and you have to understand the different national cultures. With Westinghouse we have integration teams for management and services integration and also a change management team, of which I am a member.

> "However, we have found that when we put together a mixed team of German and US employees the language or cultural problems are not a big issue. What people need and respond to is a clear vision of what they are doing and clear goals and targets. We are finding it is better to focus on vision and targets and then sort out any cultural differences. And I must say that so far sorting out cultural differences has been relatively easy."

Forstner also stresses that it is KWU's intention that the employees from Parsons and Westinghouse will benefit from all the tools that KWU uses in order to develop the same sort of results oriented culture. But he warns:

> "We have to be careful in rolling-out the tools. You can't launch the employee opinion survey, EFQM model, leadership appraisal, policy deployment, EVA, etc, all in the same year, it would be too much. We have to adapt tools and integrate them rather slowly."

Conclusion

According to Forstner, the three things that company must do right to succeed with a change programme are:

- Total commitment from all top leaders.
- Personal involvement of all top managers in communication to all levels all the time.
- Deploying policy in an efficient and systematic way – "the blue book is for everybody".

Forstner believes that, as all the improvements from the business excellence and EVA focuses start to filter through to the bottom line, the company should see a dramatic improvement in EVA and therefore its share price.

Key Learning Points

1. Organizational and cultural change within Siemens KWU was to support a clear change in corporate strategy. To change market priorities from the nuclear to fossil-based industries and to succeed in an open rather than closed market-place.

2. Devolvable vision and mission statements clearly detail the company's strategic intent.

3. EVA has been a key tool in creating a profit-focused mindset within the employee-base.

4. Similarly, the EFQM business excellence framework has been key to driving business and EVA improvement.

5. Policy deployment ensures a clear line-of-sight from employee activities to group goals and strategies.

6. Siemens KWU recognizes the absolute importance of leadership in creating an open climate focused on continuous improvement. Upwards appraisal is central to driving the correct leadership behaviours.

7. The organization uses both employee and customer opinion surveys to track cultural and business progress.

8. Internal communications has been an important component of driving change. And communication directly from the top is seen as a more powerful mechanism than a communication cascade.

9. The company is being careful to control the speed by which it rolls out continuous improvement tools to recently acquired firms.

7

ALIGNING HUMAN RESOURCES MANAGEMENT WITH CORPORATE CULTURE

Executive Summary

1. Aligning Human Resource (HR) practices with cultural goals is crucial for succeeding with a change effort; this belief is promulgated by all commentators interviewed for this Report.

2. When changing HR practices, organizations must address the legitimate employee concern 'what's in it for me'.

3. The HR function can play an enabling role in driving corporate change. However the function must be business- and customer-focused.

4. Linked to the above, research has found that devolving responsibility for the corporate culture to the HR function does not often lead to success with a culture change effort.

5. Research by Harvard Business School has also found that companies that value their employees perform significantly better than those who do not. However, another piece of research has found that companies are not presently meeting employee needs.

6. How to create culturally reinforcing practices in recruitment, performance appraisal, career development, recognition and incentives, and compensation mechanisms are explored in detail – and each area contains its own challenges.

7. Linked to the above, HR practices should reinforce each other as well as the new culture.

8. A case study on Hyundai Car (UK) Ltd, demonstrates best practice, along with case reports on Western Provident Association, Transco and Yorkshire Water.

Section A: Context

Human resource (HR) policies and procedures represent much of the formal levers of behaviour that must be aligned to the new cultural ethos. Quite simply how people are recruited, appraised, recognized, developed, promoted and compensated will prove a significant factor in shaping how they behave within the organization.

Any culture change effort that ignores these behavioural levers will almost certainly fail to take hold within the organization. After all, most people will naturally heighten and hone the attitudes and behaviours that are likely to make them successful. So, for example, if senior management proclaims that it wants its salespeople to develop strong customer relationship skills but then only measures, recognizes and compensates on revenue rates, then revenue will be what counts to the salespeople.

Aligning HR policies with new cultural goals was seen as absolutely critical by every adviser and practitioner interviewed for this Report. As an example, Dr George Labovitz, chairman of the US-headquartered performance measurement and change consultancy Organizational Dynamics Inc (ODI), comments:

> "It's fundamental. If you don't align career development, remuneration and promotion, for example, with what you want the culture to be then you're theory espoused. The culture change you will get you almost certainly won't like, as people recognize the hypocrisy of theory espoused versus theory practised."

Interestingly, Labovitz relates that he spoke to the HR heads of Federal Express, Xerox and Motorola shortly after each had won the prestigious and annual US-based Malcolm Baldrige National Quality Award (which assesses performance in five main areas: customer satisfaction, financial and market results, human resources, suppliers and partners, and organization-specific). He recalls that they all regretted that when moving their organizations towards a total quality culture, they did not focus on aligning their performance management systems earlier than they did. They all stated, according to Labovitz, that they would have created the intended culture much quicker if they had.

According to Labovitz, aligning HR policies and procedures with cultural goals is a hard-soft dynamic. He says:

> "The hard stuff are the HR systems, policies and procedures and performance measurement. The soft part are the values, strategic direction etc. If you can successfully align hard and soft you'll get cultural change."

What's In It For Me?

Tellingly, a number of commentators interviewed for this Report stated that too often in a culture change programme the legitimate employee question 'what's in it for me?' is not addressed. As Luca Mortara, managing director of ASI (UK), states:

"When in the acceptance stage of any change effort, employees need to see something matching their own goals and aspirations."

Therefore this Chapter will analyse how advisers believe companies should align HR practices with cultural goals, and it will show how exemplary companies demonstrate this alignment in practice. The Chapter will consider changes to:

1. Recruitment practices.

2. Appraisal mechanisms.

3. Career development and Training.

4. Recognition and Incentives.

5. Compensation.

Section B: The Role of the HR Function

The HR function itself has a role in driving culture change. However, as research later in this Chapter will suggest, giving overall responsibility for culture change to the HR function does not often lead to a successful change outcome. Of course, organizations must have effective HR methodologies to succeed with culture change, but do companies actually need a HR function for this purpose? Julian Stainton, chief executive officer of the Bristol, UK-based specialist health insurer Western Provident Association (WPA), is remarkably candid in his scathing views on the function. He says:

"You have to dismantle the HR Function. They tend to get involved with things that are nothing to do with them, while at the same time washing their hands of any responsibility for serving customers. What inevitably happens in human resources departments is that over a period of time they control the agenda. Not in what goes into the agenda but what is released from it."

Within WPA there are just two people in personnel-type roles. Responsibility for all other aspects of HR, such as training, recruitment, etc, is fully devolved to the people who run the business units and who serve the customers. Details of WPA's approach to culture change can be found later in this Chapter and in Chapter 4.

At Hyundai Car (UK) Ltd, the case study to accompany this Chapter, a converse approach to HR was taken. On the appointment of Sue Stoneman as HR director, she was the only full-time HR person; today there is a 12-strong team. A key reason for this transformation was that a key strategic thrust of the company was to mobilize human resources within both the organization itself and its dealer network. Therefore, a well-staffed HR function was seen as vital in driving this strategy network-wide. For example, it would not have been possible, the company believed, to devolve HR responsibility directly to individual franchisees as they did not have the resources or expertise to drive this change forward, let alone create a unified approach throughout the network. Indeed, providing this support from the centre was seen as an added-value service by the franchisee network.

The HR function has also played a pivotal role in driving cultural change within other case study companies. At Continental Airlines, senior HR staff played a key role in enabling change and, as shall be shown later, oversaw some innovative HR approaches. At DSM Resins, the HR function was central in supporting business units develop staff in accordance with the new cultural behaviours. At Millennium Chemicals Inc, the HR function has created a 'people policy' which directly supports the strategic goals of the organization.

Being Customer-focused

What these HR functions have in common is that they have clearly become customer-focused. In essence, by focusing on meeting the HR needs of 'internal' customers they are helping focus organizational attention onto the requirements of external customers. Rather than build empires for the sake of it, these exemplary HR functions have focused on enabling the development of employee capabilities that support the change objectives.

Hyundai Car (UK) Ltd's Stoneman explains why focusing *internally* will lead directly to improvements from the external customer perspective:

> "I believe that a lot of companies fail with customer improvement programmes because they do a lot of tactical things around customer service but forget about mobilizing their employees behind this service goal. They then wonder why the initiatives don't work. If you don't get employees to be passionate, you're whistling in the wind."

At Continental Airlines, the case study to support Chapter 1, HR itself has been transformed as part of the change effort. As explained by Michelle Meissner, the company's director of human resource development:

> "In 1994 HR was transactional in nature. Our main job was answering telephone calls, resolving employee complaints around travel abuse, and acting as the police for the corporation. HR was not adding value to the corporation."

Today, however, she says the function plays a central role in identifying and rolling-out HR best practices. Important here has been that much of HR's services are now owned and delivered by line management. As Rob Benson, pilot captain and former senior director, field services, human resources, says:

> "We believe strongly in the leader-teach role. We've done this, not through a complex manual but through a small booklet. Sections within include; filling vacancies, paying employees, creating a winning environment, maximizing performance, handling employee leave and managing progressive discipline.

> "Supervisors no longer need to come to HR and ask how to do things."

So, it is safe to say that the HR function can play an enabling role in driving culture change, but should not lead the change effort, which has to be the responsibility of senior management. However, to be effective, the function must look closely at the value it delivers to the organization and how it itself supports the strategy and new cultural ethos of the organization. If it does not, the function, as with other functions such as IT, may well prove more of a hindrance than a help. (Readers who wish to know more about how HR can be altered as part of a change effort may wish to read the Business Intelligence Report, *Transforming HR to Support Corporate Change*.)[1]

Section C: Research Findings

'Culture and Change Management' Survey Findings

'Culture and Change Management',[2] a 1998 research survey by Business Intelligence of 236, mainly large, organizations from Europe, USA and the Rest of the World (commissioned exclusively for this Report, the results of which are analysed in detail in Chapter 3) found that new roles and responsibilities was the top ranked mechanism out of six choices for bringing about change in the way the organization operates and performs.

On this list the bottom two mechanisms in order of importance were 'retraining' at fifth, with a mean score of importance of 4.02 (on a scale of 1 to 5, with 1 being the most important) and 'reward system redesign' at sixth, with a mean score of 4.12.

Interestingly, within companies who claimed to have 'extremely well defined' cultures, 'retraining' climbed just one place to fourth (with a mean score of 3.96), and 'reward system redesign' also achieved just a one place jump to fifth (with a mean score of 3.92).

The survey also found that almost 60 per cent of companies stated that it had attempted to change their corporate culture. Taking that 60 per cent as a 100 per cent, 57.47 per cent stated that an action taken had included 'redesign of reward systems'. In importance this action was ranked fifth out of seven (the top ranked being 'development of new organizational structures' at 81.03 per cent). Seventh placed, at 52.87 per cent was 'the introduction of new skills'.

So it would appear from this study that the HR practices of retraining and reward system redesign are not high on the list of priorities of organizations undergoing cultural change. This seems somewhat contrary to the views of advisers for this Report.

Tellingly, the Business Intelligence research also revealed that in 19.54 per cent of companies the HR function held responsibility for the corporate culture. However, in organizations with 'extremely well defined' cultures this fell to 12 per cent, but ballooned dramatically to 50 per cent in companies with 'very poorly defined' cultures.

Given the fact that this research found that companies with 'extremely well defined' cultures are substantially more likely than those with 'very poorly defined' cultures to achieve the intended results of a change efforts, this gives some credence to the statement in Chapter 4 that it is the top team who should be the guardians of corporate culture and not any specific function.

Harvard Research

A usual reason for changing HR practices in companies, and especially true in culture change efforts, is to create a greater sense within the employee-base of being valued. The belief being, of course, that employees who feel valued will perform better.

In their seminal 1992 work, *Corporate Culture and Performance*,[3] the Harvard Business School professors John Kotter and James Heskett found a correlation between companies valuing employees and business success. From an original study of 207 companies, the authors chose 22 who they classified as having strong cultures. Based on relative economic performance from 1977 to 1988, 12 of these were further defined as being higher performing and the remaining ten as lower performing. The authors asked industry analysts a series of questions about the sample of 22 related to each company's culture which the interviewees had to rate on a score from 1 (definitely not) to 7 (absolutely yes).

To the question 'how highly does [a specified organization] value its employees', the 12 better performing firms averaged a score of 5.8, with the very lowest score given as 4.8. The lower performers averaged 4.1 and only two of these firms scored higher than 4.8.

More on the Kotter and Heskett research findings can be found in Chapters 2 and 4.

The Global Needs of Employees

An interesting piece of international research about the workplace needs of employees was conducted in 1998 by the US-headquartered Yankelovich Partners and commissioned by the global consultancy Gemini Consulting.[4]

The study surveyed 10,339 workers in 13 nations, including ten European countries, Russia, the United States, and Japan. Somewhat surprisingly, and of real interest to organizations rolling-out global change efforts, employees, from whichever nation, consistently identified the same top five key attributes in a job. Although the order of importance varied slightly. These were:

* ability to balance work and personal life
* work that is truly enjoyable
* security for the future
* good pay or salary
* enjoyable co-workers.

Specifically, workers emphasized the importance of advancement potential and the opportunity to build skills as a way to maintain employability and job security.

Although more than one-third of workers would leave their current jobs for a 10 per cent salary increase or flexible work hours, nearly half of the workforce (44 per cent) – including workers who said they enjoy their current jobs – would leave their positions tomorrow for more potential for advancement.

Further analysis of responderts' comments showed sizeable gaps between what workers say they want and what they say they are getting from current jobs. Among the largest gaps are in the areas of providing good pay or salary, the ability to balance work and personal life, and the feeling that they are secure in the future – the attributes that workers said they value most.

Additionally, just 27 per cent of all workers feel their employers are preparing them for a good future. Says Gemini Consulting principal Jayne Buxton:

> "The study showed us that workers feel employers are not meeting core needs. In an economy where knowledge, information and the quality of workers are vital to competitive advantage, this failure to meet employees' needs could represent a threat to competitiveness itself.

> "Those employers that re-examine traditional workplace models especially in terms of time, opportunities and incentives and build a truly two-way employment contract will be the ones with the best chance to thrive today and in the future."

Case Study Examples

Many of the best practice companies profiled for this Report are clearly making significant strides in making employees feel valued. For example, Millennium Inorganic Chemicals, the case study to accompany Chapter 3, has a People Policy (formulated by its parent company Millennium Chemicals) which sets out how to achieve Millennium Inorganic's key strategic guideline to 'invest in our people to realize their full potential'. The People Policy states that:

> 'We will enable our people to excel by:
>
> - creating a safe, innovative work environment, which responds to human needs for support at the workplace and at home
>
> - designing and delivering competitive compensation and people support programmes
>
> - meeting strategic business needs for knowledge and skills and our people's needs for growth, mobility and team-building
>
> - communicating openly to promote respect and trust
>
> - building an increasingly productive, multi-cultural and diverse work-force
>
> - developing fair and consistent human resource policies and services
>
> - sharing responsibility for people management between all Millennium managers and human resources.'

To make the people policy meaningful in the workplace, Millennium is, during 1999, launching both HR and line management sponsored initiatives.

Similarly, Continental Airlines realized that to build sustainable success required people to be a significant part of its strategic Go Forward Plan. As Michelle Meissner, director of Human Resource Development, says:

"We have found, as other research has, that external customer satisfaction correlates almost exactly with internal employee satisfaction. Therefore to deliver a winning strategy in the eyes of our customers means we have to develop our people."

Mutually Reinforcing Practices

It is interesting to look at how discrete human resource practices can be changed to be aligned with new cultural goals. However, as an overview to this, Philip Sadler, chairman of the UK-based Centre for Tomorrow's Company, makes a valuable observation:

"Alignment means not only aligning the HR policies with the cultural goals but making sure the various elements of the HR policies are naturally reinforcing and providing a total system.

"Very successful companies tend to have the same bundle of HR practices. The mistake is to cherry pick. It is the total package that makes the difference."

This point about ensuring that HR practices are mutually reinforcing was made by a number of the advisers interviewed for this Report.

Section D: Recruitment

Recruitment is a valuable starting place as, the research finds, exposure to an organization's culture happens as soon as a new employee walks through the door. Organizations can go a long way to ensuring that employees have the requisite behavioural traits for the new culture during the recruitment process itself.

Case Report: Western Provident Association

Julian Stainton, chief executive officer of Western Provident Association is a firm believer in the efficacy of effective recruitment practices, being certain that unless you have the right people you will not succeed with the business, and that finding the right people starts at the recruitment stage. He says:

"What we look for in our staff is attitude, attitude, attitude. We need people who are obsessed with the quality of service. And this comes from the heart and not from any text-book. So when we recruit we look for people who are enthusiastic, people-focused and who naturally emanate our service ethic."

The right stuff

According to Stainton you can tell in 90 seconds whether an applicant has the 'right stuff'. Once the people with 'the right stuff' are recruited, they are further imbued with the absolutely critical importance of the service ethic on day one. This is explained by Adrian Schuler, WPA's director of best practices:

> "One thing we do with inductees on their first day is to give them some money and send them to a large retail establishment and ask them to buy something or to ask for advice. On their return, we get them to tell us about their experiences. The customer service at this particular store is lousy and the inductees tell us this. So we say 'that's how you're not to do it'. So what we're doing on day one in getting the customer service ethos right up front with new recruits."

Julian Stainton also makes the interesting observation that too many organizations believe it is a judicious practice to minimize what people are paid. However, he states that this then makes it much more difficult to recruit people of calibre. He says that 'low pay' will also add to creating a total picture in the minds of potential applicants of a company that's not worth joining. He says:

> "When I joined the company we would advertise for one or two vacancies, for which we would receive one or two replies, which would translate into one or two appointments. However, when working for WPA became seen as an excellent personal investment, the response rates to advertisements went up spectacularly."

Case Study Examples

Restructuring the recruitment process was also fundamentally important at Continental Airlines. Michelle Meissner recalls a time when securing employment within the company was essentially through a pre-employment test called 'fogging the mirror'. She says:

> "If you could breathe and fog the mirror you were eligible for a job at Continental."

Now, however, the recruitment process is completely different. As with WPA, this had a lot to do with the fact that Continental Airlines is now rightly perceived as a winning company, whereas previously it was an organization that many employees were ashamed to say they worked for. Says Meissner:

> "We now look for a motivational fit, meaning people who enjoy team-working, are willing to treat everyone with dignity and respect, can grow in their position, can add new ability to the organization and are imbued with a service ethic.

> "We believe strongly that employing the right people with the right attitude who enjoy working for the organization will lead to customer satisfaction, which directly leads to revenue growth and profitability."

Developing the right attitude, or right stuff, is also critically important at Superdrug, a case study to support Chapter 5. As part of the interview process, applicants have to go into the stores and find out about the company's mission, brands, and products. Says the company's head of total quality Peter Raine:

"As a key staff competency is about approaching customers and being friendly as they do this, then it is sensible to include that in the recruitment programme. And it also means that the store team, who interviewees approach with questions, get involved in the selection of future colleagues."

At Hyundai Car (UK) Ltd, changing recruitment also plays a key role in ensuring a fit between the culture and the people. For example, take the organization's customer service staff. Historically, a new recruit would be chosen from a selection of candidates forwarded by an agency. The applicants would then receive a traditional face-to-face interview.

However, knowing that these employees will spend most of their time dealing with customers over the telephone, candidates are now first subjected to a ten minute telephone 'chat' to get a feel for how their personalities come across on the telephone and so how they were likely to interact with customers.

Following this initial screening process, candidates then go through a full day assessment. This includes structured interviews, two letter writing exercises (an important customer-facing competence), customer service profiling and measurement against brand values.

Recruit passion

Hyundai Car (UK) Ltd's director of customer satisfaction, Sue Stoneman, is particularly inspired by a quote by the US-based management guru Tom Peters:

"Recruit passion, hire passion, protect passion and promote passion. I'll trade you an ounce of passion for a page of vision and a pound of business plans any day, especially tomorrow."

What comes across strongly from the above examples is that changing recruitment practices can prove a powerful lever for creating lasting culture change. If culturally aligned people are first recruited, then developed and promoted, people with the 'right stuff' will soon populate the various levels within the organization. If managed correctly this will, in time, lead to the withering of insidious cultural characteristics that may lurk, causing untold damage, within the company.

Section E: Performance Appraisal

Another critical area of HR focus that must be aligned with the new cultural goals is performance appraisal. Quite simply espousing the importance of one set of attributes and behaviours and appraising another will at best create a confused culture and a worst, and more likely, create a culture focused on the 'really important' values, ie, the ones appraised against (especially if appraisals, as is often the case, are tied to compensation mechanisms). Therefore, organizations should not underestimate the importance of appraisal, and any changes to the appraisal system should apply to each level of the organization, including the most senior.

measures are directly linked to strategic measures identified through, for example, a Balanced Scorecard. When so aligned they can prove a powerful technique for clearly prioritizing the actions of employees and for ensuring a behavioural congruence. Indeed some forward-thinking companies such as the US-based insurer The UNUM Corporation, Whirlpool Europe and BP Chemicals use personal scorecards for each individual employee thus creating a line of sight from employee goals to strategic goals.[5] An example of a personal scorecard, which includes team and corporate targets, is shown in Figure 7.1.[6]

Corporate Objectives
- Double our corporate value in seven years
- Increase our earnings by an average of 20% per year
- Achieve an internal rate-of-return 2% above the cost of capital
- Increase both production and reserves by 20% in the next decade

Corporate Targets*			Scorecard Measures	Businesss Unit Targets			Team/Individual Objectives and Initiatives
1997	1998	1999		1997	1998	1999	
160	180	250	Earnings (in millions of dollars)				1.
200	210	225	Net cash flow				
80	80	70	Overhead and operating expenses				
73	73	64	Production costs per barrel				2.
93	93	82	Development costs per barrel				
108	108	110	Total annual production				
Team/Individual Measures				**Targets**			3.
1.							
2.							
3.							4.
4.							
5.							
Name							5.
Location							
* 1995 level = 100							

(left margin label: Operating Financial)

Figure 7.1: The Personal Scorecard

In concluding this section it is safe to say that, as with employee or customer surveys (see Chapter 5 for further information on these), appraisal findings will only be useful if they lead to measurable performance improvement actions. Appraising once a year because an organization thinks it has to and then doing nothing until the following year is normally a waste of time and effort, with the usual output being employee discontent.

Section F: Career Development

Career development is a further area that needs to be aligned with the new cultural ethos. Indeed career development, and the process for internal promotion, often means changing formal processes by understanding the informal 'unwritten rules of the game' (which are dealt with in more detail in Chapter 5).

Within his book, *The Unwritten Rules of the Game*,[7] consultant Peter Scott-Morgan explains that when a written rule says, 'to become a top manager you need broad experience', the unwritten counterpart may be, 'job hop as fast as possible'. Where the written rule says, 'the best performing managers get accelerated promotion from their boss', the unwritten one interprets it as, 'keep your boss happy', 'stand out from the crowd' and 'avoid association with failure'.

The important point here is that employees quickly get to understand the real levers of advancement within an organization, so companies must ensure that these levers, both informal and formal are working in unison to drive the new cultural ethos.

Peter Raine of Superdrug states that he believes it is more than coincidental that a significant number of those employees who volunteered to act as facilitators for their cultural change programme have since being promoted.

Case Report: Transco

Of course career development is not just about climbing the organizational hierarchy, but also includes job rotations and secondments to other functions, countries or discrete projects. The latter approach is proving valuable in creating a high-performing culture at the UK-based gas supplier Transco, as managing director Phil Nolan explains:

> "One thing we've done is create Change Laboratories, which the leading change consultant Richard Pascalle helped us with. This is really about workplace learning through simulated learning.

> "What we do is take a big issue facing the company and get a group of people together who have the expertise required to make real progress, who want to be part of the solution and can be spared from their operations for a specified time period. We give them a brief and open access to everyone in the organization and they come back with recommendations for solving the original challenge. It's an intense experience and people with all the qualities we need from good leaders, such as drive, ambition, sensitivity to others, develop from this process."

Nolan explains that a valuable outcome of this exercise is that when people return to their normal workplace from these change laboratories they behave differently, in that they no longer complain about problems but rather seek a solution:

> "This is infectious and it puts pressure on managers who have to lead people who now have their own leadership skills. So the managers have to learn a more interactive set of skills."

Training

The research shows that an important aspect of creating a new cultural ethos is the organization's approach to training. After all, employees will probably need to be trained in new skills (such as being customer-focused, or for teamworking) as part of the change effort.

Training has been revolutionized within some of the case study companies. At Hyundai Car (UK) Ltd, for example, training spend, which includes Hyundai staff and those in its dealer network, has risen from £100,000 in 1994 to an allocation of £1.5 million for 1999.

In addition to training mechanisms such as leadership and employee behavioural workshops, the company has focused on using training to transform everyday skills that irritate customers. For example, based on dealer feedback, the company realized it was poor at writing letters. Says Stoneman:

> "We hid behind jargon. As an example, we would say 'the repair has been done to manufacturers' specifications'. We weren't saying 'to the customer's satisfaction', but rather that the manufacturer would be pleased with it. Consequently, we trained staff to change their use of language to talk directly to customer needs."

Investor In People (IIP)

Within many UK companies, career development and training have been interwoven within the Investor In People (IIP) standard. Essentially, IIP is a framework which ties individual training and development to business goals, and it consists of four key components:

1. Senior management has to publicly commit to the standard and either self-assess against the standard or receive a 'health check' from the local Training and Enterprise Council (TEC).

2. Training needs are then reviewed for all employees against business goals, leading to action plans which addresses identified gaps.

3. The launch of these training and development action plans for employees.

4. The training is assessed for effectiveness.

External assessment against the IIP standard is based on completion of the action plan, and submission of a portfolio of evidence to the local TEC, who validates this by site visits and interviews with employees.

The Inland Revenue Accounts Office, Cumbernauld, the case study to support Chapter 2, committed to IIP in 1992 and was awarded IIP status in 1994. According to the Office's director Andrew Geddes (who is now a director of IIP Scotland), IIP provided the right training and development to meet the Office's business objectives.

Central to this has been the creation of focused personal development review systems and plans. Through this a dialogue between manager and direct reports identifies individual skills requirements and how these are aligned to business priorities.

Employees do seem to be satisfied with how they are treated and how their skills are developed. An independent survey scored job satisfaction within the Office at 74 per cent, which was among the top survey scores.

Section G: Recognition and Incentives

Changing how people's performance is recognized and/or incentivized is also, the research finds, crucial to succeeding with a culture change programme.

Recognition systems, which may or may not include financial incentives, can have a powerful effect on the corporate culture. This includes changing the criteria by which people are celebrated, thus ensuring that those who receive the greatest recognition are those who are demonstrating the key values of the organization.

New Heroes

As an example, at KFC, the case study to support Chapter 4, the company has started to tell success stories and create new heroes. At their Louisville, Kentucky, headquarters there is an underground tunnel which connect two buildings. This has been transformed into a 'walk of leaders' containing photographs of outstanding performers throughout the restaurant system. Some people have even been taken to Kentucky to see their photographs.

At Western Provident Association (WPA) a graduated recognition programme has been instigated. At the lowest level it has a 'GOTCHA' recognition process. This has a relatively low monetary value of about £20 and is a reward that team leaders can give in recognition of someone whose done something over and above their normal job. This may be taking mail to the post office rather than the post room because a customer needs it urgently or it could be for a process improvement.

At the highest level, WPA has an Employee of the Month Award, which is not always awarded. This is for an individual or individuals who during the previous month made a significant contribution over and above what is expected. This reward receives great recognition within the organization. The only reserved car space in car park is for the employee of the month winner, their face appears on a flag which is flown from the company's flagpole for the month and there is also a financial reward of about £250. About this award Adrian Schuler, WPA's director of best practices, says:

> "The recognition that employees get from other members of the organization is a far greater motivator than the monetary portion."

Car Incentives

Interestingly, in two of the case study companies, prize draws through which the winners receive new cars have been used as an effective mechanism to incentivize employees to focus on issues of current importance to the organizations. At Siemens KWU the carrot of the car was used to incentivize people to attend a short presentation explaining the meaning of Economic Value Added (EVA) and why it had become an important strategic focus for the organization.

At Continental Airlines the car prize draw was used as the incentive for a perfect attendance programme. Basically, if an employee attends work without a sickness break for a six month period they become eligible to enter the draw to win one of three or four fully loaded Ford Explore vehicles.

In the last six months of 1998, 14,000 (35 per cent) employees were eligible for the draw. And if awarding cars for full attendance sound like an extravagance, Meissner points out:

> "The programme costs us about $700,000 a year and our loss-time is down 25 per cent. It more than paid for itself in the first year of its implementation."

Bonus Plans

Continental Airlines also demonstrated how bonuses can be effective in hitting key targets. Its on-time bonus plan was first introduced to offer employees a $65 bonus for every time it ended in the top five out of ten US airlines tracked by the US Department of Transport for on-time scheduling. The company had been a constant poor performer against this measure but the introduction of the bonus helped enable a dramatic improvement in performance. In one month it moved from bottom to seventh and is now regularly coming first.

Interestingly, the bonus plan rewards all management and staff equally. According to Mike Campbell, the organization's senior vice president, human resources and labour relations, this removed a great deal of the divisiveness in the organization, which he stresses can be an unintended outcome if you reward sections of the employee-base and not others. He says:

> "We wanted to send a clear message that we would all win together or lose together."

At Millennium Inorganic Chemicals, getting employees to 'think like owners' is a key strategic thrust, and therefore a new incentive plan has been launched through which employee bonuses are paid and corporate stock allocated due to EVA performance.

At Millennium top management are also mandated to take a significant equity stake in the company, thus demonstrating in a practical way their commitment to the strategic goals of the organization. This is also true at

Tricon (the parent company of KFC) which has also launched 'Yumbucks', an innovative programme that grants each Restaurant General Manager (RGM) an initial $20,000 in stock options, with the likelihood of more based on the annual performance of his or her restaurant. Therefore, RGM performance is directly tied to restaurant performance.

In the above cases it is clear that companies are using recognition and incentive systems as key tools in creating high performing cultures focused on corporate priorities. Through bonus systems they are ensuring that elements of the compensation package rewards strategic priorities.

Section H: Compensation

Changing the whole compensation system, the research finds, is crucial to aligning behaviour with change goals. Indeed it is certainly one of the most powerful mechanisms for changing behaviour. After all, people do tend to do what they are paid to do. Therefore, in a culture change programme if an organization, for example, states that it wants to become 'team-based' and 'customer-focused' then the compensation system must reflect this. If it still pays employees for functional competencies, and disregards teamwork and customer-facing performance, then it easy to see where the individual's focus will rest.

Pay as an Inhibitor of Change

Changing pay systems is one of the most difficult areas to get right. Several advisers suggested that the underlying reason for this is largely because the compensation practices in place today have developed slowly throughout the industrial era. They are therefore out of tune with the needs of the knowledge era and most actually inhibit, rather than promote, change.

Mark Krueger, managing director of the US-based consultancy Answerthink, for example, observes:

> "Most current remuneration policies essentially reward the work that's currently being done, and therefore does not necessarily support future direction. Programmes today often do not reward risk taking, and simply reward people for meeting objectives, not exceeding them. For most change efforts today, compensation systems will have to change."

Changing compensation systems is, according to advisers, the litmus test of whether senior management is really serious about change. As David Miller, managing director of ODR Europe, succinctly puts it, "this is where senior management tend to get scared".

Pay Research

However, there are examples of organizations willing to fundamentally appraise pay systems and attune them to the new cultural ethos. Indeed, a 1998 survey by Business Intelligence, 'Rethinking Pay, Compensation and

Performance',[8] found that 60 per cent of the 105 responding organizations had rethought pay systems to support a major change initiative, and taking the 60 per cent as a 100 per cent, 10 per cent had done so to support culture change. This represented a ten fold increase over a similar Business Intelligence survey in 1995.[9]

The 1998 survey was commissioned to support the Business Intelligence report, *Strategic Compensation*, which explores in detail how to align performance, pay and rewards to support corporate transformation. According to the author, strategic compensation has many elements which should be integrated into a continuous process. These are:

- using strategic foresight to identify business needs and priorities

- deciding on new requirements for performance and capability

- rationalizing and valuing work across the organization and among its people

- setting new standards and targets for performance, competency and behaviours

- adequately rewarding the achievements of those standards

- rethinking performance management processes

- incentivizing people as a motivator, and reinforcer

- recognizing accomplishments and contribution

- resourcing the expectations that people have to do their work as effectively as possible

- enabling a more participative environment through relational reward which genuinely engages people to use their different talents and give discretionary effort.

Case Report: Yorkshire Water

Within *Strategic Compensation*, a case report on the UK utility Yorkshire Water, showed how rewards and performance management had been rethought to support business re-engineering, and in doing so align the culture to its mission to become known as a values-driven, customer-focused business.[10]

Indeed this mission is nothing short of a survival issue for the organization. Its licence to operate can be revoked by the industry watchdog Ofwat if its performance is poor or it could become a prime acquisition target.

Organizational change

To align the performance and behaviour of the employee-base with the mission, organizational change during 1996 and 1997 was systemic. As examples:

- restructuring has created two business units for clear water and waste water

- the new structure is based on five directorates which operate across the business units – customer services, finance and regulation, strategy development and IT, capital investment, and HR

- a new managing director and board members have been appointed

- through re-engineering, internal processes are now aligned with Ofwat standards, targets and measures for each directorate

- a balanced scorecard approach to performance measurement has being introduced.

Amanda Stainton, Yorkshire Water's manager of reward and employee relations, explained how changing compensation systems has been central to creating the new organizational culture:

> "We are shifting from an entitlement, rule-based public service ethos to a performance-driven one. In the past, annual pay increases were negotiated by unions and awarded with no account being taken of whether performance was good or poor.

> "As we believed that changing our reward policies would help enable cultural change, they were completely overhauled to realign them and HR strategy with the new business strategy and change programmes."

This overhaul has comprised:
- a rigid structured grading system being replaced by six broad bands

- a new performance management process was introduced in 1997 based on contribution and competence which links pay increases to individual performance

- a competency framework has been developed which has 21 competencies grouped into four clusters, for all personnel irrespective of band – personal (4); process and business focus (11); people (5); and one job-specific technical/professional competency

- annual executive director performance bonus payments have been extended to the top two management tiers and may eventually be used throughout the organization

- the principle of variable bonus payments provides a percentage of pay at risk – split evenly between company, team and individual performance – which will help distinguish between, and reward accordingly, good, average and below-average performance.

The case report goes on to explain that the pay mix within the organization now has four elements:
1. Performance-related pay.
2. Broadbanding based on competencies.
3. Variable pay.

4. Profit-related pay (though this is being phased out due to changes to UK Inland Revenue regulations).

Four main 'people effects' are anticipated:

1. Aligning individual performance with corporate objectives.

2. Recognition by employees that rewards are fair.

3. Higher levels of motivation and personal and team challenge.

4. Becoming recognized as an employer of choice.

Stainton added:

> "We sought to undo established fundamentals. The former incremental structure had gone, giving more rewards flexibility, and, as pay integrates with performance, it is having an impact on business strategy and organizational effectiveness."

Learning points

Stainton emphasized two key learning points. First, that rethinking performance and the aligned reward mechanisms is a continuous process with distinct phases of implementation. Second, that there are significant challenges along the way. For Yorkshire Water these included:

- Overcoming union resistance to new pay and working practices – three ring binders of procedures are being radically simplified and negotiations with the company's five unions have been replaced by single table agreements.

- Tightly managing the annual salary bill to avoid pay drift.

- Setting more specific targets and personal objectives required for performance using the competency framework, especially for behavioural elements or more 'unique' jobs which are difficult to evaluate.

- Ensuring that managers', supervisors' appraisals as well as self-appraisals are conducted as objectively and professionally as possible.

Crucially, addressing these challenges, the case reported, required a significant involvement in internal communications, training and company-wide involvement. The competency framework, as an example, was shaped by involving 400 employees.

In addition, the company's 200-plus managers were fully briefed on the design of the performance management process in order for them to understand and champion its requirements and over 70 per cent of the 3100 strong workforce were trained in appraisal techniques. Stainton concluded:

> "Clearly, changing rewards became a major communications issue because people had to understand what we were doing and what the new business requirements were."

Compensation Transparency

Stainton's point here is critical. According to research for this Report, if organizations are to fundamentally alter compensation systems to support change goals, then the whole employee-base has to fully understand why these alterations are taking place and how they will affect them as individuals. They must also be as transparent as possible, so that employees can see what behaviours and aspects of performance are being rewarded. If the rewards are fully aligned with the cultural goals then this can have a dramatic effect on focusing the minds of employees onto any change initiative. For as John Childress, chief executive officer of the cultural change specialists Senn-Delaney Leadership Consulting Group, laconically states, "if you want people to pay attention, fiddle with their wallets".

Conversely, the recent history of changing pay systems to support change objectives is littered with examples of employee discontent and resistance. These can severely undermine, if not destroy completely, any culture change effort.

Section I: Conclusion

It is clear from the research that transforming HR practices is fundamental to succeeding with a cultural change effort. This transformation should cover the full spectrum from recruitment through appraisal and career development, to recognition, incentives and compensation.

Changing HR practices can prove difficult as they directly impact employees' sense of self-worth and development as well as their pocket. Handled insensitively HR changes may destroy a culture change effort, but if handled properly they may prove to be the glue that aligns behaviour and performance to the new cultural ethos and through to the achievement of strategic goals.

Changes to HR practices, especially compensation, the research found, must be communicated clearly if employees are to fully buy into the proposed alterations. Such internal communication, fundamental to a culture change effort, is the subject of the next Chapter.

Key Learning Points

1. Redesigning HR practices can be a powerful mechanism for aligning employee behaviours and performance with a new cultural ethos. It is clear that ignoring these behavioural levers will do significant damage to a change effort.

2. Changing HR practices should include recruitment for three key reasons:

   - employees are exposed to an organization's culture from day one and so can learn constructive or destructive cultural characteristics

   - an organization can heighten the possibility of recruiting culturally aligned people

   - by recruiting and then developing and promoting, culturally aligned people, companies can, over time, destroy culturally insidious characteristics.

3. Companies must also ensure that their appraisal systems focus on the desired values and behaviours. Appraisal change should start at the top of the company; tools such as upwards and 360 appraisal are valuable assessment mechanisms.

4. Career development is a vital piece of the culture change jigsaw. Not least because how people are promoted or developed is a key factor in the behaviours employees develop.

5. Financial and non-financial recognition systems should focus on promoting those who demonstrate excellence against new behavioural and performance expectations.

6. It is absolutely fundamental that organization align compensation systems with cultural goals. As one commentator said, "if you want people to pay attention, fiddle with their wallets".

7. Changes to HR practices should be communicated clearly throughout the organization and be as transparent as possible, so that employees know which behaviours and performance characteristics are being rewarded.

CASE STUDY: HYUNDAI CAR (UK) LTD

Summary

Hyundai Car (UK) Ltd has achieved a dramatic turnaround in profitability by creating a culture focused on achieving competitive advantage through service leadership. Key implementation frameworks have been the celebrated Harvard Business School's Service-Profit Chain and a six-step approach to change.

Introduction

Owned since 1994 by the automotive and support services giant Lex Services plc, Hyundai Car (UK) Ltd exclusively imports, markets and distributes cars manufactured in Korea by Hyundai Motor Corporation (which is not owned by Lex).

Headquartered in High Wycombe, Buckinghamshire, Hyundai Car (UK) Ltd has two customer sets. The first set are the independent dealers who purchase and sell the cars direct to Hyundai's second customer set, the car drivers themselves.

Hyundai has approximately 100 Lex employees with around a further 2000 people independently employed within its more than 160-strong dealer network. Instilling a strong ethic of customer service within these employee groups became the focal point of Hyundai's successful culture change programme.

The Need for Change

Culture change within Hyundai Car (UK) Ltd, as with many of the organizations profiled within this Report, was driven by a need to dramatically improve business results. In 1993, for example, only 9200 cars were sold through the Hyundai dealer network, accounting for just 0.48 per cent of the UK car market. Dealers were making very low profits from new cars (thus focusing most energy into selling used cars) and their relationship with Hyundai Car (UK) Ltd was typical of the industry.

However, before achieving a revolutionary turnaround in both financial performance and dealer relationships, Hyundai's performance would get worse. In 1995 it reported a £7 million loss to Lex, thus calling into question Hyundai Car's future within the Lex stable. Hyundai Motor Corporation was equally wanting more from its UK distributor.

Structural Problems

The poor financial performance was underpinned by an internal structure that was not geared to creating value in the customer chain. Sue Stoneman, customer service director, Lex Service plc, joined the group as Hyundai Car (UK) Ltd's human resource director in April 1994 from cultural change benchmark company British Airways. She explains:

> "At the time activities in the company were not terribly well co-ordinated. For example, sales had its priorities and marketing a different set, so sales would decide to launch an aggressive sales campaign but this would not always be supported by a relative increase in marketing activity."

Another structural problem was that the salesforce and after-sales force were managed as separate, and sometimes conflicting, entities. Stoneman continues:

> "We had a culture that believed that if dealer X sold 100 new cars a year he was a great dealer. However, the after-sales director was saying that view was wrong because after-sales were being inundated with complaints about that dealer.

> "This, therefore, meant that we did not have anyone with overall responsibility for the total performance of the dealership and so had no standard measurements of dealership performance."

This structure meant that nobody owned a particular customer, who would often be passed between sales and after-sales or indeed any other department. Stoneman explains how this led to substantial dealer frustration:

> "A dealer might contact us two or three times a day However, there were at least 36 different people they could talk to, so they were unlikely to get the same person twice. As a result, the dealer had to repeat himself with each telephone call."

Another challenge to be addressed by the change programme was that, since the mid 1990s, the culture of Hyundai could be characterized as parochial, functional and suppressed. Also, the poor financial performance had the effect of creating a somewhat deflated culture. Says Stoneman:

> "There was lots of unexploited potential within the company. The senior management had made a lot of promises about training and making it a great company to work for, etc, but due to other pressures these were not delivered on. So people were disenchanted and living with a command and control leadership style which had the effect of suppressing employee creativity and innovation."

This state was epitomized by the fact that front-line staff could not make even basic decisions without asking the permission of superiors.

Employee Opinion Survey

As a key step on the road to culture change, the human resources team conducted Hyundai Car (UK) Ltd's first employee opinion survey. The results told them that about 40 per cent of the workforce were afraid to openly say what they thought, and that employees felt undervalued. Although the feedback was rather negative, this did give the senior management team unambiguous data with which to plan the change programme.

Strategic Thinking

Stoneman's brief on joining Hyundai was to design an organizational structure capable of delivering strategic objectives. Therefore, in 1994, the management team was taken off-site for two days of strategic thinking, facilitated by the consultancy Coopers & Lybrand (since merged into PricewaterhouseCoopers). Stoneman says:

> "During this session we looked at three performance dimensions which companies have to be good at in order to compete – brand management, operational leadership and service leadership. We understood that to gain a competitive edge we would have to excel at one of these, while being competent in the other two."

First, the senior management team considered brand management. Although a longer-term aim is to leverage benefits from the Hyundai brand, the team recognized that with so many strong marques in the market-place, it would be unlikely that Hyundai could quickly secure a brand leadership position.

The focus then fell on to operational leadership. Although optimizing operational efficiency would become a key area for improvement, the team recognized that as Hyundai Car (UK) did not manufacture the cars they could only exercise operational control within clearly defined limits.

Finally, therefore, the team considered service leadership and declared this to be its best option for leveraging competitive advantage in a crowded, mature market-place. This was going to prove a complex challenge, as at the time the company did not have a recognizable service culture.

The Service-Profit Chain

The team decided to use the well-known Harvard Business School designed performance improvement framework, the Service-Profit Chain, as its primary tool for building service leadership. Stoneman had seen this work successfully within British Airways.

The Service-Profit Chain had four key links. Link one, profit and growth, is driven by link two, customer satisfaction and loyalty. This is a result of link three, service value, which in turn is determined and enhanced by link four, employee satisfaction and loyalty (see Figure 7.2).

According to Stoneman, the power of the Service-Profit Chain is that to succeed you have to look at the whole of the chain and not just one element. She explains:

> "This was quite a shift in thinking for the management board at Hyundai Car (UK) as they, like many UK boards, had traditionally been interested only in the final link in the chain – making money."

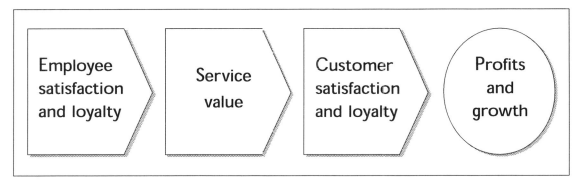

Figure 7.2: The Service-Profit Chain

So Hyundai Car (UK) Ltd began to look holistically at employees, customers and financial return.

However, at the start of the change programme the company was performing poorly against each link in the chain, so it began to talk to employees and dealers about how best to become a customer-orientated organization. The resultant feedback made it clear that a critical requirement was dramatic internal restructuring.

Therefore a new structure was designed for Hyundai. Essentially, the UK was spilt into three regions with a dedicated team headed by a director accountable for all activities within the regions' 50-plus dealerships.

Accordingly, one person was now responsible for total dealer performance and relationships, meaning the historic sales and after-sales conflict could be resolved. Dealer points of access were reduced from 36 to 12, thus immediately improving dealer satisfaction, and of the then 110 Hyundai jobs, 95 were changed overnight to be far more customer-facing. About the latter point Stoneman says:

> "This was quite chaotic and stressful and I would not do it this fast again. I would do it *much* more slowly."

Stoneman became one of the three regional directors (since moving on to become customer service director for the whole of the Lex Group). The other two directors were Nick Smith, who was from a marketing background, and John Hockley, previously head of sales operations. This change of leadership, says Stoneman, freed up a lot of energy in the organization.

Six Step Approach to Change

To create service leadership, and thus actualize the Service-Profit Chain, Hyundai Car (UK) Ltd chose a six step approach to change. The steps were:

1. Sharpen strategic vision.
2. Building customer loyalty.
3. Mobilizing human resources.
4. Quality and productivity.

5. Achieving total customer satisfaction.

6. Envisioning the future.

Sharpen Strategic Vision

Hyundai Car (UK) Ltd knew that it wanted to place the customer at the heart of the organization and that its vision had to reflect that. So in 1996 the senior management team spent a considerable amount of time debating what this vision should say and what it would mean to its stakeholder groups. In all the process took about 12 months. The thinking was aided by an MBA student who undertook specific research around service leadership qualities from the employee, dealer and end-customer perspectives. The agreed Hyundai Car (UK) vision became:

> 'We will win and retain our *chosen customers* through the *unbeatable value* of our products and the *intimate ownership experience* we provide.'

Stoneman outlines the key components of the vision:

- **'Chosen Customers'**:

  "In the past our advertising had been quite general and aimed at all car drivers. However, we were becoming much more sophisticated in pinpointing the differing types of customers who would purchase our cars, and why they made that buying decision. So we would no longer target all car drivers, so the words 'chosen customers' would remind us to focus."

  This understanding of customer groups was largely the work of the marketing director Ken Lee (who, like Stoneman, was from outside the automotive industry). Lee fundamentally believed that Hyundai needed to understand better what markets the Hyundai product was appealing to – and why.

- **'Unbeatable Value'**:

  "People buy Hyundai cars because the product does represent good value for money. So we had to start working hard to get that message across. However, such value is replicable by competitors, which is why we made the link between value and intimate ownership experience."

- **'Intimate ownership experience'**:

  "We probably spent months just defining what that word 'intimate' meant for a customer and, from research undertaken, we realized that our customers want a 'value-adding' experience when buying a car. This means a relationship with the dealers which was much more intimate than just being sold the car."

Although Stoneman is a firm believer in the power of a compelling, understandable and measurable vision statement, she does believe that creating the words is the easy bit. She says:

> "The difficult bit is getting your people to be energized and excited about the vision. Critical here is that senior management must live the vision. If they tell the organization one thing and behave completely differently then the vision will be meaningless."

Equally vital, according to Stoneman, is communication. She says:

> "We invested a considerable amount of time into communicating both the vision and the change process."

An important mechanism here is Hyundai's quarterly communications days. Early events focused on employees building their own picture of what the change process would look like, what the vision would mean to them in practical terms, and to articulate the values and behaviours that they would expect from a leading service organization. Says Stoneman:

> "In short, it was about employees taking ownership of the change process. We said here's A, where we are today, and over there's B, where we want to get to. Now you tell us how to get there."

Other communication mechanisms launched included a newspaper and monthly industrial society team briefings. Also any training that people go through always starts with a 15 minute introduction reinforcing what the change programme is all about and how the training supports the vision statement and the Service-Profit Chain. Says Stoneman:

> "Hyundai has created a lot of mechanisms through which to talk to our people, and we have to exploit all of those."

She believes that getting people to buy-in to a change programme is about telling people, telling them again and telling them what you have told them. She says:

> "Remember that people have to cope with and internalize change while doing their normal jobs. So, if senior management communicates the change vision just once a year, then employees soon forget because of day-to-day work pressures."

Building Customer Loyalty

Building customer loyalty, the second step in the six-step process, also represents the critical Service-Profit Chain link between people and profits. To help understand the drivers of loyalty, Hyundai has appointed a customer retention manager, Mark Say, to identify and disseminate 'loyalty best practice'. Say's brief is to:

- build a customer-led database
- develop an understanding of Hyundai's customer retention programme
- develop and implement an innovative, long-term retention strategy.

A key element of the strategy is a bi-monthly, 52-page customer magazine which provides a platform for dialogue and end-customer involvement. Local dealer involvement is also a key factor.

Such a focus on the end-customer does appear to be paying dividends. Customer retention rates rose from 25 per cent in 1995 to 38 per cent in 1997.

Understanding the value that customers ascribe to Hyundai vehicles, and so making them more likely to repurchase, also acts as an innovative mechanism for connecting the Service-Profit Chain links three and four, 'service value' and 'employee satisfaction and loyalty'. Stoneman says:

> "Research by the marketing director Ken Lee had found that end-customers ascribe six key values to Hyundai vehicles – confidence, value, warmth, reliability, style and honesty.

> "These are great attributes that could describe an excellent organization as well as a car. Therefore we formulated our approach to brand internalization. Through this these six Hyundai brand values also became the core values of the organization. So instead of having separate brand values and organizational values they are one and the same thing.

> "This has proved an excellent way of focusing attention on the whole of the Service-Profit Chain and not sub-optimizing the process by focusing just on discrete chain elements."

Making these values come alive required their translation into key behaviours that would prove their outward manifestation. Consequently, the whole Hyundai organization, over a two-day period, went through teambuilding exercises under the titles customer loyalty, employee loyalty and profit (which, in line with the Service-Profit Chain, are the three objectives of the business).

The question was posed, 'what are the key behaviours that everyone has to display if we are to meet these objectives?'. Hyundai management was surprised by the teams' answers. Stoneman explains:

> "The consistency was amazing with about 98 per cent correlation on what people perceived as critical behaviours."

Consequently, these behaviours were distilled into ten key performance criteria:

- Be willing to make significant change in the way we do things now in order to create greater value for customers.

- Make only those commitments you honestly expect to be able to meet; genuinely try to deliver as promised.

- Review both success and mistakes to find ways to improve for the future.

- Provide/seek out appropriate training, guidance and support.

- Keep abreast of customers'/clients' needs and priorities.

- Organize activities and timescales to achieve objectives on schedule.

- Let people know that their efforts are appreciated and valued.

- Seek feedback from customers on individual and departmental activities/contribution.

- Suggest ways to improve the way we do things.

- Support and co-operate with other departments.

Stoneman continues:

> "We mandated that everyone in the organization had to demonstrate these behaviours and that they would be built into the performance management system.

> "For instance, an employee may have a goal of selling dealers 300 cars in a month, which is the hard performance measure, but they would also have to demonstrate development against these behaviours. This gives ownership of behaviour to the people. And to be at all meaningful, values and behaviours have to become a 'live tool'."

Leaders in Hyundai are assessed against their own set of behaviours through 360 degree appraisal. However, according to Stoneman, it is one thing to tell people that they have to act and behave in new ways, and indeed measure them against these behaviours, but this mandate must be supported by excellent training. This leads to the third in Hyundai's six step approach to change – mobilizing human resources.

Mobilizing Human Resources

At Hyundai Car (UK) Ltd the purpose of mobilizing human resources is to ensure that human resource policies and processes, and the skills of the workforce, are aligned to the company's strategic aim of service leadership. Says Stoneman:

> "It is about having good processes for hiring, training, compensating and managing performance. Something the motor trade has historically not been renowned for."

Stoneman believes that human resource excellence is not just a matter of ensuring the formal procedures and policies are as good as possible. She says:

> "Much more than that it's about grabbing people's hearts and minds and getting them excited about their work, delivering service excellence and the need to change."

And this, she says, is a significant challenge:

> "It's easy to stand up and tell people that we have to do change because if we don't we'll go out of business. As managers we may know this to be true, but people on the front-line may think 'yes fine, but I've heard all this before and I've had this job for years and it will probably always be here'."

To turn these people into advocates of the change, coming up with and driving new ideas forward is a major issue for all managers, believes Stoneman, adding:

> "We have to find a new way of leading people which motivates them, excites them and liberates them to be exceptional."

Stoneman is particularly inspired by a quote by the US-based management guru Tom Peters:

> "Recruit passion, hire passion, protect passion and promote passion. I'll

trade you an ounce of passion for a page of vision and a pound of business plans any day, especially tomorrow."

Stoneman agrees that passion is the key emotion to nurture if Hyundai is indeed to gain competitive advantage through service leadership. She says:

"We and our competitors all use similar technologies, methodologies, processes and systems. The performance dimensions that will set us apart is the passion and the type of service we are delivering to our customers.

"I believe that a lot of companies fail with customer improvement programmes because they do a lot of tactical things around customer service but forget about mobilizing their employees behind this service goal. They then wonder why the initiatives don't work. If you don't get employees to be passionate, you're whistling in the wind."

At Hyundai the process of developing employees who are passionate about delivering outstanding customer service starts with recruitment. The company has invested a significant amount of time understanding the service they want employees to deliver and therefore their skills requirements.

Customer service staff provides a powerful example of how this understanding has led to changes in the recruitment process. Historically, a new recruit would be chosen from a selection of candidates forwarded by an agency, who would then receive a traditional face-to-face interview.

However, knowing that these employees will spend most of their time dealing with customers over the telephone, candidates are now first subjected to a 10 minute telephone 'chat' to get a feel for how their personalities come across on the telephone and so how they are likely to interact with customers.

After this effective screening process, candidates then go through a full day assessment. This includes structured interviews, two letter writing exercises (an important customer-facing competence), customer service profiling and measurement against brand values.

Hyundai is rigorous about ensuring applicants meet the requisite criteria. Says Stoneman:

"Quite simply if candidates don't score well where they need to, then they won't get the job. And this is equally true for internal applications. However, if they fail to make the grade we will create for them a development plan to develop the required competencies."

Hyundai has also altered its bonus system to better reflect the new cultural goals. For example, only salespeople previously received bonuses and just for hitting targets; now a company-wide scheme exists, based on wider performance criteria including customer and internal dimensions.

Vitally, the process of, and indeed attitude to, training has been revolutionized within Hyundai. At the start of the change process there was no HR function within the company, other than Stoneman herself; today there is a 12-strong HR and training team headed by Mandy Spooner, another 'big-hitter' from British Airways. In 1994 employees received about two days training, whereas in 1998 this had risen to seven days. Training spend, which includes Hyundai staff and the dealer network, has risen from £100,000 in 1994 to an allocation of £1.5 million for 1999.

In addition to training mechanisms such as leadership and employee behavioural workshops, the company has focused on using training to transform everyday skills that irritate customers. For example, based on dealer feedback, the company realized it was poor at writing letters. Says Stoneman:

> "We hid behind jargon. As an example we would say 'the repair has been done to manufacturers' specifications'. We weren't saying 'to the customer's satisfaction', but rather that the manufacturer would be pleased with it. Consequently, we trained staff to change their use of language to talk directly to customer needs."

A further aspect of mobilizing human resources has been to involve employees in the company's decision-making processes. Mechanisms include an employee steering group with representatives from all parts of the business. This employee steering group meets with the managing director and HR team to discuss specific process problems.

Driving change through the dealerships

Given the nature of Hyundai's operations, mobilizing human resources also, and crucially, means training and encouraging people in the dealer network to deliver service leadership. Says Stoneman:

> "Anything we do with our own people, we then do with our dealers. Indeed, Hyundai's courses on behavioural training now include, on the same courses, their own in-house staff and employees from the dealerships."

This in itself signals a major cultural shift within Hyundai. Prior to the launch of the change programme an atmosphere of mutual distrust, and indeed antagonism, characterized the dealer network and Hyundai relationship.

Rolling-out change to the networks followed change implementation within Hyundai itself, as the company firmly believed that dealers would only change if they really believed that Hyundai itself had changed. Therefore, dealers had about a year's experience of the 'new' Hyundai before they were brought into the change process, and indeed factored into the whole Service-Profit Chain. Says Stoneman:

> "We went to the dealers with our vision and asked 'what stops you from delivering this vision?'. Feedback strongly stated that they wanted to change but didn't know how to. To do so they said they needed three things from Hyundai:
>
> 1. Management training for the senior people in their dealerships.
> 2. Customer service training for their people. Consequently, Hyundai designed a two day customer service workshop for dealer staff, which all will have completed by the end of 1999.

3. Help with local area marketing. For this Hyundai has launched a dedicated help team to works directly with the dealerships."

In addition, all the principals within the dealerships, eg general managers, are going through a three-day 'how to lead in service industry' workshop. They then run these for their own people, backed by focused service improvement sets and calendarized action plans. Such an approach was revolutionary within the dealerships, as many at the time were not even holding team meetings.

Hyundai's own people have been through coaching and mentoring courses so they can help guide and assist dealerships through the change process.

Hyundai has also conducted more than 150 dealer evening sessions explaining what an ideal dealership looked like in terms of business management. This required significant improvement within many dealerships where effective business systems or processes were not in place. Says Stoneman:

> "This was acceptable when they were selling around 80 new cars a year, but to sell around 200 new cars a year, business systems have to be substantially slicker."

Hyundai also implemented 'how you deliver exceptional customer service' via service improvement evenings at each dealership. Hyundai's Regional Management Team went to all 150 dealerships and ran this session. She says:

> "This was about giving ownership for delivering service excellence to the dealerships. But importantly we said that we would help them make the requisite improvements."

Key to effecting significant improvement within the dealerships was the crafting of service standards, which outlined benchmark standards of customer-facing excellence.

Hyundai also developed dealer manuals on customer service, managing your market-place and people values. These include simple checklists that dealer principals can use to assess themselves and their teams against ideal dealership profiles. For example, it helps them diagnose how well they hand over a car and how well they treat customers when they have to do extra work on cars. Says Stoneman:

> "The work we've done helping dealers deliver to our vision has so far cost us about £1 million. This in itself demonstrates that we are serious about change."

Quality and Productivity

According to Stoneman, quality and productivity, the fourth step in the six-step approach to implementing change, is about ensuring that the systems and processes are in place to deliver the previous steps. Therefore, a lot of work has gone into training employees in total quality management tools and techniques. This has included the setting up cross-functional and cross-hierarchical service excellence teams, tasked with solving problems identified in the quarterly communication days.

Stoneman believes that step four is where the company presently is on the six-step journey. However, it is proactively working on step five, 'achieving total customer satisfaction'. For example, the company is developing a one-stop shop for dealers and end-customers. This means a significant investment in call centre technology and an artificial intelligence support system combined with a large investment in behavioural training for the support centre team.

According to Stoneman, step six, 'envisaging the future', will be about looking at emerging trends, benchmarking what is happening in different industries and using this knowledge to further develop its service leadership ethos. She says:

> "Eventually, we want Hyundai to be the company that sets the standards that others follow."

Change Results

Given the significant time and resources invested by the company into its change programme, the big question is 'has the bottom-line benefited?'. The results speak for themselves. The company has transformed a £7 million deficit in 1995 to a near £9 million profit in 1998 (and this against the background of the Korean economic crisis); average dealer profit jumped from £51,500 in 1995 to £80,000 in 1997; and market share has grown from 0.45 per cent in 1993 to 1.18 per cent in 1997. Table 7.1 shows the upward trend in Hyundai Car (UK) Ltd's performance in the period 1993–1997.

	1993	1994	1995	1996	1997
Market share	0.48%	0.64%	0.72%	0.94%	1.18%
No. of retail cars sold per dealer	56	68	80	106	150
HCUK profit (loss) £000s	(1605)	(4930)	(7079)	2086	8962
Average dealer profit £000s	NA	NA	51	72	80
Total cars sold	9200	12,247	13,948	18,959	26,074

Table 7.1: Hyundai Car (UK) Ltd Performance Statistics 1993–97

As for other evidence of success, employee satisfaction grew from 60 per cent in 1995 to over 80 per cent in 1998. And the Sewell's Industry Survey (an independent ranking of dealers satisfaction) ranked Hyundai fifth out of the forty marques represented in the UK in 1998, up from 15th place in 1996.

On top of this, the company has started to win customer service awards from its end-users, such as the Cornhill Insurance Customer Service Award.

Conclusion

Within Hyundai Car (UK) the journey towards service excellence is never-ending and their next challenges include:

- Piloting and delivering a robust customer relationship management programme that seeks to create, sustain and engender a dialogue with the end-customer, thus adding value to the intimate ownership experience.

- Further improving and developing robust, efficient measurement and tracking systems to enable the company to measure key performance criteria in relation to customer loyalty.

- Fully understanding each dealer's ability to grow with the franchise, eg through extended product range and Hyundai's demands for increased professionalism.

- Introducing a methodology to really understand profitability by dealership and make each dealer development manager profit responsible.

- Focusing on employee retention, eg succession planning, training and career paths, development plans and revised contracts for employment.

- Linking customer satisfaction and loyalty to staff compensation schemes.

- Building brand desirability and familiarity through strong national advertising which emphasizes the 'experience' of owning a Hyundai, rather than being simply product-focused.

Key Learning Points

So what have been the keys to success thus far? Stoneman identifies 12:

1. Involving the top team to the point of advocacy.

2. Structuring the organization around the customer.

3. Putting key champions and advocates in place early on.

4. Partnering marketing and HR to internalize the brand.

5. Having a good product.

6. Having an owning board (Lex) with the belief and wisdom to let go.

7. Having a strategic sponsor with a compelling experience set.

8. Creating an holistic, integrated approach.

9. Taking the dealers with Hyundai.

10. Taking a long-term view and sticking with it.

11. Demonstrating positive impact on the bottom line.

And about the 12th point, Stoneman says:

"Sometimes, there's times when you haven't got all the data, but you can see where you want to get to, and you're in the driving seat. You've got to take a really deep breath, put your faith in those around you... and jump. You'll never get anywhere worthwhile without the occasional leap of faith."

8

THE COMMUNICATIONS IMPERATIVE – MESSAGES, MEDIA AND PRACTICES

Executive Summary

1. Excellent internal communication mechanisms are essential for successfully driving cultural change. Indeed a number of commentators stress that you cannot communicate enough.

2. Discrete communication mechanisms must be mutually reinforcing, ie, tell the same story.

3. Communication must be open, honest and clearly support the intended cultural ethos.

4. Communication, the research finds, must be two-way, thus enabling constructive feedback around change ideas and progress.

5. Research finds that companies recognize the fundamental importance of internal communications in a culture change effort, but are mixed in their assessment of its effectiveness.

6. It is critical that senior management leads the communication effort to support the change programme. Indeed advisers state that the failure of senior managers to communicate is a major cause of change failure.

7. Bad news, our research finds, must be communicated quickly and honestly and preferably delivered by senior management.

8. A well thought out internal communications plan with tailored (but consistent) messages to discrete stakeholder groups is a vital aspect of change roll-out.

9. Frameworks such as the balanced scorecard are proving powerful for communicating strategic objectives.

10. Numerous communication mechanisms are being used today. Indeed it is judicious to use a variety of techniques as people receive messages in different ways.

11. According to the research, however, face-to-face communication is still clearly the most powerful mechanism.

12. Electronic mechanisms such as corporate intranets and e-mail are proving invaluable communication mechanisms.

13. A case study on Ernst & Young demonstrates best practice.

Section A: Context

Repeatedly during the research for this Report, advisers and practitioners stressed the critical importance of internal communications in successfully driving culture change. Indeed, the words 'communicate, communicate, communicate' were often spoken, as was the sentence 'you cannot communicate enough'.

It is clear that organizations must design and implement a well thought out communication strategy in support of any change effort. The primary reasons for this are simple:

1. People need to know why a change effort, which may be painful, is taking place; essentially what the business imperatives are.

2. Employees also need to know, as early as possible, what the change programme will mean to them personally. The 'what's in it for me' question which, according to advisers, is too often overlooked in change efforts.

3. Communication is a powerful way to quickly disseminate (and, importantly, constantly reinforce) the intended cultural characteristics of the organization.

As Nancy Blodgett, president of the US-based consultancy Performance Excellence, Inc, comments:

"It's important to make the new behaviours and values explicit, otherwise people might not get the message, especially if one or more managers' behaviours and value systems runs contrary to the new culture. Employees will be more certain about what behaviour is expected of them if these are clear, written down, posted in public areas and constantly reinforced."

Such is the importance of communication that the advisers and practitioners interviewed were unanimous in their belief that a change effort cannot succeed without proactive and focused internal communication mechanisms. As this Chapter will show, there are numerous communication mechanisms being used by organizations today to drive the change message. Traditional approaches such as cascade briefings and face-to-face meetings are being supplemented by knowledge-era tools such as corporate intranets, e-mail, etc. But importantly, whatever communication mechanisms are used, they must reinforce and support a central message, ie, they must show consistency and tell the same story, and equally must enable a two-way flow of ideas, opinions and observations.

However, it must be stressed that getting the communication element of a change programme right can be difficult and senior managers often feel they have not done enough. As Dick Kline, president of the US-headquartered Lehigh Portland Cement Company (the case study to support Chapter 9), states:

> "We worked hard to communicate all the details. But one thing I've learnt about communication is that you always feel you need much more of it."

Section B: Research Findings

The fundamental importance of internal communications came through strongly in 'Culture and Change Management', a survey of 236, mainly large, organizations in Europe, the USA and the Rest of the World, exclusively commissioned for this Report (the survey findings are analysed in detail in Chapter 3).[1]

To the question, 'on a score of 1 (extremely important) to 5 (totally unimportant) how do you rate [internal communications programmes] in enabling culture to be changed?', 61.79 per cent of respondents gave the top score of 1, 26.96 per cent of companies proffered a score of 2, 10.11 per cent said 3, 1.72 per cent scored this 4 and not one organization gave a 5 score.

Interestingly, only senior managers role modeling new behaviours ('walking the talk'), received a higher 1 score rating at 88.62 per cent. This provides statistical validation to comments made earlier in this Report (especially in Chapter 4) that senior management behaviour is an even more critical factor in culture change efforts than internal communication mechanisms.

As Johan Van der Hel, human resources manager for DSM Resins' Coating Resins Business Unit (DSM Resins is a case study to accompany Chapter 5) says:

> "No matter how much internal communication you do via newsletters etc... all that expense will be wasted if management does not display the [correct] behaviours."

Language

Another problem, the research shows, is that culture can be expressed clearly but communicated incorrectly. Alison Rankin-Frost, head of the UK-based

Context Consulting, provides this example:

> "If a goal is to be open and honest or customer-focused, organizations often make the mistake of using a style of language that does not support the intended cultural ethos. A company we work with is quite old fashioned and bureaucratic. They want to transform the culture into one that is much more customer oriented and one where employees have a sense of urgency rather than being complacent. However, senior management, instead of explaining to their employees the reason why they have to change, are telling them they have to change. All this achieves is a reinforcement of the hierarchical, bureaucratic style that they wish to change."

Therefore, Rankin-Frost makes the important observation that it is not always the amount of communication that leads to failure, but the style.

The Efficacy of Communications

Indeed, although organizations responding to the 'Culture and Change Management' survey stressed the importance of internal communications and seemed to be doing a great deal of it, they were mixed in their assessment of the efficacy of communications.[2]

In answer to the question, 'on a score of 1 (completely agree) to 5 strongly disagree), please indicate your level of agreement with the following statement: [in your organization] internal communications are well managed to communicate corporate priorities and cultural values', only 11.48 per cent proffered top score of 1. Another 27.65 per cent gave a 2 score, 30.21 per cent a rating of 3, 18.29 per cent said 4, while 12.34 per cent gave the lowest score of 5.

Therefore, according to this evidence, most organizations still have some way to go before they can confidently say that they have got internal communications right.

The importance of getting internal communications right was highlighted in a 1995 survey by PA Consultants, which found that 91 per cent of quality and re-engineering programmes which failed, did so due to poor communications.[3]

Another telling statistic is provided by David Miller, managing director of ODR Europe, who says that 70 per cent of all messages that people remember comes from the lips of their leaders. This leads directly to the important role played by the senior management team in a communication effort, which is the subject of the following section.

Section C: The Role of Senior Management

Although this was covered in Chapter 4, it would be a failing to omit this vital component from a Chapter on internal communications. For as Robin Cammish, managing director of the UK-headquartered QPA Consultancy (and previously a chief architect of the culture change programme as part of the merger to create the pharmaceutical giant SmithKline Beecham), rightly states:

> "The failure of senior managers to communicate is a major cause of change failure. They must take every opportunity to talk to as many people as possible. While at SmithKline Beecham, myself and a colleague went on the road and personally spoke to 20,000 people in one-to-one sessions and in business meetings."

Independent UK-based consultant Garrey Melville reiterates the importance of the visibility of the people driving the change effort. However, he also makes the important point that the process of having senior managers out in the field talking about, and getting feedback on, the change programme can have benefits other than getting the need for change across. He says:

> "If the CEO and senior team are out there talking to people and getting feedback they will quickly discover just how much intellectual capital resides in the employee-base. And if they are seen to be receptive to new ideas, a mass of business improvement suggestions will come forward."

Case Study Examples

Putting senior managers who are receptive to new ideas out in the field was certainly the case with a number of the case study companies. At Millennium Inorganic Chemicals for instance (the case study to accompany Chapter 3), the CEO Robert E Lee and his global executive team have been unflagging in their desire to communicate the need for change to the globally dispersed workforce. As Ian Hampton, human resources director at the company's Bunbury, Western Australia plant says:

> "Our executive team has been at the forefront of announcing, leading and explaining the change process. They've been travelling all round the world to present the Better Ways (the company's culture change) programme."

With the goal of replacing detached, hierarchical communication processes with an open, direct and lively exchange of ideas and opinions, the members of the global executive committee spent the whole of October 1997 travelling the world and holding meetings to talk about the future with Millennium employees. Impressively, in nine meetings, over 60 per cent of the company's people got to meet the executive committee face-to-face and hear them describe the new global vision, mission and the search for Better Ways.

This also enabled the executive team to hear the thoughts, ideas and concerns of front-line employees. Thus enabling a crucial two-way flow of information and, as the Better Ways message was delivered directly by senior management, greatly improving the chance that it would be remembered by the employee-base.

At KFC, the case study to support Chapter 4, CEO David Novak and his senior team travelled throughout North America holding meetings with both employee and customer groups. The purpose being to uncover views on KFC, both good and bad, in order to pinpoint the key cultural drivers of change at where it mattered most, the front-line employee-customer interface.

At BT Northern Ireland, a case study to accompany Chapter 6, CEO Lucy Woods has reinforced the culture change programme through a variety of mechanisms, such as meeting every single manager for a meal once or twice a year (about 12 managers attend each meal and Woods attends about two dinners a month). She also conducts non-management breakfast meetings throughout Northern Ireland where she discusses with the employee-base subjects such as improvement plans, public image, etc.

Another mechanism used by Woods is a monthly audio-conference where she speaks for about ten minutes and then anybody can ask her live questions on any relevant subject. If she cannot provide the answer she promises to get the reply to them later.

Communicating Bad News

However, one of the most difficult aspects of the senior management's role in driving change is to personally communicate bad news as well as good. As Andrew Geddes, director of the Inland Revenue Accounts Office, Cumbernauld, Scotland (the case study to accompany Chapter 2) observes:

> "In times of change there's a natural uncertainty among staff. They want to be told the bad news as well as the good and they want managers to be open and to share a genuine two-way dialogue about the business. And it's my job as director to ensure that this two-way dialogue takes place."

It is also important, the research finds, that communications, whether they are delivering good or bad news, must be honest. Indeed, no matter how unpalatable and difficult it is to deliver news around redundancies, etc, it is better to be honest and get this out of the way as soon as possible.

It is also vital that senior managers manage this in line with the new cultural ethos of the organization. If senior management does not communicate bad news as quickly as possible, if they manage the communication insensitively, or worse if they, for example, assure employees that change will not lead to redundancies and then make swingeing job cuts, then the change effort will almost certainly lead to resistance within the employee-base. As well as maybe derailing the change effort totally, it will in all probability lead to employees treating anything their leaders say with deep suspicion. The hidden agenda will always be looked for (even if there is not one) and indeed the grapevine will probably quickly create one.

Case Report: Continental Airlines

The importance of senior management delivering bad news themselves was recognized at Continental Airlines (the case study to accompany Chapter 1). Vitally, this was also in keeping with the organization's identified values of honesty, trust, dignity and respect.

Chief operating officer Greg Brenneman explains how, when he shut down operations in Greensboro, North Carolina, the approach taken was markedly different to how it would have been handled pre-change days:[4]

> "The historical norm for delivering bad news at Continental was for a senior manager to dump the new on the local airport manager's lap and then hide in our corporate office building. But I decided to go to Greensboro myself, make the announcement to the employees, and take my punches publicly."

Taking the punches publicly not only showed that Brenneman was willing to treat the Greensboro employees according to the new values, especially honesty and respect, it would also have delivered a powerful message to the rest of the employee-base that the senior management team was willing to live by the new values, thus making organization-wide buy-in more likely.

The importance of senior management honesty and being quick in delivering bad news is of absolute importance when undertaking a merger or acquisition. Indeed, how senior management communicates in the early days is a key contributor to the long-term success of a merger or acquisition. It is important that what is communicated to the staff is factual, timely and direct in order to boost employee confidence in the management team. This is especially important because when a merger or acquisition is announced, employees are naturally concerned about issues such as job security. Dealing with such fears as early as possible will help get employees' minds focused onto the job of creating a new and better organization. This is explored in detail within the next Chapter.

So far this Chapter has argued that effective internal communication mechanisms are a prerequisite for successfully driving culture change efforts and has detailed the crucial role of the senior management team in ensuring a successful internal communications campaign. Now attention should be focused on crafting an internal communication plan and at various communication mechanisms.

Section D: Internal Communication Plans

The first important point to stress about internal communication plans is that there has to be a clear line-of-sight between communication objectives, culture change goals, and strategic objectives. A danger, the research finds, is that as an organization gets deeper and deeper into the tactical elements of culture change, it is remarkably easy to lose sight of the original point of the transformation.

According to Melville, the communication plan should, therefore, have a mission, objectives and timescales which align directly with the strategic requirements of the change programme. He also makes the point that overall responsibility of the internal communication effort should be owned by a senior team with some board representation, and that one person has to have ownership of the whole plan.

Segmenting Audiences

However, a critical problem at the start of a communications effort is identifying key audiences for the change message and tailoring the message to the needs of each discrete audience (although the messages should still 'tell the same story').

Research findings

A survey by Business Intelligence of 248, mainly internal communication managers, in support of the 1996 report, *The Strategic Management of Internal Communications*, found that 51 per cent of respondents stated that they segment audiences against set criteria (some only occasionally), 41 per cent said they did not, whereas 8 per cent were uncertain.[5]

The board/top management	37%
Senior/middle managers	52%
Supervisors and junior managers	44%
Specialist professional staff (eg, IT, legal, HR)	24%
Pensioners	9%
Others	11%

Table 8.1: Percentage of Research Carried out for Different Audiences

And to the question, 'for which of the following audiences have you carried out research to establish their communication needs?', the respondents replies are shown in Table 8.1.

The board/top management	27%
Senior/middle managers	38%
Supervisors and junior managers	28%
Specialist professional staff (eg, IT, legal, HR)	14%
Pensioners	10%
Others	10%

Table 8.2: Percentage of Audiences for whom Separate Communication Channels have been Developed

To the question, 'for which of the [same] audiences have you developed separate communication channels?', the respondents' replies are shown in Table 8.2. This same survey found that according to internal communication specialists their five most important roles were in:

1. Supporting major change programmes.
2. Communicating messages from top management.
3. Raising awareness of business issues and priorities.
4. Communicating the business mission/vision and values.
5. Facilitating feedback.

Given their comparatively poor performance in identifying and communicating tailored messages to specific groups, internal communication specialists

Small group meetings

Mark Krueger, managing director of the US-headquartered Answerthink Consultancy Group, continues the theme:

> "The most effective communication mechanisms we have seen are small group meetings and cross functional group meetings where senior and middle managers talk directly to the employee-base about the change programme, explaining how each employee can be involved and the benefit to each employee. And these groups should be no larger than 20 people, or they will lose the critical interactive element."

Monthly luncheon discussions

Krueger goes on to say that a spin on a traditional meeting-style approach currently gaining popularity is where senior executives invite representatives from different departments to monthly luncheons. He says:

> "This is normally a two hour opportunity for chatting and asking any questions and employees usually consider it an honour and privilege to attend. Often the department representative will bring multiple questions. This is an important way for senior managers to stay in touch with how the change programme is progressing and being perceived and for getting questions out and answers in via an unfiltered mechanism."

Adrian Schuler, director of best practices at the UK-based specialist health insurer Western Provident Association (a case report in Chapters 4 and 7,) explains how such an approach can led to an outpouring of new business improvement ideas.

> "I find the best way to get new ideas is to get a group of six people in a room and over sandwiches ask them for their ideas. This is where you get the best ideas, because they have them.

> "I'm always excited by the great ideas that emanate from this sort of get together."

Siemens KWU, a case study to support Chapter 6, is one company that uses a communication mechanism by which senior executives hold face-to-face meetings with employees which they call 'Monte Carlo round tables'. Through this, a high ranking leader, normally at board level or just below, randomly selects about 20 people and invites them to a round table discussion.

This discussion has no agenda so employees are free to speak openly about how they see the company progressing and any problems they are facing. The meetings are confidential and, the organization believes, proving to be a powerful way to connect senior management with the concerns of the shop floor.

Melville provides this example of the benefits that can come out of a small-group approach to rolling-out a cultural change. He says:

> "I was a facilitator on one culture change programme and we gave people an exercise to design a house magazine as it should look three years from now. We had an editor, copywriter, etc, and we had two hours to produce it."

According to Melville, what came out of this process was that people began to think positively about how they wanted the company to be perceived externally and how they wanted to be part of creating the company's success. He says:

> "During this process people envisioned shares going through the roof, customers being won, and people giving their best to create this success."

Such a technique can be powerful for getting people energized and ready to align their performance, and indeed behaviour, to the culture change objectives. Case study companies recognized the efficacy of planned events to drive home the change message and to enthuse the employee-base.

Case Study Examples: Enthusing the Employee-base

At Hyundai Car (UK) Ltd, a case study to support Chapter 7, an effective mechanism for driving change has been its quarterly communication days. Early events in the change process focused on employees building their own picture of what the change process would look like, what the vision would mean to them in practical terms, and to articulate values and behaviours that they would expect from a leading service organization. Says director of customer satisfaction Sue Stoneman:

> "In short, it was about employees taking ownership of the change process. We said here's A, where we are today, and over there's B, where we want to get to. Now you tell us how to get there."

At Siemens KWU, the company held a major communications event called the 'KWU day' in June 1998. Says director of business excellence, Dr Christian Forstner, who was in charge of its organization:

> "This was a day to celebrate our achievements and discuss our future plans. This was held on a Saturday and out of 16000 people in Germany 10200 attended. We hired four of the biggest conference centres in Germany, and used the Newcastle, UK, plant's parking lot. These centres were connected by ISDN and our board was spread out between the sites.
>
> "The day started with a presentation from the board and then a live discussion with employees based on questions selected on-line.
>
> "It also included a live discussion with customers. These were board level customers so it helped further the culture of open communications. Everybody could hear what the customer thought we were good at and where we could improve.
>
> "This event was a powerful learning experience. At the end of the day, we asked people what they had learnt and got them to create improvement action plans to take back to the workplace."

Celebrating successes is also important at BT Northern Ireland. For example, when the organization won the 1997 UK Quality Award it held a party for 6000 people (employees and partners) at the King's Hall, Belfast. According to CEO Lucy Woods, winning the Award and the celebratory event helped further the real sense of pride in achievement that is now pervasive within the organization.

A Variety of Communication Tools

There are many other internal communication mechanisms being used by case study companies such as, for example, newsletters, cascade briefings, e-mail, telephone hotlines, roadshows, videos, corporate television, etc. Indeed, using a variety of internal communication mechanisms within the one organization is almost always a judicious policy (as long as they are mutually reinforcing and delivering the same central messages), for as Blodgett comments:

> "Generally, the more ways you can communicate the messages of change, the better – so use as many as you can. This is important because not everyone pays attention to all methods of communication. For example, some people ignore inter-office mail while some ignore e-mail. That's why using a variety of methods is the most effective."

Indeed, practitioners interviewed from Superdrug (a case study to accompany Chapter 5) and Continental Airlines stressed the importance of using a variety of mechanisms.

Case Study Examples

As examples of mechanisms used, Millennium Inorganic Chemicals uses employee briefings (a prime purpose being to report information from the monthly executive committee meetings), semi-annual organizational briefings (where members of the executive committee hold update meetings with employees in their specific areas of responsibility, discussing how their activities relate to the company-wide vision and strategic plan), newsletters, e-mail bulletin boards, and a company-wide intranet. There is also an annual global conference for all employees.

Hyundai Car (UK) Ltd, has an internal newspaper, a bi-monthly 52 page customer magazine which provides a platform for dialogue and end-customer involvement, and monthly team briefings. Also any training that people go through always starts with a 15 minute introduction that reinforces what the change programme is all about and how the training supports the strategic goals of the organization.

The Inland Revenue Accounts Office, Cumbernauld, has launched management update meetings known as (MUMs). These quarterly events review the progress of the business and includes all managers and Customer Service Improvement Group and Trade Union representatives. Focus group meetings of about 100 people are held to further inform staff of business direction and gain useful feedback. The Office has also introduced a team listening system that feeds information down to the workplace in a structured way and allows teams to discuss issues and feedback. In addition, the Office has introduced an information help line which anybody in the organization can use to ask questions and they are guaranteed at least a holding answer within three hours and a full response within 24.

Continental Airlines has introduced a hotline to handle employees' suggestions, which is managed by a cross-section of the employee-base such as, for example, pilots, flight attendants, mechanics and gate agents. These employees are required to research each submitted suggestion and get back to the sender within 48 hours with one of three responses:

- we fixed it

- we are not going to fix it, and here is why

- we need to study it a little more, and will get back to you by such and such a date.

In its first three years of implementation, the hotline received, on average, more than 200 calls per week. In addition the organization has a daily two-page newspaper, monthly and quarterly magazines, weekly voice-mail messages from CEO Gordon Bethune, a corporate intranet, e-mail, bulletin boards used to update employees on progress towards the Go Forward strategic plan, and monthly meetings in the organization's Houston headquarters where people are invited to talk with Gordon Bethune.

Moreover, all Continental executive officers are assigned cities that they have to visit on a quarterly basis. When the company releases quarterly earnings, all employees can dial a toll-free number and listen to a taped conversation between a market analyst and a senior executive.

At Superdrug, a key mechanism for communicating performance against its strategic goals is its 'team time' process. This is a one and a half hour session which every team holds ten times per year. Broken down into three sections, the first focuses on improving business awareness and the second is about how the team is progressing against its 'living the mission' objectives. The third section is called 'Talkback' which focuses on team ideas for improving customer-facing performance. An innovative mechanism that comes into play during this final session is the company-wide Starfish.net. This is an 'ideas management system' where the teams forward improvement ideas to a central co-ordinating office.

During Talkback the team considers all improvement ideas that had been previously listed on a 'bright ideas' internal bulletin board and provide a yes/no decision on the validity of each suggestion. If the decision is 'yes, we want to proceed with this suggestion', then the team decides whether to categorize it as a 'quick win' or a 'big idea'.

A quick win is a good idea that the team can Plan, Do, Measure, Improve and (if it works) share with the rest of the organization via Starfish.net. A 'big idea' is a suggestion that the team needs further help in developing and implementing. The idea is captured and sent in to Starfish.net for further investigation. Importantly, the team has to consider key questions prior to forwarding the idea, such as who does the idea benefit, what are the benefits to the customer and what would it cost to do. On receiving the 'big idea' a central team acknowledges idea receipt, researches its viability, and communicates to the team whether the idea will be progressed.

Section G: Electronic Communications

Importantly, Starfish.net has been launched as a key mechanism for the electronic sharing of information and knowledge to improve performance. Electronic communication mechanisms are very important. As Melville comments:

> "You cannot underestimate the roles of intranets, e-mail and other electronic mechanisms for communication. And if used correctly technology can play an important enabling role in communicating the key messages of a change programme."

Melville stresses that such communication tools can be especially powerful for managing and sharing corporate knowledge. He says, "such tools allow a lot of valuable knowledge to be captured, analysed, and disseminated". However he warns:

> "Creating an environment conducive to using such systems and indeed sharing knowledge can be in itself be a major culture change exercise in many firms."

Case Report: BBC Worldwide

This is a challenge being faced by BBC Worldwide, the commercial arm of the BBC which, by operating within global markets, is tasked with creating non licence fee revenues from the BBC's vast range of products. Creating a culture conducive to knowledge sharing is therefore seen as a key competitive tool for such a knowledge-rich and creative organization.

However, it would be misleading to say that BBC Worldwide is undertaking a culture change programme, but rather as CEO Rupert Gavin says:

> "A culture enhancing programme to make the culture more competitive. But in such a way that doesn't compromise the inherent values that we have."

And this is an important point, for the BBC Worldwide has to perform the difficult balancing act of making money commercially while retaining the powerful public services broadcasting ethos and reputation for product excellence that the BBC is renowned for throughout the world.

Knowledge-sharing

Leveraging product excellence through a commercial lens by sharing knowledge organization-wide does lead to some fundamental problems within such an innovative organization as BBC Worldwide. As Gavin points out:

"A difficulty for us in knowledge sharing is that it is the obverse of the creative organization. Ideas are what we trade in. An individual's power is based on how many of the ideas and pieces of information he or she can keep to themselves, because that is the sum of what they are worth. It will be an interesting challenge to change that."

A twin approach

To create a knowledge-sharing environment, the organization is taking a twin approach, technological and cultural. Gavin says:

"There's a growth in the technology enabling knowledge-sharing to happen, and we're moving to an intranet environment, which is important as we straddle the word. And this will be based on our electronic mail system."

Interestingly, Gavin comments that its most recent survey of staff found that e-mail was the preferred methodology by which people wish to receive information about the organization, about change and for knowledge transfer. Gavin continues:

"We're making the intranet our nerve system for information. It will be knowledge rich rather than the point of last hope. To that end we have to be quite rigorous in killing things so that people know it's the only way. It's only when you start throwing away telephone directories, sales aids on paper, etc, that people realize that they have to do things electronically and that this is the nerve base of our operations."

About the cultural element of knowledge-sharing he says:

"This is focusing on fostering the team values that means that people are incentivized to share knowledge within the teams, and so will lead to a shift from a functional to one-organization mentality."

And he makes the important point:

"Without that mentality even the best technology would be meaningless because it won't be used."

Case Study Examples: Knowledge-sharing

Companies can go a long way to getting a 'knowledge-sharing' mentality by including measures of knowledge-sharing in performance appraisals (as is the case at Ernst & Young) and ensuring that the people who get on within the organization are those willing to proactively share knowledge and information.

Within Ernst & Young, a key tool used for sharing knowledge is the firm's KnowledgeWeb, a constantly-evolving electronic resource that can be accessed at any time, by any of its people, from any of its personal computers or laptops in the world.

Focusing on further developing knowledge-sharing capabilities is key to a number of the case study companies. BT Northern Ireland, for instance, has a member of its strategy team looking into how knowledge management and sharing can further enhance customer-facing performance. CEO Lucy Woods says:

> "It would be brilliant if the knowledge in people's heads was available for others when they needed it."

Millennium Inorganic Chemicals has put together Manufacturing Technology Teams, drawn from across locations, to find internal best practices to evaluate for usage within other sites. Team members will brainstorm ideas for improvement and then prioritize those ideas according to the impact they could have on the company. A Manufacturing Steering Committee will then review the opportunities and designate some as best practices for sites to emulate.

Knowledge, Communications and Culture

From a culture change perspective, the relationship between knowledge, communications and culture was outlined by Hubert Saint-Onge, a senior executive with the Canadian-based financial institution, the Mutual Group, in the Business Intelligence report, *Creating the Knowledge-based Business*.[8]

Saint-Onge believes that most of the tacit knowledge of an organization resides in its culture. He contrasts the mindsets of individuals with organizational 'world views'. Mindsets, he says, shape the way that individuals interpret events and see the world around them. The collective mindsets of individuals is, therefore, the tacit knowledge of the organization. It is, he says, largely implicit but affects the behaviours and assumptions of individuals. He explains:

> "Effective communications and explicit knowledge exchange is only possible within a culture that provides a minimal level of congruence of its tacit knowledge."

An important point here being that if employees share similar mindsets, then communication will be more effective as people will essentially see the same things and share a general understanding of what the messages mean in relation to 'the way we work around here'. Thus, reinforcing a central message of this Report that culture must be clearly understood if change efforts are to secure lasting benefits.

Section H: Conclusion

Internal communication mechanisms, the research finds, are crucial for effectively implementing and driving culture change deep inside an organization. But getting communication right is seen by many advisers and practitioners as one of the most difficult aspects of any change programme. Importantly, communication must be led by senior managers who should be 'out there' in the field championing the change message and talking with and getting feedback from employees at the front-line. Communicating key messages has to be an ongoing process, as constant reinforcement is key to getting the message across.

Importantly, communication must be honest and timely. Communication mechanisms, of which there are many, must be mutually reinforcing and together must help drive the new behaviours and values that will underpin the achievement of corporate strategy.

Three Stages of Communication

According to Ernst & Young's Edmund White there are three stages, or waves, for using internal communication in creating an organization aligned behind corporate strategy, and crucially, adaptive to further change. This is shown in Figure 8.1.

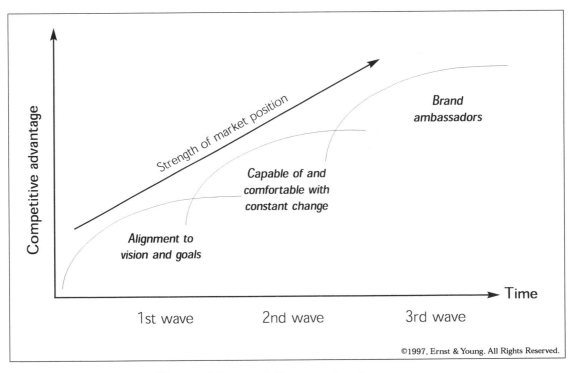

Figure 8.1: The Three Waves of Internal Communications

Depicted with a vertical axis representing competitive advantage and a horizontal axis representing time, the first wave, according to White, is about effecting employee alignment to vision and goals. The second wave is about creating a workforce and organization that is capable of and comfortable with constant change, while during the third wave employees become brand ambassadors for the firm.

White believes that during the third wave employees should be living the vision, therefore clients should be able to know what the firm stands for purely by observing the behaviour of the firm's staff.

Key Learning Points

1. Utilizing internal communication mechanisms to support a change effort is essential for success. Not least because employees need to know the business reasons for the change and what it means to them personally.

2. Indeed, it is clear from the research for this Chapter that change efforts cannot succeed without proactive and focused internal communication mechanisms.

3. However, although critical, internal communication is second in importance behind senior management demonstrating the right behaviours. As one practitioner stated:

   "No matter how much internal communication you do via newsletters, etc... all that expense will be wasted if management does not display the [correct] behaviours."

4. Linked to the above, senior management must personally lead the communication effort. Importantly, they must be receptive to feedback from the employee-base.

5. Communications must be consistent and mechanisms must be mutually supportive and reinforce the new cultural standards.

6. Organizations, the research finds, should develop a robust internal communications plan in support of the change effort and segment audiences.

7. There are a lot of communication mechanisms in use today. Although companies should use as many as possible, both traditional and electronic, the research shows that face-to-face communication is still the most powerful mechanism for delivering change messages.

CASE STUDY: ERNST & YOUNG

Summary

International financial and business advisory firm Ernst & Young has successfully created an organization focused on delivering value to its clients. Key to this has been a far-reaching culture change programme that catalysed all employees to achieve this.

Introduction

With about 85,000 employees worldwide, Ernst & Young is one of the world's leading financial and business advisers. Financial results for the UK, headquartered in London, showed fee income in 1998 at £663 million (up 19 per cent from 1997), profit per partner also up 19 per cent to £308,000 and partnership funds employed up 22 per cent to £190 million.

Impressively, this success was achieved as the firm made its greatest ever investment in service and product development, knowledge management, information technology (IT) and the development and recruitment of people.

Delivering Client Value

Active in over 132 countries, Ernst & Young, a result of a 1989 merger of the UK's financial advisory firms Arthur Young and Ernst & Whinney, has one overriding business objective – to deliver demonstrable and measurable business benefits to its clients.

According to Edmund White, the firm's national head of internal communications, this culture of client focus is firmly embedded in the minds of its employee-base. He says:

"If you ask most people in the organization to describe Ernst & Young, they'd say that we're in business for the benefit of our clients full stop.

"This, they'd say, is underpinned by demonstrating value to our employees and a performance focus on outgrowing our competitors."

As a measure of the latter, an analysis of published data by Ernst & Young's Centre for Business Knowledge of the growth of the 'big six' professional service firms from 1996 to 1998, shows Ernst & Young outpacing the competition, being a clear three percentage points ahead of its nearest rival (see Table 8.4).

Ernst & Young	31%
Andersen	28%
KPMG	23%
Price Waterhouse*	20%
Deloite & Touche	19%
Coopers & Lybrand*	17%

*Merged in 1998 to form PricewaterhouseCoopers.

Table 8.4: 'Big six' growth 1996–1998

Culture Change

Understanding the roots of Ernst & Young's growth and success requires travelling back to the early 1990s to the launch of the firm's wide-ranging culture change programme, the aim of which was to make the firm more client-focused and nimble in an increasingly competitive and demanding market-place. As White explains:

> "Historically, most of the client contacts and relationships within professional firms were acquired and developed through personal connections. Remember that until the mid 1980s firms such as Ernst & Young were not allowed to advertise, so such 'friendships' were critical. Consequently, the notion of being commercial and having to proactively sell our services was an alien concept.

> "Although that culture was successful at the time, by the start of the 1990s the market was moving on. For the first time clients were beginning to ask questions such as 'what value do we get from our auditors?', and 'why have we used this firm for the past 30 years?'."

Therefore, he says, there was a realization within Ernst & Young that future survival required nothing less than a paradigm shift in the corporate mindset, "quite simply we had to become more commercial". And this, White explains, would prove a challenge:

> "We had a lot of very successful individuals who were accustomed to a certain approach to business, and here we were asking them to change. And a lot of senior people were afraid of this because they didn't know how to go out and sell our services."

The pressures of a changing market-place were compounded by the deep recession of the early 1990s, which further squeezed fee-earning potential.

It was the above cocktail of life-threatening challenges that focused the thinking of the now-chairman Nick Land, as he explained in a Harvard Business School case study:[9]

> "One morning soon after the 1991 recession hit, I was in the kitchen... skimming the *Financial Times* when an article about another 'big six' firm caught my eye. The article featured a senior partner who was saying 'what recession?'. My first reaction was, 'if this guy really believes he can carry on as normal in this first phase of what will surely be an awful recession for professional service firms, he is a dinosaur'. That sent me bouncing around thinking about how the world was changing."

Land considered various approaches to counter the challenges of a changing business world. The hottest topic of the time was total quality management, which he rejected as it tends to focus on improving the current state whereas he knew the firm needed a massive organizational shift.

Change Steering Group

Effecting this shift would, he believed, require a radical change in the behaviour of all staff and an organizational restructuring to become truly responsive to customer needs.

Recognizing that radical change would be a huge undertaking, an initial step by Land in 1992 was to set up a steering group of senior partners to oversee the change programme.

This group realized that if there was to be any chance of the change imperatives taking hold within the firm, it would be critical to first get the partners on board and enthused. Consequently, Land and other steering group members spent the autumn of 1992 visiting partners in all the UK offices to deliver the change message. According to White, Land's visibility went a long way to convincing the partners that he was indeed serious about change.

Partner Days

Land and his team reinforced the firm's need for transformation through a series of partner days, a key goal of which was to create the classic 'burning platform' on which partners would see that due to market diktats, change had to happen, despite the firm's then profitable state. Land also outlined that this change programme would take a long time – up to ten years he warned.

These partner days were followed by workshops, organized by managing partners within each office, for managers and staff and which shared similar agendas to the partner days. All these workshops included presentations on why the firm needed to change followed by an open-floor discussion moderated by a consultant from change specialists Kinsley Lord.

Just holding these manager and staff days signalled a radical culture change within Ernst & Young, as many felt that for the first time the firm had sought the opinions of non-partners in a significant strategic issue.

During 1992 the firm articulated its vision statement, this being:

'To be recognized as the leading professional service firm which contributes most to its clients' success.'

Throughout 1993, Land or another senior partner attended over 30 training programmes to lead discussions on what the vision would mean for the firm in the future.

1993 Initiatives

The steering group, believing that a critical mass of employees at all levels had bought into the need for change, also launched ten change initiatives to be rolled-out during 1993. These were:

1. An internal communications policy: Land appointed a full-time national communications manager, and at least one person per office was assigned part-time to the role of internal communications manager.

2. Driving the use of IT throughout the firm.

3. Client care, which was broken down into three main sets of activity:
    - a survey to obtain client feedback
    - a review of the results to identify areas for improvement
    - the implementation of identified changes to improve client service.

4. Use of six-step problem-solving framework called KEY (Kaizen at Ernst & Young) to drive continuous improvement throughout the firm.

5. Business planning: employing the KEY Framework and a facilitator trained in its techniques, a team of partners and managers were designated in every office to prepare a cross-discipline business team for the following fiscal year. This proved to be a dramatic departure from the firm's traditionally functional approach to business planning.

6. The creation of performance development systems (PDS) to link individual objectives with business objectives.

7. A sales skills programme aimed at creating a sales culture in the organization.

8. A 'barrier buster' award, through which several individuals were recognized each month for exceptional efforts to break down internal barriers of hierarchy, geography or discipline.

9. An attitude survey of all partners, managers and staff.

10. Change workshops where employees could discuss and evaluate the change programme. These included bi-annual 'Leaders for Change' workshops, at the first of which Land and his steering group reported how they were going to change their own behaviour to align with the change objectives. In October 1993, the whole partnership gathered for a two-day conference entitled 'Winning Through Change', while a further round of manager and staff days were held under the heading 'One Year On'.

In addition, during 1993 and 1994, most partners attended one of a series of week-long business strategy courses which focused on how other organizations were transforming themselves. Land attended each one and led question-and-answer sessions on his view of the future and the progress of the change programme.

1994 Key Initiatives

With so many change initiatives under way, the steering group meeting in November 1993 discussed feedback from employees, which suggested that there was a sense of 'initiative overload' within the firm. There was also concern that the change process was too intangible, meaning many different things to different people.

Consequently, the steering group identified three pressing problems to focus on during the following year, each of which will be looked at in turn:

1. The need to reorganize the London office (which then accounted for about half the firms employees and revenue).

2. Overcoming widespread dissatisfaction among senior managers.

3. Countering a general frustration with a lack of a clear over-arching vision for change (although the firm did have a vision statement).

London Reorganization

White says of the London office reorganization:

"This was primarily driven by the needs of the clients, many of whom were saying 'isn't it a bit stupid that some of your people meet for the first time on a client's premises'.

"And we realized that we must be missing business opportunities if we were not able to provide our clients with the best of our collective industry knowledge.

"So, rather than being organized along traditional disciplines, for example we had a number of London audit teams who had clients in different industries, we put people from different disciplines, such as audit, tax and consultancy into the same industry-facing groups."

Examples of these were:
- Entrepreneurial Services (to serve owner-managed and smaller inward investment companies).
- Financial Services.
- Industrial and Commercial Services and Media.
- Energy and Resources Services.

In keeping with the steering group's preference for change through inclusivity, these recommendations came from a working group of London partners who spent three months analysing the existing structure and several proposed models that came out of a change workshop focused exclusively on the London reorganization.

The firm has since reorganized across the whole of the UK. Now everybody in audit and tax, for example, is aligned to an industry sector. Ernst & Young has moved from having over 20 offices run as independent businesses to four regional businesses plus national businesses such as consultancy, corporate recovery and business risk consulting. Says White:

"Our people now increasingly understand the industries they are serving and how their combined knowledge adds value to the industries they serve."

Senior Management Project

The second key area of pressing concern highlighted by the 1993 attitude survey was a growing discontent among senior management (ie, those just below partner level). This discontent, the survey found, was largely because senior managers felt unappreciated and that they were not sufficiently recognized or rewarded for their loyalty and contribution. There was also widespread dissatisfaction with the dearth of career counselling for senior managers.

A real fear for the firm was that these experienced and knowledgeable people would leave the firm once the UK recession lifted. Consequently, Land appointed a task force of nine partners and managers to work on 'the senior management project'. Based on interviews with 200 senior managers in early 1994, the task force made a number of recommendations. These included:

1. Managers, senior managers and partners need to have discernibly different responsibilities and accountabilities that reflect the job they do and that provide a distinct step change in progression.

2. Career planning should be in place for everyone in the firm and must recognize that people should have an appropriate combination of technical, business development, managerial and industry-based experience.

3. People should be given responsibility in areas in which they have special expertise, no matter if it results in a senior manager being in charge of a partner.

4. Senior managers should be informed of precisely what they have the scope to deliver without interference from partners.

5. Transparent links should be established between performance and reward.

6. People management and leadership development programmes should be provided to all partners and managers.

Despite being rolled-out during 1995, little changed. This was largely the result of being too broad and dependent on work by office managing partners. Therefore, Land appointed a new project team consisting wholly of managers to develop a more concise and instructive set of action plans. The team arrived at two recommendations:

1. The performance development system (PDS) should overlay its current 'competency framework' with a 'role framework'. The proposed role framework would mean individuals setting personal goals aligned with their offices objectives in four categories; business development, client service, product and technical development, and managing people. Employees would then be evaluated and rewarded on how well they fulfilled their pre-determined role.

2. Ernst & Young should introduce a new grade as an alternative to equity partnership. Its entrants would be a mix of senior managers with highly specialized expertise and functional specialists, such as the heads of organizational development and strategy. There would be strict criteria for admission to this grade, so it would not be considered a consolation prize for people who did not make it through to the partnership level, but rather a legitimate goal in itself.

Success Model

The third identified problem was the lack of an over-arching vision of change. Overcoming this perceived shortcoming has seen the firm invest a considerable amount of time detailing exactly what the Ernst & Young vision is, why the vision is important and articulating a set of seven building blocks that together would drive the organization to achieving its vision.

This success model has been visualized in a form that, because of it is shape, has become know within the firm as 'the rocket' (see Figure 8.2). This shows how the vision derives from the firm's characteristics, supported by the competitive advantage, and driven by the seven building blocks.

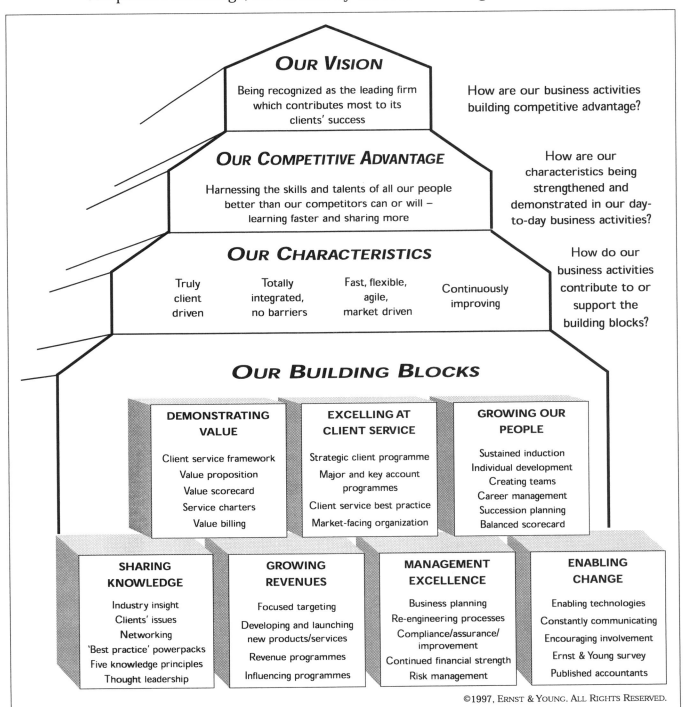

Figure 8.2: 'Living Our Vision' Success Model

First, the original vision of, 'to be recognized as the leading firm which contributes most to its clients' success' has recently been slightly modified, but the change is important, as White explains:

> "The vision is now 'Being recognized...' as it's happening, so it's now about living the vision so we can maintain this position."

Ernst & Young defines its competitive advantage as:

> 'harnessing the skills and talents of all our people better than our competitors can or will – learning faster and sharing more.'

As Land said in Ernst & Young's 1998 report and accounts:[10]

> "In common with many organizations, our only asset is our people. Their skills, knowledge and experience are complemented by determination, passion and the belief that they can make a difference to their clients and to Ernst & Young. We recognize that we need to demonstrate value to our people just as much as we do to our clients. To this end, we have created an environment where our people know they have influence and where roles, not grades, are what counts."

And White adds:

> "The culture is surprisingly non-hierarchical. There isn't really an us and them mentality. There's work we need to do and it doesn't matter who does it. There is of course a management structure, but that doesn't get in the way of getting the work done."

As will be explained later in this case study, harnessing the skills of employees has also led to Ernst & Young being recognized as a benchmark organization for knowledge management.

In the rocket model, Ernst & Young goes on to define its characteristics as:
- Truly Client Driven.
- Totally Integrated with No Barriers.
- Fast, Flexible, Agile and Market Driven.
- Committed to Continuous Improvement.

White explains:

> "We recognized that if we could demonstrate these four characteristics we would gain a competitive advantage in the market-place. However, some people did say 'yes, but what about integrity, honesty, hard work, etc'. But we said 'we take that for granted'. We're going to assume that people have integrity, are honest and work hard."

Therefore, Ernst & Young, unlike many organizations profiled for this Report, does not have a set of corporate values. An internal working group did try to articulate a set but the attempt was abandoned because in trying to gain consensus the wording became meaningless. Says White:

> "A problem with value statements is that individual's value sets are never going to be the same, except at a certain level such as 'murder is wrong'.

"Values can be 'so what', so it's better to build an environment where it is very difficult for people to behave in a way contrary to the firm's beliefs. So, at Ernst & Young it's very difficult to work in silos, to not be open or not share knowledge, as examples."

The firm's seven building blocks are:

- demonstrating value

- excelling at client service

- growing our people

- sharing knowledge

- growing revenues

- management excellence

- enabling change.

As Figure 8.2 shows each block contains specific supporting business activities.

360 Degree Appraisal

One important mechanism for ensuring that the building blocks, and indeed each element of 'the rocket', are firmly embedded into the fabric of the firm, is the organization's 360 degree appraisal system. As an example, the partners' performance contribution and measurement indicators for 1997–1998 included dimensions such as 'achieving client satisfaction' with assessment criteria such as client care, demonstrating value and risk management; 'building revenues' with dimensions such as winning new work and internal and external networking; 'coaching people and developing teams' with areas such as effective team player, demonstrating skills/commitment in coaching role, enhancing the capabilities of people; and 'living the vision' with areas such as demonstrating leadership in transforming the business, flexibility, agility, market driven, total integration and no barriers.

Knowledge Management

Assessing performance dimensions such as internal and external networking and total integration also helps the firm get knowledge management onto the corporate agenda.

Land recognized the importance of this knowledge, or intellectual capital, in gaining and sustaining competitive advantage. He said:[11]

"We not only have a culture which fosters an integrated best-team approach but have also been investing very substantially on a global basis in building world-class knowledge management. We already have a global network of five Centres for Business Knowledge [these being in London, Cleveland, Toronto, Paris and Sydney]. In the UK we have introduced an Assurance Support Centre which specifically focuses on relevant business information and insights, initially for nine key industries, for the benefit of our Business Assurance Teams."

About the firm's approach to knowledge management and sharing, the Spring 1997 edition of *Emerson's Professional Services Review* stated:[12]

> "The new Ernst & Young wants to go beyond the simple mechanics of technology and establish the foundation for an entirely new knowledge-sharing culture. This vision has not only created the new knowledge-sharing standard in professional services, but positions Ernst & Young to leverage its model to other industries worldwide."

A 1998 analysis by the UK knowledge consultancy Teleos for Business Intelligence, ranked the firm fourth in the world for knowledge management (the highest professional firm on the list) and first in the effectiveness of knowledge sharing category.[13]

A key tool is the firm's KnowledgeWeb, a constantly-evolving electronic resource that can be accessed at any time, by any of its people, from any of their personal computers or laptops anywhere in the world.

However, as White explains, creating a culture of knowledge sharing does include challenges:

> "It's not natural in Western cultures for people to give knowledge away for free. We have to constantly demonstrate the benefits for the individual and the organization.

> "Also, in our industry a lot of our knowledge comes from our clients, so a complex challenge is how we can leverage value from that knowledge while protecting our client's knowledge from falling into the hands of competitors."

Client Surveys

Crucial to the firm's success in both business and cultural transformation terms has been its use of surveys, both for its clients and staff.

For its clients Ernst & Young has designed a client satisfaction engagement questionnaire. This comprises about 20 questions measured on a scale from 1 (extremely dissatisfied) to 5 (extremely satisfied). Questions include how satisfied are you that Ernst & Young:

- Understood and helped you identify the issues key to your success?
- Demonstrated a good understanding of your business?
- Shared knowledge with you and your team?
- Provided fresh insights, ideas and suggestions?
- Demonstrated the value they added to your business?

There is also room for additional comments. Reinforcing the firm's belief in delivering exceptional customer value, White says:

> "Client handlers know that anything below five means they have to do something about it."

Employee Surveys

The firm's first employee survey was in 1994 and has grown to become a valuable database for tracking both employee satisfaction and the firm's success in creating a client-focused culture. It also, says White, provides a tremendous opportunity to learn and to prioritize action.

In addition to asking questions such as 'do I have a good understanding of the vision?', the survey also asks how the firm has progressed against areas highlighted as needing attention in the previous questionnaire. For this reason, the firm did not conduct a survey in 1998 as highlighted problems would take longer than a year to fix. As White says:

> "When you publish results, the only point is to use the findings for continuous improvement and to communicate change."

The firm is carrying out a survey in 1999. Importantly, the survey is now outsourced to specialist surveying company ISR, thus enabling Ernst & Young to benefit from benchmark comparisons drawn from ISR's extensive database.

Wherever possible Ernst & Young compares its results against two main sets of data. The first is the UK Service Sector which contains a large number of organizations from various service industries. The second is a group of organizations recognized as delivering high performance and who, therefore, provide a much higher standard against which Ernst & Young can compare itself.

The data shows how far the firm has come in creating a satisfied employee-base aligned behind strategic objectives. Results for dimensions such as communication, vision and leadership, job satisfaction, client service quality, management effectiveness and teamworking and co-operation show the firm above the UK service sector norm, and ahead of the high performance norm for communication and vision and leadership. Says White:

> "So we're sure we're doing the right things in engaging people. But we know we must still improve. For example, we haven't got our measurement system right. Reward and recognition performed relatively poorly on the survey, so we now know where we have to prioritize."

Internal Communications

White is convinced that an integral element of the successful culture change programme is the firm's total commitment to internal communications. He says:

> "We recognized that open, honest, continuous communication would make or break the programme. If we were going to succeed with such radical change then people had to understand it and be aligned to it."

Crucially, White believes that internal communications is *not* about telling people what to do, but rather engaging them in what the firm is striving to achieve.

To effect this the firm has created a network of about 40 internal communications managers. These are people in the business whose role it is to help local managers address communications issues.

In the initial period of the change programme, issues emerged that the network could not resolve at a local level. They were able to pick a phone up and get straight through to a member of the executive. Says White, "this hotline proved very effective".

According to White there are three stages, or waves, for using internal communications to transform an organization. Depicted with a vertical axis representing competitive advantage and a horizontal axis representing time, the first wave is about effecting employee alignment to vision and goals. The second wave is about creating a workforce and organization that is capable of and comfortable with constant change, while during the third wave employees become brand ambassadors for the firm (see Figure 8.1).

White believes that during the third wave employees should be living the vision, and therefore clients should be able to know what the firm stands for purely by observing the behaviour of the firm's staff.

Future Challenges

Looking into the future, Ernst & Young knows that it will have to keep improving and changing if it is to maintain its leading market position. Challenges ahead include becoming much more of a global entity.

With a similar goal in mind, two key competitors Coopers & Lybrand and Price Waterhouse merged in 1998 to create a new firm, PricewaterhouseCoopers. During the same year Ernst & Young itself considered merging with the consultancy KPMG. As Land said in the 1998 report and accounts:[14]

> "For four months of the year we were in discussions with KPMG about a worldwide merger. Having completed thorough due diligence on one another, Ernst & Young concluded that the differences between our cultures and our visions for the future were too great. We decided that full integration of the two businesses would be very a protracted affair with the inevitable impact on growth and market position.... It was a measure of our people that their knowledge of the discussions did not distract them from their focus on our markets, our clients and our business objectives."

Conclusion

In conclusion, Land commented:[15]

> "It is now six years since we began the process of fundamentally changing many aspects of the firm, in anticipation of the significant changes that would affect the business world for much of the late 1990s and beyond. During that time this process of change has brought substantial benefits to

our clients, our people and our business. Client care feedback, staff survey results, people retention rates and growth all bear testimony to the fact that Ernst & Young is an exciting, dynamic and very successful organization."

This is a belief independently supported through Ernst & Young's inclusion in 1998's *The 100 Best Employers in the UK* listing by the Corporate Research Foundation. The judges stated:[16]

"Ernst & Young... looks like a winning team in a range of growing management disciplines..."

White believes there are three key elements that a company must get right if it is to succeed with culture change:

1. **Communication**: "It has to be continuous. Once it's started it can't stop".

2. **Visible leadership**: "You cannot lead a culture change by diktat. Leaders have to be visible, respected and seen to be changing themselves".

3. **Make the success of it visible**: "Don't take even small successful change for granted. And put processes in place that say 'yes we're taking stuff away but we're putting more in'. There's a natural tendency for people to think of change as just taking things away. So you have to demonstrate that it will give more than it takes".

White also adds that there an additional point to make, "and if you wanted a fourth thing, it's fun". As a final comment White says:

"The scary stuff about change management is that most of it is simply applied common sense – but that's what makes it difficult."

Key Learning Points

Ernst & Young has succeeded with its culture change programme because it got a number of fundamentals right, and these include:

1. Basing the culture change programme on clear strategic imperatives. In Ernst & Young's case these were to realign the firm to changing market-place requirements.

2. Senior management commitment from chairman Nick Land and the other senior partners was unwavering and visible.

3. All levels of the firm were engaged in the change programme – partners, managers and staff.

4. The senior team was willing to learn from mistakes and recognized that cultural change would take a long time.

5. A model of business success was designed and forms the basis of all the firm's activities. This comprises a vision, a definition of how the firm would gain competitive advantage, key characteristics and seven building blocks.

6. Sharing knowledge is a critical focus within Ernst & Young, and the firm has invested considerable resources into facilitating this.

7. Similarly, the firm has invested heavily in internal communications, recognizing that all employees must be kept informed, and involved, in the change effort.

9

MERGERS AND ACQUISITIONS – THE CULTURAL CHALLENGE

Executive Summary

1. There has been a phenomenal growth in merger and acquisition (M&A) activity over recent years and this shows no signs of abating.

2. Despite this growth, research finds that a significant percentage of M&As fail to deliver the expected business benefits.

3. Failure, the research finds, is rarely due to price or faulty strategies, but rather to cultural issues.

4. Chief executive officers have a crucial role is creating a winning culture within unified organizations.

5. Shaping a new corporate vision can play an important role as it gives employees at all levels something tangible to work towards that is unique to the new organization.

6. Senior managers must be careful not to create a 'victor and vanquished' mentality within the new organization. This is a particular problem following a hostile take-over

7. A process of cultural due diligence will go a long way to identifying potential cultural misalignment between organizations.

8. Merger Integration Teams should focus on integrating cultural attributes as well as physical systems.

9. Unifying human resource mechanisms can prove a difficult area in the integration process, especially around the area of compensation and benefits.

10. Internal communication, the research shows, plays a pivotal role in successfully melding cultures. Communication should be honest, direct and timely, and companies should not shy from communicating bad news as quickly as possible.

11. The experiences of acquisition exemplar GE Capital provide powerful learning points for other organizations.

12. A case study on Lehigh Portland Cement Company demonstrates best practice.

Section A: Context

Whereas the previous Chapters in this Report have focused on culture change in the generic sense (ie, general principles for any culture change effort), this Chapter focuses squarely upon a specific issue – managing the cultural change aspects of merger and acquisitions (M&As).

This is important because, as shall be explained, M&A activity has experienced phenomenal growth in recent years and shows no signs of abating in the near or even medium future. However, despite this, M&As, as shall also be shown, often fail to deliver the anticipated business benefits or shareholder returns. The reason for this, the research finds, is that combining organizations rarely get the culture fit right. Indeed, they often fail to consider the cultural aspects of the relationship at all, despite the fact that cultural difficulties, as this Chapter shall show, are myriad.

Therefore, this Chapter will consider why so many M&As do indeed fail and will consider best practice processes to heighten the potential for success, such as cultural due diligence, cultural integration through post merger management, dealing with employee concerns, aligning HR systems and the important role of focused, honest and dedicated communications. First, however, it is necessary to look at the business imperatives that have led to the explosion in M&A activity.

Section B: Merger and Acquisition Activity

According to an article in the UK's *The Guardian* newspaper the largest mergers (involving European organizations) during 1998 are shown in Table 9.1.[1] According to the same article, the total value of global M&As was £1500 billion during 1998, with, it claimed, oil giant Exxon heading the pack with the largest successful bid, valued at £48 billion for Mobil, bringing together organizations with 123,000 employees.

Companies	$ billion
1. Zeneca/Astra	67.0
2. BP/Amoco	54.3
3. Daimler/Chrysler	39.5
4. UBS/SBC	23.0
5. Fortis/Generale de Banque	12.3
6. Vereinsbank/Hypo	12.3
7. Huls/Degussa	11.8
8. Commercial Union/General Accident	11.2
9. San Paolo/IMI	9.5
10. Viag/Alusise	8.6

Table 9.1: Largest Mergers during 1998 involving European Organizations ($ billion)

Key Drivers for Increased Activity

So why are M&As on the increase? According to the research for this Report there are several key drivers; globalization, achieving economies of scale to better compete (especially as competitive pressures accelerate), industry deregulation, the potential of technological exploitation, and buoyant stock markets leading to the availability of ready cash.

M&As are affecting a wide variety of organizations, be they companies leading the information and communications revolution, such as in the telecommunications industry (eg, Vodaphone and Airtouch), or companies in pharmaceuticals (Zeneca and Astra), financial services (the UK's Halifax Bank and Birmingham Midshires Building Society), car manufactures (Daimler Benz and Chrysler), food and drinks (Guinness and Grand Metropolitan), oil and gas (BP and Amoco). In short, M&As can affect any company in any industry.

The importance of scale

John Childress, chief executive officer of the culture change specialists Senn-Delaney Leadership Consulting Group, stresses the importance of scale as a key determinant of the current M&A activity. He explains that its significance is easily understood if we consider the increasingly global nature of business:

> "More and more companies are competing on a global basis, so scale helps reduce price to a competitive level. Scale gives you purchasing power that you don't normally have if you are a regional player and it also helps you to streamline processes such as manufacturing or finance."

Globalization

Childress goes on to say that if you want to expand globally there are two ways you can do it. One is organic growth, the other is through mergers or acquisitions. Organic growth, he says, is normally preferable but slow. He explains:

> "It's preferable because you can control it and you don't have the cultural challenges. However, the world is moving much too fast for this to be a viable strategy for many companies, so the other alternative, a merger or acquisition, is the most practical. And, to be honest, for most companies who wish to succeed on a global level this is the only viable option open to them."

Childress believes that M&A activity will remain buoyant as increasing number of countries open their market-places, as more and more companies start to source globally, and as the lower wage-rate countries ramp up the level of exports of their products.

However, although M&As are not a new phenomena, they are, according to research, posing some new challenges. M&As today were contrasted with M&As of the 1980s in *Mergers & Acquisitions: Getting the People Bit Right*, a 1998 report by the UK business college, Roffey Park Management Institute. The report stated:[2]

> "Mergers and acquisitions from the mid 1990s onwards are markedly different to the deals of the late 1980s. Because of the drive to focus on core activities, many are related/horizontal acquisitions. They tend to be in sectors that are experiencing rapid change or deregulation. Many are cross-border transactions. They are probably more complex and potentially problematic than the unrelated conglomerate deals that were typical of the 1980s."

Levels of M&A Failure

The failure rates are frightening and it is interesting to explore why so many mergers fail. In a November 1998 article in the UK's *Sunday Times*, Alan Crozier, a consultant with William M Mercer, provided these statistics:[3]

> "Since the mid 1980s, 57 per cent of deals worth £300 million or more have resulted in poor returns for shareholders in the following three years, relative to industry averages. Even in the 1990s, where deals have been more strategically driven, the success rate is barely 50 per cent."

He went on to claim that research shows that 61 per cent of deals failed to cover even the cost of capital; fewer than 25 per cent generated economic value for the buyer; productivity fell by as much as 50 per cent; management turnover was typically 35 per cent and in hostile take-overs 54 per cent. He said that some bidders underperformed their sector by as much as 35 per cent.

Tellingly, Crozier stated that size appears to be a factor, stating that the larger the deal, the more likely it is to fail in its strategic intent and in delivering shareholder value. A worrying statement given the present corporate predilection for 'mega-mergers'.

And, importantly, he says that the reason lies not in the price, nor in faulty strategy:

> "The main cause of failure are cultural inability to change, lack of leadership and motivation, insufficient time given to the change process and inadequate communication."

Failure Examples

Larry Senn, chairman of Senn-Delaney, quoting from research within the US-based *Training Magazine*, states that up to one third of mergers fail within five years, and as many as 80 per cent never live up to their full expectations.

As examples of failure (and crucially why these were due to a cultural mismatch), Senn provided several high profile examples. AT&T's failed acquisition of NCR being one instance, where losses quickly reached two billion dollars. Senn writes:

> "While the companies looked similar on the surface, the cultures were different in important ways. NCR was conservative and AT&T politically correct. NCR had always been tightly controlled from the top and AT&T more decentralized. AT&T was heavily unionized and NCR non-union. Problems became evident whenever they came together. At one point they tried something as simple as sharing facilities but had to give up on it due to lack of compatibility."

Another example of a cultural clash quoted was the merger of Price Club and Costco Wholesale to create Price/Costco Inc, which became the world's second largest operator of warehouse clubs. About the problems here, Senn quoted from Michael Shea of the US-based Charter Investment Group, who said:

> "The Price guys had much more of a real estate... mentality. The Costco guys were the type who started working at grocery stores bagging groceries when they were ten years old and worked their way up the ladder. Since no team alignment work was systematically done to bridge the gap, the combination was deadly."

Why Culture is Overlooked

According to the research the strategic fit is rarely a cause of failure. Dr George Labovitz, chairman of the US-headquartered organizational change and performance measurement consultancy Organizational Dynamics Inc (ODI), espouses the view of many commentators interviewed for this Chapter when he says:

> "There are two things you need for a successful merger, a good strategic case and good chemistry, and you must have both. Most fail because the chemistry's bad, not the strategic case. Actually it's fairly straightforward to make the strategic case for a merger, but that in no way guarantees success."

The excitement of 'doing the deal'

A specific problem with the M&A process, according to our research, is that the process of 'doing the deal' is exciting and companies spend a disproportionate amount of time on this. As Suzanne C Francis, an expert in the cultural elements of M&As and a senior partner with the US-based consultancy Robert H Schaffer & Associates, comments:

> "The hard work is making it happen after the deal, which is a lot less interesting, it's dirty work. A disproportionate amount of time and resources is expended on doing the deal and little energy, money or people allocated to making it work."

This, she says, is unsurprising, given that 'deal doers' are paid exceptionally well, whereas line managers (those who have to make it work in practice) tend to be paid much less.

Continuing with the theme, Childress adds that a big reason for M&A failure is that they are driven by investment banking firms who normally do not want anything to get in the way of the transaction and their fees. He says:

> "They are purely transaction driven. Whether it succeeds after the deal is done is not their concern. They're paid as a percentage of the deal.

> "It's a very myopic system right now. And I think companies are being badly served by an investment banking community which does not get involved or care about whether or not this will eventually be a workable merger or acquisition."

Quoting from *Training Magazine* , Senn adds:[5]

> "The majority of merger shortfalls are due to human factors, not to quantitative analysis. You can run all your discounted cash flows and have the numbers come out perfectly, but it's the human resources side of a merger or acquisition that spells failure or success."

However, according to our research, such failing caused by being purely financially driven is starting to change, albeit slowly, as the importance of the cultural integration of merging organizations gains credence. Indeed the past year has seen a significant rise in newspaper and magazine column inches dedicated to this issue. This, coupled with the appalling failure statistics, is going some way to making CEOs sit up and take notice.

Section C: The Role of the CEO

When looking in detail at some of the key cultural reasons for M&A failure it is helpful to start with the role of senior management, as it will be they who will need to champion and lead the employee-base through the potentially painful process of integration.

A difficult problem at the beginning, especially within a full-blown merger, is for the appointed CEO (and this choice in itself can cause problems, especially if two merging companies possess powerful CEOs) to pull together into one team the new executive board. This was the case at Lehigh Portland Cement Company (the case study to accompany this Chapter), where the most senior managers from the merging Lehigh and CBR cement companies had significantly different managerial styles. To help overcome this the top leaders spent a considerable amount of time crafting a new vision for the organization, and one that 'both sets' of managers could commit to, and a planning guide for operationalizing the new strategy of the merged organization.

Creating a New Vision

Indeed, our research finds, creating a new vision for the merged organization is critical as it helps the new company gain its own identity and gives employees something concrete to focus on and work towards. About the vision for Lehigh Portland, 'working together to build our communities', vice president of total quality Peter Tait says:

> "Although a short vision, it neatly explains what we do. Working together as a merged company, working with customers, with suppliers and with communities."

It is also important for the senior management team to spend time developing, resourcing and communicating a clear transition plan for the new company. A merger integration team, for example, was central to merger success at Lehigh Portland. Pivotal indeed as the management styles of the two companies were quite different. Lehigh was centralized and hierarchical whereas CBR was decentralized and highly participative. Such differences, the research finds, often lead to M&A failure, but are too often overlooked in the post-merger process as senior managers often, and somewhat arrogantly, believe that employees will accept the new culture when they see its efficacy in everyday operations.

It is also important to note that whoever gets the top jobs will be watched carefully during the merger process. Insensitivity here can lead to a hugely damaging victor and vanquished mentality emerging in the two 'separate' organizations, which is the topic of the next section.

Section D: The Victor Versus Vanquished Mentality

The danger of creating a victor versus vanquished, or 'winners and losers', mentality within merging organizations is, according to the research, a significant challenge in an M&A activity. Although a danger in any merger or acquisition it may be especially problematic if one company was subject to a 'hostile' take-over. The danger of the acquired employees feeling defeated in a corporate war and therefore being at the mercy of the 'conquering army' (and expecting the punishment that this may bring) should not be taken lightly.

According to the research, how senior managers of the 'winning' company approach this victor versus vanquished mindset will go some way to determining the M&A's eventual success. Francis comments:

> "If you act like a victor and expect people to bow down to you then you're going to got problems. You have to look to ways to manage that doesn't create an adversarial situation.

> "If you say that nothing's negotiable then people are more likely to feel vanquished. However, if you say lets plan this together and there are things that are negotiable then this will create a much firmer foundation for going forward."

According to Senn, a related problem is that the acquiring company typically wants to impose changes, and tends to view those in the acquired company as highly resistant to change. He writes:[6]

> "The most frequent complaint of companies that are being acquired is that the new owners 'don't appreciate us; we don't get any credit for what we've done and what is working. They only point out how their way is better'."

During such times, he says, it is critical for the acquiring firm to go out of its way to acknowledge as many positive aspects of the acquired firm as possible. At the same time, it should set expectations and create an environment in which there is a high level of openness to change.

Therefore companies can go a long way to minimizing this danger by recognizing that there will be positives and negatives in both the combining organizations. As creating a 'new and improved' organization is normally a key goal of any M&A, this can prove a powerful opportunity to analyse strengths and weaknesses within both companies and selecting the best practice process from each or indeed creating a new process altogether, an approach taken by Lehigh Portland. Therefore, the 'stronger' organization, if there is one, must not presume that their way is necessarily best and must go out of its way to acknowledge and raise to the ascendancy the best practices of the other company. This will go some way to getting 'buy-in' from the employees from the 'weaker' organization.

Roffey Park Research

However, and on the surface somewhat surprising, the Roffey Park researchers found that, in some cases, employees from the 'losing' company are relieved to be acquired, whereas some from the 'winning' company feel they do not get the full benefit of their 'victorious' position. The authors write:[7]

> "[Our research found that] sometimes, if there were poor relations between senior managers and staff or between the management team and its parent company, employees were relieved to be sold. Instead of being resentful and uncooperative, they exhibited a positive and helpful attitude to their new owners."

And, with reference to the successful merger between UK-based drinks retailers Threshers and Peter Dominic, they write:

> "Some of the Thresher middle managers... considered that the allocation of jobs turned them from considering themselves winners into losers when they found themselves reporting to a more experienced Peter Dominic manager. They could not understand why, if they were part of the dominant group, they were being asked to change roles, and people took the matter to heart. They also blamed senior management, complaining that they had not been communicated with enough and that all the attention was being lavished on Dominic staff."

The key points here are that senior management must communicate with, and pay attention to the concerns of, both sets of employees in a merger or acquisition process, and should not underestimate the potential dangers of victor and vanquished mindsets.

So, knowing that cultural misalignment is almost certainly a key reason for M&A failure, and that a multitude of cultural barriers may need to be overcome, how can an organization begin to tackle these problems?

Section E: Cultural Due Diligence

According to the research, a process of cultural due diligence must play a central role in the M&A process. We find that, quite properly, financial due diligence receives a lot of attention during M&A exercises. However, cultural due diligence receives substantially less attention. But this is a dangerous approach, as Alison Rankin-Frost, head of the UK-based Context Consulting, points out:

> "Financial due diligence only shows what has happened up until that point of time. Cultural due diligence will show if there are problems to be faced in the future. It can take a long time to merge two companies and therefore senior management may have to think through whether they have the time or the money to manage that merger."

According to Senn, an internal resource specialist or outside consultant should assist in the culture aspect of due diligence. This, he says, would include the following:[8]

1. Developing a simple and quick profile of the culture of the acquisition (or merger) candidate and be aware of similarities and differences.

2. Determine similarities and differences in the internal reinforcement systems, including:
   - compensation/benefit systems
   - performance review systems
   - performance criteria (written and unwritten)
   - hiring and firing criteria and practices.

3. Compare philosophies of the dominant leaders, especially if they are both to stay on.

4. Openly discuss not only financial considerations, but the similarities and differences in culture and the proposed nature of cultural integration, ie, autonomous organizations, assimilation, or procreation of a new entity.

Undertaking a Cultural Audit

An important aspect of the due diligence process, the research shows, is conducting a cultural audit of an organization which you are going to acquire or merge with. As Childress says:

"You have to know what to look for. It's usually not in the numbers. It's usually in the history, in the habits, beliefs and values of the organization. One way to find that out is to ask employees. Another way is to ask customers.

"If you know what to ask for, you can really get to see what the real cultural strengths of the organization are. You can pull together views from both organizations and quickly see where the overlaps are and where the differences are."

For the auditing process, Childress states that the two organizations should complete a cultural profile of their own organization (using a profile tool such as the one shown in Chapter 5, Figure 5.1) and then use an outside consultant to interpret the findings and highlight similarities and potential problems. With this information a strategic plan for dealing with the difficulties, and indeed for leveraging benefits from the cultural similarities, can be created.

Alignment Diagnostic

A recently developed mechanism that can be used for assessing cultural similarities is the Alignment Diagnostic tool designed by ODI. This tool is also shown in Chapter 5, and essentially is an electronic application which enables a computer-based graphical analysis of how well the organization is aligned. It asks employees a series of questions which they have to answer using a scale of strongly agree to strongly disagree. Lawrence Brink, ODI's vice president for marketing/product development, says:

"By using the Diagnostic organizations can pinpoint where there's going to be cultural issues such as contrasting management styles, customer focus, approaches to teamworking etc, that will need to addressed. You really need to look below the surface of organizations to see how they actually work on a day-to-day basis, and you can only get that from the people who work deep inside the companies."

He adds that in M&As there has to be a point where the new entity is a fully functioning whole, and if intervention strategies to resolve cultural disconnects can be deployed early in the integration process then this may save the new company millions of pounds.

Case Report: Ernst & Young

It is interesting to note that following a due diligence process, one of the case study companies, Ernst & Young (the case study to accompany the previous Chapter) decided not to proceed with proposed merger with its rival consultancy KPMG.

Writing in the firm's 1998 report and accounts, chairman Nick Land explained why:[9]

> "For four months of the year we were in discussions with KPMG about a worldwide merger. Having completed thorough due diligence on one another, Ernst & Young concluded that differences between our cultures and our visions for future were too great. We decided that full integration of the two businesses would be a very protracted affair with the inevitable impact on growth and market position."

In short, therefore, cultural due diligence will provide a clear analysis of cultural similarities and differences will enable merging organizations to pinpoint potential cultural problems in advance and so prepare intervention plans. It will also show when the merger or acquisition is not as viable as it may first appear on paper.

However if, after cultural due diligence, the decision is made to progress with the merger or acquisition, the management of the new entity then faces the complex problem of post-merger management.

Section F: Merger Integration

Commonly, organizations in this phase will set up a merger integration team consisting of representatives of both organizations. In addition to financial and physical integration the team should consider cultural integration, as was the case at Lehigh Portland Cement Company.

According to Senn-Delaney, the key steps in the cultural integration plan should be:[10]

* Complete and extend the cultural profiling and analysis of cultural similarities and differences begun during the due diligence process.

* Begin development of a new shared vision, mission, and values set. They define a new culture which incorporates and builds upon the best of each organization.

* Develop communication plans and strategies.

* Create a more detailed organizational structure and reporting relationship.

* Develop the personal plan, including:

  - Benefit packages
  - Compensation packages.

According to Ron Duboff of William M Mercer Management Consulting, writing in the December 1997/January 1998 edition of the UK magazine *Focus on Change Management*, an examination of those companies that have successfully used acquisitions to generate profitable growth reveals that strong post-merger management has three characteristics, each of which, he writes is intrinsically linked to strong leadership. These being:[11]

1. **An ambitious vision**: a vision of strategic value over the long term, usually extending beyond the immediate deal.

2. **Effective alignment**: a comprehensive integration plan for aligning structures, processes, systems, and culture with the vision

3. **Fast and focused transition**: quick actions to capture key opportunities and accelerate the transition to a single, new company.

Within the *Sunday Times* article mentioned earlier, Alan Crozier, also of William M Mercer, made the critical point that at the start of an integration process managers have to answer two key questions:[12]

1. How do they get the people in their enlarged companies to realize there is a new agenda and they have a role to play?

2. How do they prevent them becoming demotivated as colleagues face the chop?

He says that critical here is the first 100 days of the new entities existence:

> "In this period, leaders must articulate their vision and agenda for change. They must build understanding and encourage and reward the behaviour that will deliver the results promised to shareholders [and] the communication must be honest and robust to win respect.

> "Challenges need to be faced. At all levels there will be a hunger for information. Redundancy fears will trigger anxiety about job security and career progress and produce a scramble for survival and promotion."

Case Report: GE Capital

The first 100 days is seen as critical at acquisition exemplar GE Capital Services, a global financial services organization comprising 27 separate businesses and totalling more than 50,000 employees (nearly half of them outside the United States), with a net income in 1996 of $2.8 billion.

The company made more than 100 acquisitions from 1993 to 1997 inclusive, resulting in a 30 per cent increase in its workforce, the rapid globalization of the business and a doubling of its net income. Unsurprisingly successful acquisition and integration has become a core capability to the organization.

Writing in the *Harvard Business Review*, GE Capital executives Ronald N Ashkenas and Lawrence J DeMonaco, along with Robert H

Schaffer's Suzanne C Francis (who has worked with GE Capital on a number of acquisitions), stated that the company had learnt four critical lessons in making an acquisition work financially and organizationally. A summary of those lessons follows.[13]

Lesson 1: Ongoing integration

According to the authors, acquisition integration is not a discrete phase of a deal and does not begin when the documents are signed. Rather, they say, it is a process that begins with due diligence and runs through the ongoing management of the new enterprise.

The authors admit that for many years at GE Capital integration did begin once the deal was done, but that in most cases that approach to integration was less than effective. Integration, they say was slow and costly.

The approach changed in the mid 1980s, when GE Capital acquired Dart & Kraft Leasing (D&K) and Kerr Leasing, intending to integrate Kerr into D&K. In the midst of that integration process, GE Capital acquired Gelco Corporation, a much larger leasing company that also included other financial services businesses. At that point, the acquisition strategy called for integrating both D&K and Kerr into Gelco's auto-fleet leasing business, spinning off some other pieces of Gelco into free-standing businesses, and selling some non-strategic pieces of the company. The authors write:

> "In short, this was no simple acquisition integration, and many of GE Capital's senior executives were concerned that the standard approaches to integration would be inadequate.

> "As a response, a human resources executive suggested that the company's communications experts use the regulatory review period *before* the Gelco acquisition closed to create a comprehensive communications plan for the forthcoming integration. But instead of just a communication plan, what emerged was the framework for an entire integration strategy. The strategy included a 48-hour communication blitz directed at employees immediately after the deal closed; the formulation of a role in the new organization for the former Gelco, D&K and Kerr executives, a strategy for presenting the acquisition to the media; a way to handle some necessary consolidations of headquarters staff; and an outplacement plan."

Most importantly, they say, the framework signalled a new way of thinking about integration – a recognition that there were predictable issues that could be anticipated long before the deal actually closed. Indeed the authors write that GE Capital found that being sensitive to acquisition issues during the due diligence phase began to foster better decisions about whether to proceed with an acquisition at all.

Lesson 2: Integration is a full-time job

The second key lesson, according to the authors, is that integration management is a full-time job and needs to be recognized as a distinct business function, just like operations, marketing or finance.

They state that a common problem is a due diligence team often includes people from different functions, but it is rarely clear which one person will become responsible for ensuring that the new company becomes a fully functioning, high-performing part of the acquirer. At GE Capital, responsibility for integration ended up as part of the remit of the leader of the acquiring GE Capital business, but other demands, and a lack of knowledge about certain integration issues, made it impossible for him or her to give it their full attention.

Recognizing that the integration manager is a key, and discrete, role, GE Capital now generally appoints two types of people as integration managers – the *high potential* individual and the *experienced hand*. They write:

> "The high potential manager is usually a less seasoned person with strong functional credentials who is viewed as a future business leader. That type of person is widely employed in small, straightforward or highly structured integration efforts. For more complex acquisitions or those that incorporate multiple businesses, an experienced hand – someone who knows GE Capital well and has proven management skills – usually takes on the integration job.

> "In all cases, the integration managers that have been most effective have served on the due diligence team. The integration manager then becomes a full-fledged member of the leadership team for the acquired business, reporting directly to its business leader. Selection of the integration manager is based as much on personal characteristics as on technical skills... all have strong interpersonal skills and are sensitive to cultural differences. All have the ability to facilitate groups and a deep knowledge of how GE Capital works. And all have the energy to do what it takes to make an integration successful."

Importantly, the integration manager is *not* accountable for the performance of the business, as GE Capital found that doing so reduces the accountability of both the business leader and the rest of the leadership team. And in reality the integration manager does not control the critical business resources. Instead of having profit and loss responsibility then, most of GE Capital's integration managers are held accountable for the creation and delivery of a disciplined integration plan and for reaching the plan's milestones.

Lesson 3: The importance of early communication

According to the authors, decisions about management structure, key roles, reporting relationships, lay-offs, restructuring and other career-affecting aspects of the integration should be made, announced and implemented as soon as possible after the deal is signed – within days, if possible. They write:

> "Creeping changes, uncertainty and anxiety that last for months are debilitating and immediately start to drain value from the acquisition."

A key recognition here, they state, is that the new managers are often excited and keen to get on with the challenge of running the new company, whereas the employees within the acquired company (at all levels from the most senior to junior) are apprehensive with worries over job security, new orders, etc. They write:

> "On one hand, when issues of security are not addressed immediately, levels of productivity, customer service and innovation quickly deteriorate as employees focus on their own needs rather than those of the company. On the other hand, if acquiring managers restructure quickly but without sensitivity, they risk beginning their tenure without the trust and respect of the remaining staff. The challenge is to avoid both traps, to make structural changes as quickly as possible but in a way that maintains everyone's dignity. If that challenge is not met, successful integration may not be possible."

They state that the acquiring company must be straightforward about what is happening and what is planned, stating that even when the news is bad, the one thing that staff of newly acquired companies appreciate most is the truth.

The authors also stress that it is critical to treat those who will be negatively affected (eg, through redundancies or who feel they lose position through structural changes) with dignity, respect, and support. Stating that not only is this the right thing to do, it is also a powerful way to show those who remain what kind of company they now are working for – and to help them develop positive feelings.

Lesson 4: Quickly becoming business-focused

The final lesson, according to the authors, is that a successful integration melds not only the various technical aspects of the businesses but also the different cultures. The best way to get to this, they say, is to get people working together quickly to solve business problems and accomplish results that could not have been achieved before.

Interestingly, that belief was espoused by Dr Christian Forstner, director of business excellence Siemens KWU (a case study to support Chapter 6), who found that when it put together a mixed team of German and US employees (following its acquisition of part of Westinghouse Electric Company) the language or cultural problems were not a big issue. Forstner says:

> "What people need and respond to is a clear vision of what they are doing and clear goals and targets."

The *Harvard Business Review* authors go on to state that GE Capital has distilled several steps business leaders can take to bridge the cultural gaps that exist when integrating any acquisition.

Meet, greet and plan (urgently)

They write that once the deal is closed and the transfer of ownership becomes official, the GE Capital business leader, with the help of the acquisition manager, organizes orientation and planning sessions for the members of the management team of the new acquisition and their counterparts in GE Capital.

The intention being to use these sessions to create a 100-day plan for acquisition integration.

Within this step, acquired managers are asked to talk about the strengths of 'their' companies, opportunities for improvement and how they see the synergies with GE Capital. Then the GE Capital business leader, integration manager and other executives describe what in means to be part of GE Capital – the values, the responsibilities, the challenges, and the rewards. That includes a presentation and discussion of the standards required of a GE Capital business unit, including a list of approximately 25 policies and practices that need to be incorporated into the way the acquired company does business. Those range from quarterly operating reviews to risk policies to quality and integrity procedures.

Following this a 100-day plan for acquisition integration is designed. The plan addresses such issues as the need for integrating functions, taking any steps necessary for financial and procedural compliance, making any shifts in compensation and benefits, and managing customer contacts.

According to the authors the 100-day timetable creates a sense of urgency, challenge and excitement. It imbues the integration with a feeling of zest and energy. At the same time, it forces the management team to move into action and avoid becoming paralysed by mixed feelings and personal politics.

Communicate, communicate – and then communicate some more

According to the authors communication should be an ongoing task and creating a communication plan during the due diligence and negotiation phase of a transaction (so that employees and external parties are informed as soon as a deal is closed) is only the first step in an effective communication programme. They write:

> "Keeping the communication process going – and making it reach broadly and deeply throughout the organization – requires more than just sharing information bulletins. It requires the creation of forums for dialogue and interaction that can help span the cultural chasm between acquirer and acquiree."

GE Capital's Private Label Credit Card business is cited as one example of GE Capital's communication process. The plan identified several distinct audiences:

- the senior managers of both organizations
- the integration manager and his team
- all the employees of the acquired organization
- all of GE Capital's employees – the customers, clients and vendors of the combined company
- the community
- the media.

The appropriate time to communicate was identified for each audience; before the deal was closed, for instance, or at closing, or perhaps 60 days after the closing. And for each audience, the appropriate mode of communication was selected, ranging from newsletters and memos to videos and small-groups, to town meetings and visits from management.

However, in GE Capital's experience, such intensive communication, even when combined with extensive integration planning, is sometimes not enough to bridge deep cultural integration gaps. A more direct approach to cultural integration is often needed.

Address the cultural issues head-on

Therefore, to deal with potential difficulties around cultural misalignment, GE Capital, with assistance from a consulting firm, has constructed a systematic process of cross-cultural analysis, leading up to a structured three-day 'cultural workout' session between GE Capital and the newly acquired management team. That process is now applied in most of GE Capital's acquisitions, especially when there is a significant non-US component.

Here is how the process works. First, using the results of focus groups and interviews with customers and employees, a computer-generated analysis is developed that plots the acquired company's culture on a scattergram across four dimensions: costs, technology, brands, and customers. The analysis also contrasts how employees see the company with the way customers see it. A similar survey is done for the GE Capital business.

Once the survey results are ready, the managers from both GE Capital and the acquired company meet for the three-day cultural workout. (If everything is on schedule, this meeting takes place at or as close to the end of the first 100 days). At that session, the data from the two companies are compared to highlight areas of convergence and difference.

With facilitative help, the results are used to focus discussions about cultural differences and similarities and their implications for doing business. The authors write:

> "By the third day of the session, participants shift their focus from the past to the future. Based on what has been accomplished in the first

100 days they are asked two questions. Where do they want to take the company and what kind of future do they want to create? That discussion results in a written outline of a new business plan for the acquired company, based on the goals that were established as part of the original deal, now augmented by the collective dreams and aspirations of the new management team. After the first 100 days, the stage is set for continuing the integration and development process over the next six months or more on the basis of a shared understanding of cultural differences and a concrete plan for bridging the gaps."

The results of the cultural workout are then normally shared organization-wide through small-group meetings, videos and other channels. That gives the wider employee population access to the same body of cultural data as the management team has – and the same opportunity to digest it and consider the implications for the integration. These are supported by specific action projects, using employees from the acquiring and acquired companies focused on critical business goals.

Crucial to successful integration at GE Capital is understanding the HR challenges and the role of effective internal communications. And the following sections will look at these two components of M&A activity.

Section G: Integrating Human Resources Mechanisms

According to research for this Report, pulling together discrete HR mechanisms can be a major challenge in an M&A exercise. Not least because the HR functions themselves may be completely different in the two organizations. This was the case at Lehigh Portland Cement Company, where the Lehigh function was centralized and therefore senior HR managers would direct services throughout the organization, whereas at CBR (with whom Lehigh merged), HR was decentralized. Following the decision to decentralize as much of HR as possible, a Merger Integration Team and Process Ownership Groups played a critical role in designing and embedding the new decentralized approach, as they did with other corporate services such as purchasing and engineering.

Of course there may be significant differences in HR services such as career development, appraisal, promotion, training and compensation and benefits.

How people are promoted, the research finds, will be watched carefully by the newly integrated employee-base. They will be watching to see which of the combined organizations are taking ascendancy. As Lehigh Portland president Dick Kline says:

"There was an initial tendency for people to count how many executives came from CBR and how many from Lehigh. People were very interested in who got what jobs."

Who gets promoted and why will also play a critical role in defining both the formal and informal cultural influences on 'the way we work around here', as people will begin to see promotion as the rewards of living by the 'new' cultural standards. But of course these standards may just as easily be 'unwritten' as 'written'. Therefore, organizations should be careful here to ensure that, as with any culture change programme, formal and informal cultural levers are working in unison to embed the new culture. More on the problems of unwritten and written rules during a culture change programme can be found in Chapter 5, Section E.

Compensation and Benefits

A particularly difficult problem in M&As, the research finds, is in unifying compensation and benefit systems. As Francis says:

> "This can be particularly troublesome. Often compensation and benefits will be very different in the two organizations and how this is dealt with will go a long way to securing buy-in to the new company."

She says that employees from both organizations will look at the pay and benefits of the other, compare these with their own and, quite naturally, want the best of both to be brought together to create the new compensation and benefits package.

Creating the new compensation package can take some time. At Lehigh Portland, for example, although compensation systems were largely the same within the combining entities, there were differences in benefit packages. At the time of writing the case study, new standardized company policies were still being prepared.

The time it can take to get the 'pay' aspect of an M&A right was outlined in the 1998 Roffey Park research. The authors write:[14]

> "New pay systems normally involve formal negotiating processes and these are rarely concluded in the few months usually allowed for this task. Employee representatives are often going through a merger process too and struggles for control are as common in Trade Unions as in the boardroom. In some [of our case studies] the harmonization of pay was not immediately affordable and phased in. It may often be more realistic to implement interim terms and conditions of employment, and then set a timetable for agreeing new pay and grading systems - that often takes a year or more in complex mergers."

Case Report: Hoeschst Marion Rousell

Redefining HR mechanisms was an important element of aligning the UK sites following the creation of the global pharmaceuticals company Hoeschst Marion Rousell. The challenges were explained by manpower development manager Richard Nicholson at the Business Intelligence conference *The New Change Management Agenda*.[15]

Nicholson admits that all the merger activity was unsettling, especially as all the restructuring led to redundancies and some people did not get the jobs in the new organization that they expected. However, on the positive side Nicholson said that people really did want the merger to work and there was a general willingness to accept and try new ways of working.

Redefining relationships

To create a new sense of oneness in the UK, the company decided to redefine relationships throughout the organization on four levels:

1. One-to-one relationships.
2. Teams.
3. Between teams.
4. Across the company.

The UK operation worked out of three sites : Denholm, near Uxbridge, Middlesex; Milton Keynes, Buckinghamshire; and Swindon, Wiltshire. Said Nicholson:

> "We wanted to create a sense of identity and not just be this amalgam of three different organizations."

Values

The first thing the company did was create a set of consistent, ground rules which all could work to. Key to this was crafting a new set of shared values: ambition, integrity, urgency and ownership. Said Nicholson:

> "The values gave us a constant with which to build the various initiatives and programmes that we put together."

Workshops were held throughout the organization looking at how individuals in their own terms could define these values.

Performance management

Importantly these values were built into the performance management process. The first element, however, was to create a performance management process that took the new strategy of the organization and broke it down from its broad headings to become meaningful for each individual.

Basically a system of cascade objectives was created which made people clear as to what their job was, what they were supposed to be doing and the output the company was looking for. Nicholson commented:

> "Objective setting and clarity was critical. Appraisals are often once a year process. However, we put in place a performance tracker which meant that on a three monthly cycle we talked about performance with individuals and progress towards objectives."

The company also used bonuses to reward individuals for excellent progress, but importantly these were tied earlier to the actual event being rewarded rather than a once a year payment.

For training and development the company put together personal development plans for each employee. Therefore, each individual had something tangible they could be measured against.

A 360 degree feedback mechanism was also introduced (more on this appraisal system can be found in Chapter 7, Section E). Nicholson said that this showed that the organization was serious about relationships, and at the time of his conference presentation about three-quarters of people in leadership positions had been through this process.

Also important was team-building exercises, such as ten-pin bowling and climbing mountains. Everyone in the company, over an 18 month period, went through some element of team-building. According to Nicholson the main reason for this was to get the relationship-building process in place.

The UK management of Hoeschst Marion Rousell also used communication mechanisms in pursuing their goal of creating unity. In addition to briefing groups the company created a 12 page journal. Based on focus groups the company ensured that issues covered were the ones that people wanted to focus on and indeed what they were worried about. This journal was sent out to everybody in the company. Nicholson said:

> "The journal content was discussed in individual teams and feedback helped focus the content of the next issue.

> "From the first issue we got about 250 questions. There's no management input as such as they don't say what should go in the journal. Rather the content is driven by submitted questions and managed by a people from different parts of the company."

However, Nicholson stresses that although this bi-monthly journal has proved invaluable it does not remove the need for face-to-face contact. Thus, reinforcing a crucial point made in the previous Chapter about communication efforts to support any change effort.

Section H: Internal Communications

Internal communications, our research finds, plays a crucial role in an M&A activity and they must be robust at the start of a merger of acquisition process and active throughout. As Childress succinctly states, "people want honest, direct and timely communication".

He adds that it is better for companies to over-communicate rather than under-communicate during this time, saying that anything that can be communicated should be communicated, since people can better face the known than the unknown.

First, the research finds, it is important to explain the business rationale of the merger or acquisition, as employees are more likely to buy-in to a new company if they can clearly see the reasons. Also if one company is acquiring another, senior management from the acquirer should talk personally to employees from the acquired company. As Senn says:[16]

> "It is easier to be resentful towards an unknown, invisible ogre, than it is to be resentful about a person you have personally experienced as being real, rational and concerned."

And, the research finds, honest, direct and timely communications are especially important if the merger or acquisition is going to result in redundancies. Childress says:

> "It is better to deliver the bad news early. Get all the gnashing of teeth over with quickly so that the people left can get on with the job."

How Not To Communicate

An example of how not to communicate was given in 'Merger Mania – Coming to a Company Near You', an article that appeared in the January 23rd 1999 edition of *The Guardian*. First, the authors recounted a tale from a survivor of the 1980s merger that created the pharmaceuticals giant Glaxo Wellcome:[17]

> "The only way I was going to keep sane was just to ignore everything, put my head down and do my work."

According to the authors it took a full nine months before staff in that deal learned whether they would keep their jobs:

> "Then, on two ghastly days in October 1987... more than 1000 employees were each given an appointment at which they would be told their fate. Employees were directed in small clusters to a waiting room and then on down a corridor. Those sent to an office on the right were reprieved and given a perfunctory welcome to their new job. Those sent to an office on the left were sacked. One employee commented, 'it was like being led to the slaughter'."

The authors also write that after the take-over of Union Bank of Switzerland by Swiss Bank Corporation (SBC), employees in London were told they were out – because SBC's information technology was better and so were its people.

Losing Key Staff

Even if job losses are not an intended outcome of an M&A then this itself should also be communicated early, as was the case at Lehigh Portland and at Bristol & West, the case report below. This is important because people will naturally fear the worst during a merger or acquisition.

Another problem here is that companies may face the danger of losing key staff who fear that either they will lose their jobs or be overlooked in the corporate reshuffle. As Childress says:

> "Head-hunters have a field day when a merger or acquisition is announced. Uncertainly breeds insecurity and fear. What often happens is there's a series of revelations. First, the new entity announces the top team, then a month later the next layer is announced, then the following month the next layer. And what happens is people's résumé's are quickly on the streets. Most of the good people leave, not because the new organization didn't want to keep them but they just didn't talk to them soon enough."

So a danger here is that key competitors become beneficiaries of the merger process. Therefore the new organization must do all it can, as quickly as possible, to reassure key staff that their future is even brighter within the new organization. Staff leaving due to uncertainly at the start of an M&A process is a common problem that organizations should be aware of. Losing staff at any level may prove extremely damaging, but losing key staff, whose knowledge, experience and skills may be very difficult to replace, may prove a potentially disastrous problem.

Indeed, organizations must accept that people will, quite naturally, be worried about their futures when a merger or acquisition is announced. Allaying these fears as quickly as possible will make it much more likely that the employees will remain and will help free-up employees minds to focus on the real goal of the merger or acquisition which is to create a new and better organization.

Case Report: Bristol & West

Communicating quickly to staff was felt to be vital by the senior managers of the UK-based mortgage lender Bristol & West (B&W) during its acquisition by the Bank of Ireland, as outlined in the Roffey Park research.[18]

The Bank of Ireland acquisition of Bristol & West is a somewhat unusual acquisition as it was initiated by B&W itself, who believed that expansion and focusing on its core assets would be best served by finding an 'out-of-market' buyer. Also important here was that in doing so would minimize the risk of redundancies and allow B&W management to retain autonomy. Bank of Ireland became interested in B&W because it had been looking to expand its mortgage operations in the UK.

Allaying fears around job losses

The merger announcement was widely, and largely positively, covered by the media. However, much of the early comment concentrated on the question of whether the deal would result in redundancies at B&W.

The authors say:

> "The [B&W] executive team was prepared for this, knowing full well that this was a paramount concern to its 2200 employees and gave fulsome assurances that no job losses would ensue."

Despite the public assurances, director Kevin Flannagan believes that the executive team were not quite believed and therefore it was necessary to keep repeating the message. A B&W employee agrees, admitting:

> "The biggest issue for most of the staff was whether we would have a job. Many of us didn't dare to believe the initial message that there would be no redundancies."

Therefore, in addition to the usual communication processes, B&W installed a 'questions and answer clearing house' operating through e-mail. Through this, employees could ask any question about the proposed sale, and receive an answer ideally within 24 hours.

According to the authors, this service was used intensively by staff and mainly concentrated around their concerns about job losses and whether the transfer of ownership would affect their terms and conditions of employment. And, the authors state, B&W's senior management believes that this service proved both rapid and flexible and helped substantially to alleviate staff concerns immediately after the announcement.

Case Report: Lehigh Portland Cement Company

Early communication was also critical at Lehigh Portland. Once the merger was announced a letter was sent by the new president Dick Kline to every employee. This detailed why the new organization was being created and what it intended to achieve. The senior team also explained the role of the Merger Integration Team and follow-up letters explained how the Team was progressing and reported key findings.

Kline explains that a key reason why they were careful to keep employees fully briefed on the Team's progress was, unsurprisingly, that if the work of such a team is not communicated fully and honestly, it lends itself to potentially damaging rumours, especially around job losses. And downsizing was not a merger objective.

In addition to this communication mechanism, the company ensured that managers received further briefings on progress and they were mandated to brief their own departments.

Section I: Conclusion

It is clear from the research that the chances of succeeding with a merger or acquisition are significantly enhanced if the cultural aspects of integration receives at least as much attention as the financial and physical integration.

Cultural integration should begin as early in an M&A process as possible and should receive concerted attention for a considerable amount of time after the deal is done. As this Chapter has shown there are a plethora of potentially fatal cultural barriers to M&A success, and senior management would be judicious to pay attention to them all.

Roffey Park Ten Key Learning Points

According to the Roffey Park's research for the report, *Mergers & Acquisitions: Getting the People Bit Right*, the managerial challenges of an M&A can be distilled into ten key learning points:[19]

1. Consciously manage the merger process.

2. Parcel the merger or acquisition into a number of simple and easily understood stages.

3. Set short-term goals for the business at each stage.

4. Try to map and plan for the various emotional waves that will sweep through the organization as different groups of employees work through the changes brought about by the merger/acquisition.

5. Communicate at every step – even when there is no news.

6. Get people on board as quickly as possible.

7. Protect the core business.

8. Adopt a phased and professional approach to HR issues.

9. Accept that it is at the local, micro level where differences in working practices and underlying values are resolved.

10. Do not try to 'paint the culture on afterwards'.

Key Learning Points

1. As cultural issues seem to be a primary cause of M&A failures, companies should pay attention to the challenges in melding cultural characteristics as early in the M&A process as possible.

2. Linked to the above, companies intent on integration should beware of getting too wrapped up in the excitement of 'doing the deal' at the expense of looking at the cultural issues.

3. Chief executive officers should not underestimate their crucial role in shaping a unified culture for the new organization.

4. It often happens that one side in the integration process feels they are the 'victors' while the other feels they are 'the vanquished'. The strengths of these emotions should not be underestimated and organizations should work hard to understand, and deal with, these feelings.

5. Cultural due diligence should be a critical part of any integration effort. It will help identify similarities and differences, and indeed companies may decide to walk away from a deal at this stage.

6. Merger Integration Teams should focus on cultural as well as physical integration.

7. Companies should play close attention to the inherent problems associated with merging HR systems, especially around compensation and benefits.

8. Internal communication is a critical enabler of successful integration processes. Companies should not underestimate the anxiety that a merger or integration causes within the employee-base, and companies should over-communicate rather than under-communicate.

CASE STUDY: LEHIGH PORTLAND CEMENT COMPANY

Summary

A merger of US-headquartered Lehigh Portland Cement Company with the North American operations of Cimenteries CBR is proving successful due to sensitivity to cultural issues, proactive leadership of the executive team and a well defined new way of working based on the principles of total quality and a participative approach to management.

Introduction

With more that 6000 employees Lehigh Portland Cement Company operates 12 plants in North America and more than 200 concrete, aggregates and related construction materials businesses. The Lehigh name has been synonymous with cement production in the US for over 100 years, since it was first established in the limestone-rich Lehigh Valley in the US state of Pennsylvania.

In 1978, Lehigh, a publicly traded US company was acquired by the German company Heidelberger Zement. Lehigh's operations were mainly centred in the north-east, mid-west and south-eastern United States. Cimenteries CBR, SA, a Belgian cement and materials manufacturer acquired its North American assets in 1986. These operations were centred on the west coast of the United States and the western provinces of Canada.

Subsequently, in 1995, the Heidelberger Zement Group acquired control of Cimenteries CBR SA in Belgium which included CBR's North American operations.

At that time it was decided to merge the North American assets of Heidelberger and CBR. The reason for the merger, says Dick Kline, president of Lehigh Portland, was quite simply to consolidate the activities of the two companies, harness the potential managerial and operational synergies and to position the company as a much larger combine in North America.

Interestingly, the organizations decided to combine under the Lehigh Portland name, a decision that met little resistance from the CBR staff because employees from both companies (and these were, at about 3000 people each, of essentially equal strength) recognized that the Lehigh brand was strong in North America and so value could be leveraged from the name.

A Decentralized Approach

Planning the operational and cultural dimensions of the merger started in 1995 and an early decision was to base the new organization largely around the existing CBR structure and management approach. Explains Peter Tait, vice president, total quality, who, like Kline, came from the CBR half of the business (although Kline had previously worked for Lehigh):

> "Lehigh was a highly centralized company while CBR was highly decentralized. Dick Kline strongly believed that a decentralized approach to running the new company would be more effective. Also, CBR took a participative approach to management whereas Lehigh was more of a command and control culture. Dick Kline felt that participation was a more effective way to gain employee commitment. On top of this CBR had always been profitable, which was not the case for Lehigh. Therefore, the companys' owners said go with the CBR approach."

Another structural challenge to face was that CBR was set up as vertically aligned organization, whereas Lehigh was focused around product lines. This did cause some cultural problems, says Tait, as CBR management were more accustomed to seeing the 'big' company picture whereas Lehigh managers had been trained to view operations purely from a functional perspective, such as manufacturing or marketing, etc.

Kline explains that integrating the managerial approach posed, and is posing, an interesting challenge. He says:

> "As CBR was decentralized, operating units were autonomous and their presidents have complete general management control of their units, which was clearly not the case at Lehigh. Consequently, we found that managerially we spoke different languages.

> "And as Lehigh managers moved into operational units they had the challenge of contending with a far greater managerial breadth. They had to understand the manufacturing side of operations, financial and administration responsibilities as well as sales and marketing."

So let's look at the process by which the 'new' company started to address such challenges and indeed how it managed to successfully merge the organizations' operational and cultural dimensions.

The Merger Integration Team

A crucial decision pre-official merger was to set up a Merger Integration Team, consisting of nine senior managers from each company to make the strategic recommendations for the operational and cultural merger process. The team was co-chaired by Al Watt, who was then president of CBR's Vancouver-based business unit and Al Stauss, Lehigh's then vice president of sales and marketing.

The team was cross-functional and all economic business units and staff departments were represented, thus ensuring as wide a view as possible of the two companies' operations and activities.

Al Watt, now retired but previously president of the CBR-owned Tilbury Cement company, which covered the British Columbia region of Canada and the US states of Washington and Oregon, outlines a key goal of the team:

> "As part of moving to the decentralized approach to working, Dick Kline wanted to re-establish Lehigh's cement operations on a regional basis and so most corporate services had to be transferred to the regions. Therefore we had to examine how to do this for services such as purchasing, engineering, human resources and legal."

The Merger Integration Team was broken down into the various service areas, and these sub-teams would identify the present processes within each company and take what was best from both and report back to the executive committee with merger recommendations.

According to Kline this process of identification and recommendation in itself provided an excellent learning opportunity for the team members and therefore the organization. He says:

> "We took time to evaluate how each company was functioning and this was a major accomplishment. Usually managers and companies are too busy to step back and look at the whole picture, so by completing this exercise we were provided with the rare opportunity for experts who knew their fields to thoroughly review operations, create best practice processes and where necessary rewrite procedures."

An external consultant was used to facilitate this evaluation, which provided further expert input into the redesign process. It should also be noted that not every aspect of the services were decentralized. For example, benefits and tax became centralized services because, says Tait, it made good business sense.

The Merger Integration Team was operational for about nine months and essentially made the core decisions, which were agreed by the executive committee, as to how the new company would operate. As shall be explained later, the role of making this new structure work in practice was then devolved to Process Ownership Groups.

New Vision, Mission and Value Statements

First it is important to look at the crucial role of the new Lehigh Portland's executive committee (which comprised ex-CBR and Lehigh executives in about equal measure) in shaping the identity of the merged organization.

Kline recalls that an interesting challenge was overcoming the different cultural traits within a newly merged executive committee:

> "We had to work to find the best from both cultures and then work to exploiting the positives from each and blend them together to make something stronger."

An important step by the executive committee was to articulate a new vision, mission and set of corporate values. The vision statement reads, 'Working Together to Build Our Communities'. About this Tait says:

> "Although a short vision it neatly explains what we do. Working together as a merged company, working with customers, with suppliers and with communities."

The Lehigh Portland mission statement reads:

> 'We are committed to being the industry leader in providing outstanding value to our customers, a safe and stimulating work environment for our employees, and superior returns for our shareholders.'

And its value statement reads:

> 'Our companies are totally committed to:
>
> * providing superior quality products and services to our customers
>
> * maintaining the highest level of integrity, ethics and excellence in all aspects of our business
>
> * providing a safe, challenging and rewarding work environment for our employees
>
> * fulfilling our responsibilities to our industry, to our communities and the protection of the environment
>
> * continuously improving our people, our products, our services and our profitability.'

Creating a Planning Guide

Another important executive committee decision in creating the new merged organization, and indeed valuable for creating senior management consensus around future direction and working practices, was the formulation of a 'planning guide'.

With facilitative input from the consultancy Organizational Dynamics Inc (ODI), the guide was designed as a vehicle for achieving Lehigh Portland's vision, mission and value statements. Under the heading 'planning for world-class' the executive committee identified five critical success factors for achieving this world-class status and therefore its strategic goals. These are:

* growth strategy

* employee satisfaction

* customer satisfaction

* measurement systems

* community involvement.

Each critical success factor was supported by a goal and 'areas of focus', which is shown in Table 9.2.

CSF	Goal	Area of focus
Growth strategy	To continually improve our financial results and be recognized as a leader in our achievements of profits.	• internal growth • contiguous growth • greenfield growth
Employee satisfaction	To attract and retain employees whose goals and expectations are in alignment with our vision, mission and values.	• work environment • rewards and recognition • career opportunities
Customer satisfaction	To be the long-term provider of choice for our customers.	• product • service • relationship
Measurement system	To have a system that routinely assesses organizational performance against goals.	• availability of information • use of information • benchmarking
Community involvement	To be viewed by the communities in which we operate as a responsible corporate citizen and as a valuable asset to the community.	• local communities • industry relationships

Table 9.2: Lehigh Portland's Critical Success Factors

Within the planning guide each area of focus is detailed as a working, step-by-step, template for a business unit or department to move from existing to world-class practices. Each step is defined and supported with required actions to move to the next step. As a working tool, progress through each step is measured by guide users through dated milestones. A focus area example is shown in Table 9.3.

The planning guide is formatted as a five phase process through which business units or departments concentrate on one or two areas of focus which it believes improving performance will aid overall business performance. The guide is an ongoing performance improvement tool in that users are expected to return to the document once the actions within the chosen areas of focus have been successfully completed.

According to Tait, the facilitated work with ODI helped the executive committee to articulate what world-class would look like and exactly what the organization needed to do to get there. He says:

> "The work undertaken by the executive committee was where we really dealt with creating a new common culture. We identified our critical success factors, fully committed to them, published the guide and rolled it out deep inside the organization.

> "The guide has been tremendously useful in that employees now know what we mean by 'world-class', our goals to get there and the steps we expect them to take to move us towards achieving those goals."

Tait makes the crucial point that the planning guide is seen as a 'new' corporate tool:

> "The guide never gets referred to as an old Lehigh or CBR tool. People see it as being an output of the new Lehigh Portland Cement Company."

EMPLOYEE SATISFACTION

Goal: To attract and retain employees whose goals and expectations are in alignment with our vision, mission and values.

Areas of Focus:
- Work Environment.
- Rewards and Recognition.
- Career Opportunities.

WORK ENVIRONMENT

Steps along the scale of Work Environment	Where are you			Actions necessary to reach the next step
	Date	Date	Date	
Autocratic, top-down management, low trust, negative recognition and negative employee relations.				• introduce participation and teams • create a safe environment • conduct safety training • share business information • communicate need for change • employee training
Employee input is sought, but not used systematically.				• open communications • recognize positive employee relations are critical • continuous training and development for managers and employees • establish individual accountability
Management leads teams and identifies problems. Employee input is sought, used and recognized.				• gain and productivity sharing • continuous training and development • establish group accountability
Self-directed work groups. Management coaches. Complete employee involvement.				

Table 9.3: Area of Focus Example

Process Ownership Groups

Operational and cultural integration was further advanced through the use of Process Ownership Groups. As Tait says:

> "The combination of both the Merger Integration Team and the Process Ownership Groups proved a powerful integration mechanism."

Seven Process Ownership Groups were launched by the company, with each sponsored by a member of the executive committee. Each Group comprised of between 8 and 15 people, focused on specific organizational functions that could be standardized company-wide, such as sales and marketing, technical services and quality control, and included representatives from each economic business unit.

The Groups' Lehigh facilitators, who were trained by ODI, comprised members drawn from various levels of the organization in order to gain different process perspectives.

A valuable addition to the Groups was the use of 'sounding boards'. These were experts in the business who Group members used, on an ongoing basis, to test implementation ideas before the Group made the formal recommendation to the executive committee. Thus enabling wider consultation and input into the implementation process.

Importantly, these Groups built on the work undertaken by the Merger Integration Team, and by further analysing existing and recommended processes, ensured that robust, best practice processes were finally rolled-out throughout the organization.

Five groups were closed down after 15 months, as their work was seen as complete. Referring to the benefits gained from the groups Kline says:

> "We had regional differences and cultural differences to process implementation. And setting up these Groups certainly helped us overcome our cultural differences more quickly. They brought together people from various hierarchical levels to work on common goals and to find best practice solutions. They proved a quick way to build teamwork, friendships and create a sense of working for the same company that would otherwise have taken years to create."

Total Quality Management (TQM)

Combining the two organizations was also made somewhat easier in that both companies were already committed to the principles and practices of total quality management (TQM) although CBR had been using such an approach for a longer period of time. And as both organizations were being trained by ODI, this meant that a common language to performance improvement was already, to a certain extent, established in both companies. Indeed it was Dick Kline, as president of CBR, who had recommended ODI to the then president of Lehigh. Kline says:

> "This dual exposure to quality gave a useful foundation to develop from. Total quality principles were used by the Merger Integration Teams, by the Process Ownership Groups, and are quickly becoming the way we work around here."

Indeed all employees are receiving ongoing training in total quality tools and techniques.

The companies were also somewhat fortunate in that the compensation systems, often a stumbling block in any merger, were essentially compatible. However, there were some differences in employee benefits. At the time of writing this case study new common policies were being prepared.

Employee Perceptions

At the time of the merger the 'new' company did face some usual merger difficulties. These problems, which are largely based around perception and are ongoing, are not uncommon in the early years of a merger. As Kline explains:

> "There was an initial tendency for people to count how many executives came from CBR and how many from Lehigh. People were very interested in who got what jobs."

As research for this Report has shown, being sensitive to perceptions around 'new' appointments is critical to succeed with cultural integration. Any insensitivity here can easily lead to discontent and a 'winner and loser' mentality emerging in the two previous companies. Kline continues:

> "Step-by-step barriers are being knocked down as we move managers across the line. But there is still a general reluctance for ex-Lehigh people to bid for jobs in what were CBR locations and businesses and to some extent vice versa."

The Importance of Communication

Another ongoing challenge for succeeding with mergers is that of communication, and the new Lehigh Portland senior management team were equally sensitive to this issue from the start of the merger process. Kline explains the initial communication process used once the merger was announced:

> "A letter from myself was sent to every employee detailing why the new organization was being created and what it intended to achieve.

> "We explained what the Merger Integration Team would be doing and follow-up letters explained how the Team was progressing and reported key findings."

He explains that a key reason why they were careful to keep employees fully briefed on the Team's progress was, unsurprisingly, that if the work of such a team is not communicated fully and honestly, it lends itself to potentially damaging rumours, especially around job losses. And downsizing was *not* a merger objective.

The final recommendations of the Merger Integration Team were subsequently communicated company-wide. In addition to this communication mechanism, the company ensured that managers received further briefings on progress and they were mandated to brief their own departments. Says Kline:

> "We worked hard to communicate all the details. But one thing I've learnt about communication is that you always feel you need much more of it."

Overcoming Resistance

Interestingly, the fact that the old Lehigh moved to the old CBR decentralized and participative style of management was, believes Kline, largely supported by ex-Lehigh people. Not least because they are being provided with more responsibility and a more challenging, and indeed, more interesting working environment. However, he does admit that some people feel comfortable with a command and control style of management and for them change has been difficult.

One area which did put up some resistance was the corporate headquarters of Lehigh (which indeed became the headquarters of the new company). This is somewhat unsurprising as Lehigh headquarters were accustomed to directing plant operations. Regionalization naturally had a significant impact on the role of headquarters staff and caused some concern as to the efficacy of the new approach.

But Al Watt says that following the establishment of regional offices many headquarters staff started to see that the changes were rewarding, efficient, not threatening and indeed provided them with opportunities to learn new skills.

Merger Success

So the million dollar question is, and critical given the high failure rates of mergers, is it proving a success? According to Kline the answer is a resounding yes:

> "The merger has been a success financially, due partly to a buoyant economy but also the way the company is managed.

> "We've made a significant number of changes and we've taken a company, Lehigh, that had pretty much looked the same for 20 years and created a dynamic new entity.

> "Ex-Lehigh employees are beginning to see that the executive committee was serious when it said it wanted to create a participative cultural style and give people more freedom in how they work."

Tait says that the structure and culture of the organization has been endorsed by two members of the executive committee who had not been recruited from either Lehigh or CBR. They have stated that Lehigh Portland is the best company they have ever worked for.

Conclusion

In conclusion, the Lehigh Portland's executive team would agree that there is still some way to go before a new unified culture fully evolves. As Kline stresses, "cultures stay in place a long, long time".

Similarly Tait says that there still something of a 'CBR and Lehigh guy' mindset, but gradually this is eroding, partly due to the total quality approach being rolled-out company-wide, the strong lead given by the executive committee, the new unified vision, mission and corporate values, and the teamworking that is now in place. Tait also makes the important statement:

> "We made a conscious effort to recognize that we were dealing with different cultures and to proactively address these issues."

Kline believes that the three critical factors in succeeding with the CBR-Lehigh merger were:

1. The commitment of the people themselves. He says:

   > "The work of the Merger Integration Team and the Process Ownership Groups was phenomenal. They accomplished a great deal for the organization and people learnt a great deal in the process."

2. The support of shareholders. He comments, "they provided full support to what the new management team was trying to do".

3. The quality effort. He says, "total quality is providing a common performance language and is really helping to create a one company mindset".

Key Learning Points

1. A Merger Integration Team, comprising senior managers from both the merging organizations was set up to mastermind the strategic elements of the union.

2. Process Ownership Groups, also with representatives from the two companies, were created to operationalize the merger.

3. The executive team articulated a new vision, mission and set of values for the merged organization. This kick-started the process of creating a distinct company.

4. Similarly, the executive team created a 'planning guide' which, to a large extent, installed a continuous improvement mindset within the organization. Importantly, the guide is seen as a new company tool, and not imposed from one of the two previous companies.

5. Rolling-out total quality management tools and techniques is helping create a common cultural language and is fast becoming 'the way we do things around here'.

6. The company paid close attention to ensuring that the merger objectives and integration process were effectively communicated deep inside the organization.

10

CONCLUSIONS AND KEY LEARNING POINTS

Executive Summary

1. A 'winning' corporate culture is not just about creating a strong culture. Rather it is one that is adaptable to changing market and customer needs and flexible enough to meet the demands of changing strategic objectives.

2. A culture change programme must be in support of strategic goals or significant business imperatives, or else it will almost certainly fail.

3. It is of fundamental importance that the CEO and the senior management team support and drive the culture change effort. Equally, they must personally role model the new cultural behaviours.

4. Linked to the above, responsibility for culture change must be owned at the top of the organization, and not devolved to a specific function.

5. It is judicious, the research finds, for companies to conduct a thorough assessment of their existing culture before launching a culture change programme. This will help identify potential cultural problems and enable senior managers to build robust culture change plans that anticipate these challenges.

6. The whole of the employee-base should be involved in the culture change programme. Involvement is the most effective way to secure buy-in for the change objectives.

7. Frameworks such as the balanced scorecard and the European Foundation for Quality Management's (EFQM) Business Excellence Model can be powerful mechanisms for aligning individual behaviour and performance with strategic goals.

8. Linked to the above, organizations should not underestimate the power of measurement in creating a new culture. As one commentator says, "measures drive behaviour and behaviour creates culture".

9. It is vitally important to align Human Resource (HR) mechanisms with the new cultural ethos. Quite simply, how individuals are appraised, developed, promoted and, crucially, compensated plays a pivotal role in shaping their behaviour and therefore embedding the new culture.

10. Similarly, internal communication mechanisms play a powerful role in driving cultural change. But communication should be open, honest, two-way, mutually reinforcing and clearly support the new cultural ethos.

11. The research shows that it is cultural issues, and not faulty strategies or price issues, that lead to most merger and acquisition failures. So companies considering a merger or acquisition would be judicious to make cultural integration a key focus of the integration effort.

12. High performing cultures in the future will, according to advisers, be able to cope with constant change, be customer-focused, and amoeba-like. Accountability for performance will be devolved deep inside the organization and those at the top will demonstrate markedly different leadership styles than are generally valued today.

Section A: Context

In the introduction to this Report a winning corporate culture was defined as:

> 'Where there exists a visible set of performing enhancing behaviours which together form a recognizable corporate personality and healthy organizational mind.

> 'This organizational mind exists to deliver superior performance and as such is constantly learning about, and aligning with, changing customer and market demands.'

Note that this describes a *winning* corporate culture for, as research for this Report has shown, just having a strong culture is not in itself enough to deliver sustainable competitive advantage. Cultures must adapt to changing market and customer needs and therefore must be flexible enough to meet the demands of changing strategic objectives.

Section B: In Support of Corporate Strategy

This leads to the first key learning point of this Report. A culture change programme must be in support of new strategic or business imperatives. For as Luca Mortara, managing director of the UK arm of ASI, said in Chapter 2:

> "A culture change programme makes sense only if it contributes to a shift in strategy and planning. Culture change per se means nothing."

This is important because, as the research has found, culture change can be a painful process (although it must be said that many of the case study companies found it less painful than they first imagined) and the employee-base will, on the whole, only commit to the change if they can see the business imperatives. Also, if a cultural change effort is separated from clear business objectives then it will quickly wither in the face of more important issues.

Case Study Examples

Each of the case study companies had a clear and well communicated business case for cultural transformation. Whether they were in dire financial straits, such as Continental Airlines (the case study to accompany Chapter 1) and Hyundai Car (UK) Ltd (the case study to support Chapter 7), or doing well financially, such as BT Northern Ireland (a case study to accompany Chapter 6) and Ernst & Young (the case study to support Chapter 8), all of these companies made it clear why they wanted to transform the corporate culture, what the business outcomes would be, how the cultural change would take place, and what was expected from the employee-base.

Section C: The Role of Senior Management

Equally, each of these, and indeed the other case study companies, were aware of the paramount importance of senior management commitment to, and leadership of, the culture change process. Quite simply, the research finds, if the senior management team, or at least several influential members of the team (including the chief executive officer) are not fully behind the change effort then it is unlikely to succeed, or at least it will not secure sustainable benefits. As Dr George Labovitz, chairman of Organizational Dynamics Incorporated (ODI), said in Chapter 4:

> "Senior managers are the key to success in almost every case of culture change I know."

Indeed, 'Culture and Change Management', a survey exclusively commissioned for this Report (the findings of which are analysed in detail in Chapter 3) found that senior executives role modeling new behaviours, or 'walking the talk', was by far the most important factor in enabling cultural change. Of the 236 survey respondents, 88.62 per cent claimed this factor to be 'extremely important'.[1]

Case Study Examples

Excellent senior management role modeling examples from the case study companies include Lucy Woods, CEO of BT Northern Ireland, who conducts non-management breakfast meetings throughout the province where she discusses with the employee-base subjects such as improvement plans, public image, etc. She also holds a monthly audio conference where employees can ask her any questions.

KFC's then CEO David Novak (since promoted to CEO of Tricon, which owns KFC) and his senior team travelled throughout North America holding meetings with both employee and customer groups. The purpose being to uncover views on KFC, both good and bad, in order to pinpoint the key cultural drivers of change to where it mattered most, the front-line employee-customer interface. This played a crucial role in the then sluggish KFC experiencing four successive years of growth under Novak's leadership.

At Continental Airlines chairman and CEO Gordon Bethune and president and COO Greg Brenneman personally led the transformation effort at this ailing company. This included getting out into the airports and on the planes, loading bags and standing alongside the agents at ticket counters. As Brenneman said:[2]

> "We just talked at every opportunity about our plans for the airline and how we were going to accomplish them. In general, our communication policy changed from, 'don't tell anybody anything unless absolutely required', to 'tell everybody everything'."

Value Statements

A key leadership role, the research has found, is in crafting a set of values for the organizations, as it is values that set the new behavioural standards. Leaders must not just craft the words, but live and breathe them as the employee-base will 'ape' the actual behaviours of their leaders and not the words.

As an example, if the senior management team states that an openness to learning is a hoped for new behaviour, then they must show, and indeed communicate, examples of how they themselves are learning on an ongoing basis. For the latter, being brave enough to show how they as leaders made mistakes and how they have learnt from these mistakes will go a long way to embedding this cultural ethos.

The senior management team must also 'own' the values. As John Childress, chief executive of the culture change specialists Senn-Delaney Leadership Consulting Group, comments:

> "The organization's culture and corporate values must be centrally controlled by the senior management team. You can devolve decision-making powers, etc, but you must keep central control over the culture."

Culture as a Corporate Asset

This is an important point. Corporate culture must be managed as conscientiously any other asset – and it must be managed by the senior team. Evidence to support this statement came from the 'Culture and Change Management' survey,[3] which found that 72 per cent of companies with 'extremely well defined' cultures claimed that responsibility for culture resided at a senior level, against just 40 per cent of companies with 'very poorly defined' cultures. Notably those with 'extremely well defined' cultures were massively more likely to succeed against their change goals than their 'very poorly defined' counterparts. Interestingly, this research found 50 per cent of companies with very poorly defined cultures devolve responsibility for culture to the HR function.

So, the research would suggest that devolving responsibility for corporate culture is normally a mistake and indeed can lead to disastrous results, which will not please shareholders.

Delivering Shareholder Value

Indeed, our case study companies do believe that delivering shareholder value is a direct result of actively managing, and leveraging benefits from, the corporate culture. Hyundai Car (UK) Ltd, believes this so strongly that the Harvard Business School Service-Profit Chain framework has driven their culture change effort. Essentially, the Service-Profit Chain has four key links. Link one, profit and growth is driven by link two, customer satisfaction and loyalty. This is a result of link three, service value, which in turn is determined and enhanced by link four, employee satisfaction and loyalty. Hyundai Car (UK) Ltd, through its culture change process has transformed a £7 million deficit in 1995 to a near £9 million profit in 1998.

Such is KFC's David Novak's belief in being employee- and customer-focused that he says:

> "I hope that the results that we generate over time will demonstrate that a value-based work environment is powerful, but I think it is too early to claim victory. The proof will be in the pudding, but I'm betting my job that it will work."

At Continental Airlines, at the start of the change process in 1994, the company was facing bankruptcy for an unprecedented third time. In 1998 it reported a pre-tax profit of $770 million. Central to this was its culture change programme that supported a new strategic plan, the Go Forward Plan, comprising marketing, financial, product and people elements.

So key lessons thus far are that culture change must support business imperatives and to stand any real chance of success must be visibly led by those at the top of the organization who need to role model the new behaviours. Also creating a culture that is employee- and customer-focused, would appear to greatly enhance the prospects of delivering shareholder value.

Section D: Assessing the Existing Culture

The research also found that before rolling-out a culture change programme, it is judicious to assess the state of the existing culture. One key reason being that there are typically numerous challenges within a culture change effort, early warning signs of which can normally be found through a rigorous assessment of the culture as it is at the start of the initiative.

These challenges may be found in the 'unwritten rules' that govern behaviours deep inside the organization. These are often seen in the historic ways that employee behaviours have been rewarded and punished. They may also show up in the 'heroes' of the organization, ie, those who are celebrated. So, if an organization tends to celebrate and deify salespeople who are purely financially driven, and wants to transform to a culture that promotes customer-facing behaviours, then this will show that a lot of work will need to be done to effect such a cultural transformation.

Subcultures

A cultural assessment may also show the different behaviours that exist within organizational subcultures, be they functionally, professionally or geographically based. Indeed, within the 'Culture and Change Management' survey,[4] on a score of 1 (strongly agree) to 5 (strongly disagree), just under 50 per cent of companies gave a score of 1 or 2 to the statement, 'subcultures within our organization pose a major barrier to gaining a unified culture'.

However, according to several commentators interviewed for this Report, a common mistake here is attempting to homogenize subcultures. Rather, they stress it is better to understand that differing parts of the organization need their own cultural nuances, and allow these to exist underneath a 'super-ordinate' culture that powerfully exudes the key values and strategic goals of the organization, which all employees must sign up to.

As Philip Sadler, chairman of the UK-based Centre for Tomorrow's Company, said in Chapter 5:

> "You only have to look at companies such as HP and Johnson & Johnson. These are companies with strong cultures. Certainly there will be differences between guys in marketing and manufacturing in, for example, Johnson & Johnson, but overall the Johnson & Johnson culture is the dominant thing."

And he adds:

> "It's by focusing people's attention onto the corporate goals as a whole that helps creates the focus on the culture."

Creating a Gap Analysis

Therefore, undertaking a cultural assessment will provide senior management with a gap analysis from where they are today to where they want the culture to move to. This will enable the creation of a robust plan to move the culture forward; one which understands and has strategies for dealing with the myriad problems ahead.

A range of tools for assessing existing corporate cultures is shown in Chapter 5. However, most commonly companies use employee and customer surveys to assess, and indeed track cultural development. Case study companies such as Ernst & Young and Siemens KWU (a case study to accompany Chapter 6) both use such surveys widely. Importantly, however, both stress that the only point of doing such assessments is to create improvement plans based on the survey findings. So, the research shows, companies must act, and be seen to act, on survey findings, otherwise they are at best pointless exercises and at worst will demotivate staff and annoy customers.

Section E: Creating a 'Line-of-Sight'

It is also important, our research finds, to involve the whole employee-base in shaping the behaviours that will fashion the new cultural ethos. It is not the role of the employee-base to design the over-arching cultural standards, which is a job for senior management, but it is the employee-base that will have to commit to the hoped-for new culture and make it come alive in day-to-day working practices.

As an example of how to do this, Hyundai Car (UK) Ltd held workshops for all employees where the employee-base essentially decided on the new behaviours that would support and drive the new customer-facing strategy.

Strategy Implementation Frameworks

The research also found that many organizations are using strategy implementation frameworks such as the balanced scorecard and the European Foundation for Quality Management (EFQM) Business Excellence Model as mechanisms for aligning individual behaviour with operational performance and strategic objectives. As examples, Superdrug (a case study to support Chapter 5) and Ernst & Young use the balanced scorecard. BT Northern Ireland used the scorecard and the EFQM model. And the EFQM model is used at Siemens KWU and Inland Revenue Accounts Office, Cumbernauld, Scotland (the case study to accompany Chapter 2).

The power of such frameworks (which are explained in Chapter 6) is that they enable a measurable and trackable line-of-sight from individual performance to corporate strategy. The role of measurement, as the research finds, should not be underestimated when attempting to change a corporate culture. As Labovitz succinctly puts it, "measures drive behaviour and behaviour creates culture".

Section F: Aligning Human Resources

However, critical to creating this chain of reactions is to align human resource mechanisms to the new cultural ethos. Simply, the research finds, how individuals are appraised, developed, promoted and, crucially, compensated plays a pivotal role in shaping their behaviour. So, if senior management espouses one set of cultural traits and rewards another set, it is clear which set an employee will aspire to. Additionally, HR practices must be mutually reinforcing, so they are driving in unison the intended cultural behaviours.

The research also found that creating a sustainable new culture should start at the recruitment stage for two important reasons. First, new recruits are exposed to the new culture (formal and informal) on joining the company, so organizations can create processes, such as mentoring, whereby new recruits learn the preferred cultural behaviours. And second, by paying close attention to the recruitment process, organizations can go some way to ensuring that people with the right cultural traits are brought into the company at the start. This is found at the case study companies Superdrug, Hyundai Car (UK) Ltd and Continental Airlines, and at Western Provident Association, a case report featured in Chapters 4 and 7.

So, a key learning point here is that if employees are measured and rewarded against new performance standards that are based on cascading measures at each level of the organization, then the organization will go a long way to creating the line-of-sight from individual behaviour to strategic objectives.

Section G: Internal Communications

Also critical to succeeding with a culture change programme, the research finds, is the role of internal communications. All of the advisers and practitioners interviewed for this Report stressed the fundamental importance of communication mechanisms in driving and embedding cultural change.

Indeed 61.79 per cent of respondents to the 'Culture and Change Management' survey[5] rated internal communication programmes as 'extremely important' as a cultural change enabler. A further 26.96 per cent scores this a 2 (1 equalled 'extremely important') and not one respondent proffered a 5 score (totally unimportant).

Crucially, the research finds, communication must be open, honest and clearly reinforce the new cultural ethos. Mechanisms should enable a two-way flow of information, thus ensuring important feedback on how employees view the change programme, and, as with HR systems, be mutually reinforcing.

Electronic communication tools such as intranets and e-mail are, the research indicates, becoming key communication mechanisms within organizations. However, although important, these, and indeed more traditional mechanisms such as newsletters, are less effective than direct face-to-face communications. As UK-based independent consultant Garrey Melville said in Chapter 8:

> "Most people prefer face-to-face communications. Disseminating messages and enabling feedback through information technology is important but you can't beat sitting down and talking to other human beings. After all, change is about people."

Case Study Examples

As examples of mechanisms used, Millennium Inorganic Chemicals (the case study to accompany Chapter 3) uses employee briefings (a prime purpose being to report information from the monthly executive committee meetings), semi-annual organizational briefings (where members of the executive committee hold update meetings with employees in their specific areas of responsibility, discussing how their activities relate to the company-wide vision and strategic plan), newsletters, e-mail bulletin boards, and a company-wide intranet. There is also an annual global conference for all employees.

Continental Airlines has a hotline to solicit employee suggestions (which are all answered), a daily two-page newspaper, monthly and quarterly magazines, weekly voice-mail messages from CEO Gordon Bethune, a corporate intranet, e-mail, bulletin boards used to update employees on progress towards the Go Forward Strategic Plan, and monthly meetings in the organization's Houston, Texas headquarters where people are invited to talk with Bethune.

Moreover, all Continental executive officers are assigned cities that they have to visit on a quarterly basis. When the company releases quarterly earnings, all employees can dial a toll-free number and listen to a taped conversation between a market analyst and a senior executive.

Therefore, Continental Airlines, as with other case study companies has recognized the absolute importance of communication being led by the top, and its role in forging a tangible link between employee actions and strategic goals. The company also believes that a range of communication tools should be used as different people prefer different communication approaches.

Section H: The Cultural Factors of Mergers and Acquisitions

Communication is also critical, the research finds, in succeeding with merger and acquisitions (M&As). Commentators stated that communication should be a crucial part of the process during and for a long time after the merger or acquisition is announced. Not least because employees are naturally worried about job security and prospects when a merger or acquisition happens. If bad news, eg, redundancies, has to be communicated then this should be done as early as possible. As Childress says:

> "... anything that can be communicated should be communicated, since people can better face the known than the unknown."

Even if downsizing is not the goal of the merger or acquisition (for example, job losses was not an intended outcome of the Lehigh and CBR merger, as shown in the case study to accompany Chapter 9), then this too should be communicated early, so to avoid rumours starting and people being distracted from their real work – building a new and better organization.

Indeed, the research found that it is cultural factors and not strategic or price factors, that normally lead to M&A failure (and as the previous Chapter showed, failure rates are frighteningly high), so merging companies must pay close attention to ensuring that the cultural fit is right. Cultural due diligence, therefore, plays a crucial role in determining the cultural problems ahead. Companies must ensure that the employees from one of the combining companies are not favoured over the other, which is important in order to avoid the development of a damaging and performance sapping 'victor and vanquished' mentality.

The research shows that M&As activity is set to continue to grow dramatically over the next few years. Similarly, the focus on culture change is set to further increase in its level of importance. Indeed, the 'Culture and Change Management' survey[6] found that 79.32 per cent of respondents believe culture change to be currently a more important issue within their organizations than five years previously. And 74.44 per cent believed it would become more important over the next five years.

Section I: Tomorrow's High-performing Cultures

So what will a high-performing culture look like in the early years of the new millennium? This question was posed to a number of the advisers interviewed for this Report. First, given the speed of change these days, it is almost impossible to predict, with any accuracy, what will happen in the future. After all, how much of the present would have been forecast correctly ten years ago?

Speed and Flexibility

However, key beliefs were espoused by many of the advisers. Change will become an everyday part of life, and so being able to not just respond to, but anticipate change will become a key characteristic in successful organizations. As Childress says:

> "Speed to market, of decisions and sharing knowledge will become more important as competition intensifies and gets more global in nature. Therefore speed will be at the heart of the way successful cultures evolve."

Flexibility is another key word used repeatedly by advisers. In coping with ever-changing market and customer demands, organizations will have to become more and more amoeba-like in both their structures and cultures. Building an adaptive culture (already recognized as critical by research such as that by Kotter and Heskett; see Chapter 2, Section B) will become increasingly important. So organizations must beware of the pitfalls of building strong cultures that become inflexible. As Mark Krueger, managing director of the US-based consultancy Answerthink, says:

> "The key cultural attributes in the near future will be flexibility, risk taking and clarity of direction."

Accountability

Another key word is 'accountability'. The early years of the knowledge era will increasingly see people offered and taking responsibility for their actions, and understanding their role in making corporate strategy happen. After all, devolving accountability is a key aim of frameworks such as the balanced scorecard. As Childress says:

> "People will have to feel accountable for performance and feel an important part of the company. Employees will increasingly ask themselves the questions, 'how do I makes a difference and what am I accountable for."

And if they are not asking the question, it will be increasingly asked of them.

According to Childress, creating this accountability mindset will require massive amounts of internal training. However, he stresses that in addition to continued training in IT tools and techniques, training will also focus on areas that are largely missing from corporate training programmes today, such as building self-confidence and self-esteem, etc.

New Leadership Traits

The ability to devolve accountability will also change the nature of leadership. It is in how new leadership traits are defined that will signal the greatest change to how organizations are run and organized, and therefore create the winning cultures of tomorrow.

A new model for 21st century leadership

In their book, *In the Eye of the Storm: Reengineering Corporate Culture*, Childress and Senn provided this useful model for 21st Century Leadership, shown in Table 10.1 (this is also shown in Chapter 4).[7] As this makes clear, leaders in the future will need a diametrically opposite set of skills and behavioural traits than have been valued in this century.

Many of the advisers commented on the importance of excellent leadership in tomorrow's companies. Garrey Melville stresses that a new type of leader, one that is willing to show their emotions, will evolve. He says:

From earlier paradigm	To current and future paradigm
Being a manager	Being a leader
Being a boss	Being a coach and facilitator
Controlling people	Empowering people
Holding onto authority	Delegating authority
Micro-managing	Leading with vision and values
Directing with rules and regulations	Guiding with winning shared values
Relying on 'position power' and hierarchy	Building 'relationship power' and networked teams
Demanding compliance	Gaining commitment
Focusing only on tasks	Focusing on quality, service and the customer
Confronting and combating	Collaborating and unifying
Going it alone	Utilizing the team
Judging others	Respecting, honouring and leveraging diversity and differences
Changing by necessity and crisis	Commitment to continuous learning
Being internally competitive – win/lose	Being internally collaborative – win/win
Having a narrow focus 'me and my area'	Having a broader focus 'my team, my organization.

Table 10.1: A New Model for 21st Century Leadership

"Great companies tomorrow will be created through good corporate strategies, powerful missions, and excellent and visible leaders who demonstrate strong personal values which are shared organization-wide.

"Emotional intelligence will become more important. Senior managers in the past have not dared show their emotions. However in the knowledge economy we will see more senior managers showing their emotions. This will go a long way to making companies more like living, evolving organisms than lifeless places."

Stakeholder Relations

Philip Sadler stresses the importance of stakeholder relationships in the future, due to continued social change and the increasing tendency of people to be monitors and critical of the actions of powerful business enterprises.

Indeed, most of the case study companies are aware of this. Millennium Inorganic Chemicals and Siemens KWU, for example, both work in environmentally sensitive industries and recognize that environmental responsibility is crucial for the company's sustainable success. Sadler adds:

"There will also be much more openness within corporate cultures. The progress from hierarchical structures to egalitarian, single status will have marched on. Diversity will be seen more of a strength than something you have to do to comply with for equal opportunities regulations. And acceptance of change will be taken for granted as will customer-focus."

A Healthy Cultural Mind

In their book, *In the Eye of the Storm: Reengineering Corporate Culture*, Childress and Senn concluded:[8]

> "A healthy, high-performance culture is the greatest asset an organization or team can have.
>
> "Even though these are turbulent times, you can operate from the calm in the eye of the storm if your organization has a healthy culture and you maintain a healthy state of mind."

It is organizations that make their corporate minds – and all the component behaviours and beliefs – conscious, malleable, constantly learning, and focused on keeping aligned with ever-changing market and customer demands, which will deliver superior shareholder value in the early years of the new millennium and beyond.

APPENDIX - LISTINGS

The following organizations and consultants have kindly given their time, expertise and resources in the compilation of this Report.

ASI (UK) (formerly ODI UK)
3 Shortlands
Hammersmith
London W6 8DD
United Kingdom
Tel: +44 0 181 222 7250
Fax: +44 0 181 222 7299

Answerthink
1742 Georgetown Road
Hudson
OH 44236
USA
Tel: +1 330 656 3110
Fax: +1 330 463 5471
www.answerthink.com

Centre for the Tomorrow's Company
19 Buckingham Street
London WC2N 6EF
United Kingdom
Tel: +44 0 171 930 5150
Fax: +44 0 171 930 5155
www.tomorrowscompany.com

Context Consulting
500 Chiswick High Road
London W4 5RG
United Kingdom
Tel: +44 0 181 956 2380
Fax: +44 0 181 956 2521
www.contextweb.co.uk

Ernst & Young
Becket House
1 Lambeth Palace Road
London SE1 7EN
United Kingdom
Tel: +44 0 171 928 2000
Fax: +44 0 171 928 1345
www.eyi.com

European Foundation for Quality Management (EFQM)
Brussels Representative Office
Avenue des Pleiades 15
1200 Brussels
Belgium
Tel: +32 2 775 35 11
Fax: +32 2 775 35 35

Human Resources Institute
115 Dunder Road
Burlington
VT 05401
USA
Tel: +1 802 862 8855
Fax: +1 802 862 6389
www.healthyculture.com

The ITEM Group
Burnham House
High Street
Burnham SL1 7JZ
United Kingdom
Tel: +44 0 1628 601400
Fax: +44 0 1628 667155

Garrey Melville
11 Hampden Hill
Beaconsfield HP9 1BP
United Kingdom
Tel/Fax: +44 0 1494 672909
www.elmark.co.uk

ODR Europe
Mill House
Borde Hill Lane
Haywards Heath RH16 1XR
United Kingdom
Tel: +44 0 1444 450777
Fax: +44 0 1444 450745
www.odrinc.com

Organization Dynamics Inc (ODI)
15 New England Executive Park
Burlington
MA 01803
USA
Tel: +1 781 272 8040
       +1 800 634 4636
Fax: +1 781 273 2558
www.orgdynamics.com

Organized Change Consultancy
5663 Balboa Avenue
Suite 171
San Diego
CA 92111
USA
Tel: +1 858 694 8191
Fax: +1 858 694 8187
www.organizedchange.com

Performance Excellence Inc
(formerly QC Solutions Inc)
1038 Cooper Drive
Palatine
IL 60067
USA
Tel/Fax: +1 847 202 0857
http://people.ce.mediaone.net/nblogett

QPA
1 Pickford Street
Aldershot GU11 1TY
United Kingdom
Tel: +44 0 1252 338922
Fax: +44 0 1252 338980
www.qpa-world.com

Renaissance Worldwide Inc
189 Wells Avenue
Newton
MA 02459
USA
Tel: +1 617 527 6886
       +1 888 377 9119
Fax: +1 617 527 6999
www.rens.com

Robert H Schaffer & Associates
4 High Ridge Park
Stanford
CT 06905
USA
Tel: +1 203 322 1604
Fax: +1 203 322 3599
www.rhsa.com

Senn-Delaney Leadership Consulting Group
3780 Kilroy Airport Way
Suite 800
Long Beach
CA 90806
USA
Tel: +1 800 788 3380
Fax: +1 562 989 0878

60 St James' Street
London SW1A 1LE
United Kingdom
Tel: +44 0 171 647 6060
Fax: +44 0 171 499 0087
www.sdlcg.com

REFERENCES

Chapter 1

1.   David Harvey, *Re-engineering: The Critical Success Factors*, Business Intelligence, London, 1995.

2.   Chris Ashton, *Transforming HR to Support Corporate Change*, Business Intelligence, London, 1996.

3.   Dr David Clutterbuck and Linda Gatley, *The Strategic Management of Internal Communication*, Business Intelligence, London, 1996.

4.   Daryl Conner, 'Managing, Orchestrating and Executing Corporate Transition', presentation at *Corporate Agility 97* conference, Business Intelligence, October 1997.

5.   'Culture and Change Management' survey, Business Intelligence, London, 1998.

6.   Harvey, 1995, *op. cit.*

7.   David Harvey and Carol Kennedy, *Managing and Sustaining Radical Change*, Business Intelligence, London, 1997.

8.   Greg Brenneman, 'Right Away and All at Once: How We Saved Continental', *Harvard Business Review*, Vol 76, No 5, pp162–79, September-October, 1998.

9.   John P Kotter and James L Heskett, *Corporate Culture and Performance*, The Free Press, New York, 1992.

10.   Edgar Schein, *Organizational Culture and Leadership*, Jossey-Bass Publishers, California, 1992.

11.   Schein, 1992, *op. cit.*

12.   John R Childress and Larry E Senn, *In the Eye of the Storm: Reengineering Corporate Culture*, The Leadership Press, California, 1995.

13. Childress and Senn, 1995, *op. cit.*

14. Childress and Senn, 1995, *op. cit.*

15. Brenneman, 1998, *op. cit.*

16. Brenneman, 1998, *op. cit.*

17. Brenneman, 1998, *op. cit.*

18. Brenneman, 1998, *op. cit.*

19. Brenneman, 1998, *op. cit.*

20. Brenneman, 1998, *op. cit.*

21. Brenneman, 1998, *op. cit.*

Chapter 2

1. Rosabeth Moss Kanter, *The Change Masters: Innovation and Entrepreneurship in the American Corporation*, Simon & Schuster, New York, 1985.

2. 'Culture and Change Management' survey, Business Intelligence, London, 1998.

3. John P Kotter and James L Heskett, *Corporate Culture and Performance*, The Free Press, New York, 1992.

4. 'The Inclusive Approach and Business Success: The Research Evidence. An Interim Report', The Centre for Tomorrow's Company, London, 1998.

5. Kotter and Heskett, 1992, *op. cit.*

6. John R Childress and Larry E Senn, *In the Eye of the Storm: Reengineering Corporate Culture*, The Leadership Press, California, 1995.

7. Carole Pemberton, 'From the Top', *The Guardian*, UK, 12 December 1998.

8. Childress and Senn, 1995, *op. cit.*

9. James Creelman, *Building and Implementing a Balanced Scorecard*, Business Intelligence, London, 1998.

10. Lynne Joy McFarland, John R Childress and Larry E Senn, *21st Century Leadership: Dialogues with 100 Top Leaders*, The Leadership Press, California, 1994.

11. Greg Brenneman, 'Right Away and All at Once: How We Saved Continental', *Harvard Business Review*, Vol 76, No 5, pp162–79, September-October, 1998.

12. From material supplied by the consultancy Organizational Dynamics Incorporated (ODI).

13. Daryl Conner, 'Managing, Orchestrating and Executing Corporate Transition', presentation at *Corporate Agility 97* conference, Business Intelligence, October 1997.

14. Conner, 1997, *op. cit.*

15. Kotter and Heskett, 1992, *op. cit.*

16. Childress and Senn, 1995, *op. cit.*

17. David Harvey and Carol Kennedy, *Managing and Sustaining Radical Change*, Business Intelligence, London, 1997.

Chapter 3

1. Quoted from an article on the Millennium Chemicals' website at www.millenniumchem.com.

2. Economic Value Added (EVA) is a performance measure created by the US-headquartered consultancy Stern Stewart and Co. EVA is a measure of operating profits less the cost of all the capital employed to produce those earnings. It will increase if operating profits grow without tying up additional capital, if new capital can be invested in projects that will earn more than the full cost of capital and if capital can be diverted or liquidated from business activities that do not provide adequate returns.

3. Quoted from an article on the Millennium Chemicals website, *op. cit.*

4. SAP is a software package that eliminates the need to manually move data from one system to another, thus helping to reduce data inaccuracies and improve customer service.

5. From documentation provided by Millennium Chemicals to explain its 'people policy'.

6. 'Creating Value: Millennium Chemicals Inc, Report to Shareholders 1997'.

Chapter 4

1. 'Culture Change and Change Management' survey, Business Intelligence, London, 1998.

2. John P Kotter and James L Heskett, *Corporate Culture and Performance*, The Free Press, New York, 1992.

3. Greg Brenneman, 'Right Away and All at Once: How We Saved Continental', *Harvard Business Review*, Vol 76, No 5, pp162–79, September-October, 1998.

4. John R Childress and Larry E Senn, *In the Eye of the Storm: Reengineering Corporate Culture*, The Leadership Press, California, 1995.

5. 'Culture Change and Change Management' survey, 1998, *op. cit.*

6. Brenneman, 1998, *op. cit.*

7. Childress and Senn, 1995, *op. cit.*

8. Kotter and Heskett, 1992, *op. cit.*

9. 'Culture and Change Management' survey, 1998, *op. cit.*

10. Lynne Joy McFarland, John R Childress and Larry E Senn, *21st Century Leadership: Dialogues with 100 Top Leaders*, The Leadership Press, California, 1994.

11. Childress and Senn, 1995, *op. cit.*

12. McFarland, Childress and Senn, 1994, *op. cit.*

13. Kotter and Heskett, 1992, *op. cit.*

14. Philip Sadler, 'Leadership In Tomorrow's Company', Centre for Tomorrow's Company, London, 1998.

15. 'KFC Serves Up a Winning Partnership' *The Leader*, Vol 1 No 2, Senn-Delaney Leadership Consulting Group, California and London, 1998.

16. 'The Leader', 1998, *op. cit.*

17. 'The Leader', 1998, *op. cit.*

18. 'The Leader', 1998, *op. cit.*

19. 'The Leader', 1998, *op. cit.*

20. 'The Leader', 1998, *op. cit.*

21. 'The Leader', 1998, *op. cit.*

Chapter 5

1. John Burns, *Creating an Energized Organization: Aligning Strategy and Culture*, working paper, 1998.

2. 'Culture and Change Management' survey, Business Intelligence, London, 1998.

3. John R Childress and Larry E Senn, *In the Eye of the Storm: Reengineering Corporate Culture*, The Leadership Press, California, 1995.

4. Abridged from *Culture Change Planner* by Judd Robert Allen, PhD, Human Resources Institute Inc, Vermont, 1998. With editorial assistance from Michael O'Donnell, PhD, William Baun, MA and Shari Levine, MPH. Published on www.healthyculture.com.

5. 'Culture and Change Management' survey, 1998, *op. cit.*

6. Edgar Schein, 'Three Cultures of Management: The Key to Organizational Learning', *Sloan Management Review*, Vol 38, No 1, Autumn 1996.

7. David Harvey, *Re-engineering: The Critical Success Factors*, Business Intelligence, London, 1994.

8. Alison Rankin-Frost, 'Why Change Can Be Bad For Business – and how to make change work', *Focus on Change Management*, Issue 40, December 1997/January 1998.

9. Phil Hodges, 'Controlling the Elastic Band of Change – Identifying key players and communicating with them is the way to achieve lasting change', *Focus on Change Management*, Issue 43, April 1998.

10. Childress and Senn, 1995, *op. cit.*

11. *Aspects of Excellence*, European Quality Award 1998 Official Publication, European Quality Publications, London, 1998.

12. A balanced scorecard is a strategic management framework typically consisting of the four performance perspectives of learning and growth, internal processes, customer and financial. All of these perspectives include specific objectives, targets, measures and roll-up to support the company's vision. For more on this see Chapter 6.

Chapter 6

1. Ronnie Lessem and Dr Sudhanshu Palsule, *Managing in Four Worlds: From Competition to Co-Creation*, Blackwell Publishers, Oxford, 1997.

2. Dr David Wilkinson, 'Cultural Change, Knowledge Creation and Improved Business Performance', presentation at *Corporate Agility 97* conference, Business Intelligence, London, October 1997.

3. Wilkinson, 1997, *op. cit.*

4. Carol Kennedy and David Harvey, *Managing and Sustaining Radical Change*, Business Intelligence, London, 1997.

5. D Ulrich, 'Part iii: How Change Agents Transform the Enterprise', *Strategic Partners for High Performance*, Work in America Institute, Scarsdale, New York, 1995.

6. Dr George Labovitz and Victor Rosansky, *The Power of Alignment: How Great Companies Stay Centred and Accomplish Extraordinary Things*, John Wiley & Sons, 1997.

7. James Creelman, *Building and Implementing a Balanced Scorecard*, Business Intelligence, London, 1998.

8.   Joe Doyle, John Childress and Jim Ondrus, 'Chapter 19: Strategic Transformation – The New Game', Philip R Theibert (editor), *Lessons in Cultural Change: The Utility Industry Experience*, Public Utilities Reports, Virginia, 1994.

9.   'BT Northern Ireland: A Business Ambassador', *Aspects of Excellence*, European Quality Awards 1998 Official Publication, European Quality Publications, London, 1998.

10.   Both awards are based, as the European Quality Award is, on EFQM's Business Excellence Framework, which assesses performance against nine performance criteria areas including leadership, customer satisfaction, people satisfaction and business results.

11.   *Aspects of Excellence*, European Quality Award 1998 Official Publication, European Quality Publications, London, 1998.

12.   EVA is net operating profit minus an appropriate charge for the opportunity cost of all capital invested in the enterprise. EVA is, therefore, an estimate of true 'economic' profit, or the amount by which earnings exceed or fall short of the required minimum rate of return investors could get by investing in other securities of comparable risk.

13.   *Aspects of Excellence*, 1998, *op. cit.*

14.   *Aspects of Excellence*, 1998, *op. cit.*

Chapter 7

1.   Chris Ashton, *Transforming HR To Support Corporate Change*, Business Intelligence, London, 1996.

2.   'Culture and Change Management' survey, Business Intelligence, London, 1998.

3.   John P Kotter and James L Heskett, *Corporate Culture and Performance*, The Free Press, New York, 1992.

4.   Research about the workplace needs of employees by Yankelovich Partners and commissioned by Gemini Consulting, 1998.

5.   Case studies on UNUM Corporation, Whirlpool Europe and BP Chemicals can be found in *Building and Implementing a Balanced Scorecard*, James Creelman, Business Intelligence, London, 1998.

6.   Robert S Kaplan and David P Norton, *The Balanced Scorecard: Translating Strategy into Action*, Harvard Business School Press, Boston, 1996.

7.   Peter Scott-Morgan, *The Unwritten Rules of the Game: Master Them, Shatter Them, and Break Through the Barriers to Organizational Change*, McGraw-Hill, New York, 1994.

8. 'Rethinking Pay, Compensation & Performance' survey, Business Intelligence, London, 1998. Exclusively commissioned for the report, *Strategic Compensation*, Chris Ashton, Business Intelligence, London, 1999.

9. 'New Mechanisms for Pay, Appraisal and Career Development: A study of Success Factors and Results' survey, Business Intelligence/*Personnel Today*, London, 1995. Exclusively commissioned for the report, *Pay, Performance and Career Development*, Chris Ashton, Business Intelligence, London, 1995.

10. Chris Ashton, *Strategic Compensation,* Business Intelligence, London, 1999.

Chapter 8

1. 'Culture and Change Management' survey, Business Intelligence, London, 1998.

2. 'Culture and Change Management' survey, 1998, *op. cit.*

3. Survey by PA Consulting, cited by Janet Izatt, 'The Lost Art of Communication', *PR Week*, 27 October 1995. Quoted in *The Strategic Management of Internal Communications,* Dr David Clutterbuck and Linda Gatley, Business Intelligence, London, 1996.

4. Greg Brenneman, 'Right Away and All at Once: How We Saved Continental', *Harvard Business Review,* Vol 76, No 5, pp162–79, September-October, 1998.

5. 'Is Anyone Listening? Internal Communications in Support of Organizational Change' survey, Business Intelligence/Clutterbuck Associates, London, 1995. Exclusively commissioned for the report, *The Strategic Management of Internal Communications*, Dr David Clutterbuck and Linda Gatley, Business Intelligence, London, 1996.

6. James Creelman, *Building and Implementing a Balanced Scorecard,* Business Intelligence, London, 1998.

7. 'Culture and Change Management' survey, 1998, *op. cit.*

8. Dr David Skyrme and Debra M Amidon, *Creating the Knowledge-based Business*, Business Intelligence, London, 1997.

9. Harvard Business School case study, 1995. Two case studies were published during 1995 and provided valuable background material to this case study. The case studies were prepared by Harvard Business School Associate Kate Graff as the basis for class discussion, June/November 1995.

10. 'Report and Accounts', Ernst & Young, 1998.

11. 'Reports and Accounts', 1998, *op. cit.*

12. James C Emerson, 'Ernst & Young LLP: Setting the New Knowledge Sharing Standard', *Emerson's Professional Services Review*, March/April 1997.

13. 'MAKE^{SM}' survey, Teleos/Business Intelligence, London, 1998. Commissioned for the conference *Most Admired Knowledge Enterprises 1999*, Business Intelligence, London, 1999.

14. 'Reports and Accounts', 1998, *op. cit.*

15. 'Reports and Accounts', 1998, *op. cit.*

16. *100 Best Employers in the UK*, Corporate Research Foundation, McGraw-Hill, New York, 1998.

Chapter 9

1. Nick Pandya, *The Guardian*, 12 December 1998.

2. Marion Devine, Wendy Hirsh, with Valerie Garrow, Linda Holbeche and Chris Lake, *Mergers & Acquisitions: Getting the People Bit Right:*, Roffey Park Management Institute, Horsham, 1998.

3. Alan Crozier, *Sunday Times*, 29 November 1998.

4. Larry E Senn, *The Cultural Aspects of Mergers and Acquisitions: How to Avoid Cultural Clash*, Senn-Delaney Leadership, California, 1998. This report is one of a series on Leadership Strategy published by Senn-Delaney Leadership Consulting Group.

5. Senn, 1998, *op. cit.*

6. Senn, 1998, *op. cit.*

7. Devine and Hirsh, 1998, *op. cit.*

8. Senn, 1998, *op. cit.*

9. Ernst & Young, 'Report and Accounts', 1998.

10. Senn, 1998, *op. cit.*

11. Ron Duboff, 'Leadership for Growth', *Focus on Change Management*, Issue 40, December 1997/January 1998.

12. Crozier, 29 November 1998, *op. cit.*

13. Ronald N Ashkenas, Lawrence J DeMonaco and Suzanne C Francis, 'Making the Deal Real: How GE Capital Integrates Acquisitions', *Harvard Business Review*, Vol 76, No 1, January-February 1998.

14. Devine and Hirsh, 1998, *op. cit.*

15. Richard Nicholson, 'Developing and Educating Staff to be Able to Cope in a New Environment', presentation at *The New Change Management Agenda* conference, Business Intelligence, London, 1998.

16. Senn, 1998, *op. cit.*

17. Lisa Buckingham and Roger Crowe, 'Merger Mania – Coming to a Company Near You', *The Guardian*, 23 January 1999.

18. Devine and Hirsh, 1998, *op. cit.*

19. Devine and Hirsh, 1998, *op. cit.*

Chapter 10

1. 'Culture and Change Management' survey, Business Intelligence, London, 1998.

2. Greg Brenneman, 'Right Away and All at Once: How We Saved Continental', *Harvard Business Review*, Vol 76, No 5, pp162–79, September-October, 1998.

3. 'Culture and Change Management' survey, 1998, *op. cit.*

4. 'Culture and Change Management' survey, 1998, *op. cit.*

5. 'Culture and Change Management' survey, 1998, *op. cit.*

6. 'Culture and Change Management' survey, 1998, *op. cit.*

7. John R Childress and Larry E Senn, *In the Eye of the Storm: Reengineering Corporate Culture*, The Leadership Press, California, 1995.

8. Childress and Senn, 1995, *op. cit.*

INDEX

388

This book is due for return on or before the last date shown below.

185152